Leviathan
on the
Right

MICHAEL D. TANNER

Leviathan
on the
Right

How Big-Government Conservatism Brought Down the Republican Revolution

CATO INSTITUTE

WASHINGTON, D.C.

Library of Congress Cataloging-in-Publication Data

Tanner, Michael, 1956-
    Leviathan on the Right : how big-government conservatism
brought down the Republican revolution / Michael D. Tanner.
        p. cm.
    Includes bibliographical references and index.
    ISBN 1-933995-00-9 (hardback : alk. paper)
    1. Conservatism—United States.   2. Republican Party (U.S. :
1854-)   3. United States—Politics and government—2001-
    I. Title.

JC573.2.U6T36 2007
324.2734—dc22
                                                            2006051903

Cover design by Jon Meyers.

Printed in the United States of America.

CATO INSTITUTE
1000 Massachusetts Ave., N.W.
Washington, D.C. 20001
www.cato.org

Contents

Preface

For conservatives generally and the Republican Party in particular, now is a time of intense soul searching. For the first time in a dozen years, Republicans have lost control of Congress. As a result, they are being forced to reexamine who they are and what they stand for.

It's about time. After all, more than a decade has passed since President Bill Clinton announced in his State of the Union address that "the era of big government is over." Yet, since then, government has grown far bigger and far more intrusive. It spends more, regulates us more, and reaches far more into our daily lives than it did before the Republican Revolution. This growth of government has occurred despite the fact that the Republicans, supposedly the party of smaller government, controlled both houses of Congress from 1994 to 2006 (with the exception of the brief Jim Jeffords interregnum in the Senate) and the presidency since 2000.

Behind this alarming trend stands a variety of factors, including the institutional constraints of governing and the necessities of the war on terror. But no factor has been bigger than the rise of a new brand of conservatism—one that believes big government can be used for conservative ends. It is a conservatism that ridicules F. A. Hayek and Barry Goldwater while embracing Teddy and even Franklin Roosevelt. It has more in common with Ted Kennedy than with Ronald Reagan.

At this point, let me offer a few words on what this book is *not*. It is not a discussion of the Bush administration's foreign policy. Numerous studies and critiques already address this most controversial aspect of the Bush presidency. One can hold a variety of views on the wisdom of the Iraq war or Bush's crusade to spread democracy around the world (I personally have my doubts) while still remaining in the mainstream of traditional conservative thought. By the same token, this book will not cover the growing infringements on our civil liberties brought about by the war on terror. The delicate balance between liberty and security deserves a far more detailed and careful treatment than I would be capable of here. Instead, this book focuses on domestic policy, where a perhaps more important, if less frequently discussed, battle is being waged for the soul of the conservative movement.

Nor is this book a deep discussion of the philosophical underpinnings of conservatism. They will be discussed where appropriate, but readers seeking an in-depth discussion of the differences between Burke's and Mill's approach to governing should look elsewhere. Rather, this book is an attempt to understand the rise of big-government conservatism and examine the policies it endorses. And it is a warning that those policies will fail on a practical level while leaving America less free.

Big-government conservatism is not a single monolithic movement. Those who might legitimately be described as big-government conservatives frequently disagree among themselves. In no way am I attempting to say that every individual I identify as a big-government conservative holds identical views or supports every policy that I discuss. Yet, in the end, I think the reader will conclude, as I have, that the American conservative movement has slipped from its moorings and drifted away from its traditional belief in limited government.

Finally, throughout this book I have tended to use conservative and Republican almost interchangeably. I am aware that not all Republicans are conservative and many conservatives are not Republicans, especially if one broadens the definition of conservative to include libertarians. No doubt exists, however, that in America today the Republican Party is the conservative party. The rise of big-government conservatism has taken place in the context of Republican politics and been reflected in the policies of a Republican president and a Republican Congress. Given the difficulties that our campaign finance laws pose for third parties, any debate over the future direction of conservatism will likely be decided within Republican circles.

Therefore, as Republicans wrestle with their future, they must reject big-government conservatism and return to the essential conservative principles of small government, individual liberty, federalism, and free markets. Losing is never a pleasant experience, but it can be an opportunity. In the two years before the presidential and congressional elections of 2008, Republicans will have time to rediscover the conservatism of Reagan and Goldwater. This book is a plea that they do so.

No book like this could possibly be the work of just one person. I owe a considerable debt of gratitude to all those who helped bring it from concept to fruition. First, a great many unsung heroes contributed to the research that shows up in these pages. In particular, I would like to thank Adrienne Aldridge, Brian MacWilliams, Ashby Monk, Courtney Monk, Brooke Oberwetter, Raphael Prais, Ian Wallace, and especially Robert Herritt, who spent countless hours at libraries, scouring the Internet, fact checking, and meeting all sorts of my unreasonable demands.

Thanks also to those who provided comments, information, and corrections along the way, including Michael Cannon, Daniel Maidman, Neal McCluskey, and Steve Slivinski. A special note of appreciation should go to David Boaz, Gene Healy, and Brink Lindsey, whose assistance strengthened this book considerably, as well as to Robert Garber and David Lampo for their work in production and marketing. I also want to offer a special thank-you to Cato's president, Ed Crane. No one in Washington has been more prescient in warning about the dangers of big-government conservatism. Without his inspiration and foresight, this book would never have existed.

Finally, my most heartfelt thanks go to my wonderful wife, Ellen. Every step along the way, she provided encouragement, guidance, and critical review. Without her help, I have no doubt that this book would never have seen the light of day. Even more important, she never stops reminding me that public policy is not about economic or philosophical abstractions, but about the lives and futures of real people. That is a good lesson for all of us.

PART I

FROM OXYMORON TO GOVERNING PHILOSOPHY

Whether it's called "compassionate conservatism" or "big government Republicanism," after years of record increases in federal spending, more government is now the accepted Republican philosophy in Washington.

—Rep. Mike Pence (R-IN)

1. Big Government: It Isn't Just for Liberals Anymore

Consider the following policy proposals that have been floating around Washington in the months leading up to the 2006 election: (a) creating a new cabinet-level federal Department of Families; (b) giving every child $2,000 at birth; (c) having the federal government fund 70,000 new math and science teachers; and (d) requiring every American to purchase health insurance. One might expect that those proposals were made by liberal Democrats, perhaps Ted Kennedy or Hillary Clinton preparing for their Senate majority. In fact, every one of them was made by conservative Republicans.

Or consider President George W. Bush. Bush was the first Republican since Eisenhower to run for president without calling for cutting or abolishing a single government program. Since his election, Bush has presided over the largest expansion of government spending since Lyndon Johnson initiated the Great Society. Domestic spending has increased by 27 percent during his presidency.[1] More people now work for the federal government than at any time since the Cold War.[2] Not a single federal program has been eliminated.

The expansion of the federal government under the Bush presidency goes far beyond mere dollars, however. For example, this president has

- Enacted the largest new entitlement program since the creation of Medicare and Medicaid, an unfunded Medicare prescription drug benefit that could add as much as $11.2 trillion to the program's unfunded liabilities[3]
- Dramatically increased federal control over local schools while increasing federal education spending by nearly 61 percent[4]
- Signed a campaign finance bill that greatly restricts freedom of speech, despite saying he believed it was unconstitutional
- Authorized warrantless wiretapping and given vast new powers to law enforcement

- Federalized airport security and created a new cabinet-level Department of Homeland Security
- Added roughly 7,000 pages of new federal regulations, bringing the cost of federal regulations to the economy to more than $1.1 trillion[5]
- Enacted a $1.5 billion program to promote marriage
- Proposed a $1.7 billion initiative to develop a hydrogen-powered car
- Abandoned traditional conservative support for free trade by imposing tariffs and other import restrictions on steel and lumber
- Expanded President Clinton's national service program
- Increased farm subsidies
- Launched an array of new regulations on corporate governance and accounting
- Generally done more to centralize government power in the executive branch than any administration since Richard Nixon

Individually, the merits of each of these items can be debated. Taken as a whole, they represent an undeniable shift toward big government. We have come a long way from Ronald Reagan's warning, "Government is not the solution to our problem; government is the problem," to George W. Bush's saying, "We have a responsibility that when somebody hurts, government has got to move."[6]

As longtime Washington reporter Janet Hook wrote in the *Los Angeles Times*: "No longer are Republicans arguing with Democrats about whether government should be big or small. Instead they are at odds over what kind of big government the U.S. should have."[7]

Fred Barnes, a Bush admirer, describes Bush's philosophy this way:

> The president pays lip service to limiting the size and scope of government, but it is not a top Bush priority. In truth, his view of government is Hamiltonian: it is a valuable tool to achieve security, prosperity, and the common good. His strategy is to use government as a means to conservative ends.[8]

The Bush administration has, deservedly, come in for much of the blame (or credit) for the growth of big-government conservatism. Bruce Bartlett, a former Reagan administration economist, wrote a well-argued book claiming that Bush "betrayed" the conservative movement.[9]

Figure 1.1
GOVERNMENT SPENDING, 1994–2006

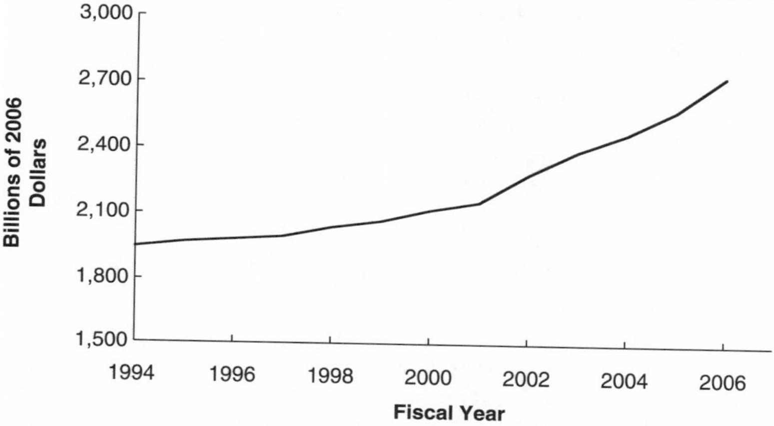

SOURCE: Office of Management and Budget.

Despite the Bush administration's many flaws, however, placing all the blame for the growth in government with the president is unfair. On those occasions when the Republicans in Congress broke with the administration, they never did so to demand *less* spending or a smaller government. A Republican-controlled Congress, after all, appropriated $91 billion more for domestic programs than the president requested during his first term.[10] Indeed, the Republican addiction to growing government began well before Bush was elected president. When Republicans took control of Congress in 1994, the federal budget was $1.9 trillion. The Fiscal Year 2006 budget totaled just over $2.7 trillion.[11] Figure 1.1 shows the growth in federal spending since 1994.

In 1994, the federal budget contained roughly 4,000 "earmarks" for specific projects in members' districts; the 2005 budget contained more than 14,000 such items.[12] The massive $286 billion 2005 transportation bill alone contained 6,371.[13]

The desire to expand government seems to have infected the Republican Party as a whole. The *Manchester Union Leader* describes an editorial board meeting with then Republican National Committee Chairman Ed Gillespie:

> The result was a surprisingly frank admission that the Republican Party defines "fiscal responsibility" as increasing the

5

federal budget at "a slower rate of growth" than the Democrats (his words). We asked him three times to explain why President Bush and the Republican Congress have increased discretionary non-defense spending at such an alarming rate, and why the party has embraced the expansion of the federal government's roles in education, agriculture and Great Society-era entitlement programs. "Those questions have been decided," he said. The public wants an expanded federal role in those areas, and the Republican Party at the highest levels has decided to give the public what it wants.[14]

It is no wonder that on election night 2006 exit polls showed that voters viewed Republicans as the party of big government by an 11-point margin. More than 39 percent of voters now believe that Republicans, not Democrats, are the party of big government. Another 16 percent of voters believe that both Republicans and Democrats support big government. That's an astounding 55 percent of voters who believe that Republicans are a big-government party. Even 29 percent of Republicans said the Republicans are the "party of big government," while an additional 17 percent of Republicans said both parties fit that description.[15]

Of course the Republican Party has always had its moderates or "wets." And many conservatives have honored their commitment to limited government more in rhetoric than in action. Unified government power, with the House, Senate, and presidency all controlled by the same party, nearly always yields more spending and bigger government than divided government.[16] But this rejection of the traditional conservative small-government agenda represents something different. The recent drift by Republicans and other conservatives toward big government is not just a result of political pragmatism, addiction to pork-barrel politics, or the desire to curry favor with constituents who appear to demand government solutions to the problems that affect them. Rather it represents a slow but steady change in conservative philosophy, one that rejects a Reaganite skepticism about government in favor of a belief that big government may not be such a bad thing after all, if it can be harnessed to conservative ends.

The Essence of Big-Government Conservatism

To understand how conservatism has been turning away from its traditional belief in small government, one has to look no further than President George W. Bush. Indeed, as John DiIulio, the first director of President Bush's Office of Faith-Based Initiatives, has pointed out; from the very beginning of his run for the presidency, Bush made clear his differences with small-government conservatives.

> His very first campaign speech, on July 22, 1999, articulated what he believed as a "compassionate conservative." Speaking before inner-city clergymen and women in Indianapolis, "economic growth," Bush preached, "is not the solution to every problem." He labeled as "destructive" the idea that government is bad and called explicitly for increasing government support for Medicaid and other federal programs. He also rebutted the notion that government needs only to step aside for families and communities to flourish. In particular he stressed that, when it comes to addressing poverty and urban blight, it "is not enough to call for volunteerism. Without more support—public and private—we are asking" local community-serving groups, both religious and secular, "to make bricks without straw."[17]

This form of conservatism is fundamentally different from the one advocated by Ronald Reagan or Barry Goldwater. That conservatism sought "to curb the size and influence of the federal establishment," as Reagan said in his first inaugural address.[18] Or as Barry Goldwater famously said in his 1960 classic, *Conscience of a Conservative*, "I have little interest in streamlining government or making it more efficient, for I intend to reduce its size."[19]

Goldwater and Reagan-style conservatism is increasingly being supplanted by a new trend in conservative thought, which might loosely be termed big-government conservatism. This type of conservatism believes in a strong and activist government that intervenes in many areas of our lives, from dealing with issues such as poverty or health care to protecting the cultural institutions of our society. Increasingly it has come to resemble contemporary liberalism in its means, if not its ends.

Of course big-government conservatism is not a monolithic movement. Indeed, calling it a movement may overstate its unity and coherence. Outside of Fred Barnes, David Brooks, and a handful of others, few directly identify themselves with the term, preferring to call themselves "compassionate conservatives," "strong-government conservatives," "progressive conservatives," or some similar euphemism. Nor do big-government conservatives agree on every policy discussed in these pages. For example, President Bush, a quintessential big-government conservative, has courageously pushed for Social Security reform despite the skepticism of many other big-government conservatives.

Rather than being a movement, big-government conservatism is more of a tendency in conservative politics and conservative thought. As such it is an amalgam of at least five currents of political thought that have been feeding into the conservative movement for many years.

- *Neoconservatives*, whose "founding fathers" were mostly former Marxists who became disillusioned with the American Left during the 1960s, have generally been identified with their support for a hawkish U.S. foreign policy and the debacle in Iraq. However, as they moved into various Republican administrations and became part of the larger conservative movement, they have also had a profound effect on domestic policy. Reflecting their roots on the left, they have not shared the traditional conservative skepticism about big government. Rather, they maintained a lingering affection for FDR and the New Deal. If they tended to reject Lyndon Johnson's Great Society, it was because they thought it had a corrosive effect on culture, not because they objected to the welfare state on principle. With conservatives in charge, they now embrace social welfare programs as an opportunity to encourage bourgeois virtues.

- *National-greatness conservatives* draw much of their inspiration from neoconservatism but take the ideas a step further. National-greatness conservatism argues that Americans need to be united around great national projects, bigger than themselves. Believers in national-greatness conservatism see Teddy Roosevelt as a hero and start from the premise that "Individual ambition and will power [should be] channeled into the cause of national greatness, and in making the nation great, individuals are able to join their narrow concerns to a larger national project."[20] Although no more than a handful of conservatives publicly identify themselves as national-greatness conservatives, they have a very loud and influential voice.

- *The Religious Right*, once content simply to be "left alone," has become increasingly comfortable with the use of government power to enforce its moral vision. Moreover, the incorporation of evangelical Protestants and ethnic Catholics into the conservative movement brought along groups of people who had little in common with economic conservatives. Indeed, many were former Democrats who were comfortable with expansive government programs.

- *Supply-siders* emphasize tax cuts rather than cutting back the size of government. Indeed, many openly argued that tax cuts would increase government revenues, making expenditure cuts unnecessary. This view meant they could avoid messy debates about the proper size and role of government. As former Rep. Jack Kemp, a leading cheerleader for supply-side economics, put it, they could govern "with no political pain, i.e., having to convince the voters to accept any real absolute cuts in government spending."[21]

- *Technophiles* embrace the idea of a "third wave" of technological change that can solve social problems.[22] Perhaps best identified with former House Speaker Newt Gingrich, they place a high value on programmatic efficiency and believe that government's role is to invest in the technologies of the future. They believe, in Gingrich's words, that "Systems, rather than individuals, should be the focus of improving production."[23]

To some extent big-government conservatives simply style themselves as realists who are adapting traditional conservative ideals to the public mood. Underlying their approach is a belief that, in the end, reducing the size of government is impossible. And, if the growth of government is inevitable, conservatives should stop worrying about the size of government and simply try to make the best of it. For example, Fred Barnes, executive editor of the *Weekly Standard*, who claims credit for coining the term "big-government conservative," criticizes those conservatives who "cling to the hope that someday, somehow, the federal government will be reduced in size."[24]

Thus, when small-government conservatives in the House, led by Rep. Mike Pence (R-IN), demanded spending reductions to offset funds that President Bush had requested in the wake of Hurricane Katrina, Barnes scoffed: "Their goal, with hurricane recovery costs soaring, is what it's always been: to hold down and restrain the growth of government. It is an impossible dream, or close to impossible."[25]

This view seems unduly defeatist. Public opinion polls consistently show a majority of Americans say they would prefer smaller government with fewer services to a larger government with more services.[26] Moreover, the political, academic, and media climates are certainly more hospitable to limited-government themes than they were in, say, the late 1970s. That was a time before the advent of conservative talk radio or think tanks. Conservative ideas like school choice or individual accounts or Social Security were little more than quaint academic concepts. Yet, that was the period when Ronald Reagan was able to rise to the presidency. In contrast, big-government conservatism appears to have led Republicans to electoral disaster.

In actuality, however, there is more to big-government conservatism than mere pragmatism. After all, the Bush administration and its big-government conservative allies in Congress have not simply acquiesced in the level of government that currently exists; they have actively sought to expand it.

Big-government conservatives see a *positive* society-shaping role for government. George W. Bush, as DiIulio pointed out, criticized what he called the "destructive mind-set: the idea that if government would only get out of our way, all our problems would be solved. An approach with no higher goal, no nobler purpose, than 'Leave us alone.'"[27] In another speech, Bush noted, "too often, my party has confused the need for limited government with a disdain for government itself."[28]

Of course the charge that traditional small-government conservatives hate government is unfair. Conservatives have always acknowledged a limited role for government. But they have been skeptical of state power, seeing government as something of a necessary evil. They share F. A. Hayek's concern that central planning and its outgrowth into the welfare state will ultimately and inevitably lead to the eclipse of liberty.[29]

Big-government conservatives dismiss such concerns. They reject Hayek's belief that we are on "the road to serfdom." They do not "feel that kind of alarm or anxiety about the growth of the state in the past century, seeing it as natural, indeed inevitable."[30] Whereas traditionally conservatives have wanted to keep government out of their lives as much as possible, big-government conservatives argue, "Wishing to be left alone isn't a governing doctrine."[31]

Therefore, as Barnes points out, "Big government conservatives are favorably disposed toward . . . a 'conservative welfare state.'"[32] They are willing to use "what normally would be seen as liberal means—activist government—for conservative ends. And they're willing to spend more and increase the size of government in the process."[33]

Traditional conservatives operated from a position of humility when it came to what government could accomplish. They rejected what Hayek called the "fatal conceit" that government can redesign society according to some sort of rational plan.[34] But big-government conservatives share with contemporary liberals a belief that government can design policies based on incentives and penalties that will result in people's behaving in exactly the way policymakers seek. For both liberals and big-government conservatives, government is neither good nor bad. It is simply a tool to be used in the pursuit of higher goals.

Thus, big-government conservatism "measures its success not by how big or small government is but by the habits it encourages in its citizens," according to Brooks.[35] Those values and habits include thrift, hard work, charity, patriotism, and especially traditional sexual and family mores.[36] If a government program advances these goals it is a good program and a proper role for government almost by definition.

For example, in his book on the Bush presidency, *Rebel in Chief*, Barnes approvingly quotes a Bush aide as saying:

> Government funding of effective teen abstinence programs is different from government funding of agencies that hand out condoms to kids. Supporting adoption centers is different from supporting abortion clinics. Supporting anti-drug efforts is different from supporting medical marijuana initiatives.[37]

As former Bush aide Daniel Casse writes, "What it comes down to is that, for Bush, there are conservative goals that take precedence over limiting the reach of government."[38]

Big-government conservatives also see an active role for government in dealing with such issues as poverty, health care, and education.[39] During his renomination speech at the 2004 Republican convention, George W. Bush expressed his belief that "government should help people improve their lives."[40] Bush has praised both FDR's New Deal and Lyndon Johnson's War on Poverty and said: "We've had enough of the stale debate between big government and indifferent government. Government must be active enough to fund services for the poor."[41]

Whereas conservatives traditionally thought social welfare to be the province of private charity and civil society, big-government conservatives believe that only government action can solve those problems. Indeed, for adherents of this philosophy, government action may not just be necessary; it may be preferable. Thus, Robert Rector of the Heritage Foundation criticizes "the mythology that the public sector welfare system is bad and corrupt and destructive. And out here there is this nonprofit private sector which is good, and vital and so forth."[42] Rector writes, "the government food stamp program [is] more conservative and more effective as a charity arm than almost any private sector food bank you could find."[43]

This does not mean that big-government conservatives are wedded to the current structures of the welfare state. They seek more "choice and accountability" in government programs. They would incorporate more market-based processes. They prefer incentives to heavy-handed regulation. But, ultimately, in contrast to the Goldwater tradition, big-government conservatism seeks to streamline government and make it more efficient, not to reduce its size.

At the same time, big-government conservatives are suspicious of unfettered free-market capitalism. Irving Kristol, the neoconservative "godfather" of big-government conservatism, famously gave capitalism "two cheers," not three.[44] Former education secretary and drug czar William Bennett criticizes "unbridled capitalism" as a "problem for that whole dimension of things we call the realm of values and human relationships."[45]

After all, markets that cater to the unregulated demands of consumers produce things such as pornography and rap music, which do not contribute to those virtues that conservatives champion. As Brooks warns, if Americans "think of nothing but their narrow self-interest, of their commercial activities, they lose a sense of grand aspiration and noble purpose."[46] This belief makes big-government conservatives far more willing to countenance business regulation than traditional conservatives. As Irving Kristol says, government must take "a degree of responsibility for helping to shape the preferences that the people exercise in a free market—to 'elevate' them if you will."[47]

Hayek spoke of "spontaneous order." Goldwater sought "freedom" first. Reagan saw government as "the problem not the solution." But, as we will see, big-government conservatives would take conservatism in a very different direction.

A New Brand of Conservatism

American conservatism is, in many ways, a sometimes uneasy mixture of two important strains of thought. On one hand is a profound classically liberal or libertarian tradition that takes its cue from John Stuart Mill's admonition: "The only part of the conduct of anyone for which he is amenable to society is that which concerns others. In the part that merely concerns himself, his independence is, of right, absolute. Over himself, over his own body and mind, the individual is sovereign."[48]

On the other hand is a strong belief in the traditions and institutions of society. Rather than Mill, it is more attuned to Edmund Burke's wisdom: "We owe an implicit reverence to all the institutions of our ancestors,"[49] and "But what is liberty without wisdom, and without virtue? It is the greatest of all possible evils; for it is folly vice and madness, without tuition or restraint."[50]

These two strains of conservatism have not always seen eye to eye. They may have very different views of what, for example, state or local drug laws should be, or what is the proper role of religion in society. But in the United States, both have been united by an opposition to overweening federal power. They share a "common dislike of the intervention of government, especially national, centralized government in the economic, social, political, and intellectual lives of citizens," in the words of conservative sociologist Robert Nisbet.[51]

Neither libertarian nor traditionalist conservatives would countenance a federal takeover of education or a massive new health care entitlement. Both are appalled by out-of-control federal spending. Both seek limits to federal power. They might disagree about what small government is, but at their heart both want a smaller government than we have today.

13

Not so big-government conservatives. Indeed, big-government conservatism has little in common with either libertarian or traditionalist conservatism. Rather, it represents something altogether new in the development of conservative thought.

Big-government conservatives recognize that they are taking conservatism in a new direction. Irving Kristol calls for converting "the Republican Party, and conservatism in general, against their respective wills, into a new kind of conservative politics suitable to governing a modern democracy."[52] Barnes says, "Bush's conservatism *is* new and different."[53]

Rich Lowry of *National Review* suggests that big-government conservatism is unlikely to survive beyond the Bush presidency.[54] He sees the recent enthusiasm for increasing the size and power of government as an aberration, but unless traditional small-government conservatives wake up and fight back, that may be just wishful thinking.

Big-government conservatism is not just a creature of the Bush administration. Big-government conservatism is evident throughout Washington these days. Congress contains few small-government conservatives. Indeed, the pressure from Capitol Hill is often for even bigger government than the White House suggests. Those few voices for small government in the Republican caucus are often marginalized or disciplined for a failure of party loyalty.

Moreover, big-government conservatives have an effective media tool in the *Weekly Standard*, which has practically become a house organ for the movement. Conservative think tanks such as the American Enterprise Institute and the Heritage Foundation are well stocked with big-government conservatives. Indeed, *Newsday* columnist James Pinkerton says of the Heritage Foundation:

> The folks at 214 Massachusetts Avenue were willing to play ball with big government. That is, they have abandoned the old Goldwaterish critique of the Leviathan State in favor of a sophisticated wonkery that seeks out Third-Way-ish approaches to thread the needle between doing nothing and doing everything. That's the art of political compromise, of course, but in so doing, Heritage abandoned black-and-white absolutism—freedom good, bureaucrats bad—for the grayer vocabulary of Benthamism.[55]

Such leading Republican candidates for president in 2008 as Sen. Sam Brownback (R-KS), Sen. John McCain (R-AZ), former House Speaker Newt Gingrich, and Massachusetts governor Mitt Romney all support different variations of big-government conservatism.

But important reasons both philosophical and practical exist to resist this trend.

A Flawed Philosophy

As we shall see in the pages to come, many of the proposals so enthusiastically supported by big-government conservatives would have precisely the opposite effects from those they desire. In the long run, big government is not likely to be compatible with either economic growth or "the bourgeois virtues" of thrift, delayed gratification, honesty, probity, and loyalty that big-government conservatives value.[56] A growing welfare state will inevitably drain resources from the private sector and put them to less efficient uses.

Moreover, by substituting government action for the voluntary activities of civil society, big-government conservatives threaten to undermine the very civic virtues that they seek to champion. If people come to believe that government will act in their place, they are less likely to become involved themselves. Indeed, we already see substantial evidence that private charitable giving tends to decline when government welfare increases.[57]

Big-government conservatives also display a great naiveté about the way government works. They appear to believe that limited programs will not grow or see their original purposes corrupted. But little in the history of government justifies such faith. Even those government programs that do the most damage today, including those decried by big-government conservatives, were devised with the best of intentions. Good intentions, however, seldom survive the realities of the programs in practice.

Big-government conservatives imagine themselves as practicing what Jonathan Rauch has called "demand-side conservatism."[58] The idea is that big government programs can be used to eliminate the conditions that create a demand for big government. Thus, if government can increase marriage, reduce out-of-wedlock births, increase saving, put people to work, educate our children, and so on, eventually less need—and less political support—will exist for government programs.

This hypothesis is sort of the conservative version of the Marxist belief in the eventual "withering away of the state." And it is likely to be about as successful. After all, can anyone recall the last time a government bureaucracy declared that it had fulfilled its mission and now should be abolished?

In their excellent history of the American conservative movement, John Micklethwait and Adrian Woodridge warn: "From a conservative viewpoint, government is usually an institution that cuts to the Left. Bureaucrats inevitably modify programs to suit their own purposes."[59] When a government program is in place, it exists for better or worse. When conservatives concede a role for government on an issue, the precedent exists, for better or worse. Thus, although the Bush administration may be pleased that the No Child Left Behind Act allows the Department of Education to impose its views and theories on the country's schools, future administrations may have very different goals and priorities. Big-government conservatives either don't understand this possibility, or don't care.

As Bruce Bartlett points out, big-government conservatism is particularly susceptible to the type of corruption that has become so prevalent in Washington in recent years. Because it has abandoned much of conservative principle and embraced the idea that government can do "good" things, not surprisingly those "good" things are often favors for favored constituencies.[60]

But big-government conservatives are wrong in a far more important and fundamental way. Our Founding Fathers set up a constitutional framework for government that strictly limited government power. They set in place barriers to the exercise of government power, devising an intricate system of checks and balances, dividing power between national and state governments as well as among three independent branches of government. And, most important, they established a government of enumerated powers, carefully spelling out those few things that the federal government could do and reserving those powers not specified to the states and the people.

These constitutional limits seem to have little meaning to big-government conservatives. With little difference from today's liberals, big-government conservatives feel free to disregard the Constitution when it serves their purpose. Where, after all, does President Bush find in the Constitution authorization for the federal government to govern local school systems?

Barry Goldwater once said, "The conservative's first concern will always be, am I maximizing freedom."[61] That is not the first or even a major concern of big-government conservatives. Former senator Rick Santorum (R-PA), who was one of the leading proponents of this line of thought during his time on Capitol Hill, wrote in his book, *It Takes A Family: Conservatism and the Common Good*, that conservatives should reject the idea of "freedom to choose, irrespective of choice." True liberty, he wrote, is not "the freedom to be left alone," but "the freedom to attend to one's duties to God, to family, and to neighbors."[62]

All of this brings big-government conservatives full circle to where, as far as the size and scope of government are concerned, little difference exists between them and modern liberals. Liberals have long held that individual preferences must give way to the "greater good" and "the needs of society." Hillary Clinton once explained her political philosophy by saying, "It's time to put the common good, the national interest, ahead of individuals."[63] How much different is that from Rick Santorum's belief that freedom does not "celebrate the individual above society"?[64] Or Brooks's admonition that the American people need to "serve a cause larger than self-interest"?[65]

Conservatives once were appalled when then vice president Al Gore said government should be "like grandparents, in the sense that grandparents perform a nurturing role."[66] But President Bush takes that attitude even further. According to his former chief of staff Andrew Card, "This president sees America as we think about a 10-year-old child."[67]

Those of us who believe in limited government and individual liberty have long become accustomed to threats from the Democratic left. But, today, an equal threat may come from the Republican right. Should big-government conservatives win the debate over the direction of conservatism, it will represent a fundamental change in the balance of political forces. Are we destined for a future of debates only between liberals who want to increase the size and power of government and conservatives who want to increase the size and power of government?

If conservatives abandon the ideal of limited constitutional government, who then will speak for liberty?

2. The Roots of Big-Government Conservatism

In one sense, the American conservative movement dates back to the founding of the Republic; yet in another, it is little more than half a century old.

Part of this seeming contradiction is semantic. That is, the elder strain of conservatism may be more properly thought of as classical liberalism, at the core of which is concern with individual liberty. According to John Stuart Mill, the great liberal theorist, the state could only justify interference with the conduct of individual citizens when doing so clearly will prevent a greater harm to others. In Mill's words: "The only purpose for which power can be rightfully exercised over any member of a civilized community, against his will, is to prevent harm to others. His own good, either physical or moral, is not sufficient warrant."[1]

For the first 150 years, that was this country's governing philosophy. It was enshrined in the U.S. Constitution that ours was to be a government of limited powers. Thus, in 1794, James Madison, debating a proposed welfare bill, rose on the floor of the House to declare, "I cannot undertake to lay my finger on that article of the Federal Constitution which granted a right to Congress" to pass such a bill.[2] That attitude still prevailed in 1854 when President Franklin Pierce vetoed a bill to give land to the states to allow them to build institutions for the insane. In his veto message, Pierce wrote: "I cannot find any authority in the Constitution for making the Federal Government the great almoner of public charity throughout the United States. To do so would . . . be contrary to the letter and spirit of the Constitution and subversive of the whole theory upon which the Union of these States is founded."[3]

But the rise of "modernism" and "progressivism" at the end of the 19th century brought a sea change in Americans' attitude toward government. Progressive reformers, drawing on the newly developing field of social science, believed that the problems wrought by urbanization, industrialization, and the aftermath of the Civil War were too overwhelming for average citizens to deal with. "Experts" were needed to deal with such important issues, and only government could provide the needed expertise. Whereas previously the purpose of government had been seen as protecting individual rights, now government was seen as a problem solver.

Gradually the idea of a government of limited, enumerated powers began to wither, replaced by the idea of a government increasingly involved in every aspect of American life and the American economy. By 1920, Owen Lovejoy, president of the National Conference of Social Work, was writing that government workers were "social engineers" imposing "a divine order on earth as it is in heaven."[4]

Government was already growing rapidly when the United States experienced one of the most traumatic and transforming events in the nation's history—the Great Depression. At its worst point, in 1933, nearly 13 million Americans were unemployed, nearly one-quarter of the labor force. Among non-farm workers, unemployment was even worse, as high as 37.6 percent. The nation's real gross national product declined by one-third between 1929 and 1933. One-third of the nation's banks suspended operations. Businesses went bankrupt and mortgage foreclosures were widespread, particularly on farms. Both traditional private charitable organizations and state and local governments were overwhelmed by the sudden demands placed on them.[5]

With Americans frightened and insecure, an enormous demand existed for government action. President Franklin Roosevelt responded by massively expanding the federal role in social welfare and in regulating the economy. When the Supreme Court tried to hold government to constitutionally imposed boundaries, Roosevelt threatened to pack the Court until it capitulated.

To provide some idea of how vast and rapid the expansion of government was, consider that in 1932 just 2.1 percent of all government social-welfare spending was at the federal level. By 1939, the federal government accounted for 62.5 percent of social-welfare spending—and that larger slice was from a much larger pie. Over that same period, welfare programs increased from 6.5 percent of all government expenditures (combined federal, state, and local) to 27.1 percent.[6] At the same time, the Roosevelt administration regulated prices, set labor standards, and subsidized commodities. Virtually no area remained off limits to federal control.

The Depression, Roosevelt, and later World War II so cemented liberalism—not the classical variety, but the modern, big-government style—as the philosophy of government that Lionel Trilling could write without fear of contradiction, "In the United States, at this time, liberalism is not only the dominant but even the sole intellectual tradition."[7]

It wasn't until the postwar era that a new brand of conservatism began to emerge to challenge the new liberal orthodoxy. The conservative revival was led on the economic front by Milton Friedman and his colleagues at the University of Chicago. But it was William F. Buckley, who founded the *National Review* in 1955, who made conservatism intellectually respectable and brought it to the masses. (Buckley also performed an enormous service by marginalizing and eventually weeding out the worst of the movement's cranks, racists, anti-Semites, and conspiracy theorists.)

This new conservative movement had two distinct, often antagonistic, strains. The first was libertarian, in the limited-government tradition of the Founding Fathers.[8] It drew on the economics of Milton Friedman and the philosophical writings of Ayn Rand and Murray Rothbard, among others.

The other strain could essentially be described as traditionalist. Its interest was in protecting the structures, culture, and mores of society against what its proponents saw as forced and radical change. It drew its inspiration not from Mill, but from Edmund Burke, who argued for a "liberty connected with order."[9] Reacting in part against the excesses of the French Revolution, Burke placed great weight on the accumulated wisdom of centuries of experience and believed that the bounds of liberty should be enlarged cautiously and slowly so as to avoid anarchy and unintended consequences.

The most important spokesman of this strain of conservatism was Russell Kirk, who laid out six canons of conservative thought:

1. Belief in a transcendent order, or body of natural law, which rules society as well as conscience
2. Affection for the proliferating variety and mystery of human existence, as opposed to the narrowing uniformity, egalitarianism, and utilitarian aims of most radical systems
3. Conviction that civilized society requires orders and classes as against the notion of a "classless society"

4. Persuasion that freedom and property are closely linked
5. Faith in prescription and distrust of "sophisters, calculators, and economists" who would reconstruct society upon abstract designs
6. Recognition that "change may not be salutary reform: hasty innovation may be a devouring conflagration, rather than a torch of progress"[10]

Both conservative strains shared a common enemy, the overweening state, as represented both by New Deal liberalism at home and by totalitarian communism abroad. United by this mutual opposition to statism, libertarians and traditionalists agreed to put aside their differences and form a common front. Frank Meyer, a Buckley confidant and coeditor of the *National Review*, called this "fusionism."

Meyer argued that libertarians were correct in seeing freedom as the "primary end" of politics, but they were wrong to the extent that they saw freedom as an "absolute end." "In the moral realm, freedom is only a means whereby men can pursue their proper end, which is virtue," he wrote.[11] But Meyer also maintained that virtue was not possible without freedom. "The simulacrum of virtuous acts brought about by the coercion of superior power, is not virtue, the meaning of which resides in the free choice of good over evil."[12] This belief meant that both libertarians and conservatives were heading in the same direction, even if they failed to agree on a final destination.[13]

Both traditionalist conservatives and libertarians shared a common enemy, the growing federal government. As conservative sociologist Robert Nisbet explained:

> Doubtless conservatives [of the Russell Kirk variety] are more willing than libertarians to see the occasional necessity of suspension or abrogation of this position toward the national government. . . . In general, however, over a substantial period of time, conservatism may be seen as clearly as libertarianism to be a philosophy anchored in opposition to statism.[14]

As a result the conservative movement was able to coalesce loosely around three basic propositions: opposition to communism; a belief that the domestic functions of government, and especially of the federal government, should be strictly limited; and a general if vague acceptance of traditional Judeo-Christian values. Both Kirkian conservatives and libertarians formed a core that could be considered small-government conservatism. The broad, overlapping constituencies had disagreements, but by and large, the movement held together over the next 40 years. Even Russell Kirk was able to conclude, "What we have seen in this country . . . is the gradual fusion of conservatives and old-fangled liberals . . . into a fairly coherent body of opinion."[15]

Politically, this unified small-government conservatism led to Barry Goldwater's 1964 presidential campaign. That campaign reflected a deep commitment to small government, a belief in the individual, and an opposition to the growing welfare state.

Goldwater, of course, went down to defeat, crushed by an electoral reaction to Kennedy's assassination. But one can hardly judge his influence by electoral vote totals. As his biographer Lee Edwards put it, Goldwater was perhaps the "most consequential loser" in American political history.[16] His campaign "marked the beginning of a tectonic shift in American politics . . . that shapes the nation to this day."[17]

Among the passionate converts to Goldwater's cause was Ronald Reagan, whose famous television speech before the 1964 presidential election summed up small-government conservatism, "Whether we believe in our capacity for self-government or whether we abandon the American revolution and confess that a little intellectual elite in a far-distant capitol can plan our lives for us better than we can plan them ourselves."[18]

Reagan's speech led directly to his election as governor of California in 1966 and eventually to the presidency in 1980. Although that presidency did less to reduce the size of government than many of Reagan's fans would like to believe, no doubt Reagan was the most conservative president of the postwar era. Reagan even reduced domestic discretionary spending by roughly 9.5 percent. Total government spending, driven by a 41 percent increase in defense spending, rose in absolute terms but declined slightly as a percentage of gross domestic product.[19] He privatized a number of government services and significantly reduced the regulatory burden on large parts of the American economy. And he accomplished this in the face of Democratic control of the House and, for part of his term, the Senate.

The Cato Institute's president, Ed Crane, points out that the grad-ual change in the nature of conservatism probably began with Ron-ald Reagan's second term. In contrast to his strongly ideological 1980 campaign, Reagan chose to run for reelection on a feel-good "Morning in America" theme that drained ideology—and ideas generally—from the campaign. Reagan won a 49-state landslide, but his reelection came without a mandate for further shrinking government. The ideological zeal of his first term largely slipped away, and what little remained was siphoned off by the Iran-Contra scandal. To make matters worse, Reagan's largely unproductive second term was followed by the presidency of George H. W. Bush, a man of no discernable ideology, who allowed government to begin growing again.[20] Total government spending under the first Presi-dent Bush grew twice as fast as it had under Reagan, and domestic discretionary spending began to rise again.[21]

A brief revival of small-government conservatism occurred with the Republican takeover of Congress in 1994, but those advances gradually slipped away in the absence of a leader firmly committed to small government in the Reagan-Goldwater mode.[22] Congress is too diffuse to provide that kind of leadership on the national stage. The only truly compelling congressional leader of this period was Newt Gingrich, but—as we will see—he was not truly ideologically committed to cutting the size of government. Bob Dole's vapid 1996 presidential campaign hardly provided a rallying point for small-government conservatives. And George W. Bush barely even pre-tended a commitment to limited government.

The ideological vacuum created by this lack of leadership was slowly filled by five currents of conservative thought that have coalesced into today's big-government conservatism.

Neoconservatives

Few groups have had as much influence over the shape of contem-porary conservatism as the neoconservatives. Of course in saying this one runs immediately into the fact that most neoconservatives deny that a neoconservative movement exists. Norman Podhoretz says that neoconservatives have "never had or aspired to the kind of central organization characteristic of a movement." He prefers to call it a neoconservative "tendency."[23] Irving Kristol speaks of a "neoconservative persuasion."[24] Irwin Stelzer notes that while broad agreement on principles exists among those considered neoconservatives, "there are non-trivial differences among them."[25]

Yet, whether self-identified or not, a group of individuals does exist who share a general background and a broad philosophical perspective that may be called neoconservative. These individuals have achieved positions of influence both inside and outside the Bush administration and the Republican Party generally. In these roles, they have been a driving force behind big-government conservatism.

Although the Jewishness of neoconservatives has often been overstated—several prominent neoconservatives are not Jewish—and often carries a hint of anti-Semitism, no doubt exists that the roots of neoconservatism can be found in the debates among a small group of Jewish Marxists in 1930s New York. Many Jewish intellectuals who had immigrated to the United States from Russia and eastern Europe brought with them a deep attachment to socialism. But they also brought with them the strong doctrinal splits that were then wracking the communist movement worldwide.

Leon Trotsky, one of the original leaders of the Russian Revolution, had broken with Stalin during the 1920s. What started as a disagreement between Stalin's emphasis on "socialism in one country" and Trotsky's call for worldwide revolution deteriorated further as Trotsky protested the increasing bureaucratization of the Soviet state. By 1929 Stalin had engineered Trotsky's expulsion from the Communist Party and forced him into exile. From France, Norway, and later Mexico, Trotsky denounced Stalin's Russia as a "degenerate worker's state" and built a rival center of Marxist ideology.

In the U.S. Marxist community, as elsewhere, some communists remained true to Stalin's communist Russia as a model for the worker's state, while others were attracted to Trotsky's camp. This latter group included many of neoconservatism's founding fathers, such as Lionel Trilling, Sidney Hook, Elliott Cohen, Stephen Schwartz, Seymour Martin Lipset, Albert Wohlstetter, Gertrude Himmelfarb, and Irving Kristol.[26]

As the 1930s progressed, the ideological debates were given an added imperative by the rise of the Nazis in Germany. Many Jewish Marxists were particularly disturbed that Stalin had ordered German communists to use their strength not to battle the rising Nazis, but to crush the Social Democrats.[27] In 1934, Lionel Trilling and Elliott

Cohen, among others, signed "an Open Letter to American Intellectuals," criticizing Stalin and the German communists for wrecking a united front against fascism. In return, the U.S. Communist Party attacked them as Zionists, Internationalists, Trotskyites, and "enemies of the communist party."[28]

Of particular importance was a group at times numbering from 30 to 100 anti-Stalin leftists, who gathered in alcove number 1 of the lunchroom at New York City College. This group, which included Trotskyites such as Kristol and Daniel Bell, democratic socialists such as Irving Howe, and socialist Zionists such as Nathan Glazer, provided a vigorous forum for intellectual debate—among themselves, with their pro-Stalin antagonists (who gathered in alcove number 2), and for the academic community at large.[29] Kristol would later describe this time as one of the best periods of his life, a place "where pure intellect . . . reigned unchallenged."[30]

After leaving college, most of the participants from alcove number 1 remained active in Marxist politics. They wrote for and edited such influential leftist magazines as *Partisan Review*, *Commentary*, and *The Public Interest*. Many joined the labor movement and were active in the Socialist Workers Party, where they became part of an anti-Stalinist faction led by Max Shachtman.

At the same time, however, they were beginning to question their allegiance to Marxism. Increasingly, they were forced to ask themselves whether Stalin was an aberration or whether something intrinsic in the Soviet system, and therefore Marxism itself, led to Stalinist totalitarianism. World War II, the Nazi-Soviet Pact, and the growing revelation of Stalin's crimes accelerated the philosophical shift. Increasingly this group saw Stalin's Russia and Hitler's Germany as two sides of the same totalitarian coin.

Irving Kristol was one of the first to leave his old political faith behind. By the beginning of the war he no longer considered himself a Trotskyite. By the war's end, he called himself a New Deal liberal. His compatriots were somewhat slower in dropping their romantic attachment to communism, but by the late 1940s, all were convinced that Stalin's Russia, and communism generally, represented a terrible threat that must be confronted. With the zeal of converts throughout history, they became as fervent in their anti-communism as they had previously been zealous in their Marxism.

For example, in 1949 Kristol, Bell, Glazer, and Trilling joined Sidney Hook in forming the American Committee for Cultural Freedom, which was designed to be a voice for intellectual anticommunism. The organization would later break up over disputes about how to respond to Sen. Joseph McCarthy's anticommunist crusade, but no doubt exists that it helped shaped the worldviews of Kristol and his colleagues.[31] In particular, they developed a strong belief that most American liberals were too weak and too willing to appease America's enemies.

During the 1950s, what was to become neoconservatism also drew strongly on two other important schools of thought. One was found in the writings of Protestant theologian Reinhold Niebuhr. Kristol cites him as one of the most significant philosophical influences on the development of neoconservatism.[32]

In addition to his writings as a theologian, Niebuhr was a prominent socialist and intellectual, long influential with the American Left. But in 1940, he broke publicly with the Socialist Party over its opposition to American involvement in Europe's fight against Nazi Germany. At the time, much of the socialist world followed the Stalinist line that the fight between Germany and the West was nothing more than a clash between rival versions of imperialism. Although agreeing that the West was full of "capitalistic and imperialistic injustice," Niebuhr nonetheless saw a moral gulf between liberal democracy and genocidal totalitarianism.[33] He argued for an aggressive response in the face of evil, suggesting that the only moral foreign policy was one that challenged such evil wherever it was found, by war if necessary.

Domestically, Niebuhr remained committed to socialism, or at least social democracy. He supported Franklin Roosevelt for the presidency, later worked with Americans for Democratic Action, and was vice chairman of the Liberal Party in New York. But Niebuhr also strongly believed in cultural values and traditional virtues. He criticized the "the idolatrous self-worship" of individualism and warned, "Freedom is an essential good, but it must serve the larger end of societal virtue."[34]

Niebuhr saw politics generally as a clash of absolutes. His seminal work, *Children of Light and the Children of Darkness*, argued "the duty of politics is to establish justice in a sinful world." The importance of this fight was such that even morally "ambiguous" methods were justified (for example, allying with dictatorships to resist Soviet advances), a school of thought he dubbed "Christian realism."[35]

In the context of the future development of neoconservatism, it is also worth noting that Niebuhr was perfectly willing to use big government to pursue his vision of justice. As he noted in *Christianity and Society*: "It is dishonest to scare people with the perils of state power if these are not considered in comparison with the perils of irresponsible economic power. The growth of state power is neither a caprice of history nor the fruit of 'paganism.' It is the consequence of the community's effort to protect itself against irresponsible economic power."[36]

Another key intellectual influence on neoconservative thought was the ideas of Leo Strauss, a German Jewish émigré who had fled to this country in the 1930s and begun teaching political science at the University of Chicago. In his horror at the rise of Nazism, Strauss blamed the classical liberalism of the Enlightenment, rationalism, and modernism for creating the conditions that led to the Holocaust. Much of Strauss's work was based on the reinterpretation of classical texts to reveal the covert teachings that he claimed the great philosophers had hidden from the masses.[37]

Of particular importance to the development of neoconservatism was his belief that liberty could deteriorate into libertinism, which posed a threat to the republican character necessary to preserve a free but stable society. In his view, classical liberalism—with its emphasis on knowledge through reason—tended toward relativism, which in turn led to nihilism and a belief that no one's values were better than anyone else's. If all values were equally valid, no moral basis existed for opposing totalitarianism. Thus classical liberalism was a form of cultural suicide. Moreover, he believed that American culture was well down that road. He looked at the United States in the 1950s and 1960s and saw the Weimar Republic, morally degenerate and incapable of self-preservation.

The only alternative was a return to traditional virtues, particularly those infused by religious faith. Strauss argued, "To preserve society, wise people must publicly support the traditions and myths that sustain the political order and that encourage ordinary people to obey the laws and live justly."[38] Interestingly, he took this position despite his own lack of belief in God. Shadia Drury, one of Strauss's biographers (and critics) explains that he was: "convinced that religion is necessary for the well-being of society. But to state publicly that religion is a necessary fiction would destroy any salutary effect it might have. The latter depends on its being believed to be true .... If the vulgar discovered, as the philosophers have always known, that God is dead, they might behave as if all is permitted."[39]

This conviction was part of Strauss's general belief in the "noble lie." Just as the ancient philosophers delivered separate messages for the masses and the educated elites, today's elites should fashion messages, whether strictly true or not, that will uplift the masses and help forge a stable society.[40] He taught Plato's maxim that, "If anyone at all is to have the privilege of lying, the rulers of the state should be the persons; and they, in their dealings either with enemies or with their own citizens, may be allowed to lie for the public good."[41]

Strauss strongly rejected Enlightenment thinking based on the philosophies of Jean-Jacques Rousseau, Thomas Hobbes, Spinoza, and others who championed the ideas of individual liberty, subjective morality, and scientific rationalism. Individualism was, he argued, synonymous with nihilism. And rationalism divorced man from eternal truths and timeless values. These ideas stripped purpose from life, leaving only the listless, meaningless life of economic man, or, in a desperate search for higher meaning, leading to dangerous experiments with new gods—such as Hitler or Stalin.

Among the neoconservatives who studied under Strauss or were strongly influenced by him were Allan Bloom; Harry Jaffa; Irving Kristol and his wife Gertrude Himmelfarb; Norman Podhoretz, his wife Midge Decter, and their son John; Paul Wolfowitz; Robert Kagan; and former Cheney chief of staff I. Lewis "Scooter" Libby. Kristol says that Strauss, along with Trilling, had the "greatest impact" of anyone on his political thinking.[42] In particular he agreed with the Straussian idea that too much freedom would result in the "release of popular passions hitherto held in check by tradition and religion with utterly unpredictable, but mostly negative, consequences."[43]

What was required, therefore, was a strong government, one capable of enforcing virtue upon the people. "Because mankind is intrinsically wicked, he has to be governed," as Strauss wrote.[44]

Neoconservative views emerged more fully from the turbulence of the 1960s. Already largely estranged from the anti–Vietnam War peace movement, the neoconservatives found their reverence for religion and tradition increasingly at odds with the counterculture's views on such things as drugs, sex, and the role of women. Intellectuals who placed a premium on academic study and debate, they were appalled by student takeovers and demonstrations. In addition, the core Jewish neoconservatives were greatly concerned at the anti-Semitism they saw among black nationalists and then the critics of Israeli policy in the wake of the 1967 war.

As Norman Podhoretz put it:

> If anti-Communism was the ruling passion of the neoconservatives in foreign affairs, opposition to the counterculture of the 1960s was their ruling passion at home. Indeed, I suspect that revulsion against the counterculture accounted for more converts to neoconservatism than any other single factor. But the revulsion was not only directed against the counterculture itself; it was also inspired by the abject failure of the great institutions of the liberal community to resist the counterculture. First the universities capitulated, then the national media, and finally even the Democratic Party. In part the problem was simple cowardice, but in part it was the sheer inability of these institutions to defend themselves intellectually when they came under attack by the counterculture.[45]

Most neoconservatives remained at least token Democrats throughout the 1970s, many aligning with Sen. Henry "Scoop" Jackson (D-WA).[46] Jackson was a labor-oriented liberal on economic issues, but an outspoken hawk on defense and foreign policy and culturally conservative. Although an opponent of détente with the Soviet Union, an outspoken supporter of Israel (he was the sponsor of the Jackson-Vanik Amendment designed to promote the right of Soviet Jews to emigrate to Israel), and a critic of the McGovern wing of the Democratic Party on Vietnam, he was a champion of national health care and had a nearly 100 percent lifetime rating from the AFL/CIO.[47] Jackson ran for president unsuccessfully in 1972 and 1976, both times attracting strong backing from neoconservatives. About that time, socialist writer Michael Harrington dubbed his one-time colleagues as "neoconservatives," a moniker that appears to have stuck.[48]

Also around that time, the loosely knit group of neoconservatives was beginning to move away from its Jewish roots and incorporate others who were making the Left to Right political journey. They included former Catholic socialists like William Bennett and Michael Novak, and New Deal liberal populists such as Jeane Kirkpatrick and James Woolsey.[49]

By the 1980s, most neoconservatives had finally crossed over to the Republican Party. Many had previously voted for Richard Nixon out of revulsion with McGovernism, but they remained uncomfortable generally with Republicans. Culturally, Republicans were not an easy fit for these sons of immigrants, and Nixon's policy of détente was hardly to their liking. Ronald Reagan changed all that. Even though many neoconservatives were suspicious of his libertarian leanings on domestic policy, the staunchly anti-communist Reagan offered an ideal vehicle for their aggressive anti-Soviet stance. Besides, Reagan was himself a former Democrat, a one-time union president, whose ability to relate to culturally conservative ethnic voters created a whole category of the electorate, "Reagan Democrat" voters.[50]

Among the neoconservatives finding a place in the Reagan administration were Podhoretz (United States Information Agency), Bennett (chairman of the National Endowment for the Humanities and later education secretary under George H. W. Bush), Kirkpatrick (Ambassador to the United Nations), Himmelfarb (National Endowment for the Humanities), Elliott Abrams (assistant secretary of state), Richard Perle (assistant secretary of defense), Paul Wolfowitz (assistant secretary of state and later Ambassador to Indonesia), Robert Kagan (a speechwriter in the State Department), and Irving Kristol's son, Bill (Department of Education).[51] As Podhoretz pointed out, by appointing so many neoconservatives to his administration, Reagan was "forging a living link between the Democratic mainstream and his own administration."[52]

Still, there were limits to neoconservative influence under Reagan. With a few exceptions, such as Bennett and Kirkpatrick, most neoconservatives held junior positions. Reagan's inner circle consisted largely of traditional conservatives who shared the neoconservatives' anti-communism and support for traditional moral values but were skeptical of their grander designs. Moreover, with very few exceptions, Reagan kept the neoconservatives far away from domestic policy.[53]

As Reagan moved in a more moderate direction, pursuing a conciliatory strategy toward disarmament and warmer relations with the

31

Soviet Union during his second term, neoconservative disillusion set in.[54] Jeane Kirkpatrick, the neoconservatives' most high-profile representative, left her post at the United Nations in 1985. Others, including James Baker and First Lady Nancy Reagan, eclipsed neoconservative influence. "Every now and then he shows a flash of the Reagan who might have been," Kristol wrote, "but these intermittent flashes are quickly dimmed."[55]

Neoconservatives also suffered a further loss of influence in the wake of their involvement in the Iran-Contra scandal. By the end of the Reagan administration, neoconservative fortunes were clearly waning. Their power under the first president Bush was much diminished, as demonstrated by their inability to persuade Bush to continue the Gulf War in an effort to unseat Saddam Hussein.

Shortly after George H. W. Bush was elected came the fall of the Berlin Wall and the end of the Cold War. Suddenly, anti-communism, one of the two raisons d'être of the neoconservative movement, was gone. When Bill Clinton defeated Bush in 1992, the remaining neoconservatives were sent into exile. They retreated to their think tanks, particularly the American Enterprise Institute, and their magazines, to reexamine their goals and to debate the direction that they felt American conservatism should take.

By the time George W. Bush was elected in 2000, they had reached a rough consensus in favor of a crusade for global democracy abroad and the remaking of culture at home. They were perfectly positioned, therefore, to move into positions of power in the second Bush's administration, obtaining levels of influence that they had never before achieved. Most of the "first generation" of neoconservatives was, of course, too old to serve in the Bush administration—though they remain influential—but their students and acolytes moved into several key positions influencing both foreign and domestic policy.[56]

A great deal, perhaps too much, effort has been expended debating the various philosophical influences on neoconservatism. Volumes have been written on whether Trotsky's concept of "permanent revolution" undergirds neoconservative foreign policy, or the degree of Straussian influence on this or that policy proposal.[57] Such speculation far too quickly descends into the fever swaps of conspiracy theories. What is clear, however, is that at each stage of their philosophical evolution—from Trotskyite to New Deal Democrat to

Scoop Jackson Democrat to neoconservative Republican—neoconservatives have been entirely comfortable with the idea of big government.

Much has been written about the neoconservative influence on American foreign policy.[58] But as their origins illustrate, neoconservatism has always been intimately concerned with domestic policy.[59] And their influence on domestic policy has been every bit as profound as it has been on foreign policy.

In a 1976 *Newsweek* article, Irving Kristol attempted to spell out the basic outline of neoconservative beliefs.[60] Among the points he made:

- "Neoconservatism is not at all hostile to the idea of the welfare state, but is critical of the Great Society version of this welfare state. In general, it approves of those social reforms that, while providing needed security and comfort to the individual in our dynamic, urbanized society, do so with a minimum of bureaucratic intrusion in the individual's affairs." He went on to say that neoconservatives specifically embraced "social security, unemployment insurance, some form of national health insurance, some kind of family-assistance plan, etc."

- Neoconservatives accept that a free market is the most efficient mechanism for allocating goods and services but are "willing to interfere with the market for overriding social purposes." In doing so, they prefer "rigging the market or even creating new markets," rather than "direct bureaucratic controls." Thus, Kristol says, neoconservatism "is more likely to prefer housing vouchers for the poor than government-built low-income projects."

- Neoconservatives are "respectful of traditional values and institutions: religion, the family, and the high culture of Western Civilization." They are unified in their "dislike of the counterculture that has played such a remarkable role in American life." They believe that an individual "who is 'liberated' from the sovereignty of traditional values will soon find himself experiencing the vertigo and despair of nihilism." Nor do they accept the idea that individuals can "create their own values and then incorporate them into a satisfying lifestyle."

Clearly, neoconservatives are comfortable with the modern welfare state. As Nathan Glazer put it, neoconservative differences with liberal advocates of the welfare state "do not have to do with deep, underlying, philosophical positions."[61] Norman Podhoretz has written, that from the beginning, "the neoconservatives dissociated themselves from the wholesale opposition to the welfare state that had marked American conservatism since the days of the New Deal."[62] Jeane Kirkpatrick pointed out that: "Every modern democracy is a welfare state in the sense that it seeks to provide basic minimum standards of well-being to its citizens. No serious political party, no serious policymaker, in this country or any other democracy, really seeks to repeal this function of government."[63] And Kristol notes that "a conservative welfare state . . . is perfectly consistent with the neo-conservative perspective."[64]

But neoconservatives do take serious issue with how most current welfare programs have been implemented. Indeed, they were among the first to demonstrate how social welfare programs have undermined the family and work ethic. That they spoke in the language of social science gave added reach and power to their arguments.[65] Welfare critics such as Daniel Patrick Moynihan and Charles Murray appeared frequently in their publications. This contribution should not be underestimated. Most of what is now regarded as conventional wisdom about the failures of welfare can be traced to neoconservatives and their allies.

Still, they saw themselves as "meliorists, not opponents," seeking ways "to improve, even reconstruct this welfare state."[66] As Kristol put it, "The welfare state is with us for better or worse . . . conservatives should try to make it better rather than worse."[67] By this, neoconservatives meant "a welfare state consistent with the basic moral values of our civilization."[68] The goal was to find ways to use the incentives of the welfare system, both rewards and penalties, to shape the behavior of the poor.

Not surprisingly, those social welfare programs that did not carry such extreme cultural consequences were perfectly acceptable to neoconservatives. They see both Social Security and Medicare, for example, as not only necessary, but also desirable. Indeed, those programs might even be made "more generous" because

> the elderly are such wonderful, unproblematic citizens. They are patriotic, they do not have illegitimate children, they do not commit crimes, they do not riot in the street; their popular entertainments are decent rather than degrading, and if they

find themselves a bit flush with funds, they happily distribute the money to their grandchildren.[69]

Thus, redistribution of wealth, the welfare state, or government power does not bother neoconservatives. Their only concern is whether the recipients act as good bourgeois citizens. As Gary Dorrien put it in his history of neoconservatism, "The neoconservatives were trying to repeal the 1960s, not the New Deal."[70]

Indeed, some would extend the welfare state, or at least the regulatory state, much further. Nathan Glazer has written of the "self-evident virtues of the European welfare states, with their universal health care, near abolition of poverty, provision of a decent and respectable life for most of the population," and called for "giving workers the full panoply of health care, vacation time, child benefits, parental leave, etc.," that exists in Europe.[71]

Having rejected Marxism, neoconservatives have shown little overt interest in the details of economics. Kristol, for one, says he "pay[s] little attention to the economics of the welfare state which I regard as a secondary issue."[72] Perhaps, this lack of interest is because they have long believed that the crisis they see facing America is not an economic one, but a cultural one. As James Piereson put it, neoconservatives believed in Adam Smith but preferred his "Theory of Moral Sentiments" to "The Wealth of Nations."[73]

To a large degree, this difference is not merely a matter of emphasis but a rejection of what Kristol calls "thinking economically." For example, he criticizes economists for their belief that "it is impossible to have an *a priori* knowledge of what constitutes happiness for other people . . . that such knowledge is revealed by the choices an individual makes in a free market." But, Kristol says, that is true only if you "define happiness and satisfaction in terms of the material production and material consumption of commodities." He believes it is entirely possible to define "the spiritual dimensions of a good life," which economic thinking ignores.[74]

He is particularly critical of conservative icon Ludwig von Mises, for saying:

> Economics is a theoretical science and as such abstains from any judgment of value. It is not its task to tell people what ends they should aim at. It is a science of the means to be applied for the attainment of ends chosen, not to be sure, a science of the choosing of ends. Ultimate decisions, the

> valuations and the choosing of ends, are beyond the scope
> of any science. Science never tells a man how he should act;
> it merely shows how a man must act if he wants to attain
> definite ends.[75]

Kristol and his fellow neoconservatives think that precisely those ends are most important. And they see the proper role of politics as determining and enforcing those ends.

To the degree that neoconservatives do consider economics, however, they are capitalists. That is, they acknowledge, "the idea of a centrally-planned and centrally-administered economy, so popular in the 1930s and early 1940s, has been discredited."[76] More affirmatively they see that capitalism was the most efficient economic system for allocating goods and services, and therefore the most likely system to advance people's material prosperity. Even more significant from their point of view, capitalism appears to be unique among economic systems in providing a foundation for freedom more generally.

However, neoconservatives are also critics of capitalism. Or, more precisely, they are suspicious of it. As Michael Joyce puts it, capitalism "is an engine of good that can be turned to evil ends if driven by base motives."[77] In *Two Cheers for Capitalism*, Kristol warns that the material prosperity brought about by capitalism creates a climate of instant gratification that is dangerous to the good order of society.[78] Don Eberly, who founded the National Fatherhood Initiative and helped set up President George W. Bush's Office of Faith-Based Initiatives, declares, "Decadence is brought to us by the marketplace."[79]

Essentially, neoconservatives have three interrelated complaints about capitalism.[80] First, they share the view of neoconservative fellow-traveler Daniel Bell that as capitalism produces prosperity it will also produce vices that will eventually erode the virtues upon which capitalism depends.[81] These virtues include "cleanliness, orderliness, thrift, and sexual propriety centered in the family."[82] By undercutting these virtues capitalism holds within it the potential seeds of its own destruction. Second, neoconservatives build on the arguments of economist Joseph Schumpeter that because capitalism is based on innovation and change, it relies on a "perennial gale of creative destruction" that inevitably undermines traditional social institutions.[83] In particular, the new technologies brought about by capitalist innovation have broken up the traditional nuclear family. And, third, capitalism, by definition, rewards production and consumption rather than virtue. Its success is unrelated to absolute values of right and wrong. As David Bosworth writes in *The Public Interest*, "Relativism is the standard operating procedure of scientific capitalism."[84] Capitalism is about individual choice. And individual choice, as Strauss taught, is the road to nihilism.

As a result, neoconservatives have no problem with regulation or other government intervention in the marketplace when they feel it serves a larger social good. As Irving Kristol explains, "if you believe that man's spiritual life is infinitely more important than his trivial and transient adventures in the marketplace, then you may tolerate a free market for practical reasons, within narrow limits, but you certainly will have no compunctions about overriding it if you think the free market is interfering with more important things."[85]

Thus, you find neoconservative support for such policy initiatives as outlawing pornography.[86] But neoconservative support for the reining in of capitalism goes beyond such obvious moral issues, extending to efforts to build what they consider to be a proper bourgeois society. For example, Eberly declares himself "anti-Wal-Mart," and blames the retailing giant for "stripping village life from American civilization."[87]

This is not to say that neoconservatives support business regulation in the same way as, say, liberal Democrats. More often than not, they have come down on the side of deregulation, particularly when the regulation involved is purely an economic question. However, they retain an underlying belief that government regulation and power can be used to order society.

Indeed, neoconservatives break strongly with traditional conservatives in that they are ultimately all too happy to *govern*. As Daniel Mahoney writes in *The Public Interest*, neoconservatives

> challenge the core libertarian presuppositions underlying conservative political rhetoric over the past two decades. For a generation now, conservatives have been the antigovernment party, championing the vitality of civil society against the intrusions of an overweening bureaucratic and regulatory state. If business oriented conservatives have been preoccupied with threats to individual liberty and unshackled economic activity, social conservatives have drawn attention to

37

the increasing hostility of the national government to traditional values. But conservative discomfort with the very idea of national government has placed them in a quandary: they wish to govern but fail to articulate a sufficient sense of the legitimacy of national government or the dignity of political life in general.[88]

Far from fearing a strong state, Irving Kristol says neoconservatives believe "a modern democratic state will be a strong one, not a weak one. There is not much point in lamenting this development . . . and no reason to do so."[89]

Because of their strong emphasis on traditional moral values, neoconservatives have found it easy to make common cause with religious conservatives despite the fact that so many neoconservatives are not only Jewish, but also actually agnostic or even atheists.[90] Differences exist between them, of course. For example, neoconservatives have by and large avoided the hot-button issues of abortion and, until recently, homosexuality. (The issue of gay marriage seems to have sparked some neoconservatives to speak out in opposition.) But the areas of overlap predominate.

As Kristol says, neoconservatives and the religious right are "united on issues concerning the quality of education, the relations of church and state, the regulation of pornography, and the like, all of which they regard as proper candidates for the government's attention."[91] Neoconservatives strongly backed President Bush's faith-based initiative and called for greater government support for religious institutions. Leading neoconservatives have even joined the Religious Right in attacking Darwin and championing creationism.[92]

More important, perhaps, neoconservatives have strongly defended the involvement of religious conservatives in politics. Norman Podhoretz, for example, wrote a famous essay in *National Review* defending the Religious Right from charges of anti-Semitism and arguing that the movement has been a positive force in society.[93] Kristol has criticized opposition of the Religious Right by many Jews, claiming that Jewish concern "has very little to do with traditional discrimination, and everything to do with efforts by liberals among whom, I regret to say, Jews are both numerous and prominent, to establish a wall between religion and society, in the guise of maintaining the wall between church and state." Kristol went on to say, "Jewish organizations proceed from the correct proposition that legally and constitutionally we are not a Christian nation, to the absurd proposition that we are in no sense at all a Christian society."[94]

When they have become involved in discussions of the nitty-gritty of economic policy, neoconservatives have tended toward supply-side economics (see below), giving space to supply-side writers in *Commentary* and *The Public Interest*.[95] Kristol raised much of the grant money that financed Jude Wanniski's supply-side treatise, *The Way the World Works*. He also arranged for Wanniski to receive a fellowship at the American Enterprise Institute. In fact, Wanniski called Kristol "the invisible hand" behind the early supply-side movement.[96]

Like other supply-siders, neoconservatives have tended to devote their efforts to cutting taxes, not cutting spending. Kristol says, "We should figure out what we want before we calculate what we can afford, not the reverse, which is the normal conservative disposition."[97] Elsewhere he boasts that neoconservatives have "a cavalier attitude toward the budget deficit and other monetary or fiscal problems."[98]

National-Greatness Conservatives

As the original neoconservatives have grown older and become less involved in day-to-day policy and politics, a new generation of their followers has picked up the torch. A small but extremely influential group has attempted to expand the doctrines of neoconservatism into something that they call "national greatness conservatism."

The link between neoconservatism and national-greatness conservatism is pretty much a straight line. One of the most outspoken advocates of national greatness, Bill Kristol, is Irving's son. And his collaborator David Brooks calls himself and his colleagues "intellectual heirs" of the original neoconservatives.[99] In many ways national-greatness conservatives resemble neoconservatives on steroids.

That is, national-greatness conservatives zealously embrace the central tenets of neoconservatism. They have no Hayekian fear of big government. As David Brooks puts it, "Just as socialism [is] no longer the guiding goal for the Left . . . reducing the size of government cannot be the governing philosophy for the next generation of conservatives."[100] Although generally dismissive of Barry Goldwater and many other conservative icons, they openly applaud liberal advocates of big government. "Are we willing to say that the country is worse off because of FDR or JFK or LBJ? I'm not willing to say that," states Bill Kristol.[101]

Accordingly, they generally support the existing welfare state, particularly as it applies to middle-class entitlements such as Social Security and Medicare. Indeed, they supported the Medicare prescription drug benefit and were skeptical of President Bush's efforts to reform Social Security.

Second, national-greatness conservatives are culturally conservative and support government action to support traditional social institutions. In Bill Kristol's words, conservatism must "revers[e] the widespread collapse of morals and standards in American society."[102] American greatness "ought to emphasize both personal and national responsibility."[103]

And this is the job of government. As Brooks explains, his version of conservatives would "understand that while culture matters most, government can alter culture."[104] In that vein, to cite one example, he applauds those "government agencies [that] are now trying to design programs to encourage and strengthen marriage."[105]

Their attitude can be seen in the reaction to President Bush's response to Hurricane Katrina. Many conservatives were appalled at the president's call for massive new government spending. But David Brooks excoriated not the president but his congressional critics because "they had no confidence that the federal government could do anything to transform the culture of poverty."[106]

Third, they are suspicious of unfettered free-market capitalism and strongly reject the primacy of individual choice. Bill Kristol calls for a conservatism in which the "fundamental mandate is to take on the sacred cow of liberalism—choice."[107] He is not speaking just of abortion, but of choice across a wide range of issues. David Brooks hails conservatism for evolving from "a movement that once lauded individual choice," to one that it is "preoccupied with family stability, civil society, and national cohesion."[108] The *Weekly Standard* has prominently featured articles calling for conservatism to move "Up from Libertarianism" or warning of "The Libertarian Temptation."[109] In the conflict between individuals and the larger society, national-greatness conservatives come down firmly on the side of society.

This view has led to increased support for government regulation. They believe that we can use "the strong-government tradition" "in the tradition of Alexander Hamilton, Henry Clay and Teddy Roosevelt" to improve "competition."[110]   Fourth, national-greatness conservatives support an expansive and aggressive foreign policy. No group has been as outspoken in favor of the war in Iraq and other foreign adventures.

But they also go one step beyond traditional neoconservatism. The essence of national-greatness conservatism is the belief that government must organize Americans "to serve a cause larger than self-interest, fuse their own efforts with those from other regions and other walks of life and cultivate a spirit of citizenship."[111]

Moreover, this "larger cause" cannot be discovered through individual choice or decision-making. Nor can it be found in individual communities. Thus national-greatness conservatives dismiss the tendency among conservatives to devolve power from the federal government to states, localities, and voluntary institutions, citing Edmund Burke's belief that effective local institutions depend on their being linked to "higher and more large regards," such as the nation. In short, they believe, "America won't be good locally if it isn't great nationally."[112] Thus, "ultimately American purpose can find its voice only in Washington," where "individual ambition and will power are channeled into the cause of national greatness, and in making the nation great, individuals are able to join their narrow concerns to a larger national project."[113]

Exactly what that project should be remains unclear. In fact, the project almost seems not to matter as long as it is something "big" and can be done by the federal government. Examples cited approvingly are as diverse as sending a man to Mars, establishing the 19th-century land-grant colleges, and creating the greatness of the Department of Agriculture.[114] According to Brooks, national-greatness conservatism

> champions a series of measures designed to remind American citizens of their common bonds. It revitalizes our transportation network, which has always bound us together. It nourishes the parks, forests, and preserves that are our common heritage. It reforms the nation's culture policy, so that museums and arts institutions that accept taxpayer dollars are more likely to explore what it means to be American than they are to nourish alienation and multicultural parochialism.[115]

Brooks has even called for the government to build more monuments like the Library of Congress, which symbolize "the greatness of the American experiment."[116] And Michael Petrilli of the Fordham Foundation has suggested that the federalization of education should be part of a national-greatness agenda. "Developing a common civic and cultural language could certainly be considered such a great national project—and would be possible through common K–12 standards," he says.[117]

But perhaps the best example of how national-greatness conservatives view the role of government is in their strong support for a national service program. David Brooks says, "[Mandatory national service] takes kids out of the normal self-obsessed world of career and consumption and orients them toward service and citizenship."[118] Tellingly, Brooks favors military-style national service, because under it, "Today's children . . . would suddenly face drill sergeants reminding them they are nothing without the group."[119]

Bill Kristol has also indicated his support for national service or possibly even the draft. And Leslie Lenkowsky, head of the Corporation for National Service under President Bush, also believes, "We need to convey this expectation, that everyone should expect to give something back to their country."[120]

National-greatness conservatives were not initially attracted to George W. Bush. Their preferred candidate was Sen. John McCain. McCain routinely echoes their call that "Americans must commit to a cause larger than their own self-interest."[121] According to McCain, we must renew "the responsibilities and obligations of citizenship to promote national greatness."[122] That is why McCain believes "national service should one day be a rite of passage for young Americans."[123]

Nevertheless, national-greatness conservatives have generally been supportive of the Bush administration and its policies. Meanwhile, through the *Weekly Standard*, their numerous television venues, and Brooks's regular column in the *New York Times*, they have kept up a steady drumbeat for their brand of conservatism.

National-greatness conservatives remain a small group. But through their media platforms and network of contacts both in and outside of the administration, they wield an influence far beyond their size.

The Religious Right

On January 22, 1973, an event occurred that would transform both American politics generally and the conservative movement in particular. On that day, the Supreme Court voted 7-2 to strike down as unconstitutional a Texas statute outlawing abortions except to save the life of the mother.[124] Before the Court's decision in *Roe v. Wade,* nearly two-thirds of the states prohibited abortion, and many others restricted it in some fashion. But suddenly, overnight, the United States found itself "with abortion laws more lenient than those of any noncommunist country in the Western world."[125] Whatever one thinks of the legal merits of the decision, there is no doubting its political impact.

America has always been a religious nation and has a long history of intersection between religion and politics. For example, the abolition and temperance movements were strongly influenced by religion. On the less savory side, the anti-immigrant and anti-Catholic movements of the mid-19th century were fueled by Protestant evangelism. The populism embodied by William Jennings Bryan had a large religious component and led to currency reform, corporate regulation, and adoption of direct democracy through initiatives and referenda.[126]

But by the mid-20th century a shift had occurred, leading to a more fragmented and less influential religious voice in politics. Catholic immigration brought a more diverse religious population and one that did not share many of the social and cultural concerns of Protestant evangelism. Indeed, in many cases the two groups were openly hostile. In the North, many Protestant denominations were moving away from a belief in biblical inerrancy, while in the South a more inward-looking Protestantism was developing. This form of Protestantism placed a primacy on being saved through faith, rather than works. Christians were expected to behave morally in their own lives and pray and work to convert others, but no expectation existed for social change in the world at large. "We are in the world, but not of it," was the guiding scripture.[127]

To the degree that Christians were politically active they showed no particular political leanings. In fact, while the relatively liberal Protestant denominations in New England and the Midwest leaned Republican, more theologically conservative denominations actually tended toward the Democrats. Catholic immigrants were a mainstay of the big-city Democratic machines that provided them with jobs and social welfare services. Rural and small-town southern Protestants were attracted to the New Deal's agricultural and poverty relief programs, becoming a firm part of the Roosevelt coalition.

If it was an issue at all, a majority of Christians saw big government as a positive force in their lives. Research by David King of Harvard's Kennedy School of Government shows that in 1954, for example, holding everything else constant, regular churchgoers were evenly divided between Republicans and Democrats.[128] Evangelical Protestants were even more reliably Democratic. In the years following World War II, they favored Democrats by nearly two to one. Roughly 70 percent of Catholics were registered Democrats.[129]

The first signs of shifting allegiance showed in 1960. When Democrats nominated Catholic John F. Kennedy, many southern Protestants held to a longstanding anti-Catholicism and crossed over to the Republican column (although they remained registered Democrats). This conservative and Republican drift continued throughout the 1960s and 1970s, spurred by reaction to the counterculture and the increasing secularization of society.

Rural and small-town America was unnerved by the social upheaval of the 1960s, and the sex, drugs, and rock and roll that seemed to define the era. As Kevin Phillips put it, "The World of Manhattan, Harvard and Beverly Hills was being exported to Calhoun County, Alabama, and Calhoun County did not like it."[130] Simultaneously, a series of court decisions seemed to further undermine the culture that evangelical Protestants had long taken for granted. In 1962, the Supreme Court outlawed school prayer. In 1971, it prohibited religious displays on public ground and blocked government funding of private religious schools. And in 1973 came the abortion decision. Conservative Protestants suddenly felt under siege and reacted with what neoconservative scholar Nathan Glazer called a "defensive offensive."[131]

By 1980, Republicans outnumbered Democrats among evangelical Protestants, and today Republicans hold a 25 percentage point edge. That may actually understate the shift because African American evangelicals remain overwhelmingly Democratic. Among white evangelicals the margin runs close to 40 percent.[132] Roughly 78 percent of white evangelicals voted for President Bush in 2004.[133] Catholics have been slower to change their allegiance, but a 73 to 25 percent

Figure 2.1
EVANGELICALS AND PARTY IDENTIFICATION

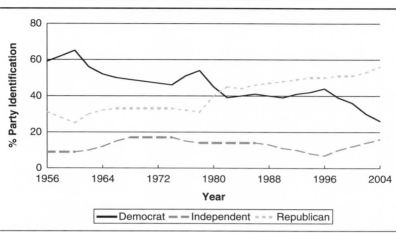

SOURCE: Pew Research Center, *Religion and Public Life: A Faith-Based Partisan Divide*, p. 7.

Democratic lead in 1960 has shrunk to just 3 percentage points, 44 to 41[134] (Figures 2.1, 2.2).

The Pew Research Center concludes, "Americans who attend worship services and hold traditional religious views increasingly vote Republican, while those who are less connected to religious institutions and more secular in their outlook tend to vote Democratic."[135] In fact, today religiously oriented voters make up a larger proportion of the Republican base vote than do wealthier Americans who are traditionally associated with conservative and Republican politics.[136]

Observers on both the Right and Left have noted that the movement of religious conservatives to the Republican Party has resulted in a shift of traditionally class-based voting. Peter Berger, for instance, argues that cultural and economic elites tend to be pro-choice, whereas the less affluent and educated are more likely to be pro-life.[137] Thomas Frank makes a similar point in his book *What's the Matter with Kansas*, arguing that Republican association with moral issues has induced working-class families to disregard their economic interest and vote conservative.[138] Frank badly misjudges

Figure 2.2
CATHOLICS AND PARTY IDENTIFICATION, 1956–2004

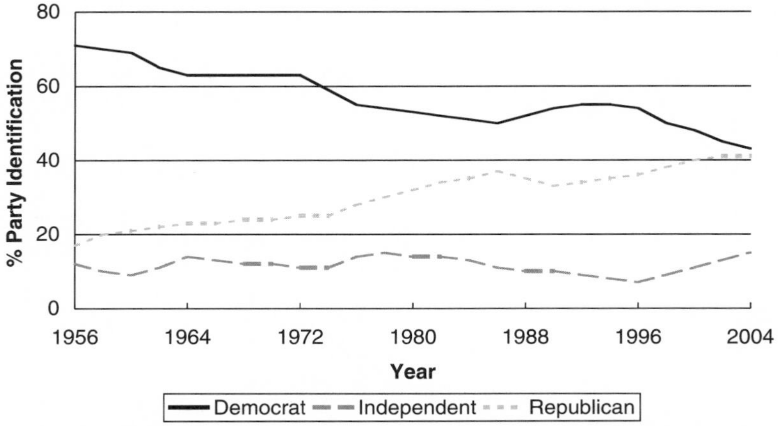

SOURCE: Pew Research Center, *Religion and Public Life: A Faith-Based Partisan Divide*, p. 7.

what economic policies actually do to benefit lower- and middle-income workers but is correct in believing that many of these people might vote Democratic if only economic issues were on the table.

This trend can be seen on a small scale among African American evangelical voters. Although the vast majority of African Americans remain firmly Democratic, Republicans have made small gains recently among religiously conservative, evangelical African Americans. The Bush administration has consciously courted this block of voters, stressing such issues as Bush's faith-based initiative and opposition to gay marriage. The success of this approach was apparent in Ohio in 2004. Bush took 16 percent of the African American vote, much better than his nationwide average of 11 percent. Most of these African American voters were motivated by opposition to abortion and gay marriage (an anti-gay-marriage amendment was on the Ohio ballot).[139] As Ohio Democratic strategist Greg Haas explained, "If [gay marriage] had not been on the ballot, John Kerry would have won Ohio."[140]

But changing political affiliation does not necessarily mean that religious conservatives have changed their views on the role of

46

government. For example, a Pew Research Center survey found that a clear majority of Catholics believe that business "makes too much profit" and that government should do more to help the needy. That poll also showed a plurality of Catholics believes that business regulation does more good than harm.[141] Another poll showed that 62 percent of Catholics favored "improving government services such as education and health care, even if it means higher spending." Even 41 percent of self-identified Catholic Republicans held that view. Only 38 percent thought "cutting taxes and reducing government spending" were more important.[142]

White Protestants have generally been somewhat less supportive of government social-welfare programs, although the Pew poll showed small pluralities holding liberal views on government's role in helping the needy and regulating business.[143] No reason exists to believe that African American evangelicals have become economically more conservative, even if some are willing to support Republicans on moral issues.

In fact, polling shows that the number of Americans who consider themselves "extremely conservative" on both cultural *and* economic issues is relatively small. Moreover, a 1992 study of data from the University of Chicago's General Social Survey suggests that no discernable correlation exists between voters' cultural and economic views.[144] Although the analysis is somewhat dated, and the increasing partisan divide may have increased conformity of views in the past few years, many religious conservatives apparently still hold moderate or even liberal views on noncultural issues.

As Adam Wolfson, former editor of *The Public Interest*, explained, "Religious conservatives are not fundamentalists when it comes to the size and role of government."[145] Indeed, as far back as the 1980s, *National Review* publisher William Rusher wrote that although religious conservatives were vital to a successful national conservative movement, welcoming them into the Republican fold would mean accommodating their view "that government may at times be a useful weapon for curbing various forms of private rapacity."[146]

The most obvious manifestation of this lack of traditional conservative principles on the part of many religious conservatives is their willingness to use government power to enforce their views on morality. No longer simply defending their communities from what they see as outside values, religious conservatives now see their mission as reforming society as a whole. Ross Douthat has written that religious conservatives are, in many ways, the heirs to the religious reformers of the past who led movements ranging from abolition to women's suffrage. He argues, not unsympathetically, that just as Victorian reformers sought to ameliorate what they saw as excesses of the industrial revolution, today's religious reformers seek to deal with the consequences of the sexual revolution.[147]

This is not a "leave us alone" stance. Gary Bauer puts it bluntly: "The question is not whether you legislate morality. The question is whose morality you're going to legislate."[148] James Dobson, the influential head of Focus on the Family, says, "The role of government is to uphold standards that are healthy for society."[149] Louis Sheldon of the Traditional Values Coalition believes the role of government is to care for and support religion as an "indispensable support of public morality."[150]

Ryan Sager notes the change in his book, *The Elephant in the Room: Evangelicals, Libertarians and the Battle to Control the Republican Party*:

> Whereas conservative Christian parents once thought it was inappropriate for public schools to teach their kids about sex, now they want schools to preach abstinence to children. Whereas conservative Christians used to be unhappy with evolution being taught in public schools, now they want Intelligent Design taught instead (or at least in addition). Whereas conservative Christians used to want the federal government to leave them alone, now they demand more and more federal funds directed to local churches and religious groups through Bush's faith-based initiative. Whereas conservative Christians used to bemoan the creation of "no fault" divorce, now many cheer as the Bush administration spends nearly $1 billion on federally funded marriage counseling and fatherhood initiatives.[151]

This belief has naturally led the Religious Right to embrace such propositions as outlawing abortion, favoring censorship, opposing gay marriage, and prohibiting stem cell research and cloning. But beyond issues of morality, the Religious Right retains an undercurrent of support for big government on a variety of issues. Catholic social-justice teaching, for example, has long stressed the "preferential option" of helping the poor.[152] This bias has led the U.S. Conference of Bishops to endorse a variety of government welfare programs and even to oppose the 1996 welfare reform.[153] Rick Santorum explained why he supports government activism—albeit conservative government activism—to combat poverty, by saying: "I'm a Catholic. How many times did the nuns beat into your brains: the poor, the poor, the poor?"[154] And Michael Gerson, President George W. Bush's former chief speechwriter and the man responsible for developing the president's theory of "compassionate conservatism," says that his politics are "drawn from Catholic social thought, which stresses that human beings are responsible for others' welfare."[155]

White evangelical Protestant groups have been less inclined to support government social-welfare programs, at least at the national level. Perhaps this reluctance reflects theological differences with Catholics, as well as the rural and small-town ties that form the evangelical heartland of America. Yet many evangelicals have ties to other government institutions—from the military to farm programs—that leave a residual appreciation for government involvement in at least some spheres of life. Many evangelicals imbibe a mix of patriotism and populism that does not lead naturally to small government.

Moreover, as with neoconservatives, economic policy is a secondary concern to much of the Religious Right. As far back as the Reagan administration, Paul Weyrich was saying:

> We can't win by defending Reaganomics. We can only win by pushing those populist/conservative anti-elitist themes which real people support. I am not going to . . . try to explain trickle down [economics] to an unemployed steelworker in Birmingham. But that same steelworker if asked to choose between our desire to see hardened criminals punished and the liberals' defense of soft-headed judges, will be with us. That's where it's at.[156]

Today, Gary Bauer says: "We can survive bad economic policies. What we can't survive is this constant attempt to strip our Judeo-Christian roots out of every nook and cranny of American life. What we won't be able to overcome is the redefinition of America as a place of merely 'do your own thing.'"[157] He goes on to criticize conservatives who would "rather discuss marginal tax rates and the gross domestic product" instead of moral values.[158]

Many on the Religious Right are deeply suspicious of big business. Gary Bauer has called for remaking the Republican Party as a party

49

"for the working American, blue collar and white collar, not just for the big corporate interests." Bauer says, "I propose that we take power out of the hands of Washington, and return it, not to the huge corporations and Wall Street investment managers, but to America's families."[159]

Bauer supported the Family and Medical Leave Act, increasing the minimum wage, and a Patients' Bill of Rights, while generally opposing free trade. He has been an outspoken critic of personal accounts for Social Security. In a scathing *New York Times* op-ed, he argued that Social Security reform would deprive stay-at-home mothers of benefits that reward them for raising children. "Why do we think the nation will be better off," Bauer asked, "by forcing workers to put their money into stock rather than, say, spending it on rearing children?"[160]

By no means do all leaders of the Religious Right share Bauer's liberal views on economic issues. Most give at least lip service to the idea of smaller government, lower taxes, and less regulation. Yet, their priorities are clear. When the Religious Right criticizes the president or the Republicans in Congress, they seldom target overspending or failing to reduce the size of government. Rather, they focus on failing to move aggressively enough on moral and cultural issues.[161]

With the grassroots holding a generally sympathetic opinion of government power, and the leadership more or less indifferent to the size of government except when they want to use it to advance their view of morality, the Religious Right has become a key constituency for big-government conservatism.

Supply-Siders

Supply-side economics is probably the most significant political movement ever begun with a cocktail napkin. At least by repute, it grew out of an afternoon lunch meeting at the Washington Hotel between economists Arthur Laffer and Jude Wanniski and Dick Cheney and his secretary Grace-Marie Arnett (now Turner). Laffer used a napkin to sketch out his theory on the relationship between tax rates and tax revenues.[162] The basic idea of the so-called Laffer curve is that:

> Changes in tax rates have two effects on revenues: the arithmetic effect and the economic effect. The arithmetic effect is

Figure 2.3
THE LAFFER CURVE

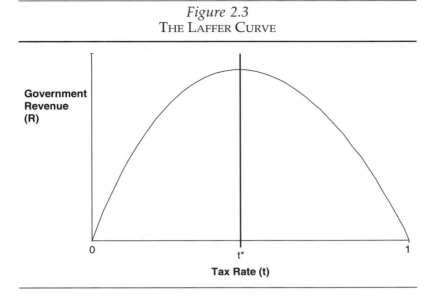

Tax Rate (t)

simply that if tax rates are lowered, tax revenues (per dollar of tax base) will be lowered by the amount of the decrease in the rate. The reverse is true for an increase in tax rates. The economic effect, however, recognizes the positive impact that lower tax rates have on work, output, and employment—and thereby the tax base—by providing incentives to increase these activities. Raising tax rates has the opposite economic effect by penalizing participation in the taxed activities. The arithmetic effect always works in the opposite direction from the economic effect. Therefore, when the economic and the arithmetic effects of tax-rate changes are combined, the consequences of the change in tax rates on total tax revenues are no longer quite so obvious.[163] (Figure 2.3)

Many observers have oversimplified this rather commonsense proposition to mean that lowering tax rates will generate increases in tax revenue, although Laffer himself warns:

> The Laffer Curve itself does not say whether a tax cut will raise or lower revenues. Revenue responses to a tax rate change will depend upon the tax system in place, the time period being considered, the ease of movement into underground activities, the level of tax rates already in place, the

51

prevalence of legal and accounting-driven tax loopholes, and the proclivities of the productive factors.[164]

This idea was not original. Norman Ture, Paul Craig Roberts, and, in particular, Nobel-laureate Robert Mundell had been making the point for some time.[165] Supply-side advocates converted this idea from an academic theory to a governing philosophy, with far-reaching consequences. On the positive side, it has helped hold down taxes. Marginal rates have been dramatically reduced since the 1990s. But, by shifting the emphasis from restraining spending to cutting taxes, supply-siders undercut the will to reduce the size of government. Taxes could be cut irrespective of spending. Indeed, if taxes were reduced, theoretically even more revenue would be produced.

Wanniski puts it in political terms: "If the Democrats are going to play Santa Claus by promoting more spending, the Republicans can never beat them by promoting less spending. They have to promise tax cuts *in order to grow the economy*—not to 'starve the government of revenue.'"[166]

As Cato president Ed Crane observed:

> When [U.S. Representatives] Jack Kemp, Newt Gingrich, Vin Weber, Connie Mack and the rest discovered Jude Wanniski and Art Laffer [in the 1970s], they thought they'd died and gone to heaven. In supply-side economics they found a philosophy that gave them a free pass out of the debate over the proper role of government. Just cut taxes and grow the economy: government will shrink as a percentage of GDP, even if you don't cut spending. That's why you rarely, if ever, heard Kemp or Gingrich call for spending cuts, much less the elimination of programs and departments.[167]

Supply-side economics received its biggest practical test with the 1981 passage of the Kemp-Roth tax cut.[168] In a very important sense, this bill, which reduced marginal income tax rates by approximately 25 percent over three years, proved the theory. As predicted, tax revenue increased significantly after the tax cuts were passed. Real income tax revenues rose by 16.3 percent from 1982 to 1989. Economic growth increased substantially as well. However, as feared, government spending also increased. In real terms, federal spending rose by 17.4 percent over that same period, outpacing increases in revenue.[169] The result was an enormous increase in budget deficits.

In the late 1990s, a combination of spending restraint and economic growth briefly produced budget surpluses, but these have ballooned again in the last five years.

In many ways, the George W. Bush presidency and the current Republican Congress represent what is both good and bad about supply-side economics. Bush pushed through the largest tax cuts since Reagan and has steadfastly resisted pressure to increase taxes. His efforts have increased economic growth despite the problems brought about by 9/11. And, in a fulfillment of supply-side theory, tax revenues have risen despite the reduction in rates. However, as under Reagan, spending has been unconstrained, resulting in budget deficits as far as the eye can see.

Supply-side economics has become an excuse for a lack of fiscal discipline. If "deficits don't matter" and voters can still be wooed with tax cuts, why bother with the dirty, sometimes painful work of cutting government? Most supply-siders do not believe in big government—although some, like Jack Kemp, clearly do—but they have provided both camouflage and a rationale for those who do.

The Technophiles

The last decades of the 20th century were a transformative period for American society, driven in large party by technological change. As the information age reached its height, traditional institutions of society often found themselves breaking down or struggling to keep up with the pace of change. Government was affected as much, if not more, than the rest of society.

This line of thinking was encapsulated by Alvin and Heidi Toffler in their best-selling book *The Third Wave*.[170] According to the Tofflers, the first wave was the agricultural revolution, which led to feudal-style social systems. The second wave was the industrial revolution, which produced "mass society" in its socialist and capitalist versions. The third wave is the postindustrial society, built around information and technology. The Tofflers warned that the new age required new institutions of governance.

No one embraced this idea with more enthusiasm than House Speaker Newt Gingrich, who led the Republican takeover of the House in 1994. Gingrich referred to *The Third Wave* as "the seminal work of our time."[171] He made the book mandatory reading for newly elected Republicans. This book says the U.S. Constitution "is increasingly obsolete, and hence increasingly, if inadvertently, oppressive and dangerous to our welfare."[172] Therefore, it should "die and be replaced."[173]

Gingrich is almost universally associated with opposition to big government. But that was not actually the case. Gingrich rhetorically criticized big government. And it served his enemies and the Clinton administration to portray Gingrich as slashing government programs. The Gingrich-inspired "Contract with America" was generally seen as a call for smaller government, although it did not actually call for cutting a single government program. (The closest it came was a call for zero-baseline budgeting.)[174]

Actually, Gingrich opposed bureaucratic government—inefficient government—not big government per se. As Gingrich said in 1994, "government plays a huge role" in society and "anybody who believes in the American Constitution ought to believe in a fairly strong government." He went on to say that he has "no particular beef with big government."[175] Or, as he said more recently, if the bureaucracies can be reformed and made more efficient, "the country could get excited about the opportunity to make government work."[176]

That is not to say that Gingrich and his followers would not like to see a smaller government. Many changes they support would indeed reduce government bureaucracies. But in the end, Gingrichism means "recognizing that even a relatively small federal or state government will be much bigger than anything the founding fathers could have dreamed of."[177]

At the heart of Gingrichism is a fascination with technology. "Technology is replacing ideology as the most powerful force for change in America and therefore in government," Gingrich says.[178] As a result, Gingrich and his fellow technophiles see technological change as both a political tactic and an answer to the issues confronting this country.

> There is a new strategy waiting to be seized that offers even a bigger step toward conservative ends: technology. Because it is new and different it will at first be resisted by conservatives . . . . Yet technology, and the efficiency it brings, contains the seeds of a transformation that would dramatically reduce bureaucracies, expand freedom and shrink the role of government. If Republicans embrace technology, they can transform

themselves from the party that cares less and spends less, to the party that modernizes a decrepit government and provides better, more-caring services.[179]

This belief in technology has led Gingrich and his disciples along three basic paths. First, they believed that government institutions needed to be reformed to make them more efficient. Most were built under an outdated "second wave" ethos. They would have to be updated for the new "third wave" technological age. Gingrich-style conservatism was about bureaucratic reform and technological innovation, not about shrinking government or individual liberty.

To see where this philosophy leads in practice, observe Gingrich's response to the question of global warming. Does Gingrich oppose the Kyoto Protocols? Well, maybe, but, "Before we spend trillions on a Kyoto policy decision, we should spend a billion or two on a ten-year total project with a systems architecture like the international geophysical year . . . aimed at saying, let's optimize our understanding of the planet's climate."[180]

Or consider this typical Gingrichism: "Imagine the speed and ease with which you use a bank-teller card anywhere on the planet and electronically verify your account and get money and then call the federal government about a case. There's no objective reason that institutions of government have to be two or three generations behind the curve in information management."[181]

Make government institutions efficient and all else will fall into place. "As a country we can give people better lives through better solutions by bringing government into conformity with the entrepreneurial systems they are experiencing in the private sector."[182] The issue is not how big government is or how much it spends; it is whether we have "the systems architecture that would spend it intelligently."[183] Traditional conservatives want the government simply to do less. But Gingrich and his fellow technophiles believe that the right systems architecture will enable the government to provide "greater goods and services at lower and lower costs."[184]

This attitude gave Gingrich conservatism its appearance of optimism. Rather than being against big government, Gingrich could be for reform. "We need to move from a 'no, because' to a 'yes, if' approach to government policy."[185] Former representative Vin Weber, one of Gingrich's followers, has also sounded the call for reforming government, rather than cutting it:

> Conservatives have to do better than simply bash govern-
> ment. We have to lead the way toward reform of government.
> We need to look at the whole government and think about
> how to empower the consumers of government benefits,
> rather than the bureaucracy. Conservatives who simply look
> to abolish agencies are going to be disappointed, but conser-
> vative reformers still have an open field.[186]

Thus one could say of Gingrich's conservatism, "while this view
did indeed see the federal government as the source of many of the
nation's troubles, it did not hold that the problem was federal power
as such. Change those wielding federal power, and the power could
be harnessed to the ends of conservative reform."[187]

Accordingly, government should play an active role in supporting
technological innovation. Gingrich believes that the federal government should "play a very powerful role in shaping the market."[188]
This role starts with government funding for scientific research and
development. "We must take steps to maintain our superiority in
Science and Technology including dramatically changing education
to incentivize advanced math and science excellence and significantly increasing the amount we invest in basic scientific research,"
Gingrich says.[189] He would double federal funding for scientific and
health research.[190]

Gingrich believes that only government, not the private sector,
can provide the needed scientific leadership.

> Basic research and development is the heart of the future, and
> we would not have had a computer without U.S. government
> funding. We would not have had the Internet without ARPA
> [Advanced Research Projects Agency] financing it; it was
> originally called ARPAnet. You can go down the list. The U.S.
> Congress paid for the first telegraph line, from Washington to
> Baltimore. We had land grants to the national railroads to
> build a transcontinental railroad. We have a long history
> in this country of effectively using government to create a
> faster future.[191]

Unless government embraces new technology, he warned, "It will
not be something that [matters] to the America people."[192]

Gingrich once called for abolishing the Department of Education,
but he has since become an enthusiastic supporter of federal-govern-
ment involvement in education. He endorsed President Clinton's

plan for the federal government to finance 100,000 new teachers and called for the government to provide Internet access to all Americans and computers to every four-year-old. He has proposed paying students for taking difficult math and science courses.[193]

Energy policy is another area where Gingrich and the technophiles support massive government intervention. Gingrich strongly supports the Bush administration's investment in trying to build hydrogen-powered vehicles. But that's only the start. He would support a host of public-private partnerships, investments in alternative fuels, and conservation measures. Almost anything goes, as long as it involves new technology.[194]

While Gingrichites correctly understood the failures of traditional welfare programs, they sought to reform not end them. "The old phrase 'conservative opportunity society' always envisioned a reformed welfare state," Weber notes.[195] A Gingrich welfare state included government-funded orphanages and "parental training" centers for single mothers.[196] He supported the Medicare prescription drug benefit and has joined with Hillary Clinton to call for the government to develop a national health care database.[197]

In some ways, Gingrich-style technophilia may seem to be a much smaller movement than those previously described. It is, with a few exceptions, largely based around one man. Yet, Gingrich has had and continues to have enormous influence over the intellectual development of both the Republican Party and the conservative movement. Given the disillusionment among Republicans with the current level of congressional leadership, nostalgia is increasing for the Gingrich era.

Newt Gingrich is widely expected to seek the presidency in 2008. His e-mail newsletter reaches more than 200,000 subscribers. Some 350 radio stations air his weekly radio commentaries. He provides one of the most frequently downloaded political podcasts on iTunes. Several think tanks provide a ready platform for his views. He has written several influential books and has recently released an updated edition of his best-selling book *Winning the Future*.[198] Many of his supporters retain key positions in Congress. By any measure, he remains a leader of the conservative movement.

But far from leading conservatism back toward the philosophy of Reagan and Goldwater, Gingrich's ideas for a technocratic, efficient, and bigger federal government have helped drive it toward the big-government conservatism that dominates today.

The Currents Flow Together

The previous discussion is not to say that these people or movements have not raised valid issues and concerns. In many cases they have brought important ideas to contemporary conservatism. Neoconservatives provided an important counterweight to the Left during the Cold War and were among the first to point out the failures of contemporary welfare policy. The Religious Right has pointed out the risks of cultural excess and brought a spotlight to the importance of the family. Supply-siders were correct on the basic economics of taxes and their efforts have helped reduce the tax burden on American workers. Newt Gingrich and his followers have raised important issues about the effect of technology on public policy.

Yet, as each of these streams of conservative thought has flowed together under the Bush administration and the Republicans in Congress, they have combined to move conservatism away from its traditional belief in limited government and toward an embrace of big, activist, and centralized government.

Though they approach issues from varied directions, each of these groups ends up at a very similar destination. The basic philosophical difference between big-government conservatives and their small-government brethren is that big-government conservatives, far from being apprehensive about the growth of government, accept it or even revel in it. They see big government as simply a means to an end—an end that is far more important than individual liberty.

In particular, big-government conservatives believe that government should promote what they perceive as virtue among the citizenry. This concept includes such values as thrift, hard work, charity, patriotism, and especially traditional sexual and family mores. In this regard, big-government conservatives are skeptical of unfettered free-market capitalism, which they regard as opening the door to immoral and unhealthy activities and choices. They are concerned that markets tend to encourage people to pursue individual self-interest rather than the greater societal good. Thus, they are willing to intervene in markets to guide citizens to make "correct" decisions. Finally, big-government conservatives see an active role for government in dealing with such issues as poverty, health care, and education. They would disagree with traditional liberals in how such programs should function, but not with the underlying rationale for government involvement.

In these beliefs, big-government conservatives share a common arrogance with contemporary liberalism. They are convinced that they know what is best for every American and because they know best, they should guide the rest of us in the proper direction. But, as we shall see in the following pages, their big-government proposals are unlikely to provide answers to the vital issues of the day, from welfare and health care to education and the entitlement crisis. Instead big-government conservatism will simply bring us ever more government intervention in and control over our lives, greater regulation, mounting debt that threatens the nation's future economic health, and less freedom for every American.

3. Proving Lord Acton Correct

No political movement can long exist in a vacuum. The philosophy must find conditions on the ground that enables it to take root and grow. The philosophical seeds of big-government conservatism fell on fertile soil in part because Republicans were making the transition from an opposition party to a governing one.

Of course, conservatives and Republicans have not been complete strangers to power. In the post–World War II era, Republicans had held the presidency more often than Democrats and briefly controlled one house or the other of Congress. They ruled the House from 1952 to 1954 and the Senate from 1980 to 1986. However, the Republican Revolution of 1994 marked the first time since 1932 that Republicans held both chambers. Moreover, they would do so on a long-term basis. When George W. Bush won the presidency in 2000, Republicans were in control of both the legislative and executive branches of government for the first time since Herbert Hoover. Although Democrats could criticize and obstruct, Republicans were responsible for governing.

It is worth reflecting on just how big (and shocking) the Republican victory of 1994 was. Before the election, the Democratic majorities looked unassailable. They held a 258 to 177 majority in the House and a 57 to 43 majority in the Senate. But the Republicans gained 54 seats in the House and 9 in the Senate. And they gained 2 more Senate seats when Colorado senator Ben Nighthorse Campbell and Alabama senator Richard Shelby switched parties. Overall, Republican candidates increased their vote totals by nine million votes over the previous election, the largest such jump in American history.[1] By contrast, in 2006 Democrats took 30 seats in the House and 6 seats in the Senate.[2]

Moreover, the Republican Party that came to power in 1994 was more avowedly conservative than at any time in recent history. A new generation of Republican members of Congress from the south and west, who considered themselves the ideological heirs of Ronald

61

Reagan, had come to the forefront, replacing many of the northeastern moderates who had controlled Republicans during their years as an opposition party.

Thus, hopes were high that the new Republican majority would, in the words of the Contract with America, "dramatically change the way Washington does business, and change the business Washington does."[3] Reason existed for optimism. On their very first day in control, the new Republican majority cut their own staff, changed budget rules to include a requirement for a three-fifths vote to raise taxes, established term limits for their leadership and committee chairs, opened committee hearings to the public while banning the practice of proxy voting in committee, ordered an audit of House finances, and applied a number of workplace regulations to Congress itself.[4] Within the first 100 days, the House had passed 9 of 10 items in the Contract with America, including tax cuts, civil justice reform, a balanced-budget amendment, and the first efforts at welfare reform.[5]

But it wasn't very long before the institutional temptations of being a governing party began to tempt these putative revolutionaries. In particular, Republicans and conservatives succumbed to three bites at the apple: a need to govern, reelection pressures, and a loss of ideological zeal.

The Pressure to "Govern"

The party in power—the "governing party"—is naturally expected to govern. Unfortunately, too often in today's political environment, governing is equated with legislating. Since Harry Truman famously ran against the "Do Nothing Congress" in 1952, unending pressure exists for the governing party to "do something" about whatever issue is on the public's mind.

To insist that an issue is not Congress's constitutional responsibility or that government can do nothing to solve a particular problem is to risk being branded as uncaring. As Fred Barnes puts it: "A governing majority stresses legislative achievement. It doesn't merely obstruct. . . . A party with a governing mentality must be prepared to take ownership of even imperfect but popular legislation. Why? Because that produces results in response to a public desire. If there are problems with a bill, the governing majority is in a position to deal with those later."[6]

Take, for example, what happened when gas prices rose during the summer of 2006. The spike in gas prices was driven by increased demand (caused in large part by the booming economies of China and India) and decreased supply (caused in part by Hurricane Katrina and short-term refinery issues). In addition, fears of turmoil in oil-producing nations in the Middle East, as well as Nigeria and Venezuela, drove up bidding on the oil spot market. None of these things was within the control of Congress. Nor was it even clear that high gasoline prices were a bad thing. Adjusted for inflation and economic growth, gas prices never exceeded their 1972 levels. The impact on economic growth and inflation was minimal, and increased costs both reduce demand and stimulate investment in alternative fuels.

Nonetheless, people were upset by the higher prices. Congress had to do *something*. Thus, in addition to the usual hearings where outraged members of Congress could berate oil company executives and increased subsidies for every energy interest imaginable, we were treated to former senator Mike DeWine (R-OH) introducing legislation that would make OPEC illegal under American antitrust laws, a proposal endorsed by the Heritage Foundation.[7] That the law is unenforceable and based on the dubious premise that foreign countries should obey domestic U.S. laws seemed not to matter. Several Republicans proposed establishing a "strategic gasoline reserve," similar to the Strategic Petroleum Reserve, although no evidence indicates that the Strategic Petroleum Reserve has reduced oil prices.[8] Indeed, such a reserve would likely increase gasoline prices.[9] But the silliest proposal of all came from Senate Majority Leader Bill Frist, who suggested giving every American a $100 check to help them pay for gasoline.[10] Fortunately, none of these measures passed and gasoline prices fell on their own.

Because big-government conservatives see an active role for government on so many issues, big-government conservatism answers this need to "do something" in a way that traditional small-government conservatism does not. Fred Barnes shows how the two fit together when he says approvingly, "Big government conservatives prefer to be *in favor* of things because that puts them on the political offensive."[11] Or as David Brooks points out, "As the governing party, Republicans [had] to betray some of the principles that first animated them."[12]

The Reelection Machine

When Republicans became the governing power, they had to deal with the entirely understandable desire to *remain* the governing party. Nothing is surprising or illegitimate in this goal. After all, a political movement cannot really be effective by losing. The central purpose of competing in the political process is to effectuate a change in public policy. That generally requires winning elections. As Mike Stokke, deputy chief of staff to House Speaker Dennis Hastert (R-IL) asked, "Is it more important to be 100 percent right or more important to be in the majority to get you toward where you want to be?"[13]

Besides, being a member of Congress is a comfortable way of life. As the National Taxpayers Union notes, members of Congress receive comfortable salaries that are often determined through legislative sleight-of-hand; pension benefits that are two to three times more generous than those offered in the private sector for similarly salaried executives; health and life insurance, whose costs are subsidized by taxpayers; limousines for senior members and prized parking spaces, both on Capitol Hill and at Washington's two major airports; travel to far-flung destinations as well as to home states and districts; and a wide range of smaller perks that have defied reform efforts, from health clubs to fine furniture.[14] Things are even better for the majority party, whose members get better offices, more staff, and the ability to control everything from travel to scheduling. Add to this the less-tangible benefits of being called "Senator, Mr. Congressman," or, better yet, "Mr. Chairman"; getting the best seats in restaurants; and being fawned over by lobbyists and the media, and one can understand why members of Congress want to remain "members of the club." As Rep. George Nethercutt (R-WA) explained in breaking his pledge to limit himself to three terms, "I didn't realize I'd be in the majority."[15]

However, for congressional Republicans, the desire to win all too soon became the desire to win at any price.

For example, shortly after coming to power in 1994, Republicans established a program to pressure Washington lobbying firms to hire Republicans and to reward those lobbyists with Republican ties with increased access to Congress, the White House, and government regulatory agencies. Dubbed the "K Street Project," the program was coordinated by Tom DeLay, Rick Santorum, and conservative activist Grover Norquist, president of Americans for Tax Reform. Norquist maintained a computer database with the party affiliation, Capitol Hill experience, and political contribution history of every registered lobbyist in Washington.[16]

Those firms that failed to fall in line were punished. In one episode, an amendment offering $1.5 billion in tax relief to the motion picture industry was stripped out of a bill after the Motion Picture Association of America hired former Clinton agriculture secretary and Kansas representative Dan Glickman as its president. Norquist declared that he considered the association's hiring of a prominent Democrat to be "a studied insult" and warned other trade associations against following suit.[17] Likewise, when the National Association of Homebuilders hired a Democrat as its chief lobbyist, its representatives were barred from participation in the Thursday Group, a weekly meeting between trade association leaders and the congressional leadership.[18] As Tom DeLay put it, "If you want to play in our revolution, you have to play by our rules."[19]

Lobbyists were also pressured for campaign contributions to Republicans and to stop contributing to Democrats. DeLay famously invited lobbyists to his office and showed them a list of "friendly" and "unfriendly" contributors. Their place on the list, he implied, would determine their treatment on Capitol Hill.[20] Ultimately, the goal was, in the words of then House majority whip Roy Blunt (R-MO), to establish "a formal, institutional alliance" between Republicans and the lobbying community.[21] This line of thinking ultimately led to the scandals involving Jack Abramoff.

Abramoff's web of dealings with Congress and others is so tangled and complex that it defies easy summary. In short, Abramoff and his associates were involved in at least four interrelated activities that either have or may ultimately lead to criminal charges.

First, he has pleaded guilty to wire fraud and conspiracy charges involving the 2000 purchase of a Florida gambling-boat venture. Abramoff admitted counterfeiting a $23 million wire transfer as part of the deal.[22]

Second, he was involved in funneling money into the political action committee run by Tom DeLay that was used to help fund campaigns for the Texas state legislature. By helping elect a Republican majority in the Texas legislature, DeLay was able to have the state's congressional districts redrawn, resulting in the election of five additional Republican representatives. Two former DeLay aides pleaded guilty, and DeLay was subsequently indicted for illegally laundering those campaign donations and resigned from Congress.[23]

Third, Abramoff has pleaded guilty to defrauding several Native American tribes and other clients with gambling interests.[24] Playing both sides of regulatory disputes over gambling on Indian reservations, he collected more than $82 million over the past decade from various tribes for lobbying and public relations. Abramoff had the tribes pay the money to a public relations firm run by his business partner, Michael Scanlon, and Scanlon would kick back half the profits from his operation to Abramoff.

Fourth, he provided gifts, travel, and jobs to the wives of members of Congress and executive branch officials in exchange for actions that helped his clients. Court papers filed in connection with his guilty pleas also suggest Abramoff arranged for $50,000 in payments to the wife of a congressional staffer in return for the staffer's help in killing an Internet gambling measure.[25] Abramoff also arranged for luxury travel for members of Congress, their families, and staff members, including golf trips to Scotland and the Mariana Islands. Among those who received favors from Abramoff and subsequently came to the aid of his clients was Rep. Robert Ney (R-OH), who subsequently pleaded guilty to bribery, fraud, and conspiracy.[26] Another was David Safavian, the Bush administration's top procurement officer, who subsequently was convicted of lying about those ties.[27]

The Abramoff scandals were different from the usual run-of-the mill bribery scandals, such as those involving Reps. Randy Cunningham (R-CA) or William Jefferson (D-LA).[28] Although Abramoff and his associates certainly used their connections to enrich themselves, the real scandal was the way the interrelation of lobbyists, the policy community, and Congress corrupted the process itself. Not surprisingly, the Abramoff scandals involve many of the same people as the K Street Project, notably Tom DeLay and Grover Norquist.[29]

Abramoff solicited campaign contributions from his Indian gaming clients and funneled that money to congressional campaigns through nonprofit public policy organizations such as Americans for Tax Reform and the National Center for Public Policy Research.[30] He paid columnists to write op-eds favorable to his clients.[31] In short, he turned the entire public policy apparatus into an electoral tool and then suborned that tool for the benefit first of his clients and, ultimately, his own gain.

"Win at any price" has seeped inside Congress as well, threatening to corrupt the legislative process itself. For example, votes were routinely held open beyond the traditional 10- or 20-minute deadline, while the Republican leadership rounded up enough votes to win. (The Medicare prescription drug vote was notoriously held open for more than four hours.) Legislation was delivered at the last minute, denying members time to study (or in many cases even read) the bills they were voting on. The rules were manipulated to prevent Democratic amendments or substitutes.

Of course, Democrats routinely abused the legislative rules as well when they were in power. And Democrats have adopted a tactic of unyielding obstructionism that often threatened to bring the legislative process to a grinding halt. But the Republican majority acted with a ruthlessness and disregard for legislative rules and norms that was truly extraordinary. Rep. David Dreier (R-CA), who was chairman of the powerful House Rules Committee, admitted at the time: "We've had to do some of the things we criticized once. But now that I'm in the majority, I have this responsibility to govern."[32]

Even the congressional reforms passed at the beginning of the Republican Revolution were eventually jettisoned. Congressional staffs and budgets have grown to pre-revolution levels. Term limits on committee chairs were weakened in the Senate in 2002, and some House chairs were granted exemptions from the limits. In early 2003, term limits on the House leadership, including Speaker Dennis Hastert, were removed.[33] Hastert eventually became the longest-serving Republican speaker in history.[34]

Big-government conservatives contributed to this type of corruption by eliminating the ideological barrier to using government to help those special interests that were in turn helping the Republican Party. Small-government conservatives were generally opposed to government interference in the marketplace, including subsidies to business. But big-government conservatives believed government had a role in shaping the market. This difference of opinion provided ideological cover for corporate welfare. As Bruce Bartlett put it, "Since it is devoid of principle, it too easily becomes an excuse to lavish gifts on those with Republican connections."[35]

Moreover, the desire for reelection at any price was not just a question of corrupt tactics. It quickly spilled over into policy decisions as well.

Newt Gingrich started the Republicans down the road to sacrificing principle for reelection, directing appropriators to steer pork to vulnerable Republican legislators in 1996.[36] He also pushed through legislation increasing the minimum wage, extending health insurance regulation, and establishing greater environmental controls—issues that were important to Republicans in marginal districts, especially in the Northeast.[37] In fact, it wasn't long before Republicans were actually attacking Democrats for failing to support pork-barrel projects. Tom DeLay criticized one vulnerable Democratic representative who voted against a pork-filled Interior Department appropriations bill, saying, "In all my years in Congress this is a first: a member of Congress actually voting against a project that would have benefited his own district."[38]

All this gamesmanship led Rep. Mark Sanford (R-SC), one of the freshmen elected in 1994, to lament, "In the first year here you deal with policy, and in year two with politics."[39]

The politicization of the policy process has only increased in recent years. The Medicare prescription drug benefit is a perfect example of policy driven by political calculation. Seniors vote in disproportionate numbers. Roughly 71 percent of those over age 65 vote, compared to less than half of those under age 30. And seniors, or at least the interest groups like AARP that claim to represent seniors, were clamoring for a prescription drug benefit. Therefore, Republicans were only too happy to oblige. President Bush and the Republican leadership made clear that they were not even particularly concerned with what the bill contained, as long as Congress eventually delivered a bill.[40] Gingrich made the case as baldly as anyone, writing, "Obstructionist conservatives can always find a reason to vote no, but that path leads right back into the minority and it would be a minority status they would deserve."[41]

Most conservative Republicans resisted campaign finance reform, saying that the curbs would infringe on free speech. Nearly all the votes against McCain-Feingold (and its House counterpart Shays-Meehan) came from conservative Republicans. But when Democrats figured out how to exploit a loophole in the law by funneling money to independent "527 groups," like MoveOn.org, Republicans came together not to defend free speech, but to try to extend campaign finance rules to these organizations.[42] In fact, House Speaker Dennis Hastert and Majority Leader John Boehner led the move to limit the ability of independent political groups to raise money.[43] Dozens of other conservatives who had voted against campaign finance reform switched sides and were unapologetic about the hypocrisy of doing so. "I think we have a system right now that is disproportionately advantageous to Democrats," said Rep. Tom Cole (R-OK).[44] Apparently, that was sufficient reason for further restricting political speech. (Democrats were no less hypocritical. Having strongly supported other campaign finance restrictions, most now voted against restrictions on 527 groups.)

For brazen cynicism the House Republican approach to legislation raising the minimum wage is hard to match. Conservatives have long opposed the minimum wage both as an unwarranted government interference in private contractual arrangements and because it drives up the cost of hiring workers, leading to a loss of jobs for the least skilled in society.[45] However, faced with pressure from Democrats and moderate Republicans to take up a politically popular wage hike, the House leadership abandoned conservative principles and instead adopted the purely Machiavellian approach of combining a minimum-wage hike with legislation to reduce the estate tax. The idea was to force Democrats to either accept the estate-tax cut or vote against the minimum-wage increase. "You've seen us really outfox you," bragged Rep. Zach Wamp (R-TN).[46]

However, the maneuver didn't just outfox Democrats. Principled conservatives were faced with the dilemma of having to vote either for a bad proposal (the minimum-wage hike) or against a good proposal (the estate-tax cut). Whether the bill passed or failed, conservative goals would be sacrificed.[47] "Every principled conservative knows this is horrible stuff," pointed out Rep. Tom Feeney (R-FL).[48]

A similar political crassness can be seen in the response of congressional leaders to President Bush's proposal for Social Security reform. Not only did Rep. Tom Davis (R-VA), chairman of the National Republican Congressional Committee, actively discourage Republican candidates from discussing the issue; he even authorized campaign commercials *attacking* Democrats who indicated that they might support Social Security "privatization."[49] As House Speaker Dennis Hastert put it in defending congressional reluctance to address the issue: "Most members, down in their heart, know that what we are trying to do is the right thing to do. It's a question of whether it's convenient politically."[50] Political convenience, not "the right thing," has become the lodestar of the GOP. As a result, barely 47 percent of Americans believe that Republicans in Congress are generally ethical. Fully 44 percent do not.[51]

While the Bush White House has occasionally been willing to spend its political capital for important issues such as Social Security reform, it too has frequently been willing to do what was politically expedient regardless of whether it was good policy. For example, Bush imposed steel tariffs in 2003 despite the unanimous opposition of his economic advisers. Karl Rove believed that the steel vote was essential to Bush's hopes in Pennsylvania and West Virginia, so free trade—a bedrock conservative principle—had to be jettisoned.[52]

The same political calculus, by both the White House and congressional leadership, can be seen in the repeated votes on emotional issues, such as constitutional amendments to ban gay marriage or prohibit flag burning. The merits of these issues aside, these amendments have no possibility of passing. Yet year after year, Congress spends valuable time debating them because they help drive the Republican base vote. As a Senate Republican leader said happily, a vote against the flag-burning amendment "would make a good 30-second spot."[53] Even the congressional intervention in the tragic case of Terri Schiavo (see Chapter 10) was driven in large part by political considerations. Sen. Mel Martinez circulated a staff memo suggesting that the Schiavo case offered "a great political issue" that would appeal to the party's base and could be used against Florida senator Bill Nelson and other Democrats.[54]

Democratic pollster Pat Cadell coined the term "the permanent campaign," arguing that "governing with public approval requires a continuing political campaign."[55] Certainly this concept has been a long-standing condition of political life, aggravated by the advent of cable television and the 24-hour news cycle. But no president has focused on this necessity with as much single-mindedness as George W. Bush. Guided by White House adviser Karl Rove, every policy is carefully tested for its political effect.[56] The result is a White House, and a Congress, where in the words of John DiIulio, the first director of President Bush's Office of Faith-Based Initiatives: "What you've got is everything—and I mean everything—being run by the political arm. It's the reign of the Mayberry Machiavellis."[57]

70

A Refuge for the Unprincipled

Finally, as Republicans consolidated power in Washington, they increasingly attracted those who joined the Republican Party because they saw it as the most direct route to power, not out of ideological conviction.

Political opportunism is nothing new. Former senator and Republican presidential candidate Bob Dole (R-KS) famously said that he became a Republican after realizing there were more Republicans than Democrats in Kansas.[58] Similarly, when he was first thinking of running for the Senate, Arlen Specter asked both Democrats and Republicans how much money they would raise for his campaign. The Republicans outbid the Democrats, so Specter became a Republican.[59]

But fewer and fewer of those coming to Washington these days seem to have the burning desire to change the world that was the hallmark of the 1994 revolutionaries. Rather, election to Congress is seen as the next step on the political career ladder. Clear evidence of this state of affairs can be seen in the fact that even first-time Republican candidates for Congress are now running campaigns based on how much pork they will bring back to their district.[60]

At the same time, the ideological fire for small government burns ever dimmer among those who remain from the revolutionary days. Washington, with its perks and power, is seductive. Study after study shows that the longer a member of Congress is in office, the more he or she spends.[61] Tellingly, a study by the National Taxpayers Union looked at 30 Republicans first elected as part of the 1994 freshman class. During their first years in Congress nearly all members of this group sponsored legislation that would have resulted in a net reduction in spending. Since 2000, however, only two members maintained that dedication to reduced spending.[62]

This lack of political conviction exists not just among the legislators but also among their staff members. Longtime political commentator Tucker Carlson tells of talking to Republican staffers and noticing their lack of attachment to or enthusiasm for any particular ideas.

> I always got the feeling they liked their candidate well enough. Their candidate was the better guy; the other guy was a pretty bad guy. Of course, they all had plans to join a lobbying shop in Washington if their guy didn't win. . . . When I went over to the other side of the room to talk to

> [Democratic staffers], they believed that their guy was a great
> guy with terrific ideas. Not only was the other guy a very
> bad guy, his ideas were terrible ideas, and if he were to beat
> their guy, the Republic would fall. If their guy won, he would
> improve not simply the life of every single American, but
> human nature itself.[63]

Indeed, when true small-government conservatives threaten the status quo, the Republican establishment often unites against them. For example, when Rep. Pat Toomey challenged Sen. Arlen Specter in Pennsylvania's Republican primary, both Rick Santorum and President Bush campaigned against him.[64] Likewise, both the White House and the Republican Party leadership backed Sen. Lincoln Chafee in his senatorial primary.[65] In the case of Sen. Chafee, this wasn't even good *politics*. Chafee went on to lose the general election, and may quit the Republican Party altogether.[66]

Similarly, when the dwindling band of small-government conservatives in Congress objects to higher spending or new programs, they are threatened with discipline by the House leadership and snubbed by the White House. For example, when Rep. Tom Feeney (R-FL) opposed the Medicare prescription drug benefit, House leaders told him that his refusal to go along would set back his bid to climb the House ladder by at least three years. He would be relegated to a position of a backbencher, they said. "Why jeopardize your career, Tom, over this one little vote?" one leader reportedly told him.[67]

Likewise when members of the conservative House Republican Study Committee, led by Rep. Mike Pence (R-IN), proposed spending cuts to offset spending for Hurricane Katrina relief, they were "taken to the woodshed." Pence and his colleagues were told "in the bluntest terms" that they were not "team players" and their careers would suffer if they continued to obstruct the leadership's wishes.[68] Things were not much different at the White House where Lawrence Lindsey, chairman of the National Economic Council, was essentially fired for telling the truth about the potential cost of the Iraq war.[69]

All of this pressure creates a climate where loyalty to the team becomes far more important than loyalty to conservative principles. The result is that principled small-government conservatives are driven out, while those who care most about "winning" rise to positions of power.

All of these trends can be seen in the Republican leadership's reaction to the Foley scandal.[70] Although Democratic claims of a cover-up were certainly overblown, no doubt exists that the leadership's reaction was based not on principle but on politics. Their performance was a mixture of self-serving opportunism, finger pointing, and general incompetence. Political columnist Robert Novak reports that many Republicans wondered whether "the sloppy treatment of Foley's conduct reflected the same leadership problems in failing to make tax cuts permanent or even to address the coming crisis in Social Security."[71] In far too many ways, it does.

The Intersection of Corruption and Big-Government Conservatism

As O'Sullivan's Law (named after John O'Sullivan, former editor of *National Review*) points out, any organization that is not explicitly conservative will over time become liberal.[72] Similarly, it might be said that a Republican Party not explicitly committed to small government will become a Republican Party that supports big government.

Soon after taking power in 1994, the Republican Party became less committed to small government than it was to keeping itself in power. Marshall Wittman, a moderate Democratic strategist, has observed: "Conservatives have become intoxicated with power. It's easy to talk about 'limited government' when you're out of power. But now that their appetites have been whetted, now that they have gained control of the leviathan state, they have found it to their liking, so they have tossed principles aside."[73] Or as former majority leader Dick Armey puts it, "Republican lawmakers forgot the party's principles, became enamored with power and position, and began putting politics over policy."[74]

Big-government conservatives gave Republicans a philosophical excuse to do those things that they wanted to do anyway. It was as if a glutton had come across an "all you can eat" diet plan. Instead of being hypocritical purveyors of pork who were using the powers of government to ensure their own reelection, they were pursuing "a positive agenda." At the same time, an influx of new legislators and staffers who lacked a sound ideological footing in small-government conservatism meant that Congress was more open to the arguments of big-government conservatives. Those few conservatives who clung to their small-government beliefs were marginalized or disciplined.

The end result, as we shall see in the chapters that follow, was a climate in Washington that was not only corrupt but far too hospitable to the idea of a growing and more powerful federal government. No longer explicitly conservative, the new "governing" Republican Party became a party of big government.

PART II

BIG-GOVERNMENT CONSERVATISM IN ACTION

We have a responsibility that when somebody hurts, government has got to move.

—George W. Bush

4. Learning to Love the Welfare State

Despite government spending of more than $9 trillion over the past 40 years on welfare programs, nearly 37 million Americans are still living in poverty.[1] They include nearly 13 million children.[2] That's 12.7 percent of the population, a decline of barely 2 percent since the start of the War on Poverty in 1965.[3] That's a pretty poor return on a $9 trillion investment.

We know that welfare is a failure.[4] It has neither reduced poverty nor made the poor self-sufficient. It has torn at the social fabric of the country and been a significant factor in increasing out-of-wedlock births with all of their attendant problems.[5] It has weakened the work ethic and contributed to rising crime rates.[6] Most tragically of all, the pathologies it engenders have been passed on from parent to child, from generation to generation.

Welfare reform made a number of significant changes in the way welfare was provided.[7] Before passage of the Personal Responsibility and Work Opportunity Reconciliation Act of 1996 (PRWORA), when most people thought of welfare, they thought of Aid to Families with Dependent Children, the country's largest cash assistance program, which provided direct cash payments to children in families where the parents are absent, incapacitated, deceased, or unemployed, as well as certain other members of the children's household, most frequently the mother. The program was funded by a combination of federal and state funds (the federal portion varied from 50 to 80 percent), with states setting benefit levels and the federal government determining eligibility requirements.

PRWORA replaced Aid to Families with Dependent Children with the Temporary Assistance for Needy Families (TANF) block grant. This change effectively abolished most federal eligibility and payment rules, giving states much greater flexibility to design their own programs. The TANF block grant was a fixed amount for each state, largely based on the prereform federal contribution to that state's Aid to Families with Dependent Children program. In addition, the block grants eliminated welfare's "entitlement" status, meaning that no one would have an automatic right to benefits.[8] States could choose which families to help. States were, however, required to continue spending at least 75–80 percent of their previous levels under the "maintenance of effort" provision.

Widespread work requirements were to be imposed on welfare recipients. Initially, states were to have at least 40 percent of their welfare recipients either working or participating in work preparation activities, increasing to 50 percent by 2002, although states were given wide discretion in designing these work programs. However, states were given various credits and exemptions that significantly reduced the number of recipients actually required to work.

PRWORA also established a time limit for welfare receipt. Recipients could not remain on the rolls for longer than 60 months (five years). However, this restriction did not apply to child-only families, where the children receive benefits but the parents do not, and states could exempt up to 20 percent of their adult recipients from time limits for "hardship" reasons. States had the option of imposing stricter time limits or using their own funds to continue paying benefits to families who exceeded the five-year time limit.

The legislation included incentives for states to establish programs to limit out-of-wedlock births. Each year, the five states that achieved the greatest reduction in out-of-wedlock birth ratios (defined as the proportion of out-of-wedlock births to total births), while also decreasing the ratio of abortions to live births, would receive $20 million in additional federal funds. PRWORA also included the following provisions targeted at out-of-wedlock births: (a) requiring unmarried teenage mothers under the age of 18 to remain in school and to live with an adult; (b) allowing states to prohibit additional benefits for women who conceive additional children while on welfare; (c) requiring states to establish numerical goals for reduction of teen pregnancy and out-of-wedlock births, and to develop specific plans for achieving those goals; (d) directing the secretary of health and human services to implement a comprehensive program to combat teen pregnancy and to ensure that at least 25 percent of American communities have teen pregnancy prevention programs in place by 2002; and (e) authorizing states to spend unused TANF funds on teen pregnancy prevention and teen parent services.[9]

In one of the more-controversial provisions, legal immigrants who arrived after 1996 and had not become citizens were made ineligible for TANF, as well as food stamps and Supplementary Security Income.[10]

Finally, rules were changed to encourage greater state efforts to determine paternity and to collect child support from absent parents. The federal government would also provide additional assistance in collecting child support.

Despite welfare reform, however, most of the mammoth federal and state social welfare complex remains unchanged. More than 70 overlapping federal anti-poverty programs still exist. PRWORA was successful in reducing welfare rolls, without increasing poverty or hardship among most former recipients, although in the last few years participation has again begun to edge upward. However, reform has not been successful in significantly reducing levels of out-of-wedlock births, nor has it enabled people to become truly self-sufficient.[11]

A Republican president and Congress might have been expected to build upon PWORA, possibly applying its lessons to other social-welfare programs. After a five-year delay, they did, in fact, reauthorize welfare reform and strengthen many of the work provisions. However, many of the gains of welfare reform are being quietly undone, while the federal government is creating new programs and expanding into new areas.[12]

Under the Bush administration, social-welfare programs have expanded at a phenomenal rate. According to an analysis of 25 major government programs by *USA Today*, enrollment increased an average of 17 percent in the programs from 2000 to 2005, while the nation's population grew by only 5 percent during that time. This increase represents the largest five-year expansion of the welfare state since the Great Society in the 1960s. Spending on these social programs was up an inflation-adjusted 22 percent since President Bush took office. Growing enrollment was responsible for most of the spending increase, but higher benefits also contributed.[13]

Big-Government Conservatives and Welfare

Big-government conservatives start with a very different attitude toward the welfare state from their small-government brethren. At heart, the former accept the idea that, as George W. Bush has said, government has a "compelling purpose" in "confront[ing] human suffering."[14] Daniel Mahoney calls on conservatives to "get over their very understandable, but ultimately self-destructive, fear of a government role in confronting poverty."[15]

If government's role is to lift people out of poverty but traditional welfare programs have clearly failed to do so, what would big-government conservatives do? Generally, they have taken two approaches.

First, big-government conservatives have long understood the importance of mediating institutions—family, church, and community—in dealing with the problem of long-term poverty.[16] The evidence is overwhelming that these nongovernmental structures are not only more effective at dealing with the underlying causes of poverty, but also they are less likely to engender unintended consequences that may make the problem worse. This finding is something that nearly all conservatives would agree with.

Several reasons exist for this outcome. First, mediating institutions are able to individualize their approach to the circumstances of the person they are trying to help in ways that governments can never do. Second, mediating institutions are much more likely to target their assistance in ways that avoid the long-term dependence that comes from government programs. Third, mediating institutions act to change the behavior of the people they are helping and may even demand such behavioral change in exchange for assistance. And fourth, such institutions are able to address problems that go beyond material poverty.

Where big-government conservatives differ from small-government conservatives is in their belief that these mediating institutions require government support in order to thrive. In the April 2001 edition of *First Things,* Richard Neuhaus took note of the different approaches to the relationship between the government and mediating institutions.[17]

> The minimalist proposition is that government should get out of the way, and let the mediating institutions—families, churches, voluntary associations, etc.—do their thing. Getting out of the way requires many changes, including changes in tax policy, professional certifications, and the freedom to hire in accord with an institution's constituting vision. The maximalist proposition goes beyond getting out of the way and suggests that the government should use the mediating institutions in achieving public purposes.

80

Big-government conservatives tend to lean toward the latter position. Small-government conservatives believe that, in the words of Charles Murray: "In a free society, a genuine need produces a response. If government is not seen as a legitimate source of intervention, individuals and associations will respond."[18] Contrast that attitude with the one expressed by former senator Rick Santorum (R-PA). Santorum says that the "get government out of the way" conservatism is "philosophical nonsense." Building the mediating institutions of society "will require a role for government that some conservatives find disquieting," but "government is as important as the other vital social structures that order our lives."[19]

As a result, big-government conservatives support proposals such as President Bush's faith-based initiative, under which the government would directly fund private, religiously based charities. The president believes that government funding of churches and other religiously based charitable activities would "unleash the armies of compassion" to lift people out of poverty. The Bush administration has taken substantial steps to shift anti-poverty funding to faith-based organizations. Such organizations now receive more than $2 billion in federal funding each year.[20]

In addition, big-government conservatives would use the power of government programs to direct or change the behavior of the poor. The Heritage Foundation's Robert Rector, for example, says, "Policymakers should recognize that America suffers largely from a problem of behavioral poverty, not material hardship."[21] Therefore, in this view, lawmakers should support "legislation requir[ing] responsible behavior as a condition of receiving welfare benefits."[22] James Q. Wilson makes a similar point, arguing that, especially as regards welfare policy, conservatives should "acknowledge the necessary involvement of government in character formation." The goal of welfare policy—indeed, public policy generally—should be to "induce persons to act virtuously."[23] As President Bush puts it, "I think part of government's responsibility is to encourage certain cultures."[24]

At its best, this attitude manifests itself in President Bush's call for an "ownership society" that would give people more control over—and responsibility for—areas of their lives such as retirement and health care. But at worst it treats poor people like children. It also leads big-government conservatives to support a host of government programs that encourage marriage, promote abstinence, restrict divorce, increase saving, encourage school attendance, and so on. In some cases receipt of benefits would be conditioned on certain behavior. In other cases new programs would be designed to "educate" the poor about how they should behave.

Clearly, poverty has a behavior-based component. Women who cannot afford to care for children should not have them. People who can work should do so. Young people should remain in school. Stable marriage provides many benefits. Thrift and savings provide a route out of poverty. We know that the best anti-poverty equation is to (a) finish school; (b) avoid pregnancy outside marriage; and (c) get a job, any job, and stick with it.

We also know that decades of liberal welfare policies have created perverse incentives and distorted behavior in ways that are harmful to the poor and their children. But oddly, big-government conservatives then turn to government to correct the problems. In fact, Robert Rector of the Heritage Foundation suggests that government can do a far better job of fighting poverty through behavioral control than can the private sector. Rather than contributing to private charities, Rector writes, "For many philanthropists, the most effective strategy may be to try to influence what the government does."[25]

Some big-government conservatives would even go so far as to pay the poor for behavior that would benefit them, such as making doctor appointments, keeping their children in school, cleaning their house, or looking for work. Newt Gingrich, for example, has endorsed a proposal by New York City mayor Michael Bloomberg for such payments.[26]

Big-government conservatives do not dispute the idea that this approach to welfare is a form of paternalism. Lawrence Mead, a leading advocate of conservative welfare reform, even titled one of his books *The New Paternalism: Supervisory Approaches to Poverty.*[27] They just believe that nothing is wrong with paternalism—as long as they get to be the parent. The big-government conservative conceit is that government not only knows what is best for each individual poor person but also can devise a mix of incentives and disincentives, rewards and punishments, that can bring about the type of behavior government seeks.

In practice, however, the policies they promote are at best unlikely to work, and at worst will create far worse problems than the ones they attempt to solve.

Government-Funded Charity

Robert Rector's views aside, little doubt exists that private charity has often succeeded where government welfare programs have failed.[28] Not surprisingly, therefore, many big-government conservatives have suggested using government funds to subsidize these charities. Particular attention, in this regard, has been focused on faith-based charities, both because of the importance big-government conservatives put on religion generally and because these groups have not historically been as likely to receive government funds as more secular charitable organizations.

Of course, faith-based organizations have had a major role in providing social services since the earliest American colonies. But for most of our history, these organizations operated without significant access to government funds.[29] Indeed, government funding of religious institutions, even charitable ones, has traditionally been viewed with suspicion.[30]

However, throughout the 1990s, increased agitation came from Christian activists and inner-city churches wishing to participate in government social-welfare initiatives. As a result, a provision was added to PRWORA to allow states to contract with religious organizations, or to "allow religious organizations to accept certificates, vouchers, or other forms of disbursement . . . on the same basis as any other nongovernmental provider without impairing the religious character of such organizations, and without diminishing the religious freedom of beneficiaries of assistance funded under such program."[31] This provision became known as "Charitable Choice" and applied to four government programs: TANF, Supplemental Security Income, Medicaid, and food stamps.[32]

Charitable Choice went much further than simply making faith-based organizations eligible for government funding. It explicitly attempted to eliminate many of the restrictions and conditions that had previously been imposed on government grants to religious organizations. Specifically, it would permit the following:

- Provision of government services in actual houses of worship
- Display by contractors of religious "art, icons, scripture, and other symbols" in areas where government services are provided
- Discrimination by religious contractors against employees on the basis of their religious beliefs

The law, however, continues to ban the use of government funds for "sectarian worship, instruction, or proselytization." It also requires states to provide an alternate secular provider for any aid recipient who does not wish to receive services through a religious institution.

The Bush administration has sought to build on Charitable Choice in several ways. First, shortly after taking office, Bush established a White House Office of Faith-Based Initiatives, as well as operational centers for faith-based initiatives in five federal agencies: the Justice Department, the Department of Health and Human Services, the Department of Labor, the Department of Education, and the Department of Housing and Urban Development.[33] In the wake of Hurricane Katrina, he even added a Center for Faith-Based and Community Initiatives in the Department of Homeland Security.[34] Second, President Bush expanded Charitable Choice to virtually all government programs. And third, he created a "compassion capital fund" to highlight best practices and provide technical assistance and start-up capital to promising faith-based programs. That fund has provided $148 million in grants to more than 3,000 organizations since it started in 2002.[35]

Allowing the government to directly fund private charitable activities, especially faith-based organizations and programs, raises many troubling questions.[36] First, of course, are a whole range of issues surrounding the separation of church and state. The law in this area is far from settled, involving court interpretation and reinterpretation of terms such as "pervasively sectarian" and "excessive involvement."[37] As a result, government grants to faith-based charities are an open invitation to litigation. Diana Etendi, an analyst with the Welfare Policy Center at the Hudson Institute, points out the many ambiguities:

> If the pastor of a church, where a new government job readiness class is starting, stops by to welcome the new group of job seeking welfare recipients and offers a prayer on their behalf, is that sectarian worship? If God or a biblical principle is mentioned during the course of counseling, is that sectarian instruction? If a client suffering a bitter divorce is invited to attend one of the church's regular support groups, is that proselytizing?[38]

Moreover, evidence indicates that the Bush administration has not been religiously neutral in determining what organizations would receive government grants. David Kuo, who served as deputy director of the Office of Faith-Based Initiatives, says that the grant review process was overwhelmingly biased in favor of conservative Christian organizations and the administration's political allies.[39]

Equally if not more important is the effect of government funding on the charities that receive those funds. Government standards and burdensome regulation intended to ensure accountability and quality inevitably come attached to government grants and contracts. These regulations can come in one of two ways. First are those regulations specifically attached to the law or policy, most of which are designed to avoid church-state entanglements, such as provisions in the 1996 Charitable Choice law, which specify government funds may not be used for "sectarian worship, instruction, or proselytization."[40] Likewise, President Bush has said that no government funds would be used under any of his proposals "for proselytizing or other inherently religious activities."[41]

Stephen Burger, executive director of the International Union of Gospel Missions, points out the difficulty of defining what terms like "proselytizing" mean, and warns, "As well intentioned as Congress is in passing [Charitable Choice], it will be the government bureaucrats and civil-libertarian lawyers who enforce it."[42] Burger and others believe that the burden will be on charities to prove that the funds they receive are being correctly used. Charitable Choice contains provisions requiring charities receiving funds to submit to a government audit.[43] As a result the government has the right to investigate a church's finances.

Unfortunately, as Melissa Rogers of the American Baptist Convention notes, the audit language of the statute is "just the tip of the regulatory iceberg."[44] Acceptance of government funds subjects an organization to a wide range of federal regulations, chief among them federal civil rights laws. According to the 1988 Civil Rights Restoration Act, a private organization "will be covered by [federal nondiscrimination laws] in its entirety, if it receives federal financial assistance which is extended to it as a whole." Among the laws it must now comply with are Title VI of the Civil Rights Act of 1964 (prohibiting discrimination on the basis of race, color, or national origin), section 504 of the Rehabilitation Act (barring discrimination on the basis of handicap), the Age Discrimination Act, and Title IX of the Educational Amendments of 1972 (prohibiting discrimination on the basis of sex and visual impairment in educational institutions and programs).[45] This government entanglement has led to both conflicts with church doctrine, especially in areas such as sexual orientation, and extensive compliance costs.[46]

Many large charities have avoided the worst of these regulatory intrusions by setting up separate, virtually secular, arms of their organizations to handle their social services. But this tactic is not easily available to the small neighborhood churches that are among the most effective. The average church in the United States has a congregation of only 75 members. Less than 1 percent of churches have congregations of more than 900 and less than 10 percent have congregations exceeding 250 people. The average annual church budget is only $55,000.[47] Faith-based initiatives not associated with specific churches are also quite small, with budgets averaging about $120,000 annually. On average, they have only two full-time and two part-time employees.[48] For these smaller churches and organizations, compliance costs can be a terrible burden.

Beyond civil rights issues, a host of labor, safety, licensing, staff training, and other regulations come into play when a charity accepts public funds. For example, contractors may be required to pay prevailing union wages.[49] And because many federal funds are routed through state agencies, state regulations may also apply. These can be as detailed and idiosyncratic as instructions on night-light placement and window-washing instructions.[50]

Even the process of applying for federal funds can be costly and time consuming, requiring detailed knowledge of the federal grant process. Applications can run to dozens, even hundreds of pages, and require extensive supporting documentation. Thus, large, established charities have an advantage in the competition for funding over the smaller, local organizations that are arguably more effective. At the very least, the process represents one more diversion of resources away from actually providing services to those in need.

Even those charities with the best of intentions will be tempted to subtly shift the emphasis of their mission to comply with the grant criteria. In some cases they will become increasingly secular in orientation, in others they may simply adopt new missions and services that distract from the faith-based charity's original goal. It is one thing for a church to open a soup kitchen because its congregation feels God has called them to do so. It is another to open that kitchen because someone dangles grant money in front of you.

The first of these two forms of "mission creep"—secularization— poses the clearest and most obvious threat to the nature of faith-based charities. Facing the threat of litigation or the loss of federal funding if they violate the First Amendment, many charities choose to err on the side of caution, virtually eliminating any religious component from their services.

But why should faith-based charities eschew proselytizing and explicitly religious functions? That is the reason for the "faith" in "faith-based" charities. These organizations believe that helping people requires more than simply food or a bed. It requires addressing deeper spiritual needs. It is, ultimately, about God. Yet in the end, Bush's proposal may transform private charities from institutions that change people's lives to mere providers of services.

Stephen Monsma, chairman of the social sciences division at Pepperdine University, examined 766 religious nonprofit groups and concluded that an inverse relationship existed between religious practices and public funding. Grading the organizations on 15 indicative religious practices, such as having religious pictures or symbols in facilities, spoken prayers at meals, and hiring practices in accordance with religious orientation as well as "encouraging religious commitment by clients," Monsma found that of those organizations scoring lowest on the religious practices scale, 44 percent received a high percentage of their annual budget from public funds. Of those organizations with the highest scores, only 28 percent received significant amounts of government funding.[51]

A second form of mission creep is subtler but can also seriously distort a charity's purpose. In the chase for government funding, charities may tailor their programs to the federal grant process rather than to the needs of their clients. Jacquelin Triston of the Salvation Army puts it this way, "If you can't do it the way you want, then you'll take your program and fit it into whatever they'll give you money for."[52] As a result, charities may find themselves taking on tasks that have little to do with their original mission or for which they are untrained or ill-equipped.

For example, Massachusetts subsidizes a large proportion of the charitable work undertaken by Catholic Charities in that state. Beginning in the mid-1990s, the state began to shift its funding priorities from other social services to substance abuse. As state funding shifted, so did the programs offered by Catholic Charities. Other programs, such as thrift shops, child-care programs, and soup kitchens, have been closed and alcohol and drug treatment programs opened. By 1995, the Massachusetts office of Catholic Charities spent 80 percent of its funds on substance abuse programs that actually served only a quarter of its clients.[53]

Stanley Carlson-Thies, director of social policy studies at the Center for Public Justice, refers to this mission creep as "vendorism," a process whereby government grants end up directing the activities of private charities, changing their direction, and turning them into mere "vendors" of government services, simply a government program wearing a clerical collar.[54]

An even more profound threat exists to the identity and mission of these charities. If the history of welfare teaches us anything, it teaches us that government money is as addictive as any narcotic. "It becomes almost like heroin," says Ed Gotgart, president of the Massachusetts Association of Nonprofit Schools and Colleges. "You build your program around the assumption that you can't survive without government money."[55]

Ironically, therefore, given that many private charities are dedicated to fighting welfare dependency, government funding may quickly become a source of dependency for the charities themselves. Lobbying for, securing, and retaining that funding can quickly become the organization's top priority. Surely we do not want to put charities on the dole. No reason exists to believe that welfare for charities would be any less destructive than welfare for individuals.

Government funding of charities also undermines one of the biggest strengths of charity—its voluntariness. As David Kelley explains, "Compassion and generosity are virtues . . . not a duty, but a value we choose to pursue."[56] It is the voluntariness of these virtues that makes them ennobling. But as Tibor Machan, professor of philosophy at Auburn University, points out, by turning generosity from a virtue to a legally compelled duty, government "limits the moral worth of generous conduct."[57] Over time, this compulsion can have a coarsening effect on society, diminishing people's desire to help, their charitableness. Rather than creating a more compassionate society, we could end up with a less compassionate one.

As evidence of this tendency, studies show that when charities receive government funds, private donations decrease because potential donors perceive less need.[58] This crowding-out effect is estimated to range from as little as 2 cents to as much as 53 cents in lost contributions for every dollar of government money received.[59]

In the end, charities come to rely more and more on government funds, and less and less on true charitable contributions. Catholic Charities now receives 62 percent of its funding from federal, state, and local governments.[60] Catholic Charities may indeed be an efficient and effective provider of government services, but at some point it becomes neither Catholic, nor a charity.

Thus, the end result of these proposals will be the substitution of coercive government financing for compassion-based voluntary giving.

Government Marriage Initiatives

One of the highest priorities of big-government conservatives has been to use government programs to promote marriage. Reauthorization of welfare reform in 2006 contained provisions for the federal government to spend $1.5 billion over five years on a "healthy marriage" initiative. The legislation would provide states with matching funds for a variety of programs designed to encourage welfare recipients, and other low-income people, to get or stay married. Among the programs that might be funded under this initiative are public advertising campaigns to promote marriage, high school education classes on the importance of marriage, marriage education and relationship-skills training for unmarried pregnant women and the fathers of their children, premarital counseling for engaged couples, mentoring programs where older married couples assist engaged couples, marriage counseling and enhancement programs, and divorce reduction programs.[61] This list includes less than what some big-government conservatives suggested. The Coalition for Marriage, Family and Couples Education, which represents some 1,600 organizations seeking federal funding under the healthy marriage initiative, is hoping to increase funding to approximately 1 percent of all TANF expenditures, roughly $400 million annually.[62] Robert Rector of the Heritage Foundation is even more ambitious. He wants to see at least 10 percent of all TANF funds used to promote marriage.[63]

In a separate proposal, Sen. Sam Brownback (R-KS) has sought $3 million for a pilot project to set up savings accounts for low-income residents, including welfare recipients, in the District of

Columbia who become engaged or agree to get married. The government would provide three dollars in matching funds for every dollar the couple saves, up to $9,000 in matching funds. The couple could also receive a $300 bonus if they complete four premarital or marital counseling classes. After the couples are married, they will be able to use the funds in their accounts to buy a home, send a child to college, or start a business. The program would also pay up to $300 toward the couple's marriage costs.[64]

Before embarking on a massive new federally funded marriage program, however, we should consider several key problems with this approach.

First, and most obvious, is the question of just who poor women, especially poor pregnant women or single mothers, are supposed to marry. William Julius Wilson and others have shown that in high-poverty areas, with their attendant crime and unemployment, relatively few marriageable men are available.[65] Several studies have looked at the fathers of children born out of wedlock and found them quite unprepared to support a family. More than a third lacked a high school degree, 28 percent were unemployed, and 20 percent had incomes of less than $6,000 per year.[66] In addition, roughly 38 percent had criminal records.[67] This last is a particular problem with young black men, nearly one-third of whom are in jail or on probation.[68] An examination of attempts to collect child-support payments from low-income unwed fathers found that a substantial number of them faced serious employment barriers, including criminal records and poor health.[69] Many single mothers may find themselves single precisely because they find their unemployed and undereducated potential partners to be unattractive marriage material.[70] Encouraging marriage to unsuitable partners may do more harm than good.

Second, marriage may do less to increase family income than supposed. Despite the evidence cited above that marriage leads to increased family income, the effect on low-income single-mothers may be less than for others. About half of unwed mothers are in fact already living with their child's father. Another third are romantically involved with the father but living separately.[71] Some evidence indicates that marrying the child's father, rather than cohabiting, leads to a greater sharing of resources and increased assistance from family and friends, and may improve the mother and children's economic well-being.[72] However, the father can be presumed to be providing at least some resources under the circumstances, so any increase would be marginal. Moreover, given the economic conditions of the fathers previously described, they may have few additional resources to bring to a marriage.

Also worth raising is the caveat that characteristics of unmarried mothers themselves may contribute to both their being unmarried and their being poor. Poverty may be less a function of family structure than of other factors that affect both family structure and poverty. Or as Theodora Ooms of the Center for Law and Social Policy asks, "Are single parents poor because they are not married, or are they not married because they are poor?"[73] The consensus of academic study currently gives more weight to family structure and nonmarital childbearing, but dissenting voices exist.[74]

Third, defining the issue as one of "marriage" may miss the real problem, that of out-of-wedlock births. Proponents of government marriage initiatives tend to lump all forms of single-parent families together, but significant differences exist between divorced families and families headed by never-married women. That is not to say that divorce makes no contribution to poverty. Divorced women are twice as likely to be poor as women in intact marriages. But divorced women are only half as likely to be poor as women who give birth out of wedlock.[75]

Several reasons explain why poverty is worse for unwed mothers than for divorced women. Unwed mothers tend to be younger, have less education and fewer job skills, and are less likely to receive child support.[76] A woman giving birth out of wedlock is more likely to drop out of school and less likely to work than are other women.[77] For example, only 59 percent of never-married mothers are high school graduates.[78] Only 38 percent are working full time.[79]

If we think in terms of preventing out-of-wedlock birth, the question becomes slightly different: should we be promoting marriage or preventing pregnancy?

After all, marriage is still the preferred family structure in America today. Most women eventually do marry, 90 percent by the time they reach age 45.[80] A strong societal trend has existed, however, toward later marriage. Between 1960 and 1999, the average age of first marriage for women increased from 20 to 25.[81] This trend has generally been beneficial, leading to greater educational and career achievement for women. On the downside, the greater interval between the onset of puberty and marriage has created a window that has led to increased out-of-wedlock pregnancy. As a result, up until their mid-20s, more women have babies than marry; afterward, the reverse is true.[82]

That means two ways exist to address the problem: reduce the age of marriage or delay pregnancies until after the women are married. Trying to change the age of marriage promises to be extremely difficult in the face of prevailing cultural dynamics. It may also have unintended negative consequences. For example, teen mothers are more likely to have a rapid second birth if they marry, which brings with it a variety of economic and other concerns.[83] They are also more likely to leave school after they become pregnant and less likely to return to school later on.[84] In addition, marriages among younger men and women are far less stable than among those who delay marriage until they are older. The former divorce more frequently and after a shorter period of marriage.[85]

Nor is marriage subsequent to an out-of-wedlock birth a panacea. As we have seen, many if not most unwed mothers are already cohabiting with their child's father, and those fathers may be unsuitable marriage partners. Even if unwed mothers later marry men other than the child's father, those men tend to be from the same disadvantaged circumstances as the mother.[86] As a result, research shows that subsequent marriage alleviates, but does not solve, the problems associated with unwed motherhood.[87]

Focusing on pregnancy prevention rather than marriage itself would therefore make sense, delaying childbearing until women have completed school, established themselves in the workplace, and perhaps married on their own.[88]

Finally, even if marriage promotion is a good idea, one should ask whether the federal government is any more likely to be successful at this effort than it has been at promoting other desirable behaviors. Although the Heritage Foundation and others are able to point to successful private-sector initiatives that encourage or sustain marriage, little evidence exists of successful government programs in this regard.[89]

KidSave

Proposals for the creation of some form of children's allowance or savings accounts have floated around the U.S. political scene at least since the 1960s without gaining much political traction.[90] In the late 1990s, they found a champion in Sen. Robert Kerrey (D-NE), who saw in the idea a way to offset needed reductions in future Social Security benefits while increasing national savings and building wealth for low-income families. Kerrey pursued several variations of the proposal, some funded from Social Security payroll taxes, some from tax credits to parents, and some from family contributions. In some versions, funds could be used for education. In others, they offset traditional Social Security benefits. Kerrey's proposals attracted significant bipartisan interest, but none ever passed the Senate.

Although Kerrey has left the Senate, a combination of the debates over welfare reform and Social Security has kept interest in his ideas alive. The New America Foundation has been one of the idea's leading proponents. The center-left organization's Asset Building Project draws on the expertise of some of the leading experts on the concept, including Michael Sherraden and Ray Boshara.

Big-government conservatives have been ardent supporters of children's allowances and other asset-building programs for the poor. For example, Rick Santorum was a cosponsor of KidSave, a plan to give every child $2,000 at birth.[91] Sen. Jeff Sessions (R-AL) has offered a plan for a $1,000 contribution.[92] David Brooks has written favorably about the idea.[93] Scholars at the American Enterprise Institute and the Heritage Foundation have come out in favor of it.[94]

KidSave and similar proposals are designed to respond to a real problem—the lack of savings opportunities for low-income Americans. As Michael Sherraden of the Washington University in St. Louis has noted, "For the vast majority of households, the pathway out of poverty is not through consumption, but through saving and accumulation."[95]

By definition, poor people lack wealth. But a difference exists between "wealth" and "income," and in this sense, the lack of wealth among the poor may be a bigger long-term problem than their lack of income. Wealth is not just an amount of money that can be used to buy things, but, as Melvin Oliver and Thomas Shapiro wrote in their seminal book, *Black Wealth/White Wealth*:

> It is used to create opportunities, secure a desired stature and standard of living, and pass class status on to one's children . . . the command of resources that wealth entails is

more encompassing than is income or education, and closer in meaning and theoretical significance to our traditional notions of economic well-being and access to life chances.[96]

Some observers suggest that the approach to defining poverty should be revised to consider the accumulation of assets or the lack of them. One common definition of "asset poverty" would define people as asset poor if they lack sufficient savings or other assets to survive for three months at the poverty level. By this definition, more than 25 percent of the population would be considered asset poor, roughly double the official poverty rate.[97] Asset poverty is a particular problem for minorities, with as many as 61 percent of African Americans and 70 percent of Hispanics among the asset poor.[98] Indeed, a lack of assets may be the biggest single reason for economic inequality between whites and minorities.[99]

It would seem, therefore, to be wise public policy to encourage asset ownership in general and among the poor in particular. But despite these good intentions, several reasons exist to be concerned about KidSave proposals.

Suppose we were to follow the recommendation of the most expensive of the KidSave proposals, HR 1041, sponsored by Rep. Jerry Weller (R-IL), and award $2,000 to families in the name of each newborn child for initiating savings accounts beginning on January 1, 2006. Suppose, also, that the amount of seed money awarded each year were increased with the rate of inflation (to maintain the investment's real value constant). Projecting the federal budget cost of this annual outlay using the Social Security Administration's estimates of births in 2006 puts the cost for 2006 at $8 billion.[100] This cost would grow with growth in the number of children born each year. Using the Social Security Administration's projections through the year 2080, the estimated present-value cost of this program would be $266 billion during the next 75 years. That is, initiating such a program would be the same as committing today to another $266 billion in federal outlays.[101]

If initiated for newborn children, considerable political pressure would exist to expand the KidSave accounts program. After all, if today's newborns are endowed with a KidSave account, why shouldn't today's one-year-olds also be provided with a similar windfall? Indeed, not doing so would provide a sharp break in the assets and resources of future retirees who happen to be born after this year compared to those born in the past. Carrying this argument forward, a case could be made for providing KidSave accounts for all children alive today. In fact, Sherraden, the intellectual godfather of KidSave, has already written positively of extending the program to all children under age 18.[102]

Suppose the age of eligibility for KidSave accounts were restricted to age 18 and younger. What would be the financial cost of awarding KidSave accounts to all of today's children? The answer, again based on the Social Security Administration's population estimates, is $414 billion.[103] To see where this largess can lead, one need only look to Europe, where children's allowances on average consume 1.8 percent of gross domestic product, with many countries spending much more. Denmark devotes 3.3 percent of gross domestic product to the program.[104]

Conceivably, expenditures of this magnitude could be justified if they would offset the expected future deficits in Social Security, that is, if account accumulations explicitly substituted for benefits under the traditional Social Security program. However, of the three main legislative proposals, only Representative Petri's bill includes this feature.

The other two plans structure their account contributions as loans. In theory, as the loans are repaid the program will, to a large degree, become self-sustaining, with repayments from one cohort funding contributions to another. However, a 30-year gap remains before the first contributions are repaid, making for a substantial increase in government spending over that period. Moreover, the Congressional Budget Office estimates that about 10 percent of all recipients will never repay their "loan."[105]

Because the federal budget is in deficit, the government will have to borrow the money used to fund the accounts. In doing so, it will have to pay interest on the incurred debt, but the account loans themselves will be repaid on an interest-free basis. The Congressional Budget Office estimates that for every $2,000 loaned in this interest-free manner, the government will incur a $1,700 cost.[106]

KidSave accounts are meant to redirect resources from retirees and workers toward children. Although nothing is wrong in principle in attempting to do that, considering the dynamic effects of such a policy on the economy is important—especially on working and saving by adults and on their provision to children of private gifts

and bequests. Given that existing federal commitments to pay entitlement benefits to current and future retirees already impose massive
tax burdens on today's workers and future generations (see Chapter
6), imposing additional burdens on taxpayers to finance KidSave
accounts would be counterproductive.[107]

Important elements common to all KidSave proposals are the
institutional details regarding ownership and management of the
funds. KidSave account proponents appear to recognize the inherent
dangers in allowing the government to invest and manage the funds
(although, curiously, some of the same policymakers and analysts
refuse to acknowledge the similar problems with investing the Social
Security and Medicare trust funds in private securities). Hence, they
specify that parents or legal guardians would serve as account custodians and make investment decisions on behalf of children until
they attain age 18.[108]

Account withdrawals would be restricted to ensure that accounts
are used for productive, asset-building purposes. Withdrawals
would be prohibited until the account owner turns 18. Thereafter,
withdrawals would be governed by rules similar to those of Roth
IRAs that permit withdrawals without penalty prior to retirement
for first-time home purchase and postsecondary education[109] Other
distributions would incur steep penalties against withdrawals of
government contributions—that is, use of funds other than for asset
building would trigger loss of all government matching funds.

Despite the apparently comprehensive safeguards against use of
KidSave funds for preretirement consumption, this arrangement also
sets up a conflict between the child as the account's owner and
its initial custodians—parents or guardians. Older generations—
parents and guardians—are expected to finance these accounts
through higher taxes. Without KidSave accounts, parents and guardians would ordinarily determine how much to save in anticipation
of the child's future needs. However, KidSave accounts would also
provide an incentive for the parents and guardians to offset their
own saving intended for their child's benefit. For families that receive
a KidSave subsidy from the government, that offset would generally
be larger than the family's tax cost for initiating the KidSave account
and making subsequent contributions into it.[110]

Thus, in spite of the seemingly elaborate safeguards included in
KidSave proposals to prevent their early withdrawal for consumption, such accounts would only enable current older generations to

exploit the new government matching grants and divert additional resources toward themselves, rather than allow those resources to flow through to their children.[111]

KidSave accounts would not treat all families equally. Families with more children would receive larger benefits. Those with fewer children would receive fewer or no benefits but would face the financial cost of a KidSave program in terms of higher taxes. The windfall reaped by many of the families with children would be in addition to the already generous subsidies allowed in the tax code for such families (currently $1,000 per child), special state-based but federally subsidized programs for child health services, child nutrition programs, and monetary assistance to families with children.[112]

Apart from the uncertainty regarding the effect of KidSave accounts on national saving and investment, the effect of such cross-family redistribution of resources on labor markets must also be considered. Such accounts would be financed out of general revenues. The benefits of KidSave accounts would flow to families with children, but the taxes used to finance those accounts would increase for everyone. Thus, financing KidSave accounts would have a negative impact on labor markets, in general, and the distortionary effect would represent a net loss of welfare.[113]

KidSave accounts are intended for long-term saving. However, withdrawals may be permitted for their use in acquiring more education and skills. Previous experience with college saving accounts—529 and Coverdell tax-saving accounts—has shown that participating households are penalized by college financial-aid policies that deny aid to those with financial resources.[114] Hence, to the extent that poorer households save in these accounts, their effort at achieving financial security for the child would be neutralized by the "college tax."

We also do not understand what the effect of KidSave will be on the serious problem of out-of-wedlock births. As mentioned earlier, academic researchers have increasingly come to accept the link between the availability of traditional welfare benefits and increased out-of-wedlock birth rates. Of course, a difference clearly exists between traditional welfare payments and KidSave. The former provide subsidies directly to parents and make those subsidies contingent in many ways on the parents' not marrying. KidSave accumulations would theoretically only be available for the child's use and that not until some time in the distant future. Moreover, the subsidy would be unrelated to marital status. Even so, parents of children receiving a KidSave subsidy are likely to feel wealthier. If so, KidSave could be perceived as a reward for having children regardless of whether the parents are married. Added to other welfare benefits, it has the potential to increase out-of-wedlock births. At the very least, this question is deserving of more study before we enact Kid-Save as national policy.

KidSave is almost paradigmatic of the big-government conservative approach to government. The problem that big-government conservatives have identified is real. But rather than rely on private and voluntary institutions or simply remove government-created barriers to saving, they have responded by calling for a massive new government program.[115]

A Conservative Welfare State Will Not Work

Conservatives have long understood the failure of government programs to deal with the problem of poverty in America. But big-government conservatives have a newfound faith in the welfare state. They believe that somehow government is capable of devising precisely the right set of incentives and disincentives to deal with the deep-rooted social, cultural, and spiritual problems of the underclass. Rather than getting government out of the business of welfare and allowing civil society to step in, they see government as a partner with traditional mediating institutions, such as family, church, and community. Indeed, they seem to believe that such institutions are incapable of operating without government assistance and direction.

But what in the record of government welfare failure indicates government is able to fine-tune the delicate balance of moral and spiritual values that hold the true solutions to poverty? Government intervention is likely only to interfere with those aspects of civil society that are already working.

5. National Health Care Lite

For all the debate over health care reform in this country, we should never lose sight of the fact that America offers the highest-quality health care in the world. Most of the world's top doctors, hospitals, and research facilities are located in the United States. Eighteen of the last 27 winners of the Nobel Prize in Medicine either are U.S. citizens or work here.[1] U.S. companies have developed half of all the major new medicines introduced worldwide over the past 20 years.[2] In fact, Americans played a key role in 80 percent of the most important medical advances of the past 30 years.[3] Nearly every type of advanced medical technology or procedure is more available in the United States than in any other country.[4] By almost any measure, if you are diagnosed with a serious illness, the United States is the place you want to be. That is why tens of thousands of patients from around the world come to this country every year for treatment.

Critics of American health care often point out that other countries have higher life expectancies or lower infant mortality rates, but those two indicators are not a good way of measuring the quality of a nation's health care system. In the United States, very low-birth-weight infants have a much greater chance of being brought to term with the latest medical technologies. Some of those low-birth-weight babies die soon after birth, which boosts the country's infant mortality rate, but in many other Western countries, those high-risk, low-birth-weight infants are not included when infant mortality is calculated.[5] Life expectancies are also affected by exogenous factors like violent crime, poverty, obesity, tobacco and drug use, and other issues unrelated to health care. In contrast, if one compares the outcome for specific diseases like cancer or heart disease, the United States clearly outperforms the rest of the world.[6]

Still, problems clearly exist with our health care system. Roughly 46 million Americans are currently uninsured.[7] We need to do more to lower health care costs and increase access to care. Both patients and providers need better and more useful information. The system is riddled with waste, and the quality of care is uneven. Government health care programs like Medicare and Medicaid threaten future generations with an enormous burden of debt and taxes.

Some have responded to these problems with calls for greater government involvement in our health care system, perhaps even a government-run national health care system. Others have suggested that what American health care needs is more choice and competition, not less.

Americans faced the choice of these two competing visions for health care reform in 1993, with the debate over "Hillarycare." That plan came down squarely on the side of government control over the American health care system. Although the Clinton administration attempted to sell the plan as expanding health coverage, in reality, the plan was a massive government rationing scheme that would have ultimately denied care and greatly diminished the quality of care for the middle class in order to control costs. The Clinton administration supported cost control as a way of obtaining funds to expand health care for the low-income population, essentially redistributing health care from the middle class. It also saw the middle class as consuming overly lavish health care and wanted to clamp down on such consumption to obtain resources for other, supposedly more urgent, "social needs." The Clinton plan would have achieved rationing through a system that would ultimately have forced everyone into heavily regulated health maintenance organizations, which would have enjoyed the ultimate power to decide what health care patients would receive and from whom. The health maintenance organizations would then have carried out the government's rationing policies. Clinton apparently hoped that indirect rationing through managed care would avoid the direct rationing caused by price controls under every other national health care system in the world. But just in case, the proposal would also have established a National Health Board, with backup authority to ration health care directly if indirect rationing failed to sufficiently reduce costs.

Fortunately, the American people rejected the idea of government-run health care. In the end, the Clinton health plan didn't even come to a vote in Congress. In fact, former House majority leader Dick Armey has said that a backlash against the Clinton plan was "the biggest reason [Republicans] took control of Congress that year."[8]

For a time Republicans actually acted like they understood this message. The growth in federal health spending fell from roughly

7 percent in 1995 to approximately 4.5 percent in 1999.[9] Several worthwhile reforms were enacted, including a pilot program for Medical Savings Accounts, precursors of today's Health Savings Accounts. Although many Democrats remained committed to national health care, even if by incremental means, Republicans appeared committed to free-market health care reform.

Today, however, big-government conservatives are blurring the distinctions between liberal and conservative approaches to health care reform. Under the Bush administration, the growth in health care spending has rebounded to more than 7 percent annually.[10] Regulation of the health care industry has increased, and the portion of health care spending paid directly by the consumer has continued to decline.

But more important, a philosophical line appears to have been crossed. Big-government conservatives appear to accept the idea that government involvement in the health care system is, if not desirable, inevitable. Thus Bill Kristol, once an outspoken opponent of Hillarycare, now argues that free-market health care is hopelessly utopian.[11] As a result, big-government conservatives have increasingly embraced proposals that take us several steps down the slippery slope to national health care.

Individual Mandates

Proposals for achieving universal health insurance coverage are again receiving serious attention. Among the ideas attracting bipartisan support are calls for an individual health insurance mandate, a legal requirement that every American obtain adequate private health insurance coverage. Those who don't receive such coverage through their employer or some other group would be required to purchase individual coverage on their own. Those who fail to do so would be subject to fines or other penalties.[12]

Such a mandate, if imposed on the federal level, would be an unprecedented expansion of government power. As the Congressional Budget Office noted when the idea was first raised in 1994, "The government has never required people to buy any good or service as a condition of lawful residence in the United States."[13]

Originally the brainchild of moderate Republicans like then-senator John Chaffee (R-RI), seeking a compromise with Hillarycare, the insurance mandate is now championed by centrist groups like the

New America Foundation. However, individual mandate proposals also have a history of support by big-government conservatives.

Among those pushing hardest for individual mandates is Massachusetts governor Mitt Romney. In April 2006, Massachusetts became the first state in the nation to pass such a mandate.[14] The bipartisan legislation was based on a proposal that Governor Romney had pushed for nearly two years. Among other provisions it will require all Massachusetts residents to have a minimum level of health insurance coverage by July 2007. Those who do not receive health insurance through their employer or government programs such as Medicare or Medicaid will have to purchase a policy on their own. Failure to do so results in financial penalties. The state will subsidize all or part of the insurance costs for low- and middle-income residents.[15]

The bill was praised by liberal Democrats like Senator Kennedy, and Governor Romney said he believes it could be a model for how Republicans can co-opt Democratic issues. "Issues which have long been the province of the Democratic Party to claim as their own will increasingly move to the Republican side of the aisle," Romney said in an interview with Bloomberg News Service.[16]

Other big-government conservatives have also embraced an individual mandate. The Heritage Foundation has supported such a mandate for more than a decade.[17] Senate majority leader Bill Frist (R-TN) has expressed general support for the idea.[18] Newt Gingrich is another avid supporter.[19] And the Weekly Standard has prominently featured articles favoring an individual mandate.[20]

Some have seen an individual mandate as an achievable step on the road to universal coverage.[21] Having long equated insurance coverage with access to health care and access to better health, they see an individual mandate as producing better health outcomes. For example, they argue, people will receive more preventive care if they are covered by insurance. In reality, however, the experience of rationing under national health insurance schemes in other countries shows that insurance coverage and access to care are entirely different things.[22] Moreover, evidence that insurance coverage or access leads to better health outcomes is uncertain at best.[23]

But the reason most big-government conservatives embrace an individual mandate is the "free-rider" problem. When an individual without health insurance becomes sick or injured, he or she still receives medical treatment. In fact hospitals have a legal requirement to provide care regardless of ability to pay. Physicians do not face the same legal requirement, but few are willing to deny treatment because a patient lacks insurance.

Such treatment is not free, however. The cost is simply shifted to others, those with insurance, or more often, taxpayers. In fact, uncompensated care costs an estimated \$40.7 billion per year, with 85 percent of that cost borne by federal, state, and local governments.[24] Thus, to a large degree individuals without health insurance are "free-riding" on the rest of us.

In addition, those most likely to go without health insurance are the young and relatively healthy. For example, although 18- to 24-year-olds are only 10 percent of the U.S. population, they are 21 percent of the long-term uninsured.[25] For these young, healthy individuals, going without health insurance is often a logical decision. However, that decision becomes a form of adverse selection. Removing the young and healthy from the insurance pool means that those remaining in the pool will be older and sicker, resulting in higher insurance premiums for those who are insured.[26]

These concerns are legitimate but smaller than commonly believed. Uncompensated care represents only about 3–5 percent of health care spending.[27] And regardless of whether a mandate solves legitimate problems in theory, the practical problems of an individual mandate make it likely to be costly and difficult to administer. More important, it would likely set in motion forces that will lead slowly, but almost inevitably, toward a government-run national health care system.

Advocates of a mandate argue that if government can mandate automobile insurance in order to protect society from the costs imposed by uninsured drivers, it should be able to do the same for health insurance. This analogy is imperfect, however. First, driving has long been recognized as a privilege, subject to all manner of regulatory requirements. If one does not like the regulations, including an insurance mandate, one can choose not to drive. A health insurance mandate would not generally give people such a choice. Second, the reason states mandate auto insurance is for the protection of *others* rather than the driver. Most states do not mandate that drivers carry insurance for their own injury or repair costs.

Mandated automobile insurance does, however, show how difficult enforcement of such mandates is. For example, 47 states have laws mandating that drivers purchase automobile liability insurance. Yet roughly 14.5 percent of drivers in those states are uninsured.[28] In some states, such as Texas, the uninsured motorist rate runs as high as 18 percent. As many as 22 percent of Los Angeles drivers are uninsured.[29] By comparison, in the three states without mandatory auto insurance, roughly 15 percent of drivers are uninsured. Thus, despite penalties that can run from loss of license to fines as high as $5,000 or even the impounding of vehicles, millions of American drivers appear to have chosen to ignore the mandate.[30] In fact, millions of Americans purchase "uninsured motorist" coverage to protect themselves from an accident where the other driver is uninsured. Interestingly, the percentage of drivers uninsured despite a mandate is roughly the same as the percentage of Americans without health insurance.[31]

The closest example to a health insurance mandate in the United States is in Hawaii, which has long mandated that all employers provide their workers with health insurance. But roughly 10 percent of Hawaiian workers remain uncovered.[32] Even under Canada's national health care system, the government has encountered difficulties in ensuring that everyone is registered and pays required premiums. For example, in British Columbia alone, an estimated 40,000 people slip through the cracks. As a result, physicians in that province provide about $5 million to $10 million per year in unreimbursed services to people without insurance.[33] Although that amount is tiny compared to the cost of treating the uninsured in the United States, it demonstrates the difficulties of forcing compliance with an insurance mandate.

The first problem is to track who is and is not insured. Here again the government's record does not inspire confidence. No federal agency invests as much time, money, and effort in tracking Americans as the Internal Revenue Service. Yet it consistently fails to track down millions of Americans who fail to file tax returns. And every 10 years a scandal arises when the Census Bureau cannot locate several million citizens. The most common solution is to require that Americans submit proof of insurance when they file their federal income taxes. But about 18 million low-income Americans are not required to file income taxes, mostly because their incomes are too low.[34] Another 9 million Americans who are required to file tax returns nonetheless fail to do so.[35] That is potentially 27 million Americans who would not be providing proof of insurance.

To deal with this situation, the New America Foundation would mandate that those who don't file income tax returns be required to submit their proof of coverage.[36] But the foundation provides no plan to deal with those who simply refuse to do so. Moreover, some of these nonfilers will be elderly, homeless, and mentally ill. Others will have changed their address, perhaps multiple times. Indeed, in Massachusetts, at least six members of the legislature have failed to file tax returns in the last few years.[37]

Furthermore, only about 30 percent of uninsured Americans have been uninsured for a full year. In fact half will regain insurance within four months.[38] Therefore many people who lack health insurance at some point throughout the year will in fact be insured at the time they file their taxes. Presumably, the "proof of insurance" could include the length of time that the person was insured, but that requirement would raise the complexity of compliance procedures considerably. It would also increase the incentive to lie.

If the government were able to determine that someone has not purchased health insurance, what penalty would apply? Ideas have been suggested ranging from loss of drivers' licenses to direct fines. However, some sort of tax penalty is the most common approach. But that is much easier said than done. As Gene Steuerle of the Urban Institute has noted, the administrative and enforcement costs of collecting the penalty would be enormous.[39] The Internal Revenue Service, for example, relies largely on voluntary compliance backed up by a slow and cumbersome legal process to collect taxes. And it does not require those with very small amounts of income to file. Even so, millions of Americans cheat or fail to file. Collecting a penalty for failure to insure would be much more difficult. "The [IRS] is simply incapable of going to millions of households, many of modest means, and collecting significant penalties at the end of the year," Steuerle warns.[40]

Also important to note is that the number-one reason people give for not purchasing insurance is that they cannot afford it.[41] Therefore, if an individual mandate for health insurance is going to be effective, some form of subsidy for low-income Americans will have to be found. As the New America Foundation notes, "Making basic coverage mandatory for individuals necessitates making coverage available and affordable for all."[42]

The cost of a health insurance policy for a family of four today averages more than $10,000.[43] Clearly, low-income individuals would have difficulty absorbing such costs. Even if the cost could be reduced by mandating a more-limited package of benefits or shifting to a high-deductible policy (with or without an accompanying Health Savings Account), the burden on low-income workers would be substantial.[44]

Subsidies will not be cheap. By some estimates, the initial cost of subsidies nationally would top $75 billion per year.[45] The subsidies under Governor Romney's plan for Massachusetts would cost about $725 million per year, with other aspects of the program driving total costs to approximately $1.56 billion.[46] To some degree, savings from uncompensated care would offset these costs.[47] Nevertheless, increased coverage would almost certainly lead to increased usage, driving up overall health care costs and necessitating increased subsidies. A legislative analysis of the plans suggests that within two years the program will face a shortfall of at least $160 billion.[48] Similar California legislation is estimated to cost as much as $9.4 billion.[49]

Moreover, when the subsidy became available to individuals purchasing insurance on their own, businesses that currently provide insurance to their workers with health insurance would either demand equivalent subsidies or drop their health coverage altogether, only too happy to shift the cost of insuring workers to the taxpayer. This behavior is already clearly visible with Medicaid.[50]

To implement an insurance mandate legislators and administrators will have to define what sort of insurance fulfills that mandate. In Massachusetts, Governor Romney originally proposed a low-cost, no-frills policy with a high deductible. However, by the time the legislature finished with the bill, the required insurance included all the state's mandated benefits.[51]

For example, the New America Foundation suggests that the Blue Cross Blue Shield Standard Benefit offered under the Federal Employee Health Benefits Program (FEHBP) provides a good model for the minimum benefits package.[52] A plan developed by Blue Cross Blue Shield of California calls for "independent medical professionals" to develop the minimum benefit package, but specifies that it should include preventive care, physician services, hospital care, and prescription drugs.[53] The Heritage Foundation has taken perhaps the least prescriptive approach, with a mandate for catastrophic coverage, defined essentially as a "stop loss" policy protecting a family against total health care costs above a certain level.[54]

Whatever the initial minimum benefits package consists of, special interests representing various health care providers and disease constituencies can certainly be expected to lobby for inclusion under any mandated benefits package. To see this process in action, one simply has to look to state mandates for health insurance benefits. The number of laws requiring that all insurance policies sold in a state provide coverage for specified diseases, conditions, and providers has been skyrocketing. In the 1960s only a handful of such mandates existed, but today there are more than 1,800.[55] The list includes mandates for coverage of hair transplants (Connecticut, Massachusetts, Maryland, Minnesota, Missouri, New Hampshire, and Oklahoma); massage therapy (Florida, Maryland, New Hampshire, and Washington); and pastoral counseling (Maine and North Carolina).[56]

Or consider Oregon's attempt to prioritize Medicaid services. In 1992, Oregon guaranteed all state residents under the poverty line a basic level of health care. At the same time, because funding was limited, the Oregon Health Services Commission drafted a priority-ranked list of medical services available to Oregonians. The state would fund services deemed priority on the basis of such factors as cost, duration of a treatment's benefit, improvement in the patient's quality of life, and community values. Services that did not qualify under these criteria would not be funded.[57] However, political calculations quickly became part of the ranking process, with the program a battleground for interests associated with various disease constituencies and health care specialties. Groups battled with each other to make sure that their needs or services were included in the list of covered services. The list was repeatedly revised to reflect not the best medical judgment but outside pressure. The legislature repeatedly intervened. The U.S. Office of Technology Assessment concluded that Oregon's prioritization plan "has not operated as the scientific vessel of rationing that it was advertised to be. Although initial rankings were based in large part on mathematical values, controversies around the list forced administrators to make political concessions and move medical services 'by hand' to satisfy constituency pressures."[58]

And when the Clinton administration proposed a minimum benefits package as part of its 1993 health care reform plan, provider lobbying groups spent millions of dollars in advertising calling for the inclusion of specific provider groups or coverage of specific conditions.

Lobbyists spent roughly $7.5 million attempting to influence the design of the new Massachusetts plan. The money appears to have been well spent. As mentioned, the legislature restored all the state's mandated benefits to the required package.[59]

Public-choice dynamics are such that providers (who would make money from the increased demand for their services) and disease constituencies (whose members naturally have an urgent desire for coverage of their illness or condition) will always have a strong incentive to lobby lawmakers for inclusion under any minimum benefits package. The public at large will likely see resisting the small premium increase caused by any particular additional benefit as unworthy of a similar effort. It is a simple case of concentrated benefits and diffuse costs.

Individual mandates cross an important practical and philosophical line. Once we accept the principle that the government is responsible for ensuring that every American has health insurance, we guarantee even more government involvement with and control over large portions of our health care system. Compulsory, government-defined insurance opens the door to even more widespread regulation of the health care industry and political interference in personal health care decisions. The result will be a slow but steady spiral downward toward a government-run national health care system.[60]

Managed Competition

The central concept behind the failed Clinton health care plan of 1993 was managed competition. The idea is to leave the provision of health care in private hands, unlike single-payer systems, but within an artificial marketplace run under strict government control. Under most iterations of managed competition, employers and individuals would join some form of purchasing pool that would negotiate with private insurers offering a government-prescribed minimum set of benefits. Individuals would choose among plans offered through the pool. Employers would continue to pay most of the premiums, but through the pool. Premiums would be community rated; that is, they could not vary according to age or health risk.[61]

Managed competition is meant to spur competition between health plans, yet competition takes place on a very limited basis. For example, health plans are not able to adjust their premiums on the basis of age, sex, current health, or other risk factors. Plans can compete on the basis of services offered, but only on the margins, because all plans are required to offer the same core benefits package. Some limited price competition is likely to occur, but because plans cannot reduce costs by managing risks or through benefit design, even that will be marginal. This situation is particularly problematic since an inability to price according to risk generally causes insurers to retreat toward the mean. This step results in an overprovision of services to the healthy and an underprovision to the sick.

Managed competition is an attempt to be a little bit pregnant on the question of markets versus government control. Or, as University of Chicago law professor Richard Epstein puts it, managed competition is "an oxymoron. One can either have managed health care or competition in health care services. It is not possible to have both simultaneously."[62]

Yet despite this view, big-government conservatives evince a strange history of affection for managed competition. For example, managed competition lies at the heart of another key part of Governor Romney's Massachusetts health reform. The legislation creates the Massachusetts Health Care Connector to combine the current small group and individual markets under a single unified set of regulations.[63] Supporters such as the Heritage Foundation consider the connector to be the single most important change made by the legislation, calling it "the cornerstone of the new plan" and "a major innovation and a model for other states."[64]

The connector would not actually be an insurer. Insurance would still be provided by the private sector. Rather, the connector would function as a clearinghouse, a sort of wholesaler or middleman, matching customers with providers and products. It would also allow small businesses and individuals to pool their resources to take advantage of the economies of scale available to large group plans.

Although the connector would not technically regulate insurance, it has wide-ranging authority to determine what insurance products it will offer. For example, the maximum deductible allowed is $2,700 for an individual and $5,450 for a family. While this conforms to current federal law, it locks in the status quo at a time when attempts are being made to change federal Health Savings Account restrictions. Moreover, individuals choosing a high-deductible policy *must* combine it with a Health Savings Account. As previously mentioned, policies must comply with the state's mandated benefits (with the exception noted below). They must also comply with the state's community-rating requirements and other restrictions designed to limit the ability of insurers to segment the market according to risk.[65]

Beyond these restrictions, the connector is authorized to offer a "connector seal of approval" to products that provide "high quality and good value." The connector itself is left to define what constitutes high quality and a good value, but significantly, that phrase frequently appears in legislation as justification for mandated benefits. The connector may choose to sell products that do not receive its seal of approval, but they are not required to do so.

No actual prohibition exists on selling small group or individual insurance outside the connector. However, because the subsidies and tax advantages are available only within the connector, and because of its competitive advantage in terms of pooling costs and risk, the connector will eventually squeeze out any outside market. In the end, the connector would become a monopsony purchaser of health insurance.

The centrality of managed competition to the Massachusetts reform should come as no surprise given the involvement of the Heritage Foundation in developing the legislation. The Heritage Foundation has promoted managed competition as part of health care reform at least since 1993 when it helped develop the Nickles-Stearns bill as an alternative to the Clinton health care plan.[66]

The Heritage Foundation believes the health insurance system is too "fragmented" and "balkanized" to work properly and argues, "Markets sometimes work more efficiently and effectively when there is a single place to facilitate diverse economic activity."[67] It cites the FEHBP as a model for national reform.[68] The FEHBP exemplifies the basic features of managed competition. First, federal employees in most places can choose from a limited array of competing insurance plans. Second, the government contributes a fixed amount, meaning that consumers choosing more-expensive plans will have to bear a larger portion of the cost. And most important, plans must accept all applicants and charge everyone the same price regardless of individual health risk, meaning insurers are prohibited from competing based on their ability to price and manage risk.

The FEHBP record on cost containment is somewhat mixed and depends on when one sets the baseline period for measurement.

Initially, the program held cost increases below both the private sector and government programs such as Medicare. However, since the mid-1990s, the rate of growth in FEHBP spending has been very high, exceeding both government plans and the plans offered by large private employers.[69] The FEHBP has also experienced an exodus of plans in recent years, generally as a result of insufficient enrollments and noncompetitive premium rates. As a result, more federal employees have coalesced into higher-cost plans.

In general, conservatives should be attempting to move the health care system toward more consumer control and freer markets, not more government regulation, controls, and subsidies. This makes their dubious flirtation with managed competition all the more puzzling.

Increased Regulation

Health care is already one of the most intensely regulated sectors of the U.S. economy. Indeed, Chris Conover of Duke University estimates that health care regulation costs consumers a net $169 billion each year.[70] However, rather than cutting back on regulation, many big-government conservatives seem perversely willing to embrace new government controls.

For example, the Bush administration strongly supports proposals to create association health plans (AHPs), group purchasing plans that allow businesses to join together and take advantage of economies of scale in purchasing health insurance. AHPs have existed for decades, both nationally and on the local level, and have proven extremely valuable in reducing health care costs for small business.[71] As currently constituted they seem like exactly the sort of market-oriented innovation that almost all conservatives would applaud.

Nevertheless, the Bush administration, unable to leave a good thing alone, wants legislation to place AHPs under federal, rather than state, regulation. No doubt exists that small businesses are being squeezed by rising health insurance premiums, and one reason is that state health insurance regulations are helping drive those premiums upward. Large employers are generally able to avoid those regulations by self-insuring under ERISA, a federal law with far less-stringent regulatory requirements. The belief is that moving the regulation of AHPs to the federal level will preempt onerous state regulations in favor of an easier federal regime.

In the long run, this abandonment of traditional conservative principles of federalism is likely to result in more insurance regulation, not less. If federal health insurance regulation is currently less burdensome than state regulation, it is because Congress has not yet been lobbied by regulation-seeking special interests to the degree that state legislators have. If Congress becomes responsible for regulating a larger portion of the insurance market, those special interests will redouble their efforts in Washington. At that point increasing insurance regulation will be even easier because lobbyists will have to focus their efforts in only one place, rather than in 50 state capitals. Moreover, interstate competition would no longer act as a barrier against overregulation.

One wonders why so much interest exists in federalizing the regulation of AHPs when a much better alternative is available. Rep. John Shadegg (R-AZ) has sponsored legislation that would allow individual consumers to purchase health insurance across state lines and in essence choose which state regulates their health insurance.[72] If a state's insurance regulations were too burdensome, purchasers could simply shop elsewhere. This possibility would put consumers in charge rather than state—or federal—regulators. Yet so far the Shadegg approach has not attracted nearly as much support as AHPs.

Big-government conservatives have also shown a willingness to use antitrust regulations to shape the health care marketplace. For example, one of the truly interesting medical innovations over the past decade has been the growth of specialty hospitals. These small hospitals generally focus on a narrower array of services than traditional full-service hospitals but perform them in greater volume. As a result, they tend to be more efficient. Studies have shown that they have lower mortality rates, shorter hospital stays, and lower rates of complications.[73]

The number of specialty hospitals has nearly tripled since 1990.[74] Their growth has threatened the market domination by large, full-service hospitals, which have naturally turned to Congress for protection. They have found support among big-government conservatives worried about protecting community hospitals. Among the most outspoken advocates of greater regulation of specialty hospitals has been Newt Gingrich. He has endorsed legislation to forbid doctors from having ownership in a hospital in which they practice and called for "requiring that specialty hospitals take all the cases in their area of specialization, the difficult and complex (and expensive) as well as the simple and profitable," in a sense a form of community rating for hospitals.[75]

Although those regulations have not yet been enacted, Congress did, as part of the Medicare Modernization Act of 2003, establish a moratorium on the creation or expansion of new specialty hospitals. In addition to prohibiting new specialty hospitals, the moratorium forbade existing ones from adding new physician investors, changing or expanding specialties, expanding facilities beyond their existing campus, or increasing the number of beds beyond specified limits.[76] Fortunately, the moratorium expired in 2005, and, although the Bush administration recommended an extension and Sen. Chuck Grassley (R-IA) introduced legislation to do so, Congress did not act on it.

In health care, as in so many other areas, big-government conservatives seem to believe that if something is a good idea it should be a legal requirement. For example, most free-market health care experts would like to see greater transparency in pricing. That is, consumers should be able to find out what doctors and hospitals actually charge. This knowledge will enable the consumer to make critical decisions about price and quality that are necessary to a fully functioning market.

The health care industry is already moving in this direction, though far too slowly. Consumer-directed health care reform will accelerate this trend. As the Federal Trade Commission has noted, "competition can help address . . . information problems by giving market participants an incentive to deliver truthful and active information to consumers."[77]

However, things are moving too slowly for some big-government conservatives. Thus, Gingrich would mandate that "every doctor, hospital, and pharmaceutical company . . . post on the Internet accurate information about price and quality," in a way that is "timely, accurate, and easy to access."[78] The Bush administration is willing to give the health care industry time to act voluntarily, but with the threat of a mandate held in reserve. If hospitals don't move quickly to make their pricing more transparent, "it's going to be imposed upon you," Al Hubbard, director of President Bush's National Economic Council, told a meeting of the Federation of American Hospitals.[79]

Big-government conservatives have also recently discovered a whole new level of respect for regulation by the Food and Drug Administration. Once, conservatives called for abolishing the FDA or cutting back its powers. But the administration used the FDA's rule-making procedures to delay making emergency contraception, the so-called morning-after pill, available without a prescription. The FDA cited concern about young teenagers' use of emergency contraception without a doctor's guidance—overruling the agency's own scientific advisers, who had overwhelmingly backed easier access.[80]

Big-government conservatives have also tried, unsuccessfully so far, to have the FDA revoke its approval for RU-486, the so-called abortion pill. RU-486, known by its brand name Mifeprex, is an early-option abortificiant for women who are eight weeks pregnant or less. Available in Europe for many years, it was approved for use in the United States in 2000, during the final days of the Clinton administration. However, the Religious Right has repeatedly peti-tioned the FDA to reverse that approval.[81] That campaign has picked up speed in the wake of reports that a small number of women may have died from complications caused by improper use of the drug.[82] Sens. Sam Brownback (R-KS), Jim DeMint (R-SC), and Tom Coburn (R-OK) have cosponsored legislation that would suspend FDA approval of RU-486.[83] Senator DeMint, normally a small-government advocate, even threatened to block the nomination of Dr. Andrew C. von Eschenbach as FDA commissioner unless the FDA removes RU-486 from the market.[84]

And when 11 states passed legislation permitting the medical use of marijuana, Rep. Mark Souder (R-IN) sought to have the FDA prevent physicians from prescribing it. The Bush FDA did issue an opinion that marijuana "has no accepted or proven medical use," ignoring its own previous findings, but has stopped short of announc-ing plans to enforce its opinion.[85]

Senate majority leader Bill Frist even wanted to expand the role of the FDA to regulate direct-to-consumer advertising. Frist was concerned that allowing drug companies to advertise on television and in magazines "can lead to inappropriate prescribing and fuel prescription drug spending."[86] Frist called for a "voluntary" two-year moratorium on such advertising by pharmaceutical companies but has also threatened government action if they do not comply.

Finally, some big-government conservatives have invoked the need for FDA drug approval as a reason for opposing prescription drug reimportation. Prices for name-brand drugs (though not necessarily for generics) are often higher in the United States than in other countries. Yet current law prohibits Americans from buying American-made drugs abroad at those lower prices and "reimporting" them to the United States.[87] Several bills have been introduced in recent years to remove that ban and allow reimportation.

Legitimate reasons exist to be concerned with the concept of reimportation generally and the bills as introduced specifically. Most such bills are poorly drafted and would result in importing foreign price controls.[88] Opponents of reimportation correctly point out that most foreign countries cap the price at which drugs can be sold, limiting the ability of pharmaceutical companies to recoup the costs of research and development. In effect, most of the world free-rides on the U.S. free-market system. Allowing reimportation of drugs sold at regulated foreign prices could force U.S. prices down to the same levels, drying up vital research and development funds.[89] In addition, reimportation opponents argue that an American ban on reimportation enforces market segmentation, allowing companies to exploit different levels of demand and maximize profits.[90]

However, many opponents of reimportation go beyond such legitimate—though fixable—concerns to argue that reimportation should be prohibited because such drugs would not have to undergo FDA review. Not surprisingly, Bush's FDA commissioner, Mark McClellan, defended his bureaucratic turf by warning that reimportation "creates a wide channel for large volumes of unapproved drugs and other products to enter the United States that are potentially injurious to public health."[91] But what should conservatives make of the Heritage Foundation's concern that "the FDA—*widely viewed as a level-headed agency*—has been quite vocal in its concern over the safety of imported drugs"?[92] Or Robert Goldberg of the Manhattan Institute, warning, "Reimportation would create a regulatory meltdown that would compromise the safety of drugs for everyone in North America?"[93]

A National Health-Information System

One of the most criticized aspects of the Clinton health care plan was its call for a national health-information infrastructure, including a personal health identification number for every American. Yet,

115

many big-government conservatives now seem to be headed down that same path.

For example, Newt Gingrich wants the federal government to spend as much as $5 billion per year (compared with the current $125 million) to create a national electronic network for health care records.[94] Gingrich and Senate Majority Leader Bill Frist have also backed Sen. Hillary Clinton's proposed legislation to create regional health-information networks to transfer health data quickly between doctors, hospitals, and nurses.[95] The eventual result would be nationwide databases containing a patient's medical information, including illnesses and genetic predispositions, alcohol and drug addiction, the medications the patient receives, and most likely, personal identifier information like Social Security numbers. Although participation on the part of patients would theoretically be voluntary, those consumers would be required to opt out of the program.

A real problem exists with medical-records technology. Too many medical records are still maintained on paper, which makes it slow and difficult to pass needed information from physician to physician. Just 17 percent of U.S. physicians are currently using electronic medical records when caring for patients.[96] Where electronic records do exist, hospital and physician systems are often incompatible. The unavailability and incompatibility of electronic medical records contributes to the unnecessary deaths of up to 8,000 people each year because of medication errors.[97] Studies also show that widespread adoption of electronic medical records could save the American health care system more than $162 billion annually.[98]

The private sector is beginning to respond. Information technology (IT) spending in the health sector is expected to increase at an annual rate of 7.4 percent from 2005 to 2010. Health care IT spending is expected to reach $39.5 billion in 2008.[99] Two-thirds of health care providers say they plan to increase their IT spending by more than 10 percent per year.[100] In fact, health care IT spending is expected to exceed IT spending in all other industry sectors.[101] Microsoft has developed electronic medical-record software.[102] Telemedicine companies, like TelaDoc, and patient advocacy organizations like PinnacleCare, collect and digitize medical records for their customers.[103]

Nevertheless, health privacy experts have raised a number of concerns with the idea of the government becoming involved with developing and mandating a single record system nationwide:[104]

- Under the proposed legislation supported by Senators Frist and Clinton, Americans' health information will be subject to the federal medical-privacy rule, which eliminates patient consent in the sharing of personal information. In other words, once individuals provide information to a regional network, they will have no say in how it is used for many purposes.
- The legislation claims to give patients the option of allowing only designated providers to see information concerning sexually transmitted disease, addiction, and mental illness. But unless patients have the absolute freedom to opt out of an electronic medical-records system and decide who can access their medical records for all purposes, their privacy cannot be guaranteed.
- Although patients could exclude certain information from the data network, the bill is unclear about whether physicians would be required to submit data about patients to Medicare or other government agencies.
- The bill directs the secretary of health and human services to establish a method for paying doctors and hospitals that provide services under Medicare. Thus doctors could be coerced into participating in the regional, that is, de facto national, networks through the government's manipulation of Medicare fees.

The Bush administration has also weakened protections for health care privacy. The Health Insurance Portability and Accountability Act of 1996 established standards for patient privacy, including a requirement that patients consent to the release of their medical records. The Bush administration revised the rules to eliminate the need for patient consent under certain circumstances. The change was a response to complaints that the existing rules were so restrictive that they sometimes delayed or prevented treatment.[105] In making the changes, however, the Bush administration opened medical records to an enormous range of potentially prying eyes. For example, under the change, the federal government could access medical records with patient consent or a judicial subpoena.[106]

Given the private sector's increasing investment in medical information technology, there is no reason to risk the downside of government involvement.

A Little Bit Pregnant?

Big-government conservatives seem to understand the dangers of a government-run national health care system. Yet they also seem to resist a truly market-based system. Their approach is to be a "little bit pregnant" on the issue, attempting to harness government regulation as a tool in forcing health care in a free-market direction—or more accurately, in the direction that they believe a free market should lead.

Big-government conservatives concede on two fundamental arguments. First, they agree that universal coverage should be the primary focus of health care policy. An assumption exists, either implicit or explicit, that success is measured by how many people have health insurance. Second, they believe health care is not like other goods and services. The usual laws of economics do not apply. Therefore, government can and should intervene to help shape the functioning of the marketplace.

These points are not minor. Rather they have long been the fundamental difference in both the practical and philosophical approach to health care reform by liberals and conservatives. Traditionally, conservatives have argued that we must shift the health care debate away from its single-minded focus on expanding coverage to the bigger question of how to reduce costs and improve quality. And conservatives have argued that health care is fundamentally no different from any other goods or services. Both consumers and providers react to normal marketplace incentives. Their behavior is rational and predictable. This set of beliefs has undergirded consumer-centered health care reforms such as Health Savings Accounts and attempts to deregulate the health care industry.

By abandoning this principled position, big-government conservatives essentially subscribe to the liberal health care agenda. Whatever short-term compromises are agreed to, they will set up an increasingly slippery slope that will slide inevitably toward a government-run health care system.

6. Blinking at the Entitlements Crisis

No greater threat exists to America's long-term fiscal heath than the skyrocketing cost of entitlement programs.[1] This year, entitlements will consume more than half of all government spending and a record 8.4 percent of gross domestic product (GDP). Moreover, entitlement spending is growing at a phenomenal rate, an annual average growth rate of 6 percent—more than double the rate of inflation.[2]

By 2040, without an enormous increase in taxes, a combination of entitlement spending and interest payments on the national debt will account for 100 percent of federal spending, leaving not a dime for any other government program.[3] By 2070, total federal taxes would have to be doubled just to support entitlement spending.[4] Federal taxes would be consuming nearly 40 percent of GDP, and still no money would be available for national defense or any other government program.[5]

Maintaining even a minimum of other government functions would push the government's share of GDP to over 50 percent.[6] Even this estimate might understate the magnitude of the problem, because it assumes slower entitlements growth than estimated by the Social Security and Medicare trustees, substantial reductions in defense and other spending, and no increase in future interest rates. Assuming more pessimistic projections in those areas leads to a potential for the federal government to consume 73 percent of GDP by 2070.[7]

At the heart of skyrocketing entitlements programs are three programs that largely serve the elderly: Social Security, Medicare, and Medicaid.[8] As Figure 6.1 shows, the cost of these three programs alone has risen from just 0.3 percent of GDP in 1950 to nearly 8 percent today.[9]

This fact should come as no surprise. Medicare and Medicaid costs are being driven to a large degree by the overall rising cost of health care. As Americans live longer, all three programs must serve

Figure 6.1
FEDERAL SPENDING ON SOCIAL SECURITY, MEDICARE, AND
MEDICAID, AS A PERCENTAGE OF GDP

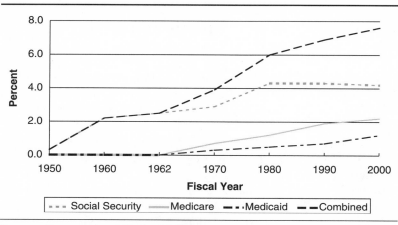

SOURCE: Congressional Budget Office.

a rapidly expanding population of seniors. At the same time, programs that operate largely as income transfers from workers to retirees are extremely sensitive to demographic changes. Because the number of workers paying taxes to support each retiree is expected to decline from 3.3 today to just 2.1 by 2030, the result is an ever-widening gap between the benefits promised under these programs and the tax revenue available to pay those benefits.[10] In fact, the total unfunded obligations facing Social Security and Medicare are more than $85 trillion.[11]

To make up this gap, Congress would have to increase taxes immediately by $3,323 per household. But even that would not be enough, and future tax increases would have to follow, rising to $4,516 by 2020, $7,472 in 2030, $9,436 in 2040, and $10,918 in 2050 (all in fiscal year 2005 dollars). In practice these increases would be the equivalent of raising the top marginal income tax rate from 35 percent to 80 percent and the typical family's marginal tax rate from 25 percent to 57 percent.[12] As an alternative, the payroll tax could be doubled.

U. S. Comptroller General David M. Walker has written that growing entitlements spending "will encumber a growing share of federal resources and test the capacity of current and future generations to afford both today's and tomorrow's commitments. Continuing on this unsustainable path will gradually erode, if not suddenly damage, our economy, our standard of living and ultimately our national security."[13]

The Congressional Budget Office is equally strong, if not stronger, in its warnings. The debt levels likely to result from rising entitlements costs "can sap national saving, slow capital formation, lower economic growth, and in the extreme, produce a substantial economic contraction."[14]

But if that level of debt is not sustainable, and if there is no reform, the only alternative will be ever-higher taxes. Former Reagan economic adviser Bruce Bartlett is one of those who warn that increasing entitlement spending makes future tax increases all but inevitable.[15] Yet tax increases carry their own risks. As Alan Greenspan warned, in his usual understated way, "Tax increases of sufficient dimension to deal with our looming fiscal problems arguably pose significant risks to economic growth and the revenue base."[16]

It is not as though no warning has been given about entitlement growth. As far back as 1995, the Bipartisan Commission on Entitlement and Tax Reform was pointing out: "If we do not plan for the future, entitlement spending promises will exceed federal resources in the next century. The current trend is unsustainable." The commissioners went on to warn, "If we fail to act, we have made a choice that threatens the economic future of our children and our nation."[17] Four years later, the National Bipartisan Commission on the Future of Medicare, although unable to reach a consensus on how to reform the program, concluded that it was unsustainable in its present form.[18] Likewise President Clinton's Social Security Advisory Council agreed that Social Security, as currently structured, could not meet its future obligations. For at least a decade—under both President Clinton and President Bush—experts inside and outside government have made clear that entitlements reform is essential to the nation's long-term fiscal health.

In the face of this looming crisis, the reaction of big-government conservatives was to enact the largest new entitlement since Lyndon Johnson established Medicare. The Medicare prescription drug benefit will cost at least $720 billion over the next decade, and perhaps twice as much. Ultimately, the program will add as much as $16.6

121

trillion to Medicare's unfunded liabilities (in present-value terms).[19] According to the Government Accountability Office, that price tag represents "one of the largest unfunded commitments ever undertaken by the federal government."[20] In practical terms, the liability translates into a required future tax increase of $2,500–4,000 for younger workers and future generations.[21]

When George W. Bush courageously attempted to reform Social Security, big-government conservatives dragged their feet, resisted any attempt to restrain benefits, and generally acted as an impediment to reform. Their reluctance to fully embrace reform was far from the biggest reason why Bush's push for reform failed, but it was one more, unneeded, obstacle.

For many big-government conservatives, entitlements such as Social Security and Medicare have never been an area of concern. As programs that primarily benefited the middle class, they were politically popular and produced fewer of the behavioral problems associated with other social-welfare programs.

Thus, as we saw earlier, neoconservatives were always supportive of these programs. When Medicare was first created, Irving Kristol praised it as "possibly the best way to deal with the problem created by the dual fact of medical care costing so much more than it used to and people living longer than they used to."[22] Kristol also has called for making Social Security "more generous," and dismissed concerns about the cost of the program as "not a conservative problem, except for those conservatives whose Good Book is an annual budget."[23]

The Religious Right has had relatively little to say on the issue one way or the other. But when its leaders have spoken out, they have tended to be skeptical of changes to the program. For example, Gary Bauer, who opposed personal accounts for Social Security as a presidential candidate in 2000, has continued to raise concerns. As recently as 2005, he warned President Bush, "Many religious voters are conflicted about whether this is something that would be good for them and their families."[24] The Family Research Council funded a study by economist and former Kemp aide John Mueller that was highly critical of personal accounts.[25] Mueller also wrote a long critical article in the *Weekly Standard* in which he accused personal account supporters of overvaluing investment in physical capital and undervaluing investment in human capital.[26]

122

The Religious Right was also angered that Bush chose to devote his political capital to Social Security reform rather than to social issues. For example, the Arlington Group, an umbrella organization representing opponents of gay marriage, wrote the president, "We couldn't help but notice the contrast between how the president is approaching the difficult issue of Social Security privatization, where the public is deeply divided, and the marriage issue where public opinion is overwhelmingly on his side."[27]

Supply-siders were somewhat latecomers to entitlements reform. Less fearful of deficits in general, they have disputed pessimistic projections of Social Security's finances, arguing that increased economic growth (stimulated by tax cuts) would provide sufficient revenue to fund future benefits. When, during the 1988 Republican presidential primary campaign, Pete du Pont suggested that younger workers be allowed to privately invest their Social Security taxes, Jack Kemp attacked him for threatening Social Security's "sacred trust."[28] One observer described Kemp as accusing Du Pont of "wild-eyed libertarianism."[29]

Newt Gingrich is another reluctant warrior when it comes to entitlements reform. He strongly supported the prescription drug benefit, saying it "added for the first time an overdue prescription drug benefit for seniors and did so at a reasonable price."[30] On Social Security, Gingrich was dragged kicking and screaming toward support for reform. In the mid-1990s, Gingrich opposed a proposal by Democratic senator Bob Kerrey (NE) to allow younger workers to privately invest two percentage points of their payroll taxes.[31] Later, he supported personal accounts funded through general revenue budget surpluses rather than a "carve-out" from payroll taxes.[32] Finally, he endorsed carve-outs, but like many supply-siders opposed any attempt to restrain benefit growth.[33]

Medicare

Even before the addition of the prescription drug benefit, Medicare was in trouble. In their 2004 annual report, the trustees of the Medicare system reported that before passage of the prescription drug benefit, the program faced unfunded obligations in excess of $45 trillion.[34] Without a drug benefit, the cost of Medicare was expected to double as a percentage of GDP by 2040.[35]

Medicare's future financial problems were easily foreseeable, the result of several readily apparent factors. First, as with Social Security and other intergenerational transfer programs, the aging of American society means there will be more and more beneficiaries compared to the number of workers paying taxes to support the program. According to Medicare's trustees, the ratio will fall from about 4 workers per beneficiary in 2003 (when the prescription drug benefit was passed) to about 2.4 workers per beneficiary in 2030, and it will continue to fall until only 2 workers per beneficiary remain in 2078.[36]

At the same time, health care costs will continue to climb. In 2003, the Congressional Budget Office estimated that a mere 30 percent of Medicare's future growth will be caused by society's aging, while 70 percent will be caused by the rising cost of health care.[37]

But despite this looming, foreseeable, and massive financial shortfall, the Bush administration and its allies in Congress decided to significantly expand the program by adding coverage for prescription drugs.[38] The result was, as mentioned, a nearly $16.6 trillion increase in the program's unfunded costs.[39]

Bruce Bartlett calls the Medicare prescription drug benefit "the worst legislation in history."[40] He may not be far off.

To begin with, the whole rationale for a massive new prescription drug entitlement was always questionable. Many, if not most, seniors already had prescription drug coverage through their Medigap, employer, or other privately purchased policies.[41] More than 70 percent of Medicare beneficiaries spent less than $500 from their own pockets for prescriptions in the year before the bill's enactment.[42]

President Bush, and some reform-minded Democrats like Sen. John Breaux of Louisiana, originally supported a prescription drug benefit in the context of overall Medicare reform. They were willing to provide the new benefit, but only if other actions were taken to encourage greater competition and hold down costs. Prescription drugs were to be offered as an additional benefit to seniors who chose to leave traditional Medicare for competing private sector plans. The competition of a private health care marketplace, combined with managed care and better integration of health services, would have helped offset the new benefit costs and served as a platform for further Medicare reforms to come.

Unfortunately, most members of Congress created a bind for themselves by promising in the previous election to pass a prescription drug plan no matter what. That sort of pandering may have made political sense—seniors constituted one in four voters in the 2002 elections. But it also meant that when faced with pressure from AARP and the institutional lobbies for seniors, they abandoned all restraint. A prescription drug benefit at all costs turned out to mean exactly that.

Attempts at larger Medicare reform were abandoned or watered down to a handful of demonstration projects that don't even start until 2010. The legislation did include provisions for the creation of Health Savings Accounts, an important reform that could be the basis for reforming the overall health care system along consumer-directed lines. But the promised fundamental restructuring of Medicare was stripped from the final bill.

Still, if one characteristic defines the Bush administration, it is stubbornness. Having committed himself to passing a prescription drug benefit, President Bush was determined to pass one. The actual details were almost irrelevant.

The administration and its allies in Congress went so far as to deliberately falsify the program's costs. They bullied the Congressional Budget Office into publishing a 10-year cost estimate for the program of $400 billion, even though Centers for Medicare and Medicaid Services chief actuary Richard Foster knew that the cost would be at least $534 billion. The *Wall Street Journal* pointed out that if the bill's true cost had been released, it would never have passed: "It is undeniable that the Medicare bill wouldn't have passed in its current form had $540 billion been the accepted cost fiction."[43] The Centers for Medicare and Medicaid Services administrator threatened Foster's job, and the true cost of the program was not revealed until after the bill had passed.[44]

The legislation's fate came down to a late-night House vote on Saturday, November 22, 2003. House Speaker Dennis Hastert was forced to hold the vote open for nearly four hours while the congressional leadership and President Bush shamelessly twisted arms to force wavering Republicans into line. When cajoling and threats were not enough, lawmakers were offered pork and campaign funds.[45] Congressional scholar Norm Ornstein called the entire exercise "the ugliest and most outrageous breach of standards in the history of the House."[46] In the end, the legislation passed 218-216.

The unsustainable and unfunded cost of the prescription drug benefit should have been enough to recommend against it even if

Figure 6.2
STANDARD MEDICARE PART D PRESCRIPTION DRUG BENEFIT, 2006

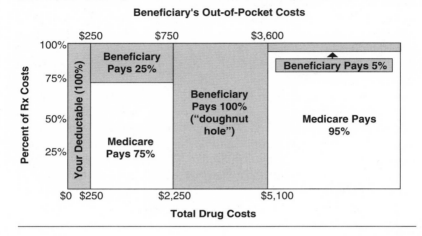

it were a good program. It is not. Under the program, Medicare recipients may choose to voluntarily enroll in the new benefit, known as Medicare Part D.[47] If they do, they will have a variety of privately managed plans to choose from, as many as 40 depending on the state where they live. They will be charged a premium that will vary depending on the plan they choose, but it is expected to average about $25 per month.

The structure of the benefit is indefensible on any public policy grounds. As Figure 6.2 illustrates, a Medicare recipient enrolled in the standard version of the prescription drug plan would pay a deductible of $250. Thereafter, Medicare will pay 75 percent of costs between $250 and $2,250 in drug spending. The patient will pay the remaining 25 percent of these costs. The patient then encounters the notorious "doughnut hole." For drug costs above $2,250 but below $3,600 in out-of-pocket spending, the patient must pay 100 percent of the costs. After that, the prescription drug plan kicks in again and pays 95 percent of costs above $3,600.[48] Because of the bill's bizarre coverage structure, many seniors will be getting far less drug coverage than they believe they will. Some may even end up paying more in premiums than they will receive in savings under the program.

126

We can expect quick and persistent political pressure to fill in the doughnut hole. The ink was hardly dry on the president's signature when AARP chief executive officer William Novelli called for eliminating the gap.[49] Already Democrats have introduced legislation to do so.[50] If they succeed, costs of the program can be expected to skyrocket dramatically.

The legislation has still more problems. As mentioned, many seniors already receive prescription drugs through their former employer's retiree health programs. However, corporations can logically be expected to try to reduce their costs by unloading seniors onto the new program.[51] In an effort to prevent this outcome, the bill contains subsidies to encourage corporations to keep their coverage. Among the companies expected to receive subsidies are such corporate giants as Alcoa, American Airlines, Bell South, Delphi, General Motors, John Deere, United Airlines, U.S. Steel, and Verizon.[52] The Congressional Budget Office estimates the cost of this corporate welfare at $150 billion over the first 10 years alone of the program.[53] Even this tax-funded bribe may not be enough to keep some companies from dropping their retirees onto the Medicare rolls, as J.C. Penney and Jostens have already done.[54] The Congressional Budget Office estimates that nearly 3 million seniors will eventually be shifted from corporate plans to Medicare.[55] That could end up costing taxpayers another $44 billion.[56]

We are living in an age of tremendous pharmaceutical breakthroughs. The pharmaceutical industry reports that more than 2,000 products are currently in development, offering new hope to those suffering from diseases ranging from cancer to diabetes to Alzheimer's disease.[57] Even more exciting is the potential for designer drugs that match our individual genetic structure.

But these new treatments can often come at great price. Consider that Erbitux, a new treatment for colorectal cancer, costs as much as $100,000 for a single treatment regimen. Avastin, another colorectal cancer treatment, costs more than $50,000. Several other cancer drugs cost $35,000 or more.[58] Medicare has no fiscally possible way to pay such costs for all the people who may ultimately need or want those drugs. As Dr. Leonard Saltz, a colon cancer specialist at Memorial Sloan-Kettering Cancer Center in New York, notes regretfully, "I don't know how much money there is in the till to pay for all this, but I have to be worried there isn't enough."[59]

127

Other countries deal with this conflict by imposing price controls, but those countries have the advantage of free-riding on the research and development conducted by the U.S. pharmaceutical industry. If price controls in this country restrict investment in pharmaceutical research, no such outlet would be available. Some research would simply not occur. Some lifesaving products will not be discovered. Yet the prescription drug benefit makes at least implicit price controls far more likely.

Finally, although media reports of the widespread confusion surrounding the plan's introduction may well have been exaggerated, no doubt problems existed.[60] Faced with a complex array of plans, offering different deductibles, copayments, and formularies, many seniors have found the program too intimidating to navigate. As a result, some 3.5 million seniors failed to sign up for the plan.[61]

Immediately following the May 15, 2006, deadline, the administration proudly announced that 29 million of 32.5 million eligible seniors had either signed up for the program or had prescription drug coverage through other sources.[62] But those numbers are misleading. Nearly 6 million of those counted as "signed up" were low-income seniors previously receiving prescription drugs through Medicaid who were automatically enrolled in the new program. Another 7 million were already participating in Medicare managed care programs that offered prescription drug coverage. And roughly another 6.9 million fall under the category of having "prescription drug coverage through other sources," primarily former employers through retiree health plans. Thus, only about 9 million voluntarily signed up for the program.[63]

Faced with the refusal of 3.5 million seniors to take advantage of subsidized drugs, the immediate reaction of big-government conservatives, led by Sens. Charles Grassley (R-IA) and Rick Santorum (R-PA), was to propose waiving the deadline and late-filing penalties. Doing so would have added $1.7 billion to the cost of the first five years of the program, with even more costs thereafter.[64]

Seniors may find more problems down the road. Plan administrators are free to change their formularies and drop coverage for particular drugs. Seniors may suddenly discover that their plan no longer covers the drugs they take, requiring them to pay more out of pocket or switch plans.[65] Some plans may stop participation altogether.

The one area where the prescription drug benefit appears success-ful is in reducing drug costs for those seniors who have enrolled.[66] It should. The federal government will spend 0.4 percent of GDP in 2006 to subsidize drug costs. That much money has to buy some-thing. But even here, benefits are wildly uneven. Some reports indi-cate that roughly 19 percent of those enrolled will actually spend more for drugs under the program.[67]

Today, the mistakes of the prescription drug program are becom-ing more widely apparent. At least two members of Congress who voted for the bill have now called for its delay or repeal. Others have said they regret their votes. One can safely say, therefore, that the program no longer commands majority support in the House. Efforts to repeal the program have also been called for in the Senate, led by Sen. John McCain (R-AZ).[68] But President Bush has warned that he would veto any attempt at repeal.[69]

When the prescription drug benefit finally passed, Sen. Trent Lott (R-MS), who voted for the bill out of party loyalty even though he thought it was a bad bill, said it was "the clearest signal I've seen yet that the revolution is over."[70] It may well provide a fitting epitaph.

Social Security

Although not in as dire shape as Medicare, Social Security none-theless is facing demographic and fiscal pressures that threaten the program's long-term sustainability.

Social Security is currently running a surplus, but according to the system's own trustees, that surplus will turn into a deficit within the next 10 years (Figure 6.3).[71] That is, by 2017, Social Security will be paying out more in benefits than it takes in through taxes. In theory, Social Security is supposed to continue paying benefits after 2017 by drawing on the Social Security Trust Fund. The trust fund is supposed to provide sufficient funds to continue paying full benefits until 2040, after which it will be exhausted (Figure 6.4). At that point, *by law*, Social Security benefits will have to be cut by approximately 27 percent.[72]

In reality, however, the Social Security Trust Fund is not an asset that can be used to pay benefits. Any Social Security surpluses accumulated to date have been spent, leaving a trust fund that consists only of government bonds (IOUs) that will eventually have

Figure 6.3
OASDI ANNUAL BALANCES (INCOME LESS COST AS A PERCENTAGE OF TAXABLE PAYROLL)

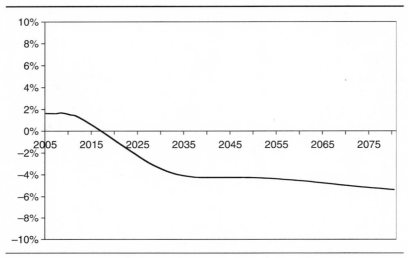

SOURCE: 2006 OASDI Trustees Report.

Figure 6.4
SOCIAL SECURITY TRUST FUND SOLVENCY

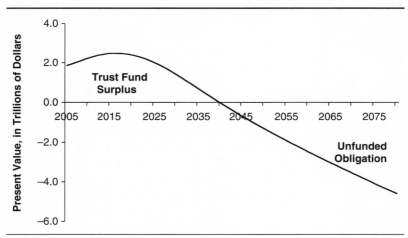

SOURCE: 2006 OASDI Trustees Report.

to be repaid by taxpayers. As the Clinton administration's FY2000 budget explained:

> These [Trust Fund] balances are available to finance future benefit payments and other Trust Fund expenditures—but only in a bookkeeping sense.... *They do not consist of real economic assets that can be drawn down in the future to fund benefits.* Instead, they are claims on the Treasury that, when redeemed, will have to be financed by raising taxes, borrowing from the public, or reducing benefits or other expenditures. The existence of large Trust Fund balances, therefore, does not, by itself, have any impact on the Government's ability to pay benefits.[73]

Even if Congress can find a way to redeem the bonds, the trust fund surplus will be completely exhausted by 2040. At that point, Social Security will have to rely solely on revenue from the payroll tax—but that revenue will not be sufficient to pay all promised benefits. Overall, Social Security faces unfunded liabilities of nearly $15.5 trillion (in present-value terms). Clearly, Social Security is not sustainable in its current form.[74]

Moreover, Social Security taxes are already so high relative to benefits that Social Security has quite simply become a bad deal for younger workers, providing a low, below-market rate of return. This poor rate of return means that many young workers' retirement benefits are far lower than if they had been able to invest those funds privately.

But the single most important failure of the current Social Security system is that workers have no ownership of their benefits. The U.S. Supreme Court has ruled, in the case of *Flemming v. Nestor*, that workers have no legally binding contractual or property right to their Social Security benefits, and those benefits can be changed, cut, or even taken away at any time.[75] This holding means that workers are left totally dependent on the goodwill of 535 politicians to determine what they will receive in retirement. And because workers don't own their benefits, those benefits are not inheritable. This factor particularly disadvantages those groups in our society with shorter life expectancies, such as African Americans.[76]

Faced with the program's unsustainability, a very limited array of options exists. As former president Bill Clinton pointed out, the only ways to keep Social Security solvent are to (a) raise taxes, (b) cut

131

benefits, or (c) get a higher rate of return through private capital investment.[77] The tax increases or benefit cuts would have to be quite large and would cause substantial problems for the economy, taxpayers, or retirees. Even worse, tax increases or benefit cuts would actually reduce the rate of return for younger workers and do nothing about the more serious issues of ownership, inheritability, and choice. President Bush, therefore, chose the third course, combining a modest and progressive reduction in the future growth of benefits with personal accounts, allowing younger workers to privately invest a portion of their Social Security taxes.

When President Bush announced his plans to make Social Security reform the centerpiece of his second-term domestic agenda, many big-government conservatives objected. No one was more opposed than Bill Kristol. As soon as the president made clear his intention to move forward on his promises to address the issue, Bill Kristol pronounced that he was "bewildered why this is such a White House priority." "I am a skeptic politically and a little bit substantively," he said.[78] Throughout the president's reform campaign, Kristol repeatedly called for Bush to "unwind" Social Security reform and "get back to the core economic message of his first term, which was economic growth and tax cuts."[79] When asked about the president's effort on *Fox News Sunday*, Kristol said flatly, "I wouldn't have done it."[80] In fact, Kristol was so upset by Bush's "mistake" in tackling Social Security that he suggested it undermined his faith in Bush's entire decisionmaking process.[81]

Other big-government conservatives also disagreed with the president's priorities. John Podhoretz argued that tackling Social Security was a "catastrophic mistake" that distracted Bush from the truly important issues of Iraq and cutting taxes. Gingrich was not actually opposed to the president's plan, but worried, "Why would you go home tomorrow having cut benefits in Social Security for a problem that might happen in 25 years?"[82] That was very similar to the sentiments expressed by Rep. Rob Simmons (R-CT), who asked: "Why stir up a political hornet's nest . . . when there is no urgency? When does the program go belly up? 2042. I will be dead by then."[83] That must have been great consolation to Simmons's younger constituents.

In Congress, both the House and Senate leadership were extremely reluctant to address the issue. It wasn't just questions about personal accounts. When pressed, they supported those. Rather they were reluctant to address the issue at all. When President Bush said, "There are a lot of people who would rather not talk about this issue," he was referring to the Republicans in Congress.[84] The Republican leadership did not disagree. As House Speaker Dennis Hastert admitted: "Most members, down in their heart, know that what we are trying to do is the right thing to do. It's a question of whether it's convenient politically."[85] Throughout the yearlong debate, they made clear that although Social Security reform was the president's top domestic agenda item, it was not theirs.

Most important, the leadership never made any attempt to force recalcitrant Republicans into line as it did with the Medicare prescription drug benefit. For increasing the size of government, the leadership was willing to twist arms. For Social Security reform, the leadership generally sat on its hands.

Some were even more obstructionist. When he was chairman of the National Republican Congressional Committee, Rep. Tom Davis (R-VA) actively discouraged Republican candidates from discussing Social Security reform. After leaving his post in 2004, Davis continued to argue against taking up the issue, calling for Republicans to "wait and see" before endorsing the president's plan.[86] He also made clear that he, himself, was opposed to making any changes to the system.[87]

Even those willing to support reform were often reluctant to make the difficult decisions. Many big-government conservatives were especially wary of Social Security reform proposals that reduced benefits, even for recipients far in the future. Some rallied around legislation by Rep. Paul Ryan (R-WI) and Sen. John Sununu (R-NH) that would have guaranteed that no future Social Security recipient would ever receive benefits lower than what the current system promised.[88] The Social Security actuaries estimated that such a guarantee would add as much as $2 trillion to the cost of the legislation (although it would have still been less expensive than preserving the current system).[89]

When President Bush called for linking the growth of Social Security benefits to prices rather than wages, thereby slowing their growth, he was attacked for advocating "the largest cut in future promised Social Security benefits in world history."[90] Supporters of reform plans that trimmed benefits were accused of wanting to "eviscerate" Social Security, not by liberals but by conservative activists like Peter Ferrara.[91]

Ultimately the president's push for reform collapsed for many reasons, not the least of which were the administration's tactical and strategic errors. The White House was never able to craft a coherent and attractive message, often ignoring the benefits of personal accounts in favor of gloomy prognostications about the program's solvency. Although accurate, the focus on solvency failed to build the grassroots enthusiasm necessary to overcome the entrenched opposition of the lobbies for seniors.[92] Second, the administration never put forward a single, detailed plan that could unite reformers. The absence of a presidential plan increased the infighting between supporters of alternative reform proposals. Third, the Iraq war sapped the president's political capital and his falling poll ratings made rallying reluctant congressional Republicans more difficult.[93] Fourth, Democrats proved surprisingly intractable, apparently having decided that their entire political strategy would be to oppose any ideas put forward by the administration. Democrats never advanced any ideas about how they would fix the program, but almost no congressional Democrats were willing to cross the line and work with the administration.[94] This partisan divide was made worse because the administration failed to reach out to congressional Democrats who might have been open to compromise.[95]

For all the administration's missteps, Social Security reform might still have passed if the Republicans had shown a genuine commitment to reducing the size of government and giving people more control over their own lives.

Perhaps the clearest example of Republican unwillingness to tackle Social Security reform came on a proposal for a very modest first step. This idea, sponsored in the Senate by Sens. Jim DeMint (R-SC) and Mike Crapo (R-ID) and in the House by Reps. Jim McCrerey (R-LA), Paul Ryan (R-WI), Sam Johnson (R-TX), and Clay Shaw (R-FL), would have rebated current Social Security surpluses to workers in the form of contributions to personal accounts.[96] Today the surplus, currently running about $87 billion per year, is used to pay for general government spending. As discussed previously, the Social Security Trust Fund is given a bond that will eventually have to be repaid out of future taxes. The proposal would have prevented Congress from spending the surplus, allowing individual workers to save that money toward their own retirement. At the same time, depriving Congress of the camouflage of the Social Security surplus might have forced it to be more fiscally responsible, curbing the growth in government spending.[97] The legislation would have had little effect, for better or worse, on Social Security's long-term finances, but it would have set the stage for more-extensive reforms.

Because the proposal did not entail any so-called transition costs or disrupt the program's short-term financing, it should have been an easy vote. In addition, politicians from both parties have long called for some form of a "lock box" to prevent Congress from spending Social Security surpluses. Yet the proposal failed in the Senate on a vote of 46 to 53 because eight Republican senators voted against it.[98] And although the "no" votes included such predictable Republican moderates as John Chaffee (RI), Olympia Snowe (ME), and Susan Collins (ME), such ostensible conservatives as Conrad Burns (MT), Pete Domenici (NM), Richard Lugar (IN), Gordon Smith (OR) and Jim Talent (MO) also voted against it.[99] As for the House—the leadership did not even bother bringing it to a vote.

In the end, the failure of the effort to reform Social Security meant that program's unfunded liabilities increased by $550 billion.[100] That is another $550 billion in debt that we have passed on to our children.

Medicaid

Medicaid is at least ostensibly designed to provide health care for low-income Americans. Enacted in 1965, at the same time as Medicare, Medicaid is jointly financed and administered by the federal and state governments. In contrast to Medicare, where eligibility is based on age, Medicaid is a means-tested program, eligibility for which is based on an applicant's income. The federal government provides between 50 and 75 percent of a state's costs according to a formula based on a state's per capita income. On average, the federal government provides 57 percent of the funding, with states responsible for 43 percent.[101]

The program's costs have been escalating rapidly in recent years. Federal Medicaid spending has risen from $129 billion when George W. Bush took office in 2001 to $190 billion today, an average annual growth 7.7 percent.[102] Although recently the rate of growth has slowed somewhat, that has been primarily because of shifting some prescription drug costs to Medicare. The administration itself projects Medicaid spending to resume its more than 7 percent per year rise after 2007. The Congressional Budget Office takes a similar view, suggesting that federal Medicaid spending will double over the next 10 years.[103]

The burden may be even greater for state governments. In fact, Medicaid is now the fastest-growing portion of most state budgets and generally trails only education as the largest single line item. The National Association of State Budget Officers reports, "Medicaid continues to hound state budgets," with every state facing pressure to hold down costs or find additional revenue to support the program.[104] The pressure reached its peak in 2003–2004, with 23 states experiencing shortfalls in their Medicaid programs in 2003 and 18 falling short in 2004. The combined shortfalls totaled more than $7 billion.[105] Although the situation improved somewhat after 2004, Medicaid continues to strain state budgets.

Unlike with Medicare or Social Security, congressional Republicans have at least made occasional attempts at reforming Medicaid. After taking control of Congress in 1994, Republicans made a major effort at Medicaid reform. Their proposal would have ended the entitlement status of Medicaid in the same way that welfare reform ended the entitlement to cash assistance. Rather, Medicaid funds would have been given to the states in the form of block grants, with states free to determine eligibility and benefits. Overall Medicaid spending would have been cut by $163 billion over five years. This proposal was part of the budget package that ultimately led to the confrontation with President Clinton resulting in the budget shutdown. The reform plans were jettisoned as part of the agreement ending that standoff. But Republicans tried again the next year, including a similar Medicaid reform measure in their proposals for welfare reform. However, when Clinton made clear that he would veto the measure, Republicans again retreated.

By 1997, their enthusiasm for both cutting government and confronting Bill Clinton waning, Republicans had made a 180-degree turn. Rather than reforming Medicaid, they now were expanding it, passing the State Children's Health Insurance Program, which extended Medicaid coverage to children in families that had incomes above Medicaid eligibility levels. In some cases, states were able to expand coverage to families earning 300 percent of the poverty level, as much as $58,000 for a family of four. The new program has added some $27.9 billion to the cost of Medicaid since its implementation.[106]

Rising complaints from governors and other state officials have again triggered interest in reforming Medicaid. This time, however, despite the fact that they presumably no longer face a presidential veto threat, Republicans have taken a far more timid approach to reform. Their efforts have been based more on the idea of making the program more efficient or trimming costs around the edges, rather than dealing with the fundamental underlying questions. For example, they have pledged to reduce Medicaid spending by $10 billion over the next five years, a little less than 1 percent of expected spending, although they have not spelled out how those savings would be achieved. And in the traditional refuge for political cowards, they have established a bipartisan advisory commission to recommend potential reforms to the program.[107]

Some recent proposals have included modest steps in the right direction, such as introducing copayments and other cost-sharing mechanisms designed to discourage overuse. Other reforms would give states greater freedom to experiment with ways to reduce costs and introduce market-based mechanisms. These initiatives generally involve such things as replacing traditional Medicaid with health care vouchers or adding health savings accounts to the program. Many of these ideas are innovative and will undoubtedly make the program more efficient.

Vouchers and health savings accounts may actually make Medicaid more attractive, bringing more people into the program. In fact, these reforms may make Medicaid more attractive than private insurance for some low-income workers, especially if Medicaid eligibility is extended up the income range as part of the reform. Big-government conservatives seem unable to completely relinquish federal control of the program. For example, Gingrich has called for the federal government to "audit states based on demonstrated improvements in health outcomes, childhood immunizations or a closing of the gap in racial health disparities."[108]

In the end, the problem stems from unwillingness to face up to the fact that Medicaid is a welfare program.[109] In fact, Medicaid provides average benefits twice as valuable as those available under federal cash assistance programs. Unsurprisingly, studies have found that Medicaid increases dependence and discourages self-reliance in the same way that other welfare programs do.[110]

Treating Medicaid like welfare would mean a return to the 1995 proposals to cap federal spending; substitute a block grant program; and give states the power to impose eligibility restrictions, work requirements, and other welfare-reform-style barriers to discourage people from becoming dependent on the program. Unfortunately, today's Republican Party is a very different one from the one that was around in 1995.

A Drop in an Ocean of Red Ink

At the beginning of 2006, Congress did manage to pass spending legislation that modestly trimmed some of the growth in smaller entitlement programs by roughly $35 billion over the next five years.[111] Although a positive step—this reduction was the first in entitlement spending since 1997—it should be placed in context. Over that same five-year period, total entitlement spending on those programs will be roughly $14 trillion. Thus, Congress successfully reduced entitlement spending by one-quarter of 1 percent.

In addition, the Republican Study Committee led by Rep. Mike Pence (R-IN) has proposed establishing an "entitlement cap" that limits total expenditures for entitlement programs and would force cuts of approximately $1.8 trillion over the next 10 years.[112] Tellingly, however, the proposal would exempt Social Security from the cap. Even more tellingly, the House leadership has shown no interest in taking up the proposal.

No meaningful effort to control the size and cost of the federal government can take place without dealing with Medicare, Medicaid, and Social Security. Ducking entitlements reform may well continue to be "politically convenient," but doing so will condemn our children and our grandchildren to a world of mounting debt and higher taxes.

7. Spending like Drunken Democrats

Although entitlement spending is the biggest fiscal problem facing this country, the rest of the federal budget is also expanding at a phenomenal rate. When the Republicans took over the House in 1994, the federal budget was $1.9 trillion (inflation-adjusted). When George W. Bush became president, it was about $2.1 trillion. The fiscal year 2006 budget, after more than a decade of Republican congressional control and five years of a Bush presidency, was $2.7 trillion![1] (See Figure 7.1.)

Of course much of this spending, especially in recent years, can be attributed to the wars in Afghanistan and Iraq as well as homeland security in the aftermath of 9/11. But domestic discretionary spending has increased for 9 of the last 10 years (Figure 7.2).[2] Since President Bush took office, domestic spending has increased by an inflation-adjusted 27 percent, a faster rate over his first 5 years in office than for any president since Richard Nixon, and nearly as fast as the rate of Lyndon Johnson (Figure 7.3).[3] In fact, by this measure, Bill Clinton was a far more fiscally conservative president than Bush.

The "revolutionary" Republicans of 1994 brought with them a genuine fervor for cutting back the size of government. Entire cabinet agencies were considered ripe for abolition.[4] More than 70 members proposed legislation that would have resulted in a net reduction in government spending.[5] Rep. Bob Livingston (R-LA), the House Appropriations Committee chairman, once actually brought a machete to his first panel meeting to dramatize his commitment to cutting programs.[6]

The high point of congressional spending restraint was in 1996, when nondefense discretionary spending actually declined for the first time since the Reagan administration.[7] But those efforts to hold down spending led to the failed standoff with President Clinton and the infamous government shutdown. Clinton skillfully used the shutdown to attack Republicans as enemies of "Medicare, Medicaid, education, and the environment." Republicans, never the most skillful at explaining their positions, became bogged down in debate

Figure 7.1
GOVERNMENT SPENDING UNDER REPUBLICAN CONGRESSES

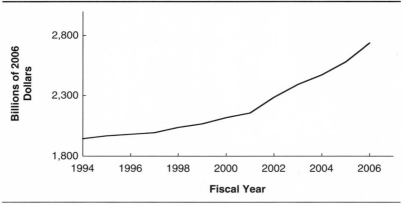

SOURCE: Office of Management and Budget.

Figure 7.2
DOMESTIC DISCRETIONARY SPENDING, EXCLUDING DEFENSE

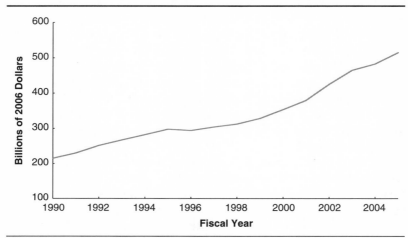

SOURCE: Congressional Budget Office.

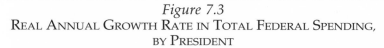

Figure 7.3
REAL ANNUAL GROWTH RATE IN TOTAL FEDERAL SPENDING,
BY PRESIDENT

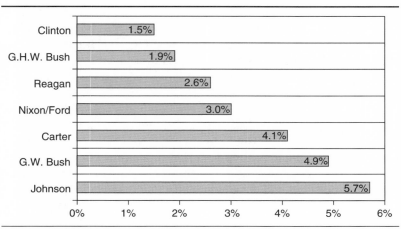

SOURCE: S. Slivinski, "Grand Old Spending Party: How Republicans Became Big Spenders," Cato Institute Policy Analysis no. 543, 2005.

over the details of budget baselines and "slowing the rate of increase." Public opinion turned against the Republicans. Although they actually achieved much of what they had sought, the episode was largely seen as a defeat.

Bloodied from their first fiscal battle, Republicans chose to retreat rather than to continue the fight. Gradually their commitment to fiscal responsibility slipped away. Those Republicans who had always wanted to spend more, but who had been kept in check by their more zealous colleagues, seized on the negative public response to the government shutdown as an excuse to resume their free-spending ways. In particular, the appropriations committee's powerful "cardinals"—the chairmen of its subcommittees—stopped cooperating with the House leadership.[8] Many other Republicans were simply terrified of Clinton's formidable political skills. The better part of valor seemed to be simply to give the president whatever he wanted and then go home to campaign.[9] In fact, in many cases the Republicans in Congress appropriated more than Clinton wanted. In contrast to Bush, who has never vetoed a spending bill, Clinton repeatedly vetoed appropriation bills that included unrequested projects or earmarks.[10] Within two years, spending on nondefense discretionary programs was higher than when the Republicans took office.[11]

At roughly the same time, a booming economy was generating ever more tax revenue. The result was a short-lived budget surplus, starting in 1999. The elimination of the budget deficit took away an important public relations weapon from those trying to hold down government spending. After that, spending began to increase rapidly.

Things went from bad to worse after George W. Bush took office. The Cato Institute's Bill Niskanen has shown that a divided government almost always produces lower levels of spending than when the legislative and executive branches are united under a single party.[12] Still, one might assume that an ostensibly conservative Republican president and a Congress with both chambers controlled by ostensibly conservative Republicans might show some measure of fiscal discipline. One would be wrong. Instead, as Rich Lowry of *National Review* explains: "[Bush] and the GOP Congress forged a mutual embrace of fiscal laxity. The GOP majority wasn't going to sink Bush's agenda, because that would hurt a Republican president and the party's fortunes. Bush wasn't going to veto congressional excess, because that would hurt the GOP majority and the party's fortunes."[13] Or as Rep. Jeff Flake (R-AZ) puts it, "When you're in control of the presidency and both houses of Congress, there's just no stop on it."[14]

By almost any measure, George W. Bush is one of the biggest-spending presidents in history. Marvin Olasky, whose writings helped form the basis for Bush's brand of "compassionate conservatism," said during the 2000 election: "Let's throw away the budget cutters. I see that coming with Bush."[15] He was correct.

As mentioned in Chapter 1, total real spending during his presidency is up 27 percent.[16] The annual rate of growth in federal outlays, on an inflation-adjusted basis, has averaged nearly 5 percent.[17]

When Bush took office, government spending accounted for just 18.5 percent of gross domestic product, a considerable decline from its peak of 22.3 percent under Bush's father, George H. W. Bush. The decline resulted from a combination of economic growth and spending restraint. But under the Bush administration, government spending has risen to 20.6 percent of gross domestic product.[18] That

Figure 7.4
GOVERNMENT SPENDING AS PERCENTAGE OF GDP

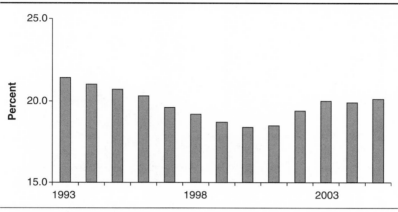

SOURCE: Office of Management and Budget.

increase represents the most rapid growth during one administration since Franklin Roosevelt (Figure 7.4).[19]

As noted, much of this spending was driven by post-9/11 defense spending, homeland security, and the wars in Iraq and Afghanistan. Defense spending has skyrocketed under President Bush, increasing at an annual rate of 8.8 percent, faster than at any time in the past 40 years (Figure 7.5). Indeed, Reagan's vaunted defense buildup in the 1980s pales by comparison. And even at the height of the Vietnam War, Lyndon Johnson didn't come close.

A large percentage of this spending is the war in Iraq, which has cost an estimated $300 billion. But defense spending outside of Iraq (and Afghanistan) has also increased dramatically. In fact, the Congressional Budget Office estimates that "war on terrorism" expenses, broadly defined to include the costs of the Iraq War, account for only about 16 percent of total defense expenditures since 9/11.[20] Besides, government spending was already rising before 9/11.[21]

Moreover, the reality is that the defense budget like every other area of government is stuffed with pork and wasteful spending. Sen. John McCain (R-AZ) has for years criticized the practice of hiding special-interest spending in defense bills.[22] Since 9/11 alone the number of earmarks in defense appropriation bills has grown from 1,409 in 2002 to 2,847 in 2006, an increase of 102 percent. The cost for the

143

Figure 7.5
TOTAL FEDERAL SPENDING ON NATIONAL DEFENSE

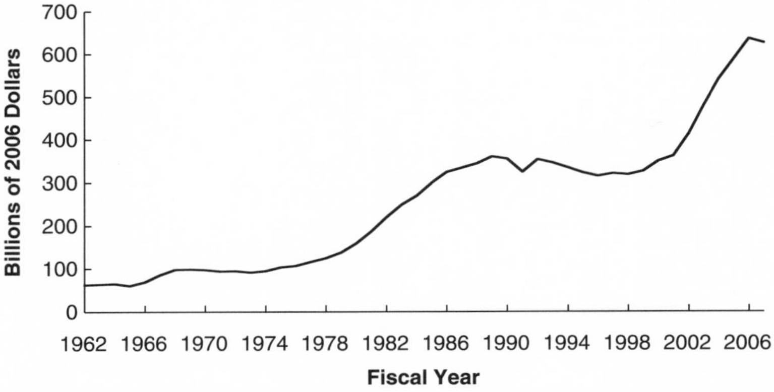

SOURCE: Office of Management and Budget.

items grew from $7.2 billion in 2002 to $9.3 billion today.[23] As McCain noted, the 2006 Defense Department Appropriations Act included "grants to dog mushers in Alaska, environmentalists in Iowa, museum curators in Texas, cranberry farmers in Wisconsin and wild-turkey hunters in the Carolinas."[24]

Many of the weapons programs currently being funded are unneeded, having virtually nothing to do with the war on terrorism or other military threats facing this country. Often they seem to have little to do with anything except interservice rivalries and the generation of jobs in key congressional districts. The Cato Institute has estimated that these unnecessary and wasteful programs cost at least $170 billion annually.[25]

As mentioned in Chapter 6, entitlement spending has also risen substantially under President Bush. In fact, it has risen at an annual rate of 4.7 percent, nearly 1.5 percentage points faster than under President Clinton.[26] The American public will not suffer the full cost of Bush's expansion of entitlement programs for many years, but the impact to come is real and substantial.

Aside from entitlements, domestic discretionary spending is where the Bush administration's big-spending ways are most readily

144

Figure 7.6
REAL ANNUAL GROWTH RATE IN FEDERAL SPENDING
(MINUS DEFENSE, HOMELAND SECURITY, AND ENTITLEMENTS),
BY PRESIDENT

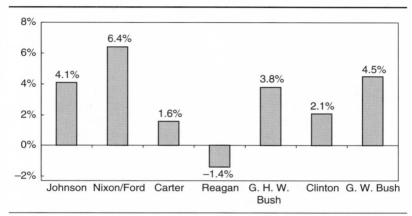

SOURCE: S. Slivinski, "Grand Old Spending Party: How Republicans Became Big Spenders," Cato Institute Policy Analysis no. 543, 2005.

apparent. As Rep. John Shadegg (R-AZ) notes, "We've had substantial spending growth over the last three years, and it cannot be blamed simply on homeland security and defense."[27]

Since taking office in 2001, Bush has allowed domestic discretionary outlays to soar by an annual average of 4.5 percent, after adjusting for inflation—compared with 2.1 percent a year under Bill Clinton, 3.8 percent under George H. W. Bush, just 1.6 percent under Jimmy Carter, and a decline of 1.4 percent under Ronald Reagan. Bush's discretionary spending increases even outpace Lyndon Johnson's. In fact, only Richard Nixon (6.4 percent), among recent presidents, increased spending at a faster rate.[28] (See Figure 7.6.)

This domestic spending is even more of a problem given the increase in defense spending discussed earlier. No president since Lyndon Johnson has tried to pursue such a "guns and butter" approach to budgeting. For example, Ronald Reagan significantly increased defense spending during his presidency. But in clear contrast to President Bush, he also cut nondefense spending.[29]

145

To make matters worse, the Bush administration has tried to cover up its overspending through what can only be considered dishonest budgeting. As the *Washington Post* notes of a typical Bush budget:

> It doesn't take into account continuing costs in Iraq and Afghanistan. It fails to address the acknowledged problem of the alternative minimum tax, which was aimed at the wealthy but is sweeping in growing numbers of ordinary taxpayers. It doesn't fully fund the administration's long-term defense spending plans. A more accurate picture of the likely deficit in 2009—even assuming the administration manages to keep to its stated spending limits—would put it more than $150 billion higher. And, of course, the surplus in government retirement accounts masks the true size of the shortfall.[30]

In addition, the cost of spending programs has continually been underestimated, often deliberately. As mentioned in Chapter 6, the administration and congressional leadership conspired to hide Richard Foster's estimate of the true cost of the Medicare prescription drug benefit—even threatening Foster's job if he revealed the truth.[31] In addition, budget gimmicks, such as pretending the tax cuts will expire or having programs start outside the budget window, have prevented an open and honest budget debate.

The Bush administration deserves all the blame it has received for out-of-control spending. Yet Congress is hardly innocent. Every year since he has been in office, President Bush has requested large increases in domestic discretionary spending. Compounding those increases, Congress has appropriated even more spending than the president asked for. For example, last year the president submitted a budget requesting $2.57 trillion, an increase of 7 percent over FY2005. Congress decided to spend $2.71 trillion, 5.5 percent more than Bush requested.

Republicans in Congress can hardly wait to spend the taxpayers' money. According to the National Taxpayers Union, in 2005 an overwhelming 184 of 218 Republicans in the House and a full 49 out of 55 Republican senators introduced legislation that would have had the net effect of increasing spending. (That is, legislation they introduced would have increased spending by more than legislation they introduced that would have cut it.)[32]

According to the nonpartisan watchdog group Citizens against Government Waste, more pork-barrel spending has occurred during the Bush administration than during any other presidency in history. The 2005 federal budget, for example, contained 13,999 pork-barrel projects at a cost to taxpayers of $27.3 billion. Compare that to 1996, right after the Republicans took control of Congress. That year, there were 958 pork projects, costing less than $10 billion.[33] When Republicans took over Congress, how many would have predicted that pork would more than double under their watch?

"Earmarks" provide another example of how Congress has failed to control spending. An earmark directs a specific amount of money to be spent by a specific federal department or agency on a specific project and is written in such a way that the money ends up in the hands of a specific recipient. Most earmarks do not go through the normal vetting or review process, and they have been at the heart of recent corruption scandals. Earmarks now show up in almost every area of federal budgeting, including defense, education, housing, scientific research, and transportation.[34] In 1994 the federal budget contained fewer than 2,000 earmarks; the 2005 budget contained nearly 14,000 such items.[35] The massive $286 billion 2005 transportation bill alone contained 6,371.[36]

Faced with public outrage and ethics scandals, fiscal conservatives forced the House leadership to accept limited earmark reform. Still, the leadership was able to water down the reforms. In particular, Appropriations Committee chairman Rep. Jerry Lewis (R-CA) and many of his fellow appropriators fought any restriction on earmarks. In the end, earmarks were still permitted, but the earmarks and their sponsors must be publicly identified.[37] Theoretically, this identification will introduce some measure of accountability. However, given the lack of success that fiscal conservatives have encountered in removing pork-barrel projects from various spending bills, the effect is likely to be minimal. Moreover, in a classic case of closing the barn door after the horse has escaped, the rule change didn't apply to any of the appropriations bills already passed. With few spending bills likely to be considered before the rule expires at the end of the year, the measure becomes far more symbolism than substance.[38] Finally, the rule applies only to earmarks funding nongovernmental organizations and entities, exempting earmarks directed to federal government agencies. Thus, about 40 percent of all earmarks, including such notorious items as the Alaska "bridge to nowhere," would be exempt from the rule.[39]

Pork seems to survive, regardless of who controls Congress. Whereas Democrats like West Virginia senator Robert Byrd were once considered the kings of pork, they were simply replaced by Republican senators like Ted Stevens of Alaska and Trent Lott of Mississippi and representatives like Don Young (R-AK) and Tom Davis (R-VA).[40]

To see how bad congressional spending has become, one just has to realize that of the 101 largest programs that the Republicans targeted for elimination when they took control of Congress, 81 are still around. In fact, spending for those 81 programs has increased by 27 percent in the last 10 years, including 14 percent under President Bush.[41]

Yet Republicans seem bizarrely proud of their fiscal irresponsibility. Tom DeLay actually said, "Republicans have done so well in cutting spending that . . . there is simply no fat left to cut in the federal budget."[42] And former Senator George Allen (R-VA) called the 2006 budget "very tight and taut."[43]

As *Wall Street Journal* columnist George Melloan put it: "Mr. Bush has few peers among American Presidents in his willingness to let Congress spend as freely as it always wants to do. And the Republican Congress has few peers in history in its willingness to take advantage of the president's generosity."[44] Or as Rep. Jeff Flake, one of the few stalwart small-government conservatives left in Congress laments, Republicans "don't even pretend to be fiscally conservative anymore."[45]

Taxes, Borrowing, and Spending

Of course the Bush administration and the Republicans in Congress have cut taxes, first in 2001 and again in 2003. Among the most important tax cuts were the following:

- A phased-in reduction in income tax rates from 39.6, 36, 31, and 28 percent to 35, 33, 28, and 25 percent, respectively. The 15 percent bracket would remain unchanged for some workers, but a new 10 percent bracket was created for low-income earners.
- Elimination of the marriage penalty.

- An increase in the child tax credit.
- Phasing out the estate tax.
- A reduction in taxes on dividends and capital gains.

These are good initiatives as far as they go. Taxes needed to be cut. When President Bush took office, federal taxes consumed 22 percent of gross domestic product. A middle-class worker earning $100,000 a year faced a 36 percent federal income tax rate. According to Cato Institute scholar Alan Reynolds, the effective marginal tax rate was actually 2 to 3 percent higher, because deductions and exemptions begin to be phased out above this level.[46] That doesn't count state income taxes, which can run as high as 9 percent.[47] The worker would also pay the 6.2 percent Social Security tax on most wages and the 1.45 percent Medicare tax on all wages.[48]

In addition to taxes on individual workers, the federal government imposed some of the industrial world's highest taxes on capital gains, interest, and investment. All of these demands significantly affected economic incentives, leading to slower economic growth.

The Bush tax cuts were, therefore, badly needed. They have stimulated the economy. Since the tax cuts were passed, tax revenues have increased significantly, cutting the budget deficit to just $248 billion.[49] In fact, the argument can be made that they were tiny compared to the country's overall tax burden. Most estimates suggest that the totality of the Bush tax cuts will save taxpayers roughly $1.7 trillion over 10 years. Although that sum may seem like a great deal, it pales in comparison to the $27 trillion in tax revenue that the government will collect over the same period.[50]

In isolation, therefore, the determination of the Bush administration and its allies to cut taxes is understandable. But because Congress has not correspondingly reduced spending, it has allowed massive deficits to accumulate (Figure 7.7).[51] And despite the recent surge in tax revenue, the Congressional Budget Office projects that without additional spending cuts, the deficit will begin rising again in 2007.[52]

As mentioned in Chapter 2, supply-siders have always put more emphasis on cutting taxes than on making the tough choices needed to reduce spending. Vice President Dick Cheney reportedly told then treasury secretary Paul O'Neill that "deficits don't matter."[53] But as Milton Friedman pointed out, the true tax on the American

Figure 7.7
FEDERAL BUDGET DEFICITS/SURPLUSES

SOURCE: Office of Management and Budget.

people is the level of government spending, no matter whether it is financed by taxes or by borrowing.[54] Congressional Budget Office director Douglas Holtz-Eakin makes a similar point.

> The projected growth of spending is important. A good (if not perfect) measure of the "size of government"—the economic burden of a government's programs—is spending. Spending on government programs diverts resources from the private sector—from consumption or investment—to the use of government. If the transfer replaces private consumption with government consumption, then the costs are felt immediately as lower private consumption. If the impact is to "crowd out" private investment, then the cost is slower growth in productive capacity. This loss persists into the future, ultimately lowering consumption at some future time.
>
> The means by which the federal government finances that spending—either via taxes or borrowing—is the mechanism by which the resources are taken from the private sector. But the key is not the particular mechanism that is used, but rather the fact that the decision to spend itself imposes the burden. Because the use of dollars for one purpose precludes their use for another, government spending always has a

burden. When Members are deciding whether to spend $1 billion for a federal program, they are choosing such a burden—even without a discussion about taxes. Unless other expenditures are reduced, current or future taxpayers will be required to pay more and give up their income to cover the costs.[55]

That is not to say that we should be completely indifferent to the mix of debt and taxes that we use to finance government. But it does mean that simply replacing a dollar of tax revenue with a dollar of debt does not solve the problem.

Of course the supply-siders have a point in that focusing too heavily on the deficit poses its own dangers. In the same way that cutting taxes can become a monomania for supply-siders, some deficit hawks allow elimination of the deficit to become an end in itself, overshadowing the more important question of the appropriate size and scope of government. This focus makes deficit hawks far too willing to raise taxes as a means of addressing the deficit. They forget that, although additional taxes may indeed bring the budget into balance, they also transfer additional resources to the government at the expense of private businesses and consumers. Making matters worse, when the taxes become too high, they become a drag on economic growth and actually reduce the amount of revenue the government receives. Relying on ever-higher taxes, therefore, can clearly be a case of diminishing returns.

In short, it's the spending, stupid.

With that idea in mind, let's look at some of the worst examples of out-of-control spending in the last few years.

The Highway Bill

Perhaps no single piece of legislation better exemplifies the fiscal irresponsibility of the Bush administration and its congressional co-conspirators than the 2005 Highway Bill. Covering an astounding 1,752 pages and costing nearly $300 billion over five years, the highway bill is the most expensive public works legislation in U.S. history.[56]

The idea of any federal highway bill is debatable. Some federal involvement in road building has always existed of course. The constitution authorizes the federal government to build "post roads," presumably to facilitate delivery of the mail, and Congress first authorized funds for such a road in 1802.[57] Modern federal involvement in roads started with the 1956 Federal-Aid Highway Act, which established the Federal Highway Trust Fund to pay for 90 percent of the proposed 41,000-mile interstate highway system. This massive undertaking was justified largely on national defense grounds.[58] Its original name, in fact, was the "National System of Interstate and Defense Highways." Eventually, the highway bill became a public works bill and was used to fund mass-transit projects and ultimately anything that could be related in some way to transportation. George H. W. Bush famously said it was about "jobs, jobs, jobs."[59] Now, highway bills are little more than a means of distributing largess to the states in a way that ensures maximum political credit for legislators.

In theory, federal highway spending is financed through the Federal Highway Trust Fund, which is funded through a dedicated tax on gasoline and diesel fuel.[60] In reality, like all federal trust funds, the highway trust fund serves as an accounting measure rather than a saving mechanism. Revenues are spent on general government operating expenses, and expenditures are ultimately financed by general revenues. For the federal government, what counts is money in and money out—not the accounting heading.

Federal funding of highways is problematic for many reasons. First, federal funding drives up the cost of building roads. The highway bill contained provisions requiring states to pay prevailing union wages (under the Davis-Bacon Act) and "buy American." These labor regulations can add as much as 30 percent to the cost of a road.[61] In addition, federal road standards are often higher, and therefore more expensive, than state standards.[62] Finally, federal administrative costs and paperwork can add as much as 5 percent to road-building costs.[63]

Second, federal funding allows highway spending to be allocated on the basis of congressional clout rather than local need or ability to pay. States whose members of Congress sit on the right committees can often obtain funding at the expense of other states. For example, Alaska receives $6.60 in highway funding for every dollar it pays in gas taxes. Other big winners are Washington, D.C., South Dakota, and Hawaii. Meanwhile, Georgia receives just 86 cents back for every dollar it pays in taxes.[64]

Third, even apart from pork (see below), federal funding encourages spending on low-priority and unnecessary projects. Because states perceive federal grants as "free" money, they are all too happy to undertake projects that they would not have funded if they had to pay for them on their own.[65]

Given these problems, some have suggested that responsibility for highways and other transportation projects be returned to the states. The Highway Trust Fund would be abolished along with the federal taxes dedicated to it; highway-financing powers and responsibility would be restored to the states. Legislation to that effect has been introduced by James Inhofe (R-OK) in the Senate and Jeff Flake in the House.[66] Not surprisingly given their colleagues' addiction to the transportation bill's pork potential, the legislation has not attracted widespread support.

The general merits of federal highway funding aside, no doubt exists that the 2005 Highway Bill was one of the true abominations of recent legislative history. President Bush initially proposed $256 billion in highway spending, a 31 percent increase over the last highway bill in 1998. But that was nowhere near enough for a pork-addicted Congress. As legislators from both parties began stuffing the bill with additional spending, President Bush made a half-hearted attempt to keep things under control, threatening to veto the bill if it exceeded $284 billion. The final bill carried a price tag of $286.5 billion, but the bill actually authorizes expenditures of $295 billion. It fictionalizes the $286.5 billion cost by assuming that, on the last day of the bill's life, Congress will rescind $8.5 billion in unused funds. The bill passed 412 to 8 in the House, 91 to 4 in the Senate.[67] Needless to say, Bush did not veto it. In fact, when he signed the bill, he said it "accomplishes goals in a fiscally responsible way."[68] Surprisingly, he was not being sarcastic.

The bill was filled with earmarked spending for individual members of Congress. To see how bad this particular bill was, consider that the 1982 highway bill contained only 10 earmarks. In 1987, Ronald Reagan vetoed a highway bill for containing just 152 earmarks, saying, "This bill is a textbook example of special-interest, pork-barrel politics at work."[69] The 1991 bill, the last highway bill passed under Democratic leadership, contained 538 such projects. But the addiction for pork has grown so large that the 2005 bill contained more than 6,000 earmarks.[70]

Perhaps the most notorious piece of pork in the highway bill was the "bridge to nowhere" that would connect the town of Ketchikan,

Alaska (population 8,900) with its airport on the Island of Gravina (population 50) at a cost to federal taxpayers of $320 million. The bridge, which would be nearly as long as the Golden Gate and higher than the Brooklyn Bridge, would replace a 10-minute ferry ride that has worked for years.[71]

The sheer absurdity of the "bridge to nowhere" made it the poster child for fiscal irresponsibility, but unfortunately it was far from unique. Consider these other projects in the highway bill:

- Another Alaskan bridge, this one costing $200 million (actually a down payment on a project estimated to eventually cost upward of $1.5 billion) that would lead from Anchorage to a rural port that has one tenant and a handful of homes. Even the Anchorage Chamber of Commerce says the project is unnecessary.[72]
- $16 million for the eponymous Nick J. Rahall II Appalachian Transportation Institute at Marshall University. The earmark was sponsored by Rep. Nick J. Rahall II (D-WV).[73]
- $5.9 million for Vermont snowmobile trails.[74]
- $4 million to reduce graffiti in New York City.[75]
- $3 million for dust control mitigation for rural Arkansas roads.[76]
- $2.75 million for the National Packard Museum in Ohio. The Packard facility isn't the only museum to get money. The Henry Ford Museum in Dearborn, Michigan, will get $1.2 million, and the Erie Canal Museum in Syracuse, New York, will receive $400,000.[77]
- $2.3 million to landscape the Ronald Reagan Freeway in California, a supreme irony given Reagan's veto of a previous pork-laden highway bill.[78]
- $2.2 million to construct a waterfront esplanade at Fort Totten in New York.[79]
- Even $200,000 for a deer avoidance system in Weedsport, New York, plus horseback riding trails in Virginia, daycare centers in Illinois, and money to refurnish the historic Harlem Theater.[80]

Congress also managed to slip into the bill several special-interest tax provisions that have little to do with transportation, including repeal of special occupational taxes on producers and marketers of alcoholic beverages, an income tax credit for distilled spirits whole-salers, a cap on excise taxes for fishing equipment, and tax exemptions for seaplanes used for sightseeing flights.[81]

Perhaps the best summary of this bill was provided by Senator McCain, who lamented, "How far and disgraceful a path we have tread in this pork-barrel laden piece of over-spending."[82]

The Farm Bill

Few government programs are as wasteful, counterproductive, and abused as farm subsidies. Most subsidies go not to small farmers but to giant agribusiness. In fact, only 33 percent of the nation's farmers received subsidies. Of those, 10 percent collected 72 percent of all money that taxpayers provided for conservation, commodity, and disaster programs over the past nine years.[83] Farm subsidy recipients include Fortune 500 companies, members of Congress, and millionaires such as Ted Turner.[84] In one particularly egregious example of agribusiness feeding at the subsidy trough, Tyler Farms of Arkansas collected nearly $32 million in farm subsidies between 1996 and 2001 by dividing one large farm into 66 legally separate corporations and signing up numerous individuals as subsidy recipients.[85]

Other money goes to people who are not even farmers and in some cases have never been farmers. Simply owning land that was used for farming at one time—even decades ago—may qualify people for payments. The *Washington Post* estimates that $1.3 billion in farm assistance each year goes to these nonfarmers.[86]

Nor do farm subsidies make sense as economic policy. They create a vicious cycle: farmers respond to subsidies by increasing production. They use existing land more intensely, increase inputs of fertilizers and pesticides (often with negative environmental effects), and put more acreage into production. The increased production can severely depress farm commodity prices. This result in turn creates pressure for still more subsidies. Consequently, more than 40 percent of net farm income comes from the federal government.[87] As the Department of Agriculture itself noted, "Government attempts to hold prices above those determined by commercial markets have simply made matters worse time after time" by encouraging unneeded output and inflating land prices.[88]

U.S. farm subsidies also contribute significantly to Third World poverty.[89] The country's combination of subsidies and trade barriers depresses the income of agricultural producers worldwide and exacerbates poverty in areas such as sub-Saharan Africa, the Caribbean, and Central Asia—where people are heavily dependent on agriculture.[90] Trade is a far more effective route out of poverty than foreign aid. Yet U.S. agricultural subsidies often make it impossible for underdeveloped nations to compete on the world market. In addition to the moral issue involved, U.S. farm subsidies contribute to anti-American attitudes around the world.

And perhaps most important, farm subsidies hurt the poor here in America. Agricultural subsidies keep the cost of food artificially high. Among the commodities most affected are such staples as milk, sugar, rice, and the products that contain them. Cotton, too, is subsidized, leading to higher clothing prices. Overall, higher U.S. food prices caused by farm programs cost U.S. consumers $16.2 billion per year, or about $146 per year per household.[91] This "food tax" falls most heavily on the poor who can least afford it and whose diets disproportionately contain the affected staples.

To their credit, when they first took over Congress, Republicans seemed to recognize the folly of American farm policy. One of the major accomplishments of the early days of the Republican Revolution was the 1996 Freedom to Farm Act. If it had been fully implemented it would have moved this country away from the command-and-control regime that had marked six decades of federal farm policy. The law increased farmers' flexibility in planting and eliminated some price supports for major crops. The law would also have significantly reduced farm subsidies.[92]

Along with welfare reform, Freedom to Farm was hailed as a clear signal that the new Republican Congress was breaking with the big-government ways of the past.[93] But in 2002, Congress and President Bush combined to undo that singular achievement.

The 2002 farm bill was a disaster in terms of cost alone. It is estimated to cost $190 billion over 10 years, an $83 billion increase over previously scheduled payments. In addition to the usual subsidies for such commodities as wheat, oats, and soy, the bill provided new subsidies to New England's dairy farmers, bailed out Connecticut oystermen, hiked subsidies to Florida citrus growers, and increased already excessive payments to Florida and Louisiana sugar barons. The bill also restored price supports for wool and mohair that had been among the few spending programs actually eliminated by Congress following the Republican takeover and guaranteed that the federal government would purchase $30 million a year of cranberry juice.[94]

But perhaps more important, the bill undid the fundamental premise of the Freedom to Farm Act. That bill was designed to wean farmers from reliance on government, allowing markets to set prices in exchange for giving farmers more freedom to decide what crops to plant. The 2002 Farm Bill reversed direction: subsidies for program crops were expanded and new commodities added. The free market was abandoned in favor of a return to bureaucratic command-and-control-style economic management. The result was to leave farmers more and more dependent on the federal government.

In signing the legislation, Bush called it "a compassionate bill," and said, "It helps America's farmers, and therefore it helps America."[95] Fiscal policy analyst Stephen Moore may have been closer to the mark when he called it "one of the most fiscally rancid pieces of legislation I've seen in 20 years of covering budget issues."[96]

Nor is the farm bill the only giveaway to agricultural interests. Congress has also passed several specialized programs. In fact, total spending for the government's Byzantine web of farm entitlements costs more than $25 billion per year.[97] For example, the Livestock Compensation Program, passed in 2002 and expanded in 2003, provides assistance to dairy farmers and ranchers hurt by drought. One might think that bad weather is a normal hazard of farming that should be borne by farmers. But regardless of whether drought assistance is justified, Congress has now expanded the program to provide assistance even when no drought exists. In 2005, more than half of the $1.2 billion distributed by the program went to farmers in areas that didn't have a drought. Farmers, in fact, are not even required to prove that they suffered an actual loss. The government simply mails them a check.[98]

Special programs for dairy farmers, corn farmers, and sugar growers also exist as well as special trade barriers against foreign sugar and milk. And special emergency relief bills are regularly passed to compensate farmers for everything from Hurricane Katrina to having debris from the space shuttle falling on their property.

In short, Republicans have not only undone their efforts to reform agricultural policies, they have made the situation worse.

Corporate Welfare

The farm bill was stuffed with giveaways to big business, but it was hardly the only example of corporate welfare that the Bush administration and Congress have passed. The Cato Institute has identified more than $90 billion annually in corporate welfare, roughly defined as "any government spending program that provides payments or unique benefits and advantages for specific companies or industries."[99] These programs range from direct cash payments to businesses to subsidized loans to insurance, research, and marketing support. Almost every agency of government manages some form of corporate welfare, but the worst offenders are the Departments of Agriculture, Commerce, Energy, Health and Human Services, and Transportation. Even defense appropriation bills are stuffed with corporate giveaways.

The Bush administration has a very mixed record regarding corporate welfare. Bush's first budget director, Mitch Daniels, said clearly, "It is not the federal government's role to subsidize, sometimes deeply subsidize, private interests."[100] And the administration has occasionally proposed to eliminate some corporate welfare programs.[101] However, it has not really fought for these cuts in the face of congressional resistance, and its own proposals, such as the energy bill, have been full of corporate subsidies.

Still, the Republican-controlled Congress has been the driving engine for corporate welfare. This congressional commitment to corporate giveaways starts right at the top. As the *Washington Post* has noted, House Speaker Dennis Hastert "makes a habit of helping Illinois-based corporations."[102] Senate Majority Leader Bill Frist has also been a prime supporter of corporate welfare bills. They have provided a solid example to the rest of Congress, which apparently believes that being in favor of free enterprise means being in favor of anything that any business may want.

Following are among the more egregious examples of corporate welfare:

- The Energy Bill: Senator McCain dubbed this monstrosity the "No Lobbyist Left Behind Act."[103] Weighing in at more than 1,200 pages and costing roughly $80 billion over 10 years, the energy bill is a swamp of corporate welfare, symbolic gestures, empty promises, and pork-barrel projects. In fact, corporate subsidies and government-funded research and development make up about $60 billion of the bill's cost. It has subsidies for fusion energy, hydrogen-powered fuel cells, "clean" coal, and other technologies. The traditional energy industries, oil and gas, also received their share of handouts, as did the nuclear power industry.[104] Naturally, the bill also contains new subsidies for ethanol, even though ethanol takes more energy to produce than is saved by using it as fuel.[105] Nevertheless, all this corporate pork will do virtually nothing to increase American energy independence or reduce costs to consumers.

- The Agriculture Department's Market Access Program provides money to corporate trade associations to advertise private products overseas. The money goes for consumer promotions, market research, trade shows, and advertising campaigns. Over the last dozen years, $1.7 billion in taxpayer money has been spent on this program with much of it benefiting large corporations. Yet Government Accountability Office studies indicate that this program has no discernible effect on U.S. agricultural exports.[106] Among those receiving money from the taxpayers through this program are Tysons Farms, Purdue, Weyerhaeuser, Archer Daniels Midland, Coors Brewing Company, and Dow Agro-Sciences.

- The Advanced Technology Program: As Brian Reidl of the Heritage Foundation notes, this $144 million per year program "does not fund basic science research. Rather, it funds the commercialization of research so that businesses can profit from it."[107] If these projects are as promising as claimed, companies should have no problem convincing their shareholders to fund them. Instead, companies such as General Electric, Hughes Aircraft, IBM, Xerox, and Honeywell, to name just a few, rely on the taxpayers to pay for what should be normal business expenses.

- The Export-Import Bank provides handouts to U.S. exporters in the form of loan guarantees, insurance, and direct loans designed to help American firms better compete for sales abroad. Very little policy justification exists for the program. The Congressional Research Service points out: "Most economists doubt . . . that a nation can improve its welfare over the long run by subsidizing exports . . . .at the national level, subsidized export financing merely shifts production among sectors within the economy, rather than adding to the overall level of economic activity, and subsidizes foreign consumption at the expense of the domestic economy."[108] Over 80 percent of the subsidies distributed by the Export-Import Bank go to Fortune 500 corporations, including such corporate giants as Enron, Boeing, Halliburton, Mobil Oil, IBM, General Electric, AT&T, Motorola, Lucent Technologies, FedEx, General Motors, Raytheon, and United Technologies.[109]

- The Overseas Private Investment Corporation (OPIC) also provides loans and investment insurance to U.S. companies doing business around the world. The majority of OPIC's largess goes to a small group of large multinational corporations and overwhelmingly supports a few highly profitable industries, such as oil and gas, financial services, and power. Among the biggest beneficiaries of OPIC handouts are Citibank, Enron, Bank of America, Intergen (a joint venture of Shell and Bechtel), and Ritz-Carlton and Hyatt Hotels.[110]

Hurricane Katrina

Hurricane Katrina was one of the largest natural disasters ever to hit this country. Undoubtedly, some kind of government response was necessary. But the answer from the Bush administration and Congress was essentially to throw money at the problem.

Within days of the disaster, before an assessment had even been made of what help was needed, Congress passed two emergency appropriations bills totaling $62.3 billion.[111] The appropriation was rushed through, outside normal procedures, with no committee hearings and little debate. As Budget Committee chairman Jim Nussle (R-IA) complained, Congress approved the disaster aid "largely without an upfront explanation of how that money would be spent, or how it would be financed."[112] The result has been an orgy of waste, fraud, mismanagement, and no-bid contracts.[113]

A handful of dedicated fiscal conservatives attempted to offset the new spending with cuts elsewhere in the budget.[114] The proposal put together by the Republican Study Committee under the auspices of Reps. Mike Pence and Jeb Hensarling (R-TX) listed more than 100 specific offset targets and their associated savings. Among them were repealing the 6,000 earmarked projects in the recent highway bill, postponing the Medicare prescription drug benefit, reducing farm subsidies, reducing federal subsidies to Amtrak, and eliminating the Advanced Technology Program. They were quickly slapped down by the Republican leadership. The leadership would not even let the proposal come to a vote, and Representative Pence was personally "taken to the woodshed" by House Speaker Hastert.[115]

When it was suggested that some of Alaska's notorious pork projects be canceled to help pay for Katrina relief, Representative Young, chairman of the House Transportation Committee, called the idea "the dumbest thing I ever heard," then angrily erupted, "They can kiss my ear!"[116] Alaska senator Ted Stevens threatened to resign before giving up any of his pork.[117]

Fiscal conservatives also warned that the lack of oversight and understanding of where all this money would go would inevitably lead to fraud, waste, and mismanagement. Such concerns were brushed aside by a Congress determined to demonstrate its compassion. But experience has proven the critics correct. As Eric Lipton wrote in a front-page story in the *New York Times*, "Among the many superlatives associated with Hurricane Katrina can now be added this one: it produced one of the most extraordinary displays of scams, schemes and stupefying bureaucratic bungles in modern history, costing taxpayers up to $2 billion."[118]

Beyond the initial appropriations, President Bush proposed a massive reconstruction package to help people in the Gulf Coast region get jobs, housing, health care, and education, pledging, "Throughout the area hit by the hurricane, we will do what it takes, we will stay as long as it takes, to help citizens rebuild their communities and their lives."[119] No one knows exactly how much his proposal would cost—the president declined to put a price tag on it—but some analysts predict it will ultimately be greater than the $300 billion dollars spent so far on the wars in Afghanistan and Iraq.[120] Another way to look at this largess is to note that the proposed Katrina-related spending could exceed $100,000 per displaced person.[121]

Michael Tackett of the *Chicago Tribune* described Bush's proposals as an "amalgam of Franklin Roosevelt and Lyndon Johnson" that draws "inspiration from the Marshall Plan, the Works Progress Administration and the Tennessee Valley Authority and social policy animated by the Great Society."[122] The *Wall Street Journal* called it "the GOP's New New Deal."[123]

Congress has been quick to spread the bounty around. The White House declared 41 states and the District of Columbia either major disaster areas or in states of emergency, allowing federal aid to flow to any state that takes in an evacuee. Sens. Charles Grassley (R-IA) and Max Baucus (D-MT) proposed a $9 billion expansion of Medicaid benefits, ostensibly to help states pay for hurricane-related emergency care, but managed to extend the added funds to 29 states, including $78 million for Alaska, which seems a long way from the hurricane zone.[124]

Some in Congress want even more. Louisiana's congressional delegation asked the federal government, without blinking, for $250 billion in aid for their state alone. That sum is the equivalent of handing every single Louisianan $56,000; paying for it would require taking an extra $1,900 from every single American household.[125] That's two and a half times what the United States spent to rebuild all of Europe after World War II (adjusted for inflation).[126]

Most of the proposals have bogged down in the legislative process. That's good news for taxpayers but bad news for the residents of New Orleans and other areas battered by Hurricane Katrina who have not received legitimate assistance.

The Inevitable Consequence of Big-Government Conservatism

Some might see this out-of-control spending as simply politics as usual, Republicans who were content to talk about fiscal conservatism when they were out of power being corrupted once they were in power. Undoubtedly there is something to this view. Republicans have become all too comfortable with the perks of power. As discussed in Chapter 3, maintaining their majority has become more important than ideology, at least since Newt Gingrich ordered appropriators to steer pork to vulnerable Republican legislators in 1996.[127]

But the spending binge by President Bush and the Republican Congress can also be seen as a direct consequence of the rise of big-government conservatism. In part, of course, spending increases because many big-government projects are expensive. In part, it is because too many big-government conservatives believe "deficits don't matter." But the true damage of big-government conservatism is more insidious. James Pinkerton points out: "There's nothing spontaneous or accidental about the spending spree. What we're seeing is the sober logic of a changing Republican Party."[128]

As the country-and-western song says, "You've got to stand for something or you'll fall for anything."[129] By abandoning their traditional belief in small government, Republicans have removed any principled objection to spending money on just about anything. Legislators have always faced a natural imperative to spend. The factors identified by public-choice economics make spending even harder to control, particularly the existence of diffuse costs and concentrated benefits.[130] As a result, even the best-intentioned and most-conservative presidents and Congresses have been able to restrain spending for only a short time. But they at least tried. The current administration and Congress have not.

When this failure of restraint is combined with an increasingly tight relationship between lobbyists and Congress, it is an open invitation to increase spending. Jacob Weisberg, a political columnist for *Slate*, calls this phenomenon "interest group conservatism," a curious governing philosophy that involves "the expansion and exploitation of government by people who profess to dislike it."[131] Why not call it what it is—big-government conservatism.

8. A National School Board

More than a little irony attaches to the fact that when terrorists attacked America on September 11, 2001, George W. Bush was sitting in a Florida schoolroom, promoting a reading program. Defending our nation from attack is a legitimate function of the federal government—indeed, the most important function of the federal government—but an education program is not. Yet such were the priorities of the Bush administration that education was receiving the president's attention.

A time existed when Republicans talked about abolishing the Department of Education. Ronald Reagan made a campaign pledge to eliminate it and renewed his promise in his first State of the Union address in January 1982, saying, "The budget plan I submit to you . . . will realize major savings by dismantling the Department of Education."[1] He was, of course, unsuccessful, but conservatives and Republicans kept trying. In 1996, the Republican Party platform said: "The Federal government has no constitutional authority to be involved in school curricula or to control jobs in the market place. This is why we will abolish the Department of Education."[2]

Today, not only have Republicans abandoned that idea, but they also have presided over the most massive expansion of federal involvement in and control over education in history. The 2004 Republican platform contained no talk about abolishing the Department of Education, instead saying: "President Bush and Congressional Republicans have provided the largest increase in federal education funding in history and the highest percentage gain since the 1960s. . . . Support for elementary and secondary education has had the largest increase in any single Presidential term since the 1960s—an increase of nearly 50 percent since 2001."[3] How far we've come. Indeed, when asked whether President Bush supported past Republican pledges to abolish the Department of Education, his education adviser Sandy Kress replied, "He never gave it a thought."[4]

No one can deny the importance of education or the need to reform our educational system. Our society is becoming increasingly divided between those with the skills and education needed to function in the increasingly competitive global economy and those without such skills and education.

Lack of education is a critical determinant of poverty. High school dropouts are roughly three times more likely to end up in poverty than those who complete at least a high school education.[5] If they do find jobs, dropouts' wages are likely to be low. Wages for high school dropouts declined (in inflation-adjusted terms) by 23 percent between 1970 and 2000.[6] As the U.S. Department of Education warns, "In terms of employment, earnings, and family formation, dropouts from high school face difficulties in making the transition to the adult world."[7] This situation is only going to grow worse as America enters a more-competitive world of global competition and commerce, which requires advanced skills and technical knowledge.

Moreover, the effect is intergenerational. Children in families where parents have not completed high school are far more likely to be in poverty than children from families where the parents have more education. Simply put, the more education, the less poverty—a cause and effect that extends across all ethnic groups, but that is particularly pronounced for African Americans.[8]

At the same time that education is becoming increasingly crucial, government schools are doing an increasingly poor job of educating children. The failures of public schools are well documented and need not be dwelled on at length here. Test scores plummeted throughout the 1960s and 1970s. The 1980s saw a slight upturn, but test scores have stagnated since.

About 10 percent of girls and 12 percent of boys do not complete school.[9] These figures may understate the real problem, however, because black and Hispanic dropout rates are nearly three times higher than dropout rates among whites, and poor children are five times more likely to drop out.[10]

Second, a quality educational system is essential to maintaining American competitiveness in a globalized economy. As the combined National Academies warned in their recent report, *Rising above the Gathering Storm*, "workers in virtually every sector must now face competitors who live just a mouse-click away."[11] To maintain our edge will require an educated workforce with the knowledge and skills appropriate to a technologically fueled global marketplace.

Yet studies repeatedly show the United States falling behind much of the world in terms of education. For example, American students score below average on math and science tests administered to students in other industrialized countries. U.S. 15-year-olds rank 21st of students from 28 countries in math and 16th in science. American students fared only slightly better in reading, scoring about average for countries that are members of the Organization for Economic Cooperation and Development.[12] This performance is not good enough, especially in today's world. Employers are aware of the problem. Some 60 percent rate the reading and math skills of their workers as "poor" or only "fair."[13]

The danger will be even greater if, as Nobel laureate Milton Friedman warned, our failing education system creates a class of workers unable to compete in world markets. Friedman feared that this new educational underclass will apply political pressure for America to withdraw from the globalized economic system for which they are ill-prepared, with profound consequences for our long-term economic growth.[14]

Conservatives have always understood the importance of education and have been among the first to raise concerns over the decline of the nation's public school system. But they have traditionally opposed federal intervention, seeing education as a responsibility of state and local governments. They agreed with the sentiment expressed by the Supreme Court in *Milliken v. Bradley* that "No single tradition is more deeply rooted than local control over public schools."[15]

But many big-government conservatives do not share this attachment to educational federalism. In fact, neoconservatives were among the first to raise the idea of national standards for education, which they saw as an antidote to the multiculturalism and liberal values being taught at the local level. Although Newt Gingrich and his technophile followers opposed federal education bureaucracies, they saw numerous opportunities for the federal government to fund and guide educational priorities. Among other things, Gingrich wants the federal government to provide every student with a laptop computer.[16] That's a proposal also endorsed by Massachusetts governor Mitt Romney.[17]

Republicans in Congress had begun increasing education spending as early as 1998. But George W. Bush took federal education

Figure 8.1
FEDERAL EDUCATION SPENDING, 1962–2005

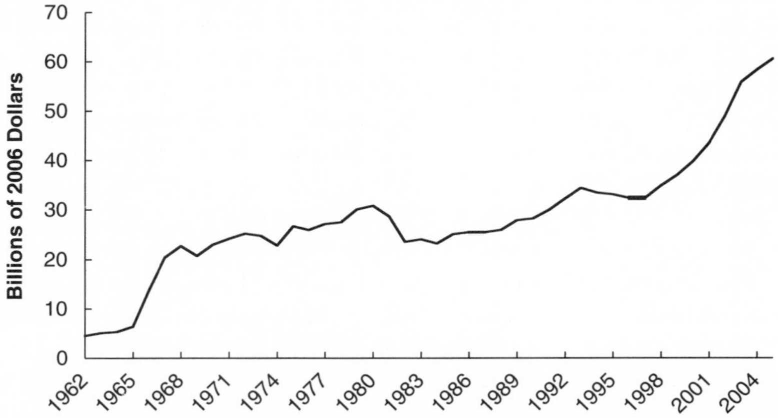

SOURCE: Office of Management and Budget.

spending to unprecedented levels. Since 2001, President Bush and the Republican Congress have increased education spending by more than 50 percent (Figure 8.1).[18] The Education Department's budget has increased from $33.6 billion to more than $60 billion.[19]

Republicans on the House Education Committee actually criticized Democrats for voting against spending increases and bragged: "The spending measure approved on the floor of the U.S. House of Representatives today provides yet another boost in education funding, bringing spending on our education priorities . . . to their highest levels in history."[20]

Senate Majority Leader Bill Frist went a step further, not only bragging about how much the federal government was spending on education but also criticizing states for failing to spend as much as he thinks they should. "This president and this Congress has [sic] demonstrated . . . a federal commitment that has not been matched by the states themselves in terms of the percentage of increase," Frist told a conference of school administrators.[21]

This massive rise in education spending occurred despite the lack of evidence that increasing the money spent on public schools will lead to increased educational performance. Education economist

Eric Hanushek of the University of Rochester reviewed 147 studies of the relationship between spending on education and student performance and concluded, "There appears to be no systematic relationship between school expenditures and student performance."[22] Likewise, John Chubb and Terry Moe of the Brookings Institution concluded: "As for money, the relationship between it and effective schools has been studied to death. The consistent conclusion is that there is no connection between school funding and school performance."[23]

Bruce Bartlett suggests that Bush's education spending was little more than a "bribe" for the soccer-mom vote.[24] But that explanation is really too cynical. In reality, Bush truly believes in greater federal government involvement in education. He has repeatedly explained, "The role of the Federal government [in education] is to insist on standards, provide resources, hold people accountable, and help school districts to meet standards."[25] Similarly, he has told audiences, "The role of the federal government is to serve as a funding source for specific projects, and an instigator for accountability systems."[26]

Traditional conservatives like Reagan and Goldwater might have believed that education was a state and—even more so—a local responsibility. George W. Bush might not explicitly disagree, but he clearly seeks to shift more of the responsibility and control to Washington.

No Child Left Behind

Perhaps the signature legislative achievement of the Bush administration is the No Child Left Behind Act (NCLB).[27] Bush himself calls it "the most important federal education reform in history."[28] That attitude is echoed by other big-government conservatives. Former Sen. Rick Santorum (R-PA) said NCLB is "the most historic legislative initiative enhancing education to pass Congress in decades."[29]

It certainly represents a major shift in federal education policy. Whether it leads to better education for our children remains very much in doubt.

NCLB was a carryover of Bush's policies as governor of Texas, where he had promoted the state's program of annually testing all students in grades 3–8 and rating schools based on their performance on the Texas Assessment of Academic Skills exams. While campaigning for president in 2000, he routinely referred to improving those exam scores, especially among black and Latino students. As president, he sought to re-create this state program on the federal level. His attitude was: "I don't want to tinker with the machinery of the federal role in education. I want to redefine that role entirely."[30]

In many ways Bush's approach to federal education reform was not original. He built on a standards-and-testing movement that had been gaining momentum since the late 1980s. Bush's father had proposed voluntary national testing tied to "world class" standards in 1989. The plan collapsed in the face of conservative opposition but was revived by President Clinton, whose "Goals 2000" provided grants to help states establish academic standards.[31] Although conservatives fought these earlier initiatives, they were not about to block their president's first major legislative achievement.

The final bill was truly bipartisan, drawing significantly on input from such liberal Democrats as Sen. Edward Kennedy (D-MA) and Rep. George Miller (D-CA). To gain Democratic support, Bush and the Republican leadership—particularly John Boehner (R-OH), at that time chairman of the House Education Committee—jettisoned conservative proposals, including private school choice, consolidation, and program flexibility.[32] They also added a number of special-interest programs, such as Ready-to-Learn Television, Star Schools, the National Writing Project, Arts in Education, Education for Native Hawaiians, and the Women's Educational Equity Act. The bill ballooned in size and cost, but that didn't seem to matter much. The final 1,100-page bill passed Congress overwhelmingly, 381-41 in the House and 87-10 in the Senate. Despite the bill's complete reversal of Republican principles, 183 of 221 Republicans in the House and 44 of 49 Republican Senators voted for the bill.

At its heart, NCLB promised billions of dollars in federal education money in exchange for establishing standards of accountability and excellence. Among the key provisions were the following:[33]

- States were required to develop a system of assessments, graduation rates, and other indicators to determine the quality of their school systems. These assessments would set standards for "adequate yearly progress."
- The assessments were to include annual standardized testing of students in grades 3–8, and once during grades 10–12 in reading and math. Standardized testing in science was required

once for students in grades 3–5, 6–9, and 10–12. Although the federal government mandated the testing, states were free to develop the actual tests themselves.

- All teachers were required to be certified in their core subject areas. Elementary school teachers were required to demonstrate their subject knowledge and teaching skills in reading/language arts, writing, mathematics, and other areas of basic elementary school curriculum. Middle and high school teachers must also pass a state test in each academic subject area they teach. Again, states were free to design their own tests and other certification criteria.
- States were required to issue detailed report cards on the performance of schools and school districts. Schools that failed to meet adequate yearly progress standards for two consecutive years were designated "in need of improvement." (In true politically correct fashion, no schools are ever labeled as "failing.")
- Students attending schools "in need of improvement" were to be able to transfer to other public schools if they wished and to be provided with tutoring and other supplemental education services. Schools designated as needing improvement must also undertake steps to improve, ranging from internal reorganization and bringing in outside experts to advise the school, to extending the school year.[34] Schools that do not improve can be taken over by the state and even turned into "charter schools."

Accountability in education makes sense. Yet great reason for concern exists over the Bush administration's approach.

Education is best handled at the local level for an important reason. Almost by definition, education involves the transmission of values. Even if we could devise a values-free way of teaching, how many parents would choose that for their children? Yet we are a pluralistic society with widely differing values and views on major social and political issues. We have already seen the disputes over such issues become the source of litigation, protests, and societal schisms. As one observer noted, these fights often end up resembling "blood feuds, ideological wars, episodes in selfishness wrapped in the rhetoric of rectitude."[35]

Think of all the areas of potential disagreement about what should or should not be taught, not just on hot-button social issues such as sex education or evolution, but which historical figures to study; how to handle issues such as slavery, the treatment of Native Americans, or Hiroshima; or what to teach about Christianity or Islam—not to mention contemporary ideological conflicts. Clearly no national consensus exists on how to approach these subjects. National agreement doesn't even exist on how much emphasis should be placed on what subjects. Science, mathematics, and reading are surely important but what about civics, history, music and the arts, or even physical education? And other questions exist about how to teach—phonics or whole language, new math or old?

Placing the federal government in charge of education risks elevating all these disputes to the national level. Potentially it would allow a single group of bureaucrats to impose their values on every student nationwide, whether or not parents or local communities share those values.

In some ways, this federal involvement might appeal to the Religious Right and some big-government conservatives who have grown frustrated with the teachers unions and what they perceive as liberal local boards of education. Senator Santorum, for example, believes that schools should teach "the truth" to help students understand "right and wrong" and make "moral choices."[36]

The first example of this congressionally dictated "truth" may have come when Congress passed an amendment to NCLB, sponsored by Senator Santorum, expressing the "sense of the Senate" that schools should teach "intelligent design" or creationism alongside the theory of evolution.[37] Although such a move may please religious conservatives, a more liberal Congress could just as easily intervene on the other side. Indeed, if some conservatives were pleased with that intervention, how would they react to knowing that the Center for Civics Education, the group funded by the federal government to promote national standards for civics and government, defines "civic virtue" as requiring "the citizen to place the public or common good above private interest"?[38]

Of course NCLB does not explicitly call for a national curriculum. In fact, President Bush has repeatedly said that he is opposed to a national curriculum. Reason exists, however, for concern that big-government conservatives are taking us in that direction.

In the long run, testing will almost certainly drive the curriculum. Little doubt exists that with academic success increasingly determined by test results, teachers will teach to the test. This outcome is not all bad. Teaching to the test ensures that certain basic information will be covered. At the same time, however, a large body of research demonstrates that high-stakes testing narrows curricula.[39] Thus, statewide testing will slowly drive individual school curricula toward statewide uniformity. And should the testing design become more national in scope, curricula will move toward national uniformity.

Some have suggested using the National Assessment of Education Progress test to "verify" performance as measured by state-designed tests. Doing so effectively creates a single national test with the potential to override state testing.[40] If states are rewarded or punished by consequence of their National Assessment of Education Progress scores, then they will teach to the test to raise those scores and receive the federal dollars for doing so. The net effect would be to create a default national curriculum.

Some big-government conservatives want to take federal influence over curricula even further. Chester Finn, who has had enormous influence on the Bush administration's education policies, and Frederick Hess of the American Enterprise Institute argue: "NCLB today is too lenient about the skills and knowledge that young Americans must acquire. . . . Washington should instead offer stricter guidance regarding the essentials that students must master." They go on to suggest, "some will decry the prospect of a national curriculum . . . most Americans would likely welcome a single set of academic standards in these most basic of skills."[41] Likewise, Diane Ravitch, another Bush education adviser, argued in the *New York Times* that we should adopt both "national education standards" and a "national core curriculum."[42] Kirk Johnson, an education analyst with the Heritage Foundation, has suggested that a national test would keep states honest, acting as "a validation check on whatever test the individual state chooses to use."[43]

Writing in support of national education testing in the *Washington Post*, William Bennett and President Bush's first education secretary, Ronald Paige, admit that "the Constitution says nothing about education," but dismiss that as outmoded "in a world of fierce economic competition." "A naïve commitment to 'states rights,'" they write, should not stand in the way of "better and more efficient ways to produce an educated population."[44]

Ample dispute exists about whether standardized testing is the best method to ensure accountability. Many experts have pointed out that such testing tends to measure a narrow range of often memorized material rather than critical reasoning skills. Students may focus on test-taking skills rather than learning generally, and those who lack test-taking skills may be unfairly penalized.[45] Studies also suggest that high-stakes testing may increase dropout rates, especially for minorities and "at risk" youths. Some estimates suggest that as many as 40,000 students drop out of school each year in part because of the pressures brought on by testing.[46] Equally valid arguments favor testing, and nearly everyone agrees that some method should exist of holding schools accountable.[47] But given the questions over the value of testing, wouldn't leaving such issues to state governments, or local school boards, be better?

NCLB also raises questions about whether it simply adds a new level of federal bureaucracy on top of state educational bureaucracies. Given the wide variation in state education regulation and standards, not surprisingly the new federal standards often differed from or even contradicted existing state standards. Too often, states responded by simply adding the federal accountability requirements on top of preexisting state plans, resulting in a dual system of accountability. Inevitably, this overlay has created confusion. For example, the federal rules identified 289 schools in Arizona as low performing, but these same schools met the state performance targets, some even earning a "highly performing" label. In Virginia, 40 percent of schools failed to meet federal goals whereas only 22 percent failed to meet state accreditation standards.[48]

Other parts of NCLB have also raised issues. For example, research clearly shows that teacher quality is a major factor in determining student academic achievement.[49] And no doubt exists that teacher quality is a significant problem in some states. NCLB both provided additional funds for teacher training and mandated that all states develop procedures to ensure that all teachers were "highly qualified." States were given some latitude in developing those procedures, but in general a "highly qualified teacher" was defined as one with full certification, a bachelor's degree, and demonstrated competence in subject knowledge and teaching. In practice, the final criterion meant passing a test in their teaching area.

States were happy to take the additional money but have done little to change their procedures for establishing teacher qualification. Apparently, not one of the 50 states will be able to meet the law's deadline for ensuring that every teacher is rated as "highly qualified."[50] Several states have attempted to write looser qualification rules and sought waivers, but the Department of Education has generally been unsympathetic to the waiver requests. "I want the states to know that Congress and the president mean business on the law," Education Secretary Spelling told the *New York Times*.[51]

As a result many states are likely to lose a substantial amount of federal funding. Although ample reason exists to question whether that money should have been offered in the first place, the sudden withdrawal of the funding will undoubtedly cause severe disruptions. Of even more concern, however, is the specter of widespread teacher shortages as teachers who fail to meet the new certification requirements are barred from the classroom by states attempting to save their funding.

Finally, NCLB perpetuates the education funding problem of throwing good money after bad. Underperforming schools qualify for additional funding. On the surface, of course, this makes sense. Those systems clearly need help more than schools that are performing well. However, providing extra help can end up rewarding failure. School districts with long, well-documented histories of failure, such as the Washington, D.C., school system, will receive tens and even hundreds of millions of dollars in additional funding. Yet no reason exists to believe that the new money will be any better spent than the old.

More than 30 states have considered or adopted measures that challenge, demand changes, or call for increased flexibility in implementation of NCLB. The most far-reaching of these is a law passed by the Utah legislature that effectively instructs the state to ignore NCLB whenever it conflicts with Utah's own education guidelines. Education Secretary Margaret Spellings has responded to the Utah challenge by threatening to withhold $76 million in federal education monies. In addition, all 50 state legislatures have signed a statement that questions the constitutionality of the act.[52]

More than two dozen lawsuits have also been filed, attempting to block parts of the program's implementation.[53] Many of these lawsuits revolve around questions of funding. For example, the National Education Association and the states of Michigan, Texas, and Vermont have sued, alleging that the federal government did not provide the states with sufficient funding for the testing, tutoring, and other new initiatives that they were required to implement under NCLB.[54] Connecticut filed a separate but similar suit. Six other states and the District of Columbia, while not parties to the suit, filed briefs in support of the plaintiffs. These unfunded costs can be a significant burden to state governments. For instance, Connecticut estimates that complying with NCLB will cost it $41.6 million.[55] A trial court dismissed the complaint, holding that Congress has the right to impose mandates on the states even if they are not funded.[56] However, the decision is being appealed.

Beyond NCLB

In addition to the No Child Left Behind Act, the Bush administration has proposed several programs to influence what subjects are taught and how they are taught. For example, the administration wants to establish a "best practices" center for educators in math, science, and reading.[57] The Bush administration has also created a new federal program to give added funding to students who complete "rigorous" high school programs. The five-year, $3.75 billion initiative would provide $750 to $1,300 grants to low-income college freshmen and sophomores who have completed "a rigorous secondary school program of study." To determine who should receive the grants the federal government will rate the academic rigor of all of the nation's 18,000 high schools.[58]

The Bush administration is also considering expansion of testing to include colleges and universities. The Commission on the Future of Higher Education, appointed by Secretary of Education Margaret Spellings, recommended national testing at the college level. Such tests "would be greatly beneficial to the students, parents, taxpayers and employers," the commission concluded.[59] The chairman of that commission also says he would like to "create a national database that includes measures of learning."[60]

Other big-government conservatives would increase the federal role in education still further. Gingrich has even suggested that the government should pay students for taking math and science classes. He worries that students see immediate financial rewards for things such as athletics, but academic students require too much delayed gratification. A new program paying students might turn that around. "That way, students wouldn't have to wait 22 years to get a paycheck, it could be every other Friday."[61] In fact, in one burst of enthusiasm, he suggests that we could send students "who have worked hard all year" to Disney World.[62]

Gingrich also wants the Department of Education to establish an "Office of Patriotic Education" to oversee programs designed to "bring patriotism back to our schools." This new agency would establish curricula and develop textbooks that combine reading instruction with patriotic stories.[63] In addition, Gingrich calls for Congress to establish standing subcommittees on patriotic education, which would enable Congress to develop standards for the teaching of patriotism. "Failure of schools to meet these standards," he says, "would result in an end to federal and state funding."[64]

Gingrich is not alone in wanting to use federal money to bludgeon education systems into ideological line. Rick Santorum has sponsored an amendment to Title IX of the Higher Education Act to require "ideological diversity" as a condition for federal funding for colleges and universities. According to Senate staffers, no official method of measuring "ideological diversity" has been set, but such factors as religion and party registration could be used.[65]

Conservatives once opposed President Clinton's proposal to have the federal government fund 100,000 new teachers.[66] Today, President Bush supports a plan to train 70,000 high school teachers to lead advanced placement courses in math and science and expand access to these challenging courses for low-income students as well as to bring 30,000 math and science professionals to teach in the classroom through an Adjunct Teacher Corps program.[67]

Federal School Vouchers

Even when they are right on general policy, big-government conservatives can't seem to resist getting the federal government involved. For example, school choice has long been a keystone of conservative education reform. Few policies would do more to help poor children escape underperforming schools. Moreover, voucher programs make schools accountable to parents. When families have the power to remove children from schools that aren't working, administrators and teachers have an incentive to provide the best educational experience for each child. Thus, even children who remain in public schools benefit from the availability of school choice.

Despite implacable opposition from the teachers unions, slow progress is being made at the state level. Some type of school-choice programs now exist, at either the city or state level, in Arizona, Illinois, Iowa, Maine, Minnesota, Ohio, Pennsylvania, Vermont, and Wisconsin, as well as the District of Columbia. Although state courts struck down a voucher program in Florida, supporters are now calling for an initiative to amend the state constitution to enable the program. These programs vary in scope and eligibility. Some offer vouchers, others tax credits.[68] Other states have not yet enacted real parental choice but have established charter schools. Still others allow a choice of public schools. Taken as a whole, they offer a variety of experiments for other cities and states to learn from. In short, states are moving forward on what should be a state issue.

Rather than step back and allow the states to work, President Bush has called for federal school vouchers in a proposal backed by the Heritage Foundation.[69] The proposal would provide $100 million in federal funds to states, local school systems, and nonprofit organizations that provide school vouchers or "scholarships" to low-income public school students. Similarly, Republicans in Congress, led by Lamar Alexander (TN) in the Senate and Howard McKeon (CA) in the House, have introduced legislation to provide parents with vouchers worth up to $4,000 per year that could be used for private-school tuition or a public school outside their local district.[70] The vouchers would be available to parents with children in schools that have failed to meet their progress goals under NCLB for at least five straight years.

This proposal seems to be another classic example of the concept that if something is a good idea it needs to be a federal program. Yet as Cato education analyst Andrew Coulson points out, federal vouchers would greatly expand federal government involvement in education. Coulson points to the Dutch experience with educational choice funded by the national government. Although the Dutch system gives parents much greater freedom to choose the school their children attend, "With government funding came government control. Today, the Dutch government defines teacher accreditation requirements, fixes salary scales, curtails the firing of teachers, sets the core curriculum, says how much will be spent, makes it illegal to charge tuition over the voucher amount, and prohibits profit-making in voucher schools."[71]

Some conservatives have been skeptical of school vouchers precisely because they worry that vouchers will be accompanied by government regulations that will, in effect, turn private schools into public schools for regulatory purposes. Federal vouchers magnify that danger by raising the threat to the federal level.

President Bush and his allies are right to favor greater choice for parents and greater autonomy for educators. However, by ignoring the proper constitutional role of the federal government, they are opening the door to even greater federal control over education. As with so many other issues, good intentions are causing big-government conservatives to abandon their principles.

This abandonment of traditional conservative principles is all the sadder because it is so unnecessary. As mentioned, progress toward educational choice is being made at the state and local levels. No need beyond impatience, combined with a desire to look like Congress is "doing something" and a love of centralized power, exists for the federal government to get involved.

The Founding Fathers would be shocked at what the president and Congress are doing today in bringing education under federal control. Congress, quite simply, has no power or authority to collect taxes for, fund, or regulate public schools. True conservatives such as Barry Goldwater and Ronald Reagan understood these limits on congressional power.

Unfortunately, true conservatives no longer fill the Republican congressional ranks. As Major Garrett, the Fox News reporter who has chronicled the Republican Revolution, sadly noted about Republican education policy, "There is no part of domestic policy on which congressional Republicans have ended up farther away from where they started. None."[72]

9. Power to the President

Perhaps no area better reflects how big-government conservatives have turned away from traditional conservative principles than the way the Bush administration, often with the active collaboration of Congress, has centralized power. Few principles have been as basic to traditional conservatism as opposition to the concentration of power in a single entity. From the division of powers established by the Founding Fathers to the federalism espoused by Barry Goldwater and Ronald Reagan, the overarching belief has been to keep government authority dispersed and as localized as possible.

But big-government conservatives have sought to reverse this allocation of power. They have sought to move power from the states to the federal government and from the legislative branch to the executive. As much as possible, they have sought to concentrate power and authority in the presidency. The implications of this philosophical change are significant.

Federalism

From its founding, our system of government has been based on the idea of federalism—the sharing of power between the states and the national government. This system was based partly on pragmatic grounds; according to the principle of subsidiarity, issues should be handled at the smallest possible level of government and the level closest to the people affected. Local levels of government were more likely to understand unique local conditions and to be more responsive to the people represented. Moreover, actions taken by diverse state and local governments allowed for greater experimentation and innovation. That is why Justice Louis Brandeis famously referred to states as "laboratories of democracy."[1]

Perhaps even more important, federalism provided a brake against an all-encompassing, overreaching central government far removed from its citizenry. Having just fought a war against the British monarchy, the Founding Fathers were determined to prevent too much power from resting in any one set of hands. Thus they divided government power, giving the newly formed federal government certain specifically enumerated powers, with remaining government authority retained by the states. As James Madison wrote in *The Federalist*: "The powers delegated by the proposed Constitution to the federal government are few and defined. Those which are to remain in the State governments are numerous and indefinite."[2]

Madison further noted that federalism provides "a double security . . . to the rights of the people. The different governments will control each other; at the same time they each will be controlled by itself."[3] Or in Thomas Jefferson's words, the states are "the most competent administrations for our domestic concerns and the surest bulwarks against anti-republican tendencies."[4]

Thus, most of the federal government's "few and defined" powers are enumerated in Article I, Section 8, of the Constitution. Further cementing the principle, the Tenth Amendment makes clear that those powers not specifically granted to the federal government "are reserved to the States respectively, or to the people."

Despite such a carefully crafted constitutional framework, a certain amount of tension has always existed between competing state and federal centers of government authority, and the balance between federal and state governments has shifted back and forth throughout our nation's history. That balance shifted dramatically as a result of the Civil War, which clearly established the federal government as the dominant partner in the federal-state relationship. The Progressive Era sped the move toward federal power, with the national government greatly expanding its role in supporting and regulating commerce. However, it was Franklin Roosevelt and the New Deal that permanently altered the relationship between the states and the federal government.

Faced with the Great Depression, Roosevelt argued that a centralized response was required to deal with the national economic crisis. Many state governments were overwhelmed and nearly bankrupt. Therefore, the national government assumed authority over large areas of economic regulation and development that had previously been the states' domain, including labor relations and agriculture. In addition, Roosevelt established nationally based welfare systems, including Social Security and Aid to Dependent Children (the precursor to Aid to Families with Dependent Children and Temporary

Assistance for Needy Families). The courts initially rejected Roosevelt's New Deal programs, but his threat to pack the court by adding judges to the court until it voted his way shifted the balance and the Court ultimately reversed itself and approved the centralization under way.[5]

Since that time Congress has subjected virtually every area of American life to federal regulation. And if the basic concept of federalism needed something further to bury it, the Civil Rights era brought attempts by southern politicians to use "states' rights" as an excuse for Jim Crow and other racist policies. This approach was not in any sense true federalism. States never had the authority to contravene basic constitutional rights, and if any doubt existed, it has been clarified by the post–Civil War amendments. However, for many people federalism had been seriously tainted by the segregationists' attempt to co-opt federalism for their own illegitimate purposes.

Even so, conservatives have long fought the federal accumulation of power and sought to revive legitimate federalism. One can go all the way back to President Eisenhower, who complained that "the Federal Government has entered fields which, under our Constitution, are the primary responsibility of state and local governments," and appointed the Kestenbaum Commission to review federal-state relations.[6] Eisenhower might not have done much to actually reverse the accumulation of federal power, but federalism remained part of established Republican and conservative doctrine. Barry Goldwater campaigned on the idea that "Freedom depends on effective restraints against the accumulation of power in a single authority," and called on "the federal government to withdraw promptly and totally from every jurisdiction which the Constitution reserves to the states."[7]

Even Richard Nixon and Gerald Ford, hardly committed conservatives, paid lip service to the idea of federalism. But no post–World War II president was as dedicated to returning to the principles of federalism as Ronald Reagan. Reagan believed, "Federalism is rooted in the knowledge that our political liberties are best assured by limiting the size and scope of the national government."[8] Reagan's embrace of federalism, while imperfect, was a legitimate attempt to establish separate state and federal spheres of government. For example, Reagan would have had the federal government assume total responsibility for the Medicaid program, while making states responsible for welfare programs such as welfare and food stamps. He sought to cut back on federal involvement in education and called for abolishing the Department of Education. The number of federal grants to state and local governments declined from 434 when Reagan took office to a low of just 303 in 1982.

The Republicans who took control of Congress in 1994 were also committed federalists, at least rhetorically. Newt Gingrich promised, "We are committed to getting power back to the states."[9] And initially they moved somewhat in that direction. Republicans made attempts to give states more leeway in using federal funds. But much of what took place was actually a form of "faux federalism," where the federal government avoided direct involvement in areas that belonged to the states but managed to keep overall control through the use of federal grants.

These grants create the illusion of state control while actually allowing for increased federal control over state responsibilities. They have provided Congress with the added advantage of minimizing political controversy by, in effect, bribing state and local officials. In addition, federal grants provide a mechanism to redistribute funds from wealthier to poorer states or regions of the country.[10]

Grants, however, are inherently inefficient and wasteful. They require states to send money first to Washington through taxes; then after the federal government takes its cut, funds are allocated through political horse-trading, then returned to the states along with a long list of complex federal regulations. Moreover, the federal government requires a massive bureaucracy to administer the grant programs. Additional and often duplicative bureaucracies are frequently required at the state and local levels. To cite just one example, the federal anti-drug "weed and seed" program requires recipients to comply with some 1,300 pages of regulation.[11]

Federal grants also disperse oversight and responsibility in a way that encourages waste and abuse. Separation of the party funding a decision from the party making the decision makes little sense. The federal government escapes blame for poor use of its funds because those decisions are made at the state level. At the same time, states are able to avoid responsibility for their decisions because it's not "their" money.

One might expect that as a former governor, George W. Bush would have some appreciation for the principles of federalism.

Indeed, shortly after he was elected, Bush pledged to "make respect for federalism a priority in this administration."[12]

However, that has not been the case in practice. As researchers at the Rockefeller Institute have concluded, "Where it really counts, the Bush II administration has paid very little attention to the niceties of federalism and the role of governors and state governments."[13] The Bush administration has not really denied this conclusion. "We have moved from devolution, which was just pushing back as much power as possible to the states," acknowledges John Bridgeland, director of Bush's domestic policy council in the first term.[14]

The Bush approach to federalism has clearly reflected the influence and attitude of big-government conservatives. At a fundamental level, big-government conservatives are much more concerned with ends than means. Something as process oriented as federalism can't be allowed to get in the way of doing things that big-government conservatives believe need to be done. When *Weekly Standard* editor Fred Barnes was asked on *Fox News* about the propriety of conservatives seeking to override states' rights in the Terri Schiavo case, he responded: "Please! States' rights? Look, this is a moral issue."[15]

Furthermore, big-government conservatives believe that a powerful and encompassing federal government is vital to their plans for remaking society. After all, if "American purpose can find its voice only in Washington," power must reside in Washington, not 50 state capitals.[16]

The Bush administration's attitude toward federalism can be seen in its pursuit of legislation such as the No Child Left Behind Act (see Chapter 8). Today, more than 700 federal grant programs exist. They range from the massive Medicaid program, costing $177 billion per year, to tiny programs like the $59 million Boating Safety Financial Assistance grant or the $10 million Nursing Workforce Diversity grant.

Equally telling are the positions the Bush administration has taken before the Supreme Court. When the cases before the Court are largely administrative questions or when the positions taken by state governments are those with which the administration agrees, the administration willingly embraces federalism. But when states are defending practices that the administration disagrees with, federalist principles are quickly abandoned. In *Raich v. Ashcroft*, the Bush administration argued that the federal Controlled Substances Act trumped California's medical marijuana law (and similar laws of 10 other states).[17] California voters had clearly spoken on this issue, enacting a law permitting persons to grow or possess marijuana for medical use when recommended by a physician, through a referendum that attracted 56 percent of the vote. Similar legislation had also been passed twice by the California legislature (though vetoed by then governor Pete Wilson).

In the case in question, the marijuana was grown entirely as part of a cooperative of patients. No money changed hands. Nothing crossed state lines. Thus, any connection to interstate commerce was tangential at best. (Lawyers for the Justice Department argued that homegrown marijuana represented interstate commerce because the locally grown marijuana would affect "overall production" of the drug.) That the Court ultimately sided with the Bush administration does not change the incongruity of the administration's intervention. Law enforcement is by right a state concern.

Likewise in *Gonzales v. Oregon* the administration unsuccessfully sought to use federal regulations to overturn Oregon's law permitting physician-assisted suicide.[18] Oregon voters had twice passed referendums to enact this law, the last time with 60 percent of the vote. The Bush administration claimed that its interpretation of the Controlled Substances Act gave the U.S. attorney general the authority to contravene the Oregon law. As with law enforcement, the regulation of medical practices has traditionally been the responsibility of state governments. But in this case, as Oregon state lawyer Robert M. Atkinson pointed out in argument before the Court, "for the first time in our history . . . a single, unelected federal official has decided what is accepted in state medical practice."[19]

The point in these cases is not whether marijuana should be legal for medical purposes or whether Oregon's assisted-suicide law is good policy. In fact, in the *Raich* case, Alabama, Louisiana, and Mississippi, states with very tough drug laws, filed an amicus brief on behalf of the defendants.[20] They intervened because: "This is not a case about drug-control policy or fundamental rights. This is a case about 'our federalism,' which 'requires that Congress treat the States in a manner consistent with their status as residuary sovereigns and joint participants in the governance of the Nation.'"[21] These conservative states recognized that, as Justice Thomas argued in his dissent, "If Congress can regulate this under the Commerce

Clause, then it can regulate virtually anything and the Federal Government is no longer one of limited and enumerated powers."[22]

The Bush administration has not been acting alone in this area. Republicans in Congress have been willing accomplices in abandoning conservative principles on federalism. A few examples suffice to show their growing addiction to federal power.

In 1995, the Supreme Court struck down the Gun-Free School Zones Act on the grounds that the law, regulating gun possession in and around schools, did not affect interstate commerce. That was the first time in more than 60 years that the Court acknowledged limits to the federal commerce power. In his majority opinion, Chief Justice William Rehnquist wrote: "We start with first principles. The Constitution creates a Federal Government of enumerated powers." Associate Justice Clarence Thomas went even further in his concurring opinion in the five-to-four case:

> If we wish to be true to [the] Constitution . . . our Commerce Clause's boundaries simply cannot be "defined" as being "commensurate with the national needs" or self-consciously intended to let the Federal Government "defend itself against economic forces that Congress decrees inimical or destructive of the national economy." Such a formulation of federal power is no test at all: it is a blank check.[23]

The *Lopez* case should have provided Congress with an opportunity to revisit its abuse of its powers under the Commerce Clause. Instead, the reaction of Congress was simply to pass the Gun-Free School Zones Act again, this time adding some boilerplate language citing the impact on interstate commerce.

In the last few years, Congress passed an energy bill that would limit the ability of coastal states to challenge offshore oil and natural gas projects. As a bonus, the legislation prohibited states from requiring more energy-efficient ceiling fans. Conservatives in Congress have also been behind an immigration, proposal, called Real ID, that dictates how states can issue drivers' licenses, and to whom. The recent Terri Schiavo case set a new level of congressional involvement in an issue that historically has been handled by the states (see Chapter 10).

One of the more obvious examples of big-government conservatism's contempt for federalism can be seen in the pursuit by many members of Congress of a constitutional amendment outlawing gay marriage. Marriage law would appear to be the quintessential state issue. Much of the congressional rhetoric surrounding this issue involves criticism of "activist judges," who are purportedly frustrating the democratically expressed wishes of local voters.[24] Yet the actual language of the proposed amendment would not just overrule judges but also forbid state legislatures from ever authorizing same-sex marriages regardless of the desires of the state's voters.[25] In fact, the people of a state would be prohibited from recognizing same-sex marriages through ballot initiative, and no state could amend its own constitution to provide for the recognition of same-sex marriages. In short, democratic politics at the state level would simply be shut down on this issue, preempted by federal fiat.

In addition, many experts believe that the language would not just outlaw same-sex marriage, but also would prohibit marriage-like arrangements, such as domestic partnerships or civil unions that accord some of the benefits of marriage to same-sex couples.[26] As Dale Carpenter, a legal professor at the University of Minnesota, points out: "Whether states should recognize same-sex marriages is one question. Whether they should be permitted to recognize same-sex marriages is a separate question. A person who opposes same-sex marriage on policy grounds can and should also oppose a constitutional amendment foreclosing it."[27]

Separation of Powers

In addition to moving power from the states to the federal government, the Bush administration has also presided over an enormous shift of power from the legislative to the executive branch.

The Constitution sets up three separate, distinct, and co-equal branches of government. The Founding Fathers, tempered by their experience with a British monarchy that ignored the will of the people and exercised arbitrary power, were at great pains to prevent the accumulation of power in a central authority. "The accumulation of all power, legislative, executive, and judiciary . . . may justly be pronounced the very definition of tyranny," wrote James Madison in *Federalist 47*.[28]

The president's powers are spelled out in Article II of the Constitution and make clear that his role is to "see that the laws are faithfully executed." That role is distinct from the legislating role of Congress.

As Chief Justice Jackson pointed out in the case of *Youngstown Sheet & Tube Company vs. Sawyer* in 1952:

> In the framework of our Constitution, the President's power to see that the laws are faithfully executed refutes the idea that he is to be a lawmaker. The Constitution limits his functions in the lawmaking process to the recommending of laws he thinks wise and the vetoing of laws he thinks bad. And the Constitution is neither silent nor equivocal about who shall make laws which the President is to execute. The first section of the first article says "All legislative Powers herein granted shall be vested in a Congress of the United States. . . ." After granting many powers to the Congress, Article I goes on to provide that Congress may "make all Laws which shall be necessary and proper for carrying into Execution the foregoing Powers, and all other Powers vested by this Constitution in the Government of the United States, or in any Department or Officer thereof."[29]

Yet the Bush administration has repeatedly sought to bypass Congress and asserted presidential authority to determine if and how laws apply to the executive branch. The administration has refused to comply with laws that it has felt unduly restrict its prerogatives and has been willing to pursue its own interpretation of what laws mean, even if its interpretation is in contradiction to the interpretation of Congress. In doing so, the administration gives the executive branch de facto legislative authority.

The most obvious and contentious assertions of executive authority by the Bush administration have been on issues involving the war on terror, such as the administration's initiation of wiretaps in contravention of the Foreign Intelligence Surveillance Act.[30] Although such issues have ignited the most public (and congressional) outrage, these are also the areas where the administration has the strongest argument. The question of presidential authority over foreign policy and national defense is clearly unsettled.

However, the Bush administration has also sought to enhance executive authority on domestic issues. For example, President Bush has made widespread use of executive signing statements. Signing statements, a proclamation issued at the time a bill is signed to explain what the president understands to be the likely effects of the bill and how it fits with the administration's views or programs, are not really a new phenomenon. They date back at least to President

Andrew Jackson, who issued a statement objecting to portions of an internal improvements bill.[31] Ronald Reagan took the idea a step further, including his signing statements in the "legislative history" section of the *United States Code Congressional and Administrative News* so that they might be used in judicial interpretation of the law.[32] As constitutional law expert Neil Kinkopf has noted, "There is nothing inherently wrong with or controversial about signing statements."[33]

However, until George W. Bush, presidents tended to use signing statements sparingly. Ronald Reagan issued 71 such statements; President George H.W. Bush issued 146 in one term; and President Bill Clinton issued 105 over two terms.[34] In fact, all presidents prior to George W. Bush issued a total of 2,175 signing statements. But in just five years in office, Bush has issued more than 700 such statements, roughly one-third as many as all his predecessors combined.[35]

Moreover, "this administration has been much more systematic and much broader in scope" in signing statements, according to Phillip Cooper, professor of government administration at Portland State University, who has studied signing statements and other executive actions.[36] Most of Bush's predecessors used signing statements for largely symbolic purposes, recognizing and rewarding constituents, mobilizing public opinion behind a preferred policy or interpretation of the law, announcing a favored interpretation of a law's intent, or generally promoting public discourse.[37] However, Bush, almost uniquely, has used signing statements to "condemn a provision of the new law as unconstitutional and announce the President's refusal to enforce the unconstitutional provision."[38]

In particular, Bush's signing statements note that he will interpret the law in question "in a manner consistent with his constitutional authority to supervise the unitary executive branch." In fact, during his first term, President Bush issued signing statements using the term "unitary executive" 95 times.[39]

This phrase is particularly important because the concept of the unitary executive underlies much of the Bush administration's efforts to centralize power in the executive branch. The theory of the unitary executive essentially holds that the executive branch of government has the power to interpret the Constitution independent of the courts and Congress.[40] Furthermore, this authority means "presidents need not adhere to 'unconstitutional' acts of Congress

or to Supreme Court decisions."[41] In short, "the President legitimately may nullify statutes and court judgments by refusing to
enforce them, acting on the basis of his independent legal
judgment."[42]

Underlying this concept is the fact that the executive branch of
government is a single unit under the control of the president, and
that, therefore, the ability of the legislative or judicial branches to
instruct, manage, or otherwise interfere with the operations of executive agencies is extremely limited.[43]

As mentioned, the most high-profile examples of the Bush administration's asserting unified executive authority in the context of
signing statements have been when Congress has attempted to limit
presidential authority in the context of foreign affairs and the war
on terror. For example, when Congress passed an amendment to an
emergency Defense Department appropriations bill that prohibits
torture during the interrogation of suspected terrorists, President
Bush signed the bill, but issued the following signing statement:

> The executive branch shall construe Title X in Division A of
> the Act, relating to detainees, in a manner consistent with
> the constitutional authority of the President to supervise the
> unitary executive branch and as Commander in Chief and
> consistent with the constitutional limitations on the judicial
> power, which will assist in achieving the shared objective of
> the Congress and the President, evidenced in Title X, of
> protecting the American people from further terrorist
> attack.[44]

Although these actions have grabbed the lion's share of the head-
lines, nearly two-thirds of the Bush administration's signing statements have concerned domestic matters, not the war on terror.[45]
Most of these statements have been in reference to presidential
appointment powers or the executive branch's internal deliberations,
but they have also touched on legislative vetoes, federalism, and a
wide range of other areas where the president believes that Congress
has gone beyond its constitutional mandate.[46]

For example, in signing the Medicare prescription drug bill, the
president objected to two provisions, a requirement that the president and executive branch officials "submit to the Congress proposals for legislation" and the establishment of a Citizen's Health Care

Working Group, whose members would be appointed by the Comptroller General, but which would have access to information provided by executive departments. The president said that he would comply with those provisions only "as the President judges necessary and expedient."[47]

Other laws and provisions the Bush administration has declared itself free to ignore include affirmative-action provisions, requirements that the administration provide information about government activity to congressional oversight committees, whistle-blower protections for nuclear regulatory officials, and congressional attempts to override White House limits on federally funded research.[48]

The President's use of signing statements in this way appears to contravene the separation of powers as envisioned by the Founding Fathers. The Constitution, after all, provides a mechanism for the president to use if he believes that a law is unconstitutional—the veto.[49] And it provides a mechanism for Congress to then override that veto by a two-thirds vote. The Constitution does not provide for the president to veto only parts of a bill. In fact, the Supreme Court has ruled that attempts to pass a "line item veto," giving the president such power, were unconstitutional.[50]

An American Bar Association task force on presidential signing statements, which included several prominent conservative legal scholars, concluded that President Bush's use of the device was virtually unprecedented and represented a "serious assault on the constitutional system of checks and balances."[51] The association has recommended that Congress pass legislation calling for judicial review of presidential signing statements.[52]

In addition to his use of signing statements, President Bush has continued the practice of using executive orders to establish policy independent of Congress. The Bush administration's use of executive orders is hardly unprecedented, of course. Every American president since George Washington has used this device, despite the fact that the Constitution contains no explicit authority for the President to do so.

The Bush administration has actually issued fewer executive orders than some of its predecessors, notably the Clinton administration, where Paul Begala once commented on the practice by saying: "Stroke of the pen, law of the land. Kind of cool."[53] Still, many of the Bush administration's executive orders have had wide-ranging effect. They include executive orders authorizing warrantless wiretapping and creating military tribunals for trying suspected terrorists (a practice overturned by the Supreme Court in *Hamdan v. Rumsfeld*, discussed later in this chapter).

As with signing statements and other tools of "the unified executive," the Bush administration has not used executive orders only in regard to foreign policy or the war on terror. For example, President Bush has used a series of executive orders to allow faith-based organizations to receive federal funds (see Chapter 4). He has issued such orders despite that fact that Congress has repeatedly rejected legislation to accomplish this end. The president, then, is not just executing the laws but making them, in clear opposition to the expressed intent of the legislative branch.

Going even further, the administration has periodically asserted its authority to act even without a specific executive order. For example, the president asserts his power to designate a person as an "enemy combatant," which allows that person to be arrested and held incommunicado indefinitely. This action amounts to a suspension of the writ of habeas corpus, the fundamental right of an accused individual to receive a hearing before an impartial judge. The Constitution grants the power to suspend habeas corpus solely to Congress, and only under extraordinary circumstances.[54] Yet the Bush administration asserts that such authority is inherent in the president's powers as commander in chief.[55] The Bush administration asserts similar authority in its position in National Security Agency wiretapping.[56]

The Supreme Court rebuked this theory of unlimited inherent presidential power in the case of *Hamdan v. Rumsfeld*. In that case, the Bush administration asserted the authority to establish special military courts to try suspected terrorists. The administration not only took this action without authorization from Congress, but it also actually rejected attempts by Congress to pass legislation authorizing the process. However, in a five-to-three decision, the Supreme Court rejected the Bush administration's claims and held that the tribunals were illegal because they were not "expressly authorized by any congressional act."[57] Although this case applied to only one particular attempt to assert executive power, it makes clear the Court's belief that presidential power does have limits.

Congress occasionally complains about presidential inroads on its authority but has done little to stop it. In part, this inaction is an outgrowth of the increased partisanship that has poisoned the atmosphere in Congress. As Thomas Mann and Norman Ornstein argue in their book, *The Broken Branch*, "members of the majority party, including the leaders of Congress, see themselves as field lieutenants in the president's army far more than they do as members of a separate and independent branch of government."[58] Because support for the president was seen as a test of party loyalty, "the uncompromising assertion of executive authority by President Bush and Vice President Cheney was met with a whimper, not a principled fight, by the Republican Congress."[59]

But Congress's failure to rein in executive authority is not just one of omission. Indeed, in many ways Congress has been complicit by delegating its lawmaking power to executive agencies. Frequently, Congress passes laws establishing broad policy goals but leaving the details up to administrative agencies. From Congress's viewpoint, this method has the advantage of allowing Congress to claim it supports some sort of noble goal, such as clean air, while letting the executive departments deal with the often unpopular tradeoffs and costs of meeting those goals. This sleight-of-hand leaves Congress free to claim credit for meeting, or trying to meet, the goal, while blaming the bureaucracy for failure or for unpopular decisions. In doing so, Congress not only is avoiding its responsibility but also is flying in the face of the constitutional requirement that only Congress can legislate.

Moreover, delegation sets up a process that almost inevitably leads to bigger government. Under the ordinary legislative process, new laws must achieve something of a consensus among a majority of legislators with differing viewpoints from two different legislative bodies and then also be approved by the president. As James Madison noted, this process was designed to be sufficiently difficult as to restrict the "facility and excess of law-making."[60] However, delegation establishes a more streamlined process, requiring a far less broad-based consensus.

In addition, by narrowing the locus of lawmaking power, delegation eases the way for special interests to assert their influence. Ordinarily, a group seeking to pass or change a law must obtain the consent of two different legislative bodies (the House and Senate) and the president. The Founding Fathers deliberately created this high bar to legislative action, ensuring that at least a reasonably broad consensus would exist before a new law could be passed. Narrow special interests or factions would find this hurdle particularly steep.

Delegation, however, by shifting the lawmaking power to a single executive agency, lowers the bar. Special interests must now gain the consent of only a single agency or bureaucrat. At the same time, by shifting lawmaking from Congress to the far less transparent bureaucracy, delegation increases the difficulty for the average citizen to have his or her input heard. Pleading your case before an agency often requires access, special legal counsel, expert witnesses, and other facilities beyond the capability of average Americans. Moreover, agency proceedings often take place behind closed doors, outside the scrutiny of the media. There are no C-SPAN cameras. Average Americans, without the ability to carefully monitor these proceedings, may not even be aware of what is taking place. The traditional legislative problem of concentrated benefits and diffuse costs becomes even more acute.

Finally, delegation effectively expands the number of potential lawmakers. David Schoenbroad and Jerry Taylor pointed out in the *Cato Handbook for Congress* that Congress's ability to legislate is limited by time and numbers, but delegation "dramatically expands the realm of the possible by effectively 'deputizing' tens of thousands of bureaucrats, often with a broad and imprecise mission to 'go forth and legislate.'"[61] Writing in *The New Republic*, Jacob Weisberg summed it up this way: "As a labor saving device, delegation did for legislators what the washing machine did for the 1950s housewife. Government could now penetrate every nook and cranny of American life in a way that was simply impossible before."[62]

The Push for Power

In their brilliantly concise analysis of the Bush presidency's constitutional record, Cato Institute scholars Gene Healy and Tim Lynch conclude, "The pattern that emerges is one of a ceaseless push for power, unchecked by either the courts or Congress, one, in short, of disdain for constitutional limits."[63] In the Bush administration's opinion, no limitation on or division of governing power exists; it all resides in the unified executive.

But the Bush administration has had an active accomplice in Congress. Not only has Congress failed to do anything meaningful to

195

check the accumulation of power in the executive branch, but also it has consistently disregarded federalist principles to shift power from the states to the federal government. Surveying the record of growing presidential power, conservative legal scholar Bruce Fein has warned of "an attempt by the president to have the final word on his own constitutional powers, which eliminates the checks and balances that keep the country a democracy. There is no way for an independent judiciary to check his assertions of power, and Congress isn't doing it, either. So this is moving us toward an unlimited executive power."[64]

This outcome is not accidental. Big-government conservatism seeks an "active," "dynamic," "strong" government. That requires the centralization of power. "National greatness" cannot take place in 50 state capitals. That is why big-government conservatives say, "Ultimately American purpose can find its voice only in Washington."[65]

But as power moves increasingly from the states to the federal government and from the legislative to the executive branches within the federal government, we confront exactly the sort of concentration of power that the Founding Fathers warned against. As James Madison put it in *Federalist 48*, "An elective despotism was not the government we fought for; but one in which the powers of government should be so divided and balanced among the several bodies of magistracy as that no one could transcend their legal limits without being effectually checked and restrained by the others."[66]

10. National Busybodies

As mentioned in Chapter 9, the federal government was set up to have only a few, enumerated powers. In particular, as Alexander Hamilton noted in *Federalist 17*, "The ordinary administration of criminal and civil justice" was a state, not a federal, responsibility.[1]

For big-government conservatives, however, no issue is too small, too personal, or too far removed from Congress's constitutional authority. In fact, sometimes any issue that hits the television news seems to become an issue that must be addressed by the federal government. And like busybodies everywhere, Congress can't help peering in our windows and telling us how to live our lives.

For example, lately Congress has taken a tremendous interest in professional sports. In 2005, both the House and Senate held hearings about whether baseball players were using steroids. When Major League Baseball owners suggested that Congress had no authority to investigate steroid use, committee chairman Tom Davis (R-VA) responded breezily that his committee "may at any time conduct investigations of any matter," a notion that while technically accurate implies an unlimited congressional reach. Besides, Davis noted: "Baseball is not just a business. It's been decreed by the courts as the national pastime."[2]

Why steroids in baseball rise to the level of federal government concern is unclear. Baseball is, after all, a private enterprise. No threat exists to public health or safety. If anyone has broken any laws, state and federal prosecutors are free to prosecute them. The best explanation Congress could muster was Sen. John McCain's (R-AZ) statement that, "fans are outraged."[3] And if anyone in America is outraged, congressional action is apparently warranted.

But if baseball fans are outraged, they can stop attending games, hurting owners where it hurts most—in the wallet. Fear of alienating potential customers provides ample incentive for baseball to develop a satisfactory steroid policy. And if fans choose to keep attending games, then they aren't as outraged as Senator McCain thinks.

But Congress couldn't wait for baseball to act. So we were treated to the sight of current and former baseball players sitting like prisoners in the dock, or mafia chieftains, being grilled by outraged members of Congress in front of the television cameras on an issue that has absolutely nothing to do with federal constitutional responsibilities. As a *National Review* editorial put it, this display was "the worst sort of congressional grandstanding."[4] Not unexpectedly the hearings provided nothing new. The steroids scandal had been building for years and baseball, responding to fan pressure, had already adopted a stricter testing policy. Yet Congress felt the issue of such importance that it held not one, but two rounds of hearings.

Switching from baseball to football, Sen. Arlen Specter (R-PA) suggested that the Senate Judiciary Committee, which he chairs, investigate the Philadelphia Eagles' treatment of wide receiver Terrell Owens, who was suspended after a series of altercations with coaches and teammates.[5] And Rep. Joe Barton (R-TX), chairman of the House Energy and Commerce Committee, called a hearing to investigate the "deeply flawed" Bowl Championship Series that determines a national college football champion.[6]

Although almost any peccadillo can catch Congress's interest, much of its time seemed to be focused on regulating the lives of average citizens—determining what we see, say, and do. For example, indecency, a frequent target of the Religious Right, was a routine subject of hearings and legislation. In 2006, Congress passed legislation that increased the maximum fine that the Federal Communications Commission could impose for violating its standards of decency from $32,500 to as much as $500,000.[7]

One can at least argue that the "public airwaves" and the interstate reach of television and radio make this topic constitutionally proper for congressional interest. But one might also suggest that parents and others who are concerned about indecency can change the channel or turn off the set. After all, relatively few complaints about indecency are actually made to those government agencies charged with policing radio and television. Not only have the number of indecency complaints fallen by roughly half since 2002, but *Media-Week* reports that 99.8 percent of all complaints to the Federal Communications Commission come from a single organization, the Parents Television Council.[8]

Some in Congress have suggested extending indecency regulation to cable television and satellite radio.[9] Going even further, Rep. James

Sensenbrenner (R-WI) has suggested applying criminal penalties for cable and satellite executives who permit the broadcast of indecent material.[10] Thus, HBO executives could potentially be jailed for broadcasting *The Sopranos*. Yet cable and satellite programming operate by subscription. Individuals who are offended by *The Sopranos* or Howard Stern can simply refuse to purchase the programming.

Of course, obscenity has long been something of an obsession with big-government conservatives. Attorney General Alberto Gonzales once said that fighting pornography was as important a priority for the Justice Department as fighting terrorism.[11] But Congress also found time to address other aspects of radio and television, such as the previously neglected issue of whether the Nielsen ratings are accurate. "It's impossible to achieve a high quality of broadcasting if shoddy audience measurement practices are permitted to proliferate," worried Sen. Conrad Burns (R-MT).[12]

Congress also voted to save us from the scourge of online poker. Approximately 23 million Americans have played poker online, betting an estimated $6 billion each year.[13] For most this activity is simply a healthy diversion or hobby. But anti-gambling activists argue that the Internet makes gambling too easy, resulting in gambling addictions and financial problems. Following a six-year campaign, the House voted in 2006 to ban online poker.[14] When the Senate did not quickly follow suit, Majority Leader Bill Frist (R-TN) added the poker ban to a bill authorizing U.S. military operations, including those in Iraq and Afghanistan.[15]

Actually, because nearly all Internet gambling sites are set up overseas where they are not subject to U.S. law, what Congress actually did was prohibit U.S. credit card companies from processing payments by people in the United States to online gambling sites.[16] In addition, law enforcement officials can order Internet service providers to block access to gambling sites. That provision will almost certainly be tested in the courts.

Once upon a time, conservatives like Barry Goldwater and Ronald Reagan told the government to "leave us alone." Today, big-government conservatives criticize the "destructive mind-set" of "an approach with no higher goal, no nobler purpose, than 'Leave us alone.'"[17]

Paternalism, Soft and Hard

Big-government conservatives' zeal for meddling in our lives is an outgrowth of a paternalistic philosophy that is deeply ingrained in the movement. In Chapter 4, we saw how big-government conservatives happily embraced paternalism as a component of welfare reform. However, in their view, not just the poor make "bad" decisions about their lives, but all of us.

Thus, we need government to nudge us in the right direction, be it through sin or vice taxes, public relations campaigns, or in some cases, outright prohibitions on substances or behavior. Sometimes this nudging is done with the tools of "hard paternalism," where some things are banned and others mandated. Other times the method of choice is "soft paternalism," where government attempts "to skew your decisions, without infringing greatly on your freedom of choice."[18] David Brooks, for example, has explicitly called for a moral and order-imposing authoritarianism aimed at providing "moral guardrails" for the untrustworthy masses.[19]

Their first choice is a sort of soft paternalism, but inside the velvet glove lurks the steel fist. Perhaps Newt Gingrich best exemplified the essence of big-government conservatism when he said government should "incentivize healthy behavior through rewards and prizes; when all else fails, mandate."[20]

Conservative paternalists often justify their proposals on the basis of externalities. That is, private behavior has consequences that affect society at large and affect us all in the long run. Yet nearly every social indicator of concern to conservatives is actually improving. Teen pregnancy is no longer rising and teens generally are waiting longer to have sex.[21] Crime rates are falling.[22] Divorce is down and marriages are healthier than they were in the 1970s and 1980s.[23] High school dropout rates are down, albeit modestly.[24] Even abortion rates are declining.[25]

Moreover, these trends have been improving since at least the early 1990s, the very time that has seen all of the culture-coarsening changes so frequently decried by conservatives: increased acceptance of homosexuality, widespread availability of pornography and gambling, and so on. This is not to argue one way or the other whether such cultural changes are desirable, but it does raise serious questions about whether government paternalism is justified on behavioral grounds, let alone constitutional ones.

Paternalists also argue that they are not really infringing on our freedoms because they are only "help[ing] you make the choices you would make for yourself—if only you had the strength of will and the sharpness of mind.''[26] Of course, one might ask exactly how the paternalists know what choices we would make for ourselves. Both liberal and conservative paternalists assume either universal consensus exists on the choices we should make, or their ideological side will always be the one with the power to make the choices. The reality is not nearly so neat, but once established the precedents are difficult to refute. Thus, *New York Times* writer Daniel Akst can slide seamlessly from applauding the congressional ban on Internet gambling to advocating a higher gasoline tax.[27]

An assumption is also made that the motives of the paternalists will always be pure, uninfluenced by rent-seeking special interests or politics. Nevertheless, more than half the members of the House Judiciary Committee, which drafted the ban on Internet gambling, are from states where casino gambling is legal, or from Florida, which allows casino gambling on cruise ships. Why then was Internet gambling singled out? In fact, the bill didn't even ban all Internet gambling. Internet betting on horseracing was exempted, as were state lotteries. Were casino interests and racetracks, which helped fund an anti-Internet gambling lobbying push, possibly interested in restricting their competition?

In addition, conservative paternalists appear to believe that somehow government is capable of developing and executing the precisely calibrated level of incentives and penalties that will make people behave in the way they want. Given the frequent failures of government to carry out its most basic tasks—remember FEMA?—there seems little reason to believe that it is capable of dealing with the myriad complexities of human motivation and behavior. From welfare to prohibition, government intervention has not only failed but also brought a host of unintended consequences, often worse than the problems it attempted to solve.[28]

Finally, government paternalism only increases the infantilization of the American public. Charles Murray famously wrote that you can't expect vibrant, healthy, active communities if you don't give them anything to do.[29] By the same token, you can't expect people to act like responsible adults if you don't let them make decisions in their lives (and take responsibility for the consequences of those decisions).

Conservatives were often the first to point out the problems that developed when modern liberals sought to protect people from the consequences of bad decisions. But rather than restoring those consequences, big-government conservatives appear to want to eliminate the choices. Perhaps we should expect no different when we have a president who "sees America as we think about a 10-year-old child."[30]

Debates will always occur among conservatives over where to draw the line in regulating personal behavior. More-traditionalist conservatives will be more favorably inclined toward such restrictions than are libertarians. But neither would be supportive of turning the federal government into a sort of national nanny, with Congress pursuing its every notion and whim at our expense.

The Schiavo Travesty

Perhaps no better example exists of big-government conservatism's willingness to ignore constitutional restraints and intervene in personal decisions than the tragic case of Terri Schiavo.

In 1990, 29-year-old Terri Schiavo collapsed from unexplained causes. She experienced both respiratory and cardiac arrest and was in a coma for roughly 10 weeks. Although she eventually emerged from the full coma, she never regained cognitive function and in 1993 was diagnosed as being in a "persistent vegetative state," that is, a state of wakefulness without detectable awareness. Medical professionals indicated that the prolonged period without oxygen had led to severe brain damage, particularly to the parts of the brain concerned with cognition, perception, and awareness.

Five years later, her husband and guardian, Michael Schiavo, petitioned the courts to remove her gastric feeding tube, claiming that it was Terri's wish that she not be kept alive by artificial means. (She had not left a living will or other directive.) Terri's parents, Robert and Mary Schindler, opposed Michael's decision. Thus began seven years of litigation, including 14 appeals and numerous motions, petitions, and hearings in the Florida courts, plus five suits in federal district court and two appeals to the U.S. Supreme Court. Those courts consistently found in favor of Michael Schiavo, and on March 18, 2005, the feeding tube was removed.[31]

At that point Congress leapt to intervene. Bill Frist, despite having never examined Terri Schiavo, nevertheless diagnosed her by looking at a videotape and concluded she was not in a persistent vegetative state.[32] (An autopsy subsequent to Schiavo's death showed that

Frist was, in fact, wrong.)[33] In record time, Congress met in executive session and passed legislation ordering a new federal court review of the case.[34] President Bush interrupted his vacation in Texas and flew to Washington to sign the bill on March 21.[35]

The Schiavo legislation violated almost every possible constitutional and conservative principle. First, the bill was not general legislation dealing with how states or federal courts should handle end-of-life issues; rather, it was aimed at a particular individual and at overturning a particular judicial decision. The legislation even stated that any findings of the court would not have precedential value. As such it comes painfully close to both a bill of attainder and an ex post facto law, both of which are constitutionally forbidden.[36]

As James Madison wrote in *Federalist 44*, "Bills of attainder, ex post facto laws, and laws impairing the obligations of contracts, are contrary to the first principles of the social compact, and to every principle of sound legislation."[37] The Supreme Court took particular note of the importance of this provision in *Brown v. United States* (1965), stating, "The Bill of Attainder Clause was intended not as a narrow, technical (and therefore soon to be outmoded) prohibition, but rather as an implementation of the separation of powers, a general safeguard against legislative exercise of the judicial function or more simply—trial by legislature."[38]

Second, Terri's Law ran roughshod over the separation of powers, even within the federal government, hopelessly blurring judicial and legislative functions. The questions in this case were not matters of policy, but questions of fact and law. As such, they were matters for the courts and had been repeatedly considered by both federal and state courts. In fact, the Schiavo legislation did not even attempt to set a broad policy. Rather, it simply ordered a new court hearing and then set a particular legal standard for that hearing, a de novo review. (A de novo review requires the court to consider the matter anew, the same as if it had not been heard before and as if no decision previously had been rendered.) Yet Congress has no power to issue injunctions in specific cases; that role is solely the judiciary's.

Third, it violated any concept of federalism. Issues such as family law, marriage, legal guardianship, and medical treatment are quintessential *state* issues. Nowhere in Congress's enumerated powers is authority given for the federal government to involve itself in such issues. As former representative Bob Barr points out, "To simply say that the 'culture of life,' or whatever you call it means that we don't have to pay attention to the principles of federalism or separation of powers is certainly not a conservative viewpoint."[39]

Finally, the attempt to force the case back into federal court reeks of the type of forum shopping that conservatives have often decried in medical malpractice or product liability cases. One side doesn't like the state court's decision, so attempts are made to move it to federal court in the hope that a different judge will give the losing side the result it wants. Moreover, as Erwin Chemerinsky of Duke Law School points out:

> Article III of the Constitution clearly limits the circumstances in which federal courts may be involved and this fits in none of the categories where federal court review is allowed. There is no question arising under federal law presented by the Schiavo case; nor does the case involve citizens of different states or any other basis for federal jurisdiction.[40]

Charles Fried, solicitor general under President Reagan, summed it up this way: "In their intervention in the Terri Schiavo matter, Republicans in Congress and President Bush have, in a few brief legislative clauses, embraced the kind of free-floating judicial activism, disregard for orderly procedure and contempt for the integrity of state processes that they quite rightly have denounced and sought to discipline for decades."[41]

None of these arguments seemed to matter to big-government conservatives. For them, the Schiavo case was a clear case of the ends justifying the means. As columnist Jim Pinkerton put it, "The social-issue core of the newly energized, southernized, and Christianized Republican party cares a lot more about its faith and its values than about the old verity of small government."[42]

PART III

DEFINING THE FUTURE

Are you willing to spend time studying the issues, making yourself aware, and then conveying that information to family and friends? Will you resist the temptation to get a government handout for your community? Realize that the doctor's fight against socialized medicine is your fight. We can't socialize the doctors without socializing the patients. Recognize that government invasion of public power is eventually an assault upon your own business. If some among you fear taking a stand because you are afraid of reprisals from customers, clients, or even government, recognize that you are just feeding the crocodile hoping he'll eat you last.

—Ronald Reagan

11. The Small-Government Alternative

As George Will has pointed out, conservatives, above all, should be realists:

> Which in government means modesty in your expectations of what government can do. Most of us do not just understand the law of unintended consequences; most of us are what we are because of that law. Which is of course that the unintended consequences of large government actions are apt to be larger than and contrary to the intended actions.[1]

We have more than a century of experience to show that ever bigger, ever more expensive, ever more intrusive government simply doesn't work. Big government has not eliminated or even significantly reduced poverty. It has not made our health care or retirement systems better. It has not improved education. It has not solved any of the myriad problems our society faces. Indeed, more often than not it has made those problems worse.

But equally important, big government comes at a big cost. This cost most obviously shows in reduced economic growth, fewer jobs, reduced take-home pay, and less overall prosperity. In an era of globalization, when Americans must compete on an international basis, taxation and regulation act as an anchor on American productivity and competitiveness. The resources that government extracts from the private sector to pay for itself are resources that are not available for the private sector to use in producing more goods and services. When the federal government takes money out of our pockets, we have less money to spend or save. When the federal government takes money from business, it has less money to use for investment, research, or payroll.

Equally important is the cost to business of complying with our dizzyingly complex tax system. Those costs may exceed $265 billion every year. Businesses bear most of this burden, spending as much as $148 billion in compliance costs. In 2005, American workers and businesses were forced to spend more than 6 billion man-hours figuring out their taxes and filing the paperwork. Putting this burden in perspective, the cost of complying with the federal tax code nearly matches the entire annual revenue of Wal-Mart ($285 billion), the second-largest corporation in America. And it is getting worse. By 2007, compliance costs are expected to surpass $480 billion.[2]

We should also recognize that taxation is a penalty on the activity being taxed. Thus taxing an activity, any activity, will reduce the level of that activity.[3] This logic is behind such policies as raising cigarette taxes to discourage smoking, but it applies equally to the impact of taxes on business decisions. Tax investment and investment will decline. Tax employment and there will be fewer employees. Tax corporate profits and businesses will be fewer.

Putting all of this together, government taxation creates a dead-weight loss of between 20 and 60 cents for every dollar of revenue raised.[4] That is, $1.00 in taxes costs the economy somewhere between $1.20 and $1.60. To cite just one example, Richard Vedder of the University of Ohio estimates that for every additional 1 percent of gross domestic product (GDP) devoted to government employment programs, unemployment *increases* by 1.3 percent.[5] Jagadeesh Gokhale has estimated that Social Security has reduced GDP by 1.1 percent from what it would have been without the cost of this program.[6]

Second, big government distracts us from the most important job of government—protecting us. America today faces a mortal threat from enemies that want to destroy us. At the same time, any number of government studies have shown not only that the 9/11 terrorist attacks were the result of a massive failure of government security effort, but also that we are still unprepared for a similar attack today.

In the months before the 9/11 attacks, one of the Bush administration's highest priority was passing the No Child Left Behind Act. On the day of the attack, President Bush was in a Florida classroom, promoting a reading program. The Constitution says that one of the purposes of the federal government is to "provide for the common defense." The Constitution says nothing about federal education programs. The time, money, and effort spent on those things that the federal government should not be involved with reduces the time, money, and effort available to keep us safe from attack.

Third, big government undermines the "bourgeois virtues" that are necessary to a democratic and civil society. Big-government conservatives believe that government can make us virtuous. In reality, the opposite is true. When government assumes more and more responsibility for our lives, less and less reason exists for us to be virtuous. We are, in effect, protected from the consequences of nonvirtuous behavior. The results are readily apparent. As government has grown, our society has become less likely to work and save, more intemperate and less concerned with the consequences of our actions, less self-reliant, and even less compassionate toward others.

Finally, and most important, big government is antithetical to freedom. Every new government program reduces our freedom just a little bit more. We are less free to manage our own lives, to decide for ourselves how to spend our money, to go into business, to plan for our retirement, to take care of our health, or to educate our children. As Ronald Reagan so correctly pointed out: "Man is not free unless government is limited. . . . As government expands, liberty contracts."[7]

Conservatives should remember Goldwater's aphorism that "A government big enough to give you everything you want is also big enough to take away everything you have."[8] That also applies to a government big enough to give conservatives everything they want.

In short, little is good about big government—conservative or otherwise.

Conservatives Need to Return to First Principles

First and foremost of these principles is a return to constitutional government.

Ronald Reagan once noted: "Almost all the world's Constitutions are documents in which governments tell the people what their privileges are. Our Constitution is a document in which 'We the people' tell the government what it is allowed to do." The Constitution is a document that established a federal government of delegated, enumerated, and limited powers. In fact, the Constitution is very specific about the powers granted to the federal government.[9] Those powers not granted to the federal government "are reserved to the States respectively, or to the people."[10] One can search the Constitution from first word to last and find no authority for Congress to involve itself in education, welfare, agriculture, health care, retirement, the arts, marriage law, or whether baseball players take steroids. Setting aside practical questions, we should recognize that for the federal government to involve itself in areas that are not within the scope of its enumerated powers is illegitimate.

Of course, on a practical level, no one expects the vast edifice of federal extra-constitutional power to be dismantled overnight. Still, upon taking office, both members of Congress and the president take an oath in which they swear to uphold the Constitution. At the very least, conservatives should approach new legislative proposals by asking where the constitutional authority to act is found.

On an even deeper level, conservatives must rededicate themselves to the ideas of limited government that animated the Constitution. As Thomas Jefferson said, "the sum of good government" is "a wise and frugal government, which shall restrain men from injuring one another, shall leave them otherwise free to regulate their own pursuits of industry and improvement, and shall not take from the mouth of labor the bread it has earned."[11] Government is a necessary evil that exists for the purpose of securing our rights.

The Founding Fathers didn't invent the idea of limited government from whole cloth. They were building on a long history of human struggle for liberty. They understood that from the biblical warning to the Israelites about the power of kings to Aristotle's explorations of a higher natural law; from the early struggle between church and state to the growth of civil society and self-governing towns in Medieval Europe; from Magna Carta to Cromwell to the Glorious Revolution of 1689; and from the Enlightenment to the writings of Adam Smith and John Locke, a conflict has existed between those who would impose their control over others and those who pursued freedom for individuals to live according to their own beliefs and desires.

This history and these ideas should animate conservatism today. Simply put, conservatism should start from a premise of individual autonomy, responsibility, and worth. This principle is what the Declaration of Independence captured when it declares "all men are created equal" and have rights to "life, liberty, and the pursuit of happiness." Every American—indeed, every person—is born free and equal, with an equal natural or God-given right to live their lives as they see fit, so long as they take responsibility for their choices and respect the rights of others, what Barry Goldwater called "the maximum amount of freedom for individuals that is consistent with the maintenance of social order."[12] This vision stands in stark contrast to both modern liberalism and big-government conservatism that see government as the shaper of society that both solves our problems and guides our morals.

The Cato Institute's founder, Ed Crane, has made the point that nearly all politics boils down to the simple question of "who decides?" Do you decide what school your child goes to or does Congress? Do you decide how to spend your money or does the government? Who picks what charities you will support, which doctor you will see, or what your retirement investments will be? In short, who decides how you will live your life? When faced with these questions, conservatives should come down firmly on the side of the individual.

Or, to sum it up as did Barry Goldwater, "For the American Conservative, there is no difficulty in identifying the day's overriding political challenge: it is to preserve and extend freedom."[13]

Political Prospects

But can a small-government agenda succeed politically? Big-government conservatives are quick to point out that despite the best efforts of small-government conservatives, government continues to grow. Fred Barnes claims:

> The possibility of smaller government has been tested twice in the past quarter century, first with the Reagan Revolution following the 1980 election, and then with the Gingrich Revolution after 1994. Both revolutions led to a single year of spending cuts, then a return to sizable annual increases, with departments and agencies targeted for extinction still intact.[14]

Even many believers in small government seem to accept the impossibility of actually cutting government. For example, Bruce Bartlett has argued that "given the extreme difficulty of making even miniscule changes in the growth path of federal spending," it is time to consider raising taxes to bring the budget into balance.[15]

First, little evidence indicates that big-government conservatism is more politically popular than its small-government competitor. The big-government conservatism of George W. Bush and the current Congress led to electoral disaster. Although the 2006 election results can certainly be blamed in part on Iraq, scandal, and traditional voter uneasiness in the sixth year of a two-term presidency,

211

the magnitude of the Republican loss clearly reflects a wider discontent. Not only did an embrace of big government fail to save the Republican majority, it likely undercut Republican efforts. Without a principled conservative difference between Republicans and Democrats, many voters had no reason to look beyond the war or the scandals. Republicans were forced to run negative, largely issueless campaigns, attacking opponents over trivialities such as whether an opponent once included racy sex scenes in a novel that he wrote.[16] Beyond being merely sleazy, such campaigns will neither motivate voters nor help build a conservative governing agenda.

Second, Barnes is wrong when he says, "Reagan and Gingrich failed for lack of public support."[17] In fact, in 1996 after two years of the most small-government-oriented Congress in recent history, Republicans gained two seats in the Senate and lost only two seats in the House. These results came in the face of Bill Clinton's overwhelming reelection as president and the fact that Republicans had to defend an enormous number of freshman House seats that had been narrowly won in 1994. In fact, those Republicans who were among the most hard-core budget cutters were reelected by even larger margins than they had received in 1994. Many of these members were specifically targeted for defeat and some were running in districts that Bill Clinton carried. Tom Coburn, for example, won by 10 percentage points while Bill Clinton carried his district by 7.[18] Even Linda Killian of National Public Radio, who chronicled the 1994 freshmen Republicans, concluded that no backlash occurred against Republican attempts to reduce the size of government.[19]

After the 1996 elections, Republicans began turning away from their government-cutting agenda. A steady erosion of electoral support followed, culminating in the debacle of 2006. As former House majority leader Dick Armey points out, the Republican defeat of 2006 was not a "repudiation of the conservative legacy that drove the Reagan presidency and created the Contract with America. To the contrary, it [represents] a rejection of big-government conservatism."[20]

Nor is it completely clear that Reagan and the House Republicans of 1994 failed. Certainly, they were far less successful in reducing the size of government than one might have hoped. Yet how much larger might government have grown in their absence?

Regardless of whether small-government conservatives were or could have been successful in the past, the question remains of

Figure 11.1
THE SUPPORT FOR SMALLER OR BIGGER GOVERNMENT

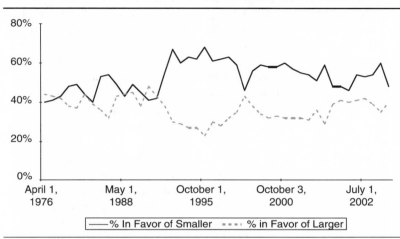

SOURCE: American Enterprise Institute, "Attitudes Toward the Federal Government."

whether a small-government agenda could succeed today. We are living in a time of both international and domestic insecurity. Dan Casse says that "reducing the size of government no longer resonates with Americans as it once did."[21] And in the population at large there may be "less popular fear of bureaucrats possessing too much control than of ungoverned forces surging out of control," as David Brooks claims.[22]

Yet public opinion polls still show that a majority of Americans say they would prefer smaller government. Since the mid-1970s, the *New York Times, CBS News, Washington Post, ABC News,* and independent pollster Scott Rasmussen have all asked voters whether they preferred "a smaller government providing fewer services" or "a bigger government providing more services." As Figure 11.1 shows, Americans have consistently supported smaller government.[23]

Moreover, support for smaller government cuts across demographic and partisan lines. Predictably 79 percent of Republicans prefer smaller government, but surprisingly so do 53 percent of Democrats (according to the most recent polling results). Even majorities of traditionally less-than-conservative categories such as women

213

(62 percent), young people (52 percent), and minorities (52 percent) favor smaller government.[24] Other polls show that by a two-to-one margin, voters believe that big government is a greater threat than big business.[25] In fact, even as Democrats were heading to victory in 2006, a CNN poll showed that by a 54 to 37 percent margin, Americans thought that government was trying to do too many things that should be left to individuals and businesses.[26] Overwhelmingly they preferred small government. This poll also showed that 72 percent of Americans thought that government had gotten bigger during the Bush administration, which may help explain Republican electoral misfortunes.[27]

Of course people may be more favorably inclined toward specific government programs than they are to big government in the abstract. But when they have the opportunity to vote directly on the size of government, they fairly consistently choose smaller government. Consider that as recently as 2002, 47 percent of voters in Massachusetts, arguably the most liberal state in the nation and home to both John Kerry and Ted Kennedy, voted in favor of a proposal to abolish the state income tax.[28] Across the country, in fact, tax-cutting initiatives nearly always pass, even in liberal states.

Those still unconvinced might say that tax cuts are easy to pass. People have always objected to paying for the government programs they otherwise want. That's a fair point. But voters also appear reluctant to approve more spending. For example, in 2006, voters in California, another solidly liberal state, defeated a universal preschool initiative by a 61 to 30 percent margin and turned down other spending initiatives. This outcome led even liberal columnist E. J. Dionne to bemoan the fact that "there remains a deep skepticism about government spending, even for the best of purposes . . . Attacks on tax-and-spend sound old and tired, but they still have force."[29]

Clearly a potent political force in favor of limited government still exists. According to Gallup polls, about 20 percent of Americans consider themselves libertarians.[30] That is, they seek smaller government on both economic and personal issues. A Pew survey puts the number of libertarians lower, at just 9 percent, but only because they classify most Americans (42 percent) as ambivalent, having no particular political philosophy.[31] However, this reasoning understates the small-government constituency because many, if not most, of those who identify themselves simply as conservative (27 percent in the Gallup survey and 15 percent according to Pew) favor smaller government as well, especially at the federal level.

In many ways, big-government conservatives are showing their contempt for voters. Dick Armey tells the story of a Republican member of Congress who approached him during the debate over welfare reform. "I know this is the right thing to do," the member said, "but my constituents just won't understand." Armey replied, "So you're telling me they are smart enough to elect you, but not smart enough to understand this?"[32]

Besides, American voters tend to like politicians who stand for something, even if they disagree with what that something is. That is the reason why "flip-flopper" was such a devastating charge against John Kerry in the 2004 election.

Republicans, of course, might worry that taking a consistently limited government position might cost them some support from religious or populist conservatives. But such fears are likely overblown. Religious conservatives are unlikely to defect to the more overtly hostile Democrats, particularly if Republicans advocate federalist principles (see below) that allow states and localities to deal with social and cultural issues. In fact, Republicans might even gain a new pool of voters. According to the Pew survey cited above, although 57 percent of self-identified libertarians voted for President Bush, roughly 40 percent voted for John Kerry.[33] These libertarian Kerry voters certainly didn't back the Senator's plans for raising taxes or increased spending. Rather they objected to Republican deficits, spending, foreign policy, and involvement in personal decision making. Consistent small-government conservatism might lure these small-government voters back to the party that claims to represent smaller government.[34]

Finally, it is important to ask whether success can be measured only in terms of electoral politics. As Richard Weaver put it in his famously titled book, "Ideas have consequences."[35] Or as George Will recently stated even more strongly, "Only ideas have large and lasting consequences."[36] By staking out principled positions in favor of limited government, conservatives can change the terms of the debate for years to come.

Barry Goldwater lost overwhelmingly, yet his campaign launched a generation of conservative politics. Indeed, without Goldwater there would have been no Reagan and no Republican Revolution of 1994. Despite the concerns I have raised about the growth of government, it is important to realize how much the intellectual and political climate has changed over 40 years. When ideas such as school choice and personal accounts for Social Security were first discussed they had little popular support. Today they are part of the political mainstream.

When President Clinton proposed a massive government takeover of the U.S. health care system, it was overwhelmingly rejected. And no serious national politician today would propose anything resembling Lyndon Johnson's Great Society. Democrats campaign today as the party of fiscal responsibility, not the party of great transformative government initiatives. True, they reflexively defend the status quo on programs like Social Security and Medicare. And they seek to spend even more than Republicans on everything from social-welfare programs to business subsidies. But in general, these increases are incremental, tinkering, or defensive reactions. There is no new New Deal.

In fact, by 1996 Bill Clinton was forced to declare, "The era of big government is over."[37] If, in the end, Clinton's claim was more rhetoric than reality, it still represented a remarkable repudiation of 40 years of political and intellectual support for big government.

That is one of the great tragedies of big-government conservatism. It is not only a poor electoral choice; it threatens to undo 40 years of conservative intellectual victory.

One last point: Martin Luther King Jr. once said, "There comes a time when one must take a position that is neither safe, nor political, nor popular—but one must take it simply because it is right."[38] The evidence suggests that reducing the size and power of the federal government *would* be safe, popular, and good politics. But ultimately, that doesn't matter. In the end conservatives should stand for limited government and individual liberty simply because it is the right thing to do.

An Agenda for Small Government

Restoring fiscal discipline and returning the federal government to its appropriate constitutional role will not come easily or overnight. Still, we will never get there if we never start. With that in mind, here are five things that conservatives could do to both reinvigorate their movement and begin to reduce the size and power of the federal government.

1. Return to Federalism

In *Conscience of a Conservative*, Barry Goldwater wrote: "The Constitution, I repeat, draws a sharp and clear line between federal jurisdiction and state jurisdiction. The federal government's failure to recognize that line has been a crushing blow to the principle of limited government."[39] Therefore, a good starting point for a new small-government conservative agenda would be to redraw the lines between state and federal responsibilities.

First and foremost, this step means the federal government should avoid involving itself in those areas that are traditional state responsibilities, including civil and, criminal justice, education, and most social-welfare issues. Congress is not a national school board, sheriff, or marriage counselor. By confining itself to legitimate federal responsibilities, Congress would free states to experiment with innovative approaches to seemingly intractable issues like health care and poverty. As issues become more and more complex, the advantages of decentralization and subsidiarity become increasingly apparent. One size seldom fits all anymore. Moreover, state and local governments are frequently more responsive to the will of the people because they are closer to the people.

Such a return to federalism would go a long way toward reestablishing the fusionism of the earlier conservative movement. The most divisive social issues, including abortion, marriage, and education, would be dealt with at the state and local levels. Here, religious conservatives, traditionalists, and libertarians would be free to disagree while they remained united on the big national issues.

Rather than the "faux federalism" discussed in Chapter 9, Congress should return to the Reagan-era policy of "turn-backs." Under this approach, specific federal programs would be terminated and, at the same time, specific federal taxes repealed. Responsibility for both collecting the revenue and spending the money would be turned back to state and local governments. The federal middleman would be eliminated altogether.

Rep. Jeff Flake (R-AZ) actually proposed this approach recently as an alternative to the massive federal highway bill.[40] Representative Flake would have cut the federal gasoline tax from 18 cents a gallon to 2 cents, allowing the states to raise gas taxes if necessary to fund projects locally. With the federal tax repealed, drivers would have been no worse off, but states would have been free to decide for themselves what projects they wanted to fund. And if Alaska truly wanted a "bridge to nowhere," the cost would be paid by Alaskan drivers.

The key is for Congress to seriously debate the areas of government that are the proper responsibility of Washington and the areas that properly belong to the states. The states, of course, will always ask for more money and complain when they don't get it. And Congress will have to restrain itself from "doing something" about every issue that reaches the news media. But in the end, a return to federalism is vital to restoring a government of limited, enumerated powers.

2. Cut Spending

Big government, of course, is not measured solely by the size of the federal budget. Even so, any attempt to reduce the size of government needs to start with a serious attempt to reduce federal spending.

Government has no money of its own. Every dollar that it spends is a dollar that is siphoned off from American workers. This spending has an economic impact because it diverts money from efficient uses in the private sector to less-productive uses in the public sector. But equally important, government spending reduces human liberty. Every dollar that the government spends is one less dollar that Americans can spend on food, clothing, housing, charitable contributions, or other goods and services of their choosing.

The Cato Institute's Chris Edwards has set out a detailed menu of potential budget cuts that would provide an excellent place to begin such a debate.[41] These cuts would total nearly $380 billion annually. If all the cuts were enacted, the federal budget would be balanced by 2011 and would generate future surpluses, while still allowing for the Bush tax cuts to be made permanent. It would also reduce federal spending from its current 20 percent of GDP to roughly 15 percent by 2015.

Lawmakers may or may not agree with any particular cut. But Congress should review each and every program, asking itself: Is this program authorized by the Constitution? Is this something that only the government can do, or is it something best left to the private sector? If only the government can do it, is the federal government better able to handle the program than state or local governments? Does the program work (and how will success be measured)? And is this program the best way to accomplish the desired goal? Does it restrict individual liberty in the most minimally necessary way? A negative answer to one or more of these questions should be reason for Congress to seriously consider reducing or eliminating the program.

Second, Congress should establish a statutory barrier against future congressional spending, similar to those in place in more than 20 states.[42] A cap on spending would link future levels of government spending to some neutral indicator such as GDP, personal income, or a combination of inflation and population growth. Total federal spending would be prohibited from increasing any faster than increases in the chosen indicator.[43] Legislation to establish a cap has been introduced by Reps. John Campbell (R-CA) and Todd Akin (R-MO).

Of course a statutory spending cap is not a substitute for the type of program-specific questioning previously described. Future congresses can always rewrite the law to avoid the restrictions. The history of spending limitations, such as Gramm-Rudman-Hollings, is one of congressional duplicity. Still, a spending cap would make congressional overspending more transparent. If Congress chooses to override the limit, it would be publicly acknowledging its fiscal irresponsibility. In this regard, spending caps may be only a speed bump to congressional spending—but sometimes speed bumps are useful. Slowed spending is still better than unfettered expansion.

3. Reform Entitlements

As discussed in Chapter 6, long-term budget control requires reform of the entitlement programs, especially the big three: Medicaid, Medicare, and Social Security. Conservatives should lead the effort for long-term reform to these programs not only out of fiscal necessity, but also because market-based reforms can give people far more choice and control over their lives.

Medicaid is now the fastest-growing portion of most state budgets. It is also a substantial burden to the federal government. It will cost more than $190 billion in 2006, and those costs are expected to rise to more than $363 billion by 2015.[44]

Most current Medicaid reforms are not truly government-limiting reforms. Most involve ideas such as replacing traditional Medicaid with health care vouchers or adding health savings accounts to the program. Many of these ideas are innovative and will undoubtedly make the program more efficient. Some may even help restrain the program's growing cost. In contrast, vouchers and health savings accounts may actually make Medicaid more attractive, bringing more people into the program. In fact, these reforms may make Medicaid more attractive than private insurance for some low-income workers. This possibility is especially likely if Medicaid eligibility is extended up the income range as part of the reform.

Medicaid reformers need to remember that Medicaid is a form of welfare. In fact, Medicaid provides average benefits twice as valuable as those available under federal cash assistance programs—and to 10 times as many recipients.[45] Unsurprisingly, studies have found that Medicaid increases dependence and discourages self-reliance in the same way as other welfare programs.[46]

As such, it should be reformed in much the same way as welfare was in 1996. Congress should cap federal funding but give states broad flexibility to target the truly needy and reduce dependence.[47] States would be free to add work requirements and programs to deal with out-of-wedlock births as well as to experiment with other restrictions. States would also be free to restrict access by those who do not truly need help, particularly middle-class nursing-home patients with sheltered assets.

Some states, such as Mississippi, Missouri, and Tennessee, are attempting to take this type of approach on their own, but these programs require congressional action to be truly effective.[48] Although Bill Clinton blocked attempts at this type of comprehensive reform in the 1990s, no such excuse exists today.

Perhaps no federal program needs reform as much as Medicare. The program's unfunded liabilities run as high as an unfathomable $70 trillion, dwarfing Social Security's financing shortfall.[49] Although the program may be politically popular, conservatives must summon the courage to make fundamental structural reforms.

Medicare reform should start with repeal of the costly and flawed prescription drug benefit. The program was always of dubious necessity and is clearly unaffordable, adding as much as $11.2 trillion to the program's unfunded liabilities.[50] In the short term, Congress can replace the current program with a more targeted benefit, providing assistance only to those seniors with low incomes or very high prescription drug costs.

On a more fundamental level, however, Medicare must eventually be transformed into a program that protects seniors from truly catastrophic illness while giving them greater control over and responsibility for the money they are spending and the choices they are making. Consensus is growing that any such reform should be based on the idea of "premium support." That is, the government would provide seniors with a fixed amount of funding per recipient, rather than paying for each service purchased. This general approach was recommended by the bipartisan Medicare reform commission in 1999.[51]

One way of achieving this outcome would be to give seniors a voucher—which seniors could supplement with their own money—to purchase health insurance from a variety of competing private insurers. Seniors could then purchase the coverage that most nearly suited their individual needs. Some might choose managed-care programs, others traditional fee-for-service coverage. Some might want plans that include prescription drug coverage, while others would prefer long-term care. Still others might deposit their funds in a health savings account and purchase catastrophic insurance with a high deductible. The vouchers could be risk adjusted so that sicker seniors would receive a higher amount.

Because the voucher would be for a specific amount of money per senior, rather than the current open-ended entitlement, such a program would allow the federal government to anticipate and limit expenditures. Furthermore, because seniors would have a financial stake in the type of insurance they purchase, they would become more cost-conscious and prudent consumers.

In the long term, Congress could go even further by allowing workers to deposit the Medicare portion of their payroll tax in a personal account to save for their retirement health needs. This system would work much like personal accounts for Social Security (see below).[52]

Finally, Congress must address the need to reform Social Security. The national retirement program is deeply flawed and facing a growing crisis. In less than 10 years it will begin to run a deficit, spending more on benefits than it takes in through taxes. The IOUs in the

Social Security Trust Fund are merely a claim against future taxes, not real assets that can be used to pay benefits. Overall, the system is more than $15 trillion in debt.[53]

Only three options really exist for fixing the problem: raise taxes, cut benefits, or invest privately. Taxes can be raised or benefits cut enough to prop up the existing system for a little while longer. But the Social Security payroll tax is already the biggest tax that the average American family pays, and cutting benefits is no better option. Already younger workers can expect a low, below-market return on their taxes. Benefit cuts would only make a bad deal worse.

More important, Social Security reform is not just about keeping the current program solvent. Conservatives should not be drawn into a "green eyeshades" debate about rates of return and actuarial solvency dates. Rather, they should see Social Security reform as an opportunity to give individual workers greater choice, control, and ownership over their retirement funds. Younger workers should be given the opportunity to privately invest as much of their payroll tax as possible through personal accounts.[54]

Doing so would treat young people, women, and minorities more fairly. It would allow low- and middle-income workers to build a nest egg of real, inheritable wealth. It would provide future retirees with higher benefits than Social Security would otherwise be able to pay. It would, for the first time, give workers ownership and a legal right to their benefits. Most important, it would shift responsibility for retirement from government to individuals.[55]

Tackling entitlements reform would require political courage and a willingness to talk straight with the American public. But without entitlements reform, no possibility exists to gain control of the federal budget or reduce the size of government. If conservatives are not willing to undertake these reforms, who will?

4. Link Future Tax Cuts to Cuts in Spending

Congress should link any future tax cuts to cuts in spending. This recommendation would not apply to making the Bush tax cuts permanent. Those tax cuts are already in place and allowing them to expire would result in an enormous tax increase for the American people. But once those tax cuts are put permanently in place, Congress should return to budget rules that require any future spending increases *or* tax cuts be offset by spending reductions.

As Milton Friedman has pointed out, the level of spending and regulation best measures the size of government, not the amount of taxes. Spending must ultimately be paid for, and regulation has costs even if they are not immediately visible. This step is especially important in the face of growing evidence that attempts to "starve the beast"—forcing spending cuts by reducing government revenues—have failed.

The Cato Institute's William Niskanen has studied the relationship between federal spending and the federal tax burden between 1979 and 2003. He concluded that contrary to "starve the beast" theory, a *negative* relationship actually existed between spending and taxes. That is, not only did tax cuts fail to reduce federal spending, but also they may actually have led to an increase in spending.[56]

Most likely, tax cuts hid the cost of that spending. Instead of having an honest debate about whether a particular program was worth paying for, we simply shifted the cost of that program onto future generations by deficit spending. Evidence of this hypocrisy can be seen in the fact that members of Congress who signed the president's "No New Taxes" pledge circulated by Americans for Tax Reform were actually more likely to vote for spending increases than those who did not. For example, six of every seven members of Congress who signed the pledge voted in favor of the Medicare prescription drug bill. Moreover, pledge signers voted for the 2002 farm bill by a three to one margin. And three-quarters of the signers supported the highway bill in the House.[57]

As long as Congress can hand out goodies today but pass on the bill to future Congresses (and future generations of Americans), it will have no incentive to reduce spending. In contrast, by tying taxes and spending more closely together, Congress will be forced to ask itself whether the marginal value of a federal program or activity is greater than the marginal cost of the taxes necessary to fund that activity. Asking that question will be a welcome change, as well as a welcome restraint on federal spending.

Democrats are expected to try to restore "pay as you go" rules for tax and spending bills, requiring that they be deficit neutral. Republicans should join them in this effort. This change, however, should be delayed until after Congress makes the current tax cuts permanent. An argument may well have been made in favor of linking spending cuts to the tax cuts *before* they were passed; however, they were passed. As a result American taxpayers have adjusted their working, saving, and investment behavior to the current tax rates. Currently, federal taxes equal 17 percent of GDP. If those tax cuts expire as scheduled starting in 2010, the tax burden on the economy would jump to 20 percent of GDP by 2014.

The evidence is overwhelming that these tax cuts have affected the economy beneficially. GDP has grown and nearly 2 million jobs have been created. The stock market has rebounded from its post-9/11 collapse. Federal revenue has increased, although not by enough to offset spending increases. Raising taxes now would reverse this growth. Therefore Congress should make the tax cuts permanent, establishing a long-term baseline for government revenues, then make any future changes dependent on reductions in spending.

5. Pass Term Limits

Few things would do as much to reinvigorate small-government conservatism as enacting term limits for members of Congress.

The Founding Fathers considered and rejected including term limits in the Constitution because they were confident that sufficient safeguards already existed, including a tradition of voluntary retirement, to prevent political careerism—something they correctly saw as a vice. For more than a hundred years they were correct, and a tradition of voluntary retirement after only a few terms (often as few as one or two) in the House lasted until nearly the end of the 19th century. However, from about 1860 on, partly as a result of the introduction of congressional seniority as a principle for committee membership and congressional leadership, the length of time that members serve has steadily increased.[58]

During the 1990s, a strong grassroots movement sought to limit terms for politicians at all levels. Some 18 states passed term limits for state legislators. More important, voters in 21 states approved term limits for their members of Congress.[59] In fact, in every case where term limits appeared on the ballot, voters approved it overwhelmingly.

Unfortunately, congressional term limits were narrowly overturned in a 5-4 decision by the Supreme Court.[60] The Court's reasoning, that states may not set qualifications for federal office, was dubious on constitutional grounds, but it effectively ended the state-level movement for congressional term limits.[61] That result left any hope for term limits up to Congress, the one body least likely to act.

The Contract with America called for a vote on term limits within the first 100 days after the Republicans took control of Congress, and they held to this deadline. However, most of the Republican leadership, including Newt Gingrich, did not really support term limits. (Gingrich notably had once called term limits "a terrible idea," although he later reluctantly gave them lip service.[62]) The Republican leadership maneuvered to prevent a vote on the type of serious term limits supported by grassroots groups, eventually supporting a measure that would have established a limit of six terms (12 years) for representatives and two terms (12 years) for senators. (Most grassroots organizations supported a three-term limit in the House.) The leadership-supported bill would also have preempted state laws that established shorter term limits. Even then, the leadership did little to rally support behind the proposed constitutional amendment. In the end, the bill received a simple majority but fell 63 votes short of the two-thirds required for passage.[63]

Having failed to get a constitutional restriction on how long legislators could serve, term-limits supporters attempted to get members of Congress to voluntarily limit their terms. They asked members and candidates to take a pledge that they would serve no more than three terms. However, the results were decidedly mixed. Roughly 18 members took and honored such a pledge, including three who were later elected to the Senate: Tom Coburn (R-OK), Jim DeMint (R-SC), and John Thune (R-SD). Three other former House members who honored their pledges were later elected governor: John Balducci (D-ME), Bob Riley (R-AL), and Mark Sanford (R-SC).[64]

However, at least 17 other members took the pledge but later broke it.[65] Today, few lawmakers self-limit.

Studies make clear that "the longer a congressman serves in Congress and is exposed to pro-spending stimuli, the more in favor of spending he becomes," as James Payne pointed out in his seminal book, *The Culture of Spending*.[66] More-recent studies have shown the same undeniable trends. Junior members of Congress are far less likely to support new spending, are more likely to vote for spending cuts, are more likely to introduce bills and amendments to cut spending, and are more likely to seek entitlements reforms.[67]

Term limits would also strengthen the willingness of Congress to resist the institutional pressures that lead toward big government, including pressure from the president and congressional leaders.

As former representative Matt Salmon (R-AZ), who honored his pledge to serve only three terms and left Congress in 2000, said, "The independence that comes from limiting my terms has enabled me to vote against the bloated budget deal of 1997, and to challenge my own party's leadership."[68] Likewise, Sanford, one of the earliest supporters of Social Security reform, noted, "If I'd viewed my career in Congress as the next 30 years of my life, I think I would have been a lot more hesitant to bring up Social Security."[69]

The Small-Government Alternative

Big government is not inevitable. Conservatives can restrain and even reverse the growth of government, if they will return to their principles. As Andrew Busch, author of *Reagan's Victory: The Presidential Election of 1980 and the Rise of the Right,* has pointed out, principle is particularly important in advancing a conservative or small-government agenda.[70] The Democratic agenda is easy to understand—they want to give people things. Small-government conservatives want people to take more responsibility for their own lives. That's a more complicated and often more difficult message. The American people will ultimately accept and even embrace it. But only if a clear philosophically and economically principled case is made to them. If they come to believe that the choice is between liberal Democrats who will give them lots of things and big-government conservatives who will give them a little bit less, they will choose the liberal Democrats.

Conservatives, therefore, must articulate a clear, principled vision. A small-government agenda will reduce the welfare state, not seek to use it as a way to control behavior. It will seek to empower health care consumers and give them more control over their money and their decisions, not increase government regulation, mandates, and controls in the cause of "ordering the marketplace." Likewise, a small-government agenda will tackle entitlement reform in a way that gives American workers greater ownership and control over their money. It will not sacrifice our children's future to ever-greater debt and government spending. A small-government agenda will respect the constitutional limits of executive and federal power. It will leave issues like education to the states, where they belong. And it will let us live our lives free from micromanagement by Congress and a Washington elite.

This is a winning agenda. It will restore American prosperity. It will increase opportunity and give everyone a shot at the American dream. Most important, it will ensure that America will always remain "the land of the free."

12. The Coming Debate

Conservatives now have an opportunity to rediscover their principles. Having been banished to the wilderness after the 2006 elections, Republicans will have to develop new policies and ideas if they hope to regain the Congress in 2008. In addition, George W. Bush will soon leave the scene, and a new group of Republican candidates will be seeking the presidency. The next few years will see an intense debate over what direction conservatives and the Republican Party will take.

Similar reappraisals by conservatives have taken place before and have led to both a reinvigorated movement and renewed electoral success. For example, Britain's Conservative Party used the time after the 1974 defeat of Edward Heath to jettison the stale, class-oriented conservatism that had settled over the Tories and develop an aggressive new brand of conservatism based on cutting taxes, privatization, and a reassertion of British pride. The result was Margaret Thatcher and four straight Tory election victories.[1]

In the United States, the Republican Party was forced to regroup after being crushed in the post-Watergate 1974 midterm elections and then losing the presidency in 1976. The party abandoned Nixonian domestic liberalism and embraced Goldwaterish small-government conservatism.[2] Four years later came the Reagan Revolution. Looking back at forced Republican reappraisal, Bruce Bartlett says, "There is no doubt in my mind that the ideas about tax-cutting and supply-side economics would have died in their crib without the political decimation of the Republican Party in 1974 and 1976."[3]

After losing the White House in 1994, Republicans replaced the "get along" leadership style of Minority Leader Bob Michel with the aggressiveness of Newt Gingrich. The result was the Contract with America and the Republican Revolution of 1996.[4] The latest loss gives conservatives another opportunity to define what it truly means to be a conservative.

Some have suggested the focus of the coming conservative debate will be over foreign policy. No doubt significant differences exist

229

between neoconservatives, paleoconservatives, libertarians, and others over what the extent and direction of American engagement around the world should be. And conservatives are increasingly split over the war in Iraq.

Yet conservatism must answer a more fundamental question. Will it return to its traditional opposition to big government, or will it embrace this new brand of conservatism that promotes big government as a tool for the remaking of society? It must choose between the conservatism of Barry Goldwater and Ronald Reagan and the conservatism of George W. Bush, Gary Bauer, Newt Gingrich, and Bill Kristol.

Carryovers occur to the foreign policy debate, of course. Many of the advocates of big-government conservatism at home are among the most strident advocates of American interventionism abroad. And as Robert Higgs has demonstrated, an undeniable link exists between war and the growth of government.[5]

But these disagreements are to a large extent only about tactics. We are at war and threatened by an enemy that has both the intent and capability to do us harm. National defense is one of the few attributes of modern government firmly anchored in the Constitution. And politically, for all the internal disagreements, support for a strong national defense remains the glue that holds the various wings of the Republican Party together.[6] The debate that will truly matter is whether or not conservatives still believe in small government.

Unfortunately, most of those expected to seek the Republican presidential nomination in 2008 fall firmly in the big-government camp. Massachusetts governor Mitt Romney was the driving force behind a managed-competition health care reform proposal that includes an individual mandate for health insurance. In the Cato Institute's biannual ranking of governors on fiscal issues, Romney received a grade of only "C." The report noted that his proposed 2006 budget included some $170 million in increased business taxes. This increase comes on top of previous business tax increases of $140 million during his term, as well as some $500 million in increased fees and other forms of revenue.[7] His philosophy of governing can be seen from his comment, "I'd be embarrassed if I didn't always ask for federal money whenever I got the chance."[8]

Former Speaker Newt Gingrich has been riding a wave of nostalgia for the Republican Revolution of 1994.[9] The recent Republican Congress was so incompetent and so inclined toward big government that 1994 looks like the golden age. But Gingrich was not and is not a small-government conservative. His support for a host of big-government programs is detailed in Chapter 2. They range from the Medicare prescription drug benefit to greater federal involvement in education. Indeed, listening to Gingrich, one gets the distinct impression that he doesn't care how big government grows—as long as it uses computers.

Bill Frist (R-TN) backed No Child Left Behind, the drug benefit, and the transportation bill. Sam Brownback (R-KS) voted against the pork-filled highway and agriculture bills, but backed both No Child Left Behind and the prescription drug benefit. According to the National Taxpayers Union, over the past three sessions of Congress combined, Frist sponsored legislation calling for just $42 million in spending cuts. He didn't sponsor a single cut during the 109th Congress. Brownback did better, but only by comparison, sponsoring legislation that would have cut $214 million.[10]

Of the candidates most commonly mentioned, only Sen. John McCain (R-AZ) has been a consistent fiscal conservative. He opposed the prescription drug benefit, and he has been an outspoken opponent of pork-barrel spending. He was an early supporter of Social Security reform, including personal accounts. However, he supported No Child Left Behind. More important, he is also the principal author of a campaign finance bill that severely restricts political speech. He has said that he "would rather have a clean government than one where, quote, First Amendment rights are being respected, that has become corrupt. If I had my choice, I'd rather have the clean government."[11] He has embraced heavily regulatory environmental policies and compulsory national service. And he has shown a disturbing predilection for elevating every personal pet peeve, from steroids in baseball to airplane service quality, to a federal issue.

Nor do other potential candidates, such as former New York City mayor Rudy Giuliani, Mississippi governor Haley Barbour, or Arkansas governor Mike Huckabee, have strong small-government records. Huckabee, for example, received a grade of "F" on Cato's gubernatorial report card. He presided over a massive increase in state spending, including an expansion of Medicaid, and approved increases in the sales, income, and cigarette taxes. Barbour earned a grade of "C." Real per capita state spending increased by 5 percent per year under his watch.[12] In short, no one has yet seized the banner of small-government conservatism.

Nor does much hope exist for small-government conservatism from other directions. The newly victorious Democratic Party stands for even bigger government than the Republicans. Democrats have almost unanimously opposed any Republican attempt to cut the budget, especially for domestic discretionary spending, and have generally sought higher spending. The Democrats' fiscal year 2007 budget proposal called for $16 billion more in spending than the Republican budget, and $177 billion more over the next five years. And that was put forward when they were in the minority!

House Speaker Nancy Pelosi (D-CA), for example, introduced 22 bills in the first half of 2006 that would have increased spending by more than $42 billion, while introducing only 1 that would have cut spending (by $200 million).[13] That record was nothing compared to new chairman of the Ways and Means Committee Charles Rangel (D-NY). Rangel introduced 80 bills in 2006 that would have increased spending and just 3 that would have cut it. The net result of his proposed legislation would have been to increase spending by *$1.6 trillion.*[14] No one in Congress is more dedicated to pork barrel spending than Sen. Robert Byrd (D-W.V.), the new chairman of the Senate Appropriations Committee. According to the National Taxpayers Union, the average Democrat in the House voted for lower taxes and spending only 17 percent of the time. That record was actually better than the Senate's, where Democrats voted for lower taxes and spending just 12 percent of the time.[15]

Although many of the newly elected Democrats ran as moderates or conservatives, they did so primarily on social issues such as abortion, gay marriage, and gun control.[16] On economic issues, they appear to be as liberal as their incumbent brethren, favoring higher taxes, more government spending, protectionism, and national health care.[17] It may make some conservatives feel good to claim them as their own, but to the degree that these new Democrats are conservative at all, they are big-government conservatives.

Nor can we expect a third party to ride to the rescue. The Libertarian Party remains captive to ideological absolutists who argue, for example, for the abolition of all taxes, rather than presenting a realistic and obtainable program for reducing the size of government. Moreover, even if the Libertarian Party—or another third party—

were to develop a credible small-government platform, campaign finance laws and ballot access barriers make it virtually impossible for a third party to be competitive.

Yet the outcome of this battle is not determined. For a long time, many conservatives withheld their criticism of the Bush administration and Congress because the alternatives seemed worse. Particularly after 9/11, they followed an instinctual need to rally around the president. The often-hysterical criticisms from the Left only created greater solidarity on the Right. But discontent with the war and the Bush administration's obvious incompetence in waging it has undermined this solidarity. And the election results prove that the threat of Speaker Pelosi was no longer enough to frighten conservatives back into line.

Of course not everyone sees the need for change. Some, like Americans for Tax Reform president Grover Norquist, suggest that those who complain about the Bush administration or Republicans in Congress are just "whining."[18] Norquist also said that the Republican loss in 2006 was nothing more than a small bump on an otherwise smooth road to conservative dominance.[19] Others say that the Republican defeat in 2006 was solely caused by discontent with the war in Iraq, that no widespread conservative dissatisfaction exists. Bill Kristol, for example, dismisses talk of conservative unhappiness with Republican big spending. "I have heard almost no one talk about it one way or the other," he told the *New York Times*.[20] David Brooks argues that the rejection of Republicans "was not philosophical."[21]

But beyond the Washington beltway, the rumblings of conservative discontent are growing louder. Grassroots organizations, such as Americans for Limited Government, the Club for Growth, and FreedomWorks, have become increasingly outspoken in their criticism of big-government conservatism. Former member of Congress Pat Toomey, who now heads the Club for Growth, says that the conservative base feels "disgust with what appears to be a complete abandonment of limited government."[22]

It wasn't evangelical Christians or so-called "values voters" who deserted Republicans. Roughly 70 percent of White evangelicals and born-again Christians voted Republican in 2006, just a fraction less than in 2004.[23] It was suburbanites, independents, and others who were fed up not just with the war and corruption, but also with the

Republican drift toward big government. On election night, more than 65 percent of voters believed that "The Republicans used to be the party of economic growth, fiscal discipline, and limited government, but in recent years, too many Republicans in Washington have become just like the big spenders that they used to oppose."[24] These disaffected believers in small government will demand that the Republican Party change. If it doesn't, the 2006 elections are likely to be just a taste of things to come. As Dick Armey notes, "Republicans have been setting the stage for [losing] for nearly a decade, running from themselves and their principles."[25] They will only return to power by "returning to their Reagan roots."[26]

But this debate is not just about who wins elections. In the long run, politics—all politics—is about human liberty. Two hundred years ago, Thomas Jefferson warned, "The natural progress of things is for liberty to yield and government to gain ground."[27] If big-government conservatives win, if we end up with nothing in Washington more than a debate between big government and bigger government, our children will inherit an America that is less prosperous and less free.

Ronald Reagan laid down the challenge for us: "You and I have a rendezvous with destiny. We will preserve for our children this, the last best hope of man on earth, or we will sentence them to take the first step into a thousand years of darkness. If we fail, at least let our children and our children's children say of us we justified our brief moment here. We did all that could be done."[28]

It is time for conservatives to answer that challenge. Is the conservative legacy to be one of Ronald Reagan and Barry Goldwater? Or is it to be one of George W. Bush and his fellow big-government conservatives?

It is time to decide.

Notes

Chapter 1

1. This figure is calculated on an inflation-adjusted basis. In nominal terms, the increase was more than 45 percent. Stephen Slivinski, *Buck Wild: How Republicans Broke the Bank and Became the Party of Big Government* (Nashville: Nelson Currant, 2006).

2. Kevin Hassett, "Where Clinton Beats W," *National Review*, November 6, 2006.

3. This figure represents the present value of the expected funding shortfall over an infinite horizon as estimated by the trustees of the Social Security and Medicare systems. Cited in Testimony of Cato Institute senior Fellow Jagadeesh Gokhale to the Committee on Homeland Security and Government Affairs, Subcommittee on Federal Financial Management, Government Information, and International Security, 109th Cong., 1st sess., September 22, 2005, http://hsgac.senate.gov/_files/092205 Gokhale.pdf.

4. Jonah Goldberg, "George W. Bush, Preservative," *National Review Online*, January 21, 2004, http://www.nationalreview.com/goldberg/goldberg200401211053.asp.

5. Clyde Wayne Crews, "Ten Thousand Commandments: An Annual Snapshot of the Regulatory State," Competitive Enterprise Institute, June 28, 2006.

6. Ronald Reagan, "First Inaugural Address" (Washington, DC, January 20, 1981); George W. Bush, Remarks to Ohio Operating Engineers (Richfield Training Center, Richfield, OH, September 1, 2003, http://www.whitehouse.gov/news/releases/ 2003/09/20030901.html).

7. Janet Hook, "President Putting 'Big' Back in Government," *Los Angeles Times*, February 8, 2005.

8. Fred Barnes, *Rebel in Chief: Inside the Bold and Controversial Presidency of George W. Bush* (New York: Crown Forum, 2006), p. 26.

9. Bruce Bartlett, *Impostor: How George W. Bush Bankrupted America and Betrayed the Reagan Legacy* (New York: Doubleday, 2006).

10. Stephen Slivinski, "The Grand Old Spending Party: How Republicans Became Big Spenders," Cato Institute Policy Analysis no. 543, May 3, 2005.

11. *Federal Budget, FY 2007, Historical Tables* (Washington: Government Printing Office, 2006), Table 1.1: Summary of Receipts, Outlays, and Surpluses or Deficits, 1789–2011.

12. An "earmark" directs a specific amount of money to be spent by a specific federal department or agency on a specific project and is written in such a way that the money ends up in the hands of a specific recipient. Most earmarks do not go through the normal vetting or review process; they have been at the heart of recent corruption scandals. Chris Edwards, "Nearly 14,000 Pork Projects in Federal Budget This Year," *Budget & Tax News*, October 1, 2005.

13. "Highway Bill Has Record Number of Lawmaker-Requested Projects," *CNN.com*, August 2, 2005.

14. "Yes Rush, It's True: RNC Chief Rejects GOP Traditions," *New Hampshire Union Leader*, September 3, 2003.

15. Poll conducted by the Club for Growth, November 7, 2006. Available at http://www.clubforgrowth.org/2006/11/new_poll_people_want_limited_g.php.

16. William Niskanen, "A Case for Divided Government," *Cato Policy Report* 25, no. 2 (March/April 2003).

17. John DiIulio, "Are Conservative Republicans Now America's Permanent Ruling Class?" *Chronicle of Higher Education*, January 20, 2006.

18. Ronald Reagan, "First Inaugural Address" (Washington, DC, January 20, 1981).

19. Barry Goldwater, *The Conscience of a Conservative* (Shepherdsville, KY: Victor Publishing, 1960), p 17.

20. David Brooks, "One Nation Conservatism," *Weekly Standard*, September 13, 1999.

21. Quoted in Richard Ebeling, review of *Dead Right*, by David Frum (New York: Basic Books, 1994), *Freedom Daily*, April 1995. (The quote appears in Ebeling's review, not in Frum's book.)

22. The "third wave" concept was popularized by Alvin Toffler and posits a postindustrial society driven by technology and information. Alvin Toffler, *The Third Wave* (New York: Random House, 1987).

23. Newt Gingrich, *To Renew America* (New York: HarperCollins, 1996), p. 44.

24. Fred Barnes, *Rebel in Chief: Inside the Bold and Controversial Presidency of George W. Bush* (New York: Crown Forum, 2006), p. 175.

25. Fred Barnes, "Pence on Fire," *Weekly Standard*, October 3, 2005.

26. See, for example, ABC News/Washington Post Poll, June 17–20, 2004, *PollingReport.com*, http://www.pollingreport.com/institut.htm.

27. George W. Bush, address to the Front Porch Alliance (Indianapolis, IN, July 22, 1999, http://www.cpjustice.org/stories/storyreader$383).

28. George W. Bush, address to the Manhattan Institute (New York, NY, October 5, 1999, http://www.manhattan-institute.org/html/bush_speech.htm).

29. See F. A. Hayek, *The Road to Serfdom*, 50th anniversary edition (Chicago: University of Chicago Press, 1994). Of course Hayek famously wrote that he was not a conservative but a classical liberal. "Why I Am Not a Conservative," in *The Constitution of Liberty* (Chicago: The University of Chicago Press, 1960). But terminological disputes aside, Hayek's warning about the growth of government is paradigmatic of traditional conservative attitudes toward government. Adam Wolfson, "Conservatives and Neoconservatives," in *The Neocon Reader*, ed. Irwin Stelzer (New York: Grove Press, 2004).

30. Irving Kristol, "The Neoconservative Persuasion," *Weekly Standard*, August 25, 2003.

31. David Brooks, "How to Reinvent the GOP," *New York Times Magazine*, August 29, 2004.

32. Fred Barnes, "A Big Government Conservatism," *Wall Street Journal*, August 15, 2003.

33. Ibid.

34. F. A. Hayek, *The Fatal Conceit: The Errors of Socialism* (Chicago: University of Chicago Press, 1989).

35. David Brooks, "How to Reinvent the GOP," *New York Times Magazine*, August 29, 2004.

36. Of course most small-government conservatives are also believers in such traditional moral values. But they have generally followed Barry Goldwater's admonition that "man's development, both in its spiritual and material aspects, is something

that cannot be directed by outside forces." Barry Goldwater, *Conscience of a Conservative* (Shepherdsville, KY: Victor Publishing, 1960), p. 6.

37. Fred Barnes, *Rebel in Chief: Inside the Bold and Controversial Presidency of George W. Bush* (New York: Crown Forum, 2006), p. 168.

38. Daniel Casse, "Is Bush a Conservative?" *Commentary* 117, no. 4 (February 2004), p. 25.

39. That is not to say that traditional small-government conservatives have been blind to these problems, but they have generally emphasized the need for cutback on government interference in order to allow the free market and the voluntary sector (civil society) to work. Government intervention was seen as a last resort.

40. George W. Bush, address to 2004 Republican National Convention (New York, NY, September 2, 2004, http://www.whitehouse.gov/news/releases/2004/09/20040902-2.html).

41. George W. Bush, "Remarks by the President in Commencement Address at the University of Notre Dame" (South Bend, IN, May 20, 2001, http://www.presidency.ucsb.edu/ws/index.php?pid=45893).

42. Robert Rector, address to a conference on "Compassionate Welfare Reform: Empowering Charities and Private Citizens" (sponsored by the Beacon Hill Institute and the David R. Macdonald Foundation, Washington, DC, December 12, 1996).

43. Ibid.

44. Irving Kristol, *Two Cheers for Capitalism* (New York: Basic Books, 1978).

45. William Bennett, speech to National Press Club, quoted in E. J. Dionne Jr., "Why Civil Society? Why Now?" *Brookings Review* 15, no. 4 (Fall 1997): 4–8.

46. David Brooks, "A Return to National Greatness; A Manifesto for a Lost Creed," *Weekly Standard*, March 3, 1997.

47. Irving Kristol, *Reflections of a Neoconservative: Looking Back, Looking Ahead* (NY: Basic Books, 1983).

48. John Stuart Mill, *On Liberty and Other Writings* (Cambridge: Cambridge University Press, 1989), p. 13.

49. Edmund Burke, *A Vindication of Natural Society: Or, a View of the Miseries and Evils Arising to Mankind from Every Species of Artificial Society* (1756; Indianapolis: Liberty Classics, 1982), pp. 15–16.

50. Edmund Burke, *Reflections on the Revolution in France* (1790; Oxford: Oxford University Press, 1993), p. 246.

51. Robert Nisbet, "Uneasy Cousins," in *Freedom and Virtue: The Conservative / Libertarian Debate*, ed. George Carey (Wilmington, DE: ISI Books, 2004), p. 42.

52. Irving Kristol, "The Neoconservative Persuasion," *Weekly Standard*, August 11, 2003.

53. Fred Barnes, *Rebel in Chief: Inside the Bold and Controversial Presidency of George W. Bush* (New York: Crown Forum, 2006), p. 161. Emphasis in original.

54. Rich Lowry, "W's Big Gov't Debacle," *New York Post*, February 21, 2006.

55. James Pinkerton, "What Would Kirk Do? The Medicare Bill Was Inevitable," *National Review Online*, November 26, 2003, http://www.nationalreview.com/comment/pinkerton200311260919.asp.

56. Mark Gerson, *The Neoconservative Vision* (Lanham, MD: Madison Books, 1997).

57. See, for example, Arthur Brooks, "Public Subsidies and Charitable Giving: Crowding Out, Crowding In, or Both?" *Journal of Policy Analysis and Management* 19, no. 3 (2000): 451–64.

58. Jonathan Rauch, "The Accidental Radical," *National Journal*, July 25, 2003.

59. John Micklethwait and Adrian Woodridge, *The Right Nation: Conservative Power in America* (New York: Penguin Books, 2004), p. 260.

60. Bruce Bartlett, *Impostor: How George W. Bush Bankrupted America and Betrayed the Reagan Legacy* (New York: Doubleday, 2006), p. 17.

61. Barry Goldwater, *The Conscience of a Conservative* (Shepherdsville, KY: Victor Publishing, 1960), p. 8.

62. Rick Santorum, *It Takes A Family: Conservatism and the Common Good* (Wilmington, DE: ISI Books, 2005), p 44.

63. Quoted in Beth Fouhy, "San Francisco Rolls Out Red Carpet for the Clintons," Associated Press, June 28, 2004.

64. Rick Santorum, *It Takes A Family: Conservatism and the Common Good* (Wilmington, DE: ISI Books, 2005), p. 44.

65. David Brooks, "How to Reinvent the GOP," *New York Times Magazine*, August 29, 2004.

66. Quoted in David Henderson, "The Joy of Freedom," *Hoover Digest* 2 (Spring 2002), http://www.hooverdigest.org/022/henderson.html.

67. Quoted in Sarah Schweitzer, "Card Says President Sees America as a Child Needing a Parent," *Boston Globe*, September 2, 2004.

Chapter 2

1. John Stuart Mill, *On Liberty and Other Writings* (Cambridge: Cambridge University Press, 1989), p. 13.

2. *Annals of Congress*, 3rd Cong, 1st sess., vol. 4, p. 179.

3. Quoted in Charles Warren, *Congress as Santa Claus: Or National Donations and the General Welfare Clause of the Constitution* (1932; repr. New York: Arno, 1978), pp. 62–63.

4. Owen Lovejoy, "The Faith of a Social Worker," *Survey*, May 18, 1920, p. 209.

5. Blanche Coll, *Safety Net: Welfare and Social Security, 1929–1979* (New Brunswick, NJ: Rutgers University Press, 1995), pp. 1–3.

6. Michael Katz, *In the Shadow of the Poorhouse: A Social History of Welfare in America* (New York: Basic Books, 1986), pp. 85–86.

7. Lionel Trilling, *The Liberal Imagination* (New York: Doubleday, 1953), p. 5.

8. Here we encounter the question, both semantic and philosophical, of whether libertarians or believers in the classical liberal tenets of individual liberty are properly described as part of the modern conservative movement. The Cato Institute's David Boaz notes the difficulty in applying labels, citing how a "*Washington Post* story datelined Moscow reported that 'liberal economists have criticized the government for failing to move quickly enough with structural reforms and for allowing money-losing state factories to continue churning out goods that nobody needs.'" Yet, Boaz points out that when "economists such as Milton Friedman make similar criticisms in the United States . . . the *Post* calls them conservative economists." David Boaz, *Libertarianism: A Primer* (New York: Free Press, 1998), p. 24. Hayek, as mentioned, wrote that he was not a conservative. "Why I Am Not a Conservative," in *The Constitution of Liberty* (Chicago: The University of Chicago Press, 1960). When William F. Buckley wrote *God and Man at Yale* (Washington, DC: Regnery, 1951), he called himself not a conservative, but an "individualist." And when Barry Goldwater was elected to the Senate a year later, he also eschewed the conservative label, referring

to himself as a "progressive Republican" and "Jeffersonian Republican." Obery Hendricks, "Class, Political Conservatism, and Jesus," *Cross Currents* (Fall 2005). Yet Buckley and Goldwater both eventually saw themselves as part of a larger conservative movement, and Hayek has been adopted into the conservative canon. Undoubtedly significant differences exist between libertarianism and traditionalist conservatism, in terms of both their philosophical antecedents and their approach to contemporary political issues. See, for example, George Carey, *Freedom and Virtue: The Conservative/Libertarian Debate* (Wilmington, DE: ISI Books, 2004). However, most observers treat libertarianism as a strain of current conservative thought. For example, Peter Berkowitz, *Varieties of Conservatism in America* (Stanford, CA: Hoover Institution Press, 2004). Perhaps, Ronald Reagan put it best, "The basis of conservatism is a desire for less government interference or less centralized authority or more individual freedom and this is a pretty general description also of what libertarianism is . . . libertarianism and conservatism are traveling the same path." "Inside Ronald Reagan: A Reason Interview," *Reason* (July 1975). Because both libertarianism and traditionalist conservatism share a common opposition to the big-government statism advocated by contemporary liberalism (and by the big-government conservatism that is the subject of this book), I believe it is fair to treat them as part of the same small-government movement.

9. Edmund Burke, *The Works of the Right Honorable Edmund Burke,* vol. 2 (Boston: Little Brown and Company, 1877), p. 87.

10. Russell Kirk, *The Conservative Mind: From Burke to Eliot* (New York: Regnery, 2001).

11. Frank Meyer, "Freedom, Tradition, Conservatism," *Modern Age IV* (Fall 1960): 355–63, available at http://www.freerepublic.com/focus/f-news/1289523/posts.

12. Ibid.

13. That does not mean that relations between libertarians and traditionalists have always been smooth. There has frequently been as much competition as cooperation, some of it quite vitriolic. But, in the end, for reasons both philosophical and pragmatic, fusionism has formed a workable majority conservative coalition for roughly half a century. For an excellent discussion of the ups and downs of fusionism, see Ryan Sager, *The Elephant in the Room: Evangelicals, Libertarians, and the Battle to Control the Republican Party* (Hoboken, NJ: John Wiley & Sons, 2006).

14. Robert Nisbet, "Uneasy Cousins," in *Freedom and Virtue: The Conservative / Libertarian Debate,* ed. George Carey (Wilmington, DE: ISI Books, 2004), p. 42.

15. Russell Kirk, "Conservatism Is Not an Ideology," *National Review,* January 30, 1962, reprinted in George Carey, ed., *Freedom and Virtue: The Conservative /Libertarian Debate* (Wilmington, DE: ISI Books, 2004), p. 12.

16. Lee Edwards, "Barry Goldwater: The Most Consequential Loser" (remarks to a conference on "The Conservative Movement: Its Past, Present and Future," Princeton University, NJ, December 1, 2003), http://www.heritage.org/Press/Commentary/ed12805a.cfm.

17. Ibid.

18. Ronald Reagan, "A Time for Choosing," NBC, October 27, 1964.

19. Stephen Slivinski, *Buck Wild: How Republicans Broke the Bank and Became the Party of Big Government* (Nashville: Nelson Current, 2006).

20. Edward Crane, "The Rise and Fall of the GOP," *Cato Institute Policy Report* 25, no. 6 (November/December 2003).

21. Stephen Slivinski, "The Grand Old Spending Party: How Republicans Became Big Spenders," Cato Institute Policy Analysis no. 543, March 3, 2005, citing *2005 Budget of the United States, Historical Tables*.

22. For a discussion of the Republican record in Congress since 1994, see Chris Edwards and John Samples, eds., *The Republican Revolution Ten Years Later: Smaller Government or Business as Usual* (Washington: Cato Institute, 2005).

23. Norman Podhoretz, "Neoconservatism: A Eulogy" (American Enterprise Institute Bradley Lecture, Washington, DC, January 15, 1996).

24. Irving Kristol, "The Neoconservative Persuasion," *Weekly Standard*, August 11, 2003.

25. Irwin Stelzer, "Neoconservatives and Their Critics," in *The Neocon Reader*, ed. Irwin Stelzer (New York: Grove Press, 2004), p. 4.

26. Jacob Heilbrunn, "The Neoconservative Journey," in *Varieties of Conservatism in America*, ed. Peter Berkowitz (Stanford, CA: Hoover Institution Press, 2004).

27. Ibid.

28. Alan Wald, *The New York Intellectuals* (Chapel Hill: North Carolina University Press, 1987), p. 63.

29. Michael Gill, "Arguing the World," *Humanities* 19, no. 1 (Jan/Feb 1998). An excellent documentary film on this period and the activities in alcove number 1, *Arguing the World*, was produced by Joseph Dorman in 1998.

30. Irving Kristol, "Memoirs of a Trotskyist" *New York Times Magazine*, January 23, 1977.

31. In the 1960s, it was revealed that the CIA had helped fund the organization, and questions were raised about its independence.

32. Irving Kristol, "My Cold War," *National Interest*, Spring 1993.

33. Reinhold Niebuhr, "The End of Illusions," *The Nation* 150 (1940): 778–79.

34. Quoted in Mark Gerson, *The Neoconservative Vision* (Lanham, MD: Madison Books, 1997), p. 18.

35. Reinhold Niebuhr, *Children of Light and the Children of Darkness* (New York: Charles Scribner's Sons, 1944), p. 114.

36. Reinhold Niebuhr, "Christianity and Society," in *Love and Justice: Selections from the Shorter Writings of Reinhold Niebuhr*, ed. D. B. Robertson (Cleveland, OH: The World Publishing Company, 1957), p. 114.

37. Strauss believed that the writings of classical philosophers contained both an *exoteric* (public) and *esoteric* (private or hidden) teaching that was kept from the masses, from either fear of persecution or a general desire to present their most important teachings to those most receptive to them. http://www.straussian.net/straussianism.html.

38. Quoted in Ronald Bailey, "Origin of the Specious: Why Do Neoconservatives Doubt Darwin?" *Reason*, July 1997.

39. Shadia Drury, *The Political Ideas of Leo Strauss* (New York: St. Martin's Press, 1988), pp. 34–35.

40. William Pfaff, "The Long Reach of Leo Strauss," *International Herald Tribune*, May 15, 2003.

41. Plato, *The Republic*, trans. Rachana Kamteker and Desmond Lee (New York: Penguin Classics, 2003), p. 339.

42. Irving Kristol, *Neo-Conservatism: The Autobiography of an Idea* (Chicago: Ivan R Dee, 1999), p. 6.

43. Ibid., p. 8.

44. Quoted in Jim Lobe, "Leo Strauss's Philosophy of Deception," in Clint Willis and Nate Hardcastle, *Jesus Is Not a Republican: The Religious Right's War on America* (New York: Thunder's Mouth Press, 2005), p. 21.

45. Norman Podhoretz, "Neoconservatism: A Eulogy" (American Enterprise Institute Bradley Lecture, Washington, DC, January 15, 1996).

46. Richard Perle, Elliot Abrams, Paul Wolfowitz, Frank Gaffney, and Douglas Feith were all aides to Senator Jackson. Bill Kristol was a campaign worker. Norman Podhoretz and Irving Kristol were leading members of the Committee for a Democratic Majority, which was founded by Jackson. Wolfowitz still calls himself a "Scoop Jackson Republican."

47. "Henry 'Scoop' Jackson vs. Joe Lieberman—or Why It Is Time for Joe to Go," *DailyKos*, February 2, 2004.

48. As related by Irving Kristol, "Forty Good Years," *The Public Interest*, Spring 2005.

49. Michael Lind, "A Tragedy of Errors," *The Nation*, February 23, 2004.

50. James Nuechterlein, *First Things* (May 1996): 14–15.

51. Gary Dorrien, *The Neoconservative Mind: Politics, Culture, and the War of Ideology* (Philadelphia: Temple University Press, 1993), p. 10.

52. Norman Podhoretz, "The Reagan Road to Détente," *Foreign Affairs* 63, no. 3 (1984): 449.

53. Philip Gold, *Take Back the Right: How Neocons and the Religious Right Have Betrayed the Conservative Movement* (New York: Carroll & Graf, 2004), pp. 247–48; Dorrien, *The Neoconservative Mind*, p. 11.

54. Stefan Halper and Jonathan Clarke, *America Alone: The Neoconservatives and the Global Order* (Cambridge: Cambridge University Press, 2004), pp. 68–73.

55. Irving Kristol, *Neo-Conservatism: The Autobiography of an Idea* (Chicago: Ivan R Dee, 1999), p. 357.

56. Among current or former Bush administration officials who can reasonably be considered neoconservatives are Vice President Cheney's former chief of staff, I. "Scooter" Libby, Elliott Abrams (National Security Council), John Bolton (undersecretary of state and later ambassador to the United Nations), Jay Lefkowitz (director, domestic policy council), Les Lenkowsky (director, Corporation of National and Community Service), Leon Kass (director, President's Council on Bioethics), Richard Perle (assistant secretary of defense), Matthew Scully (speechwriter), Joseph Shattan (another speechwriter), Peter Wehner (still another speechwriter), and Paul Wolfowitz (deputy secretary of defense, later appointed head of the World Bank).

57. For examples of this debate, see Michael Lind, "A Tragedy of Errors," *The Nation*, February 5, 2004; Justin Raimondo, "Trotsky, Strauss and the Neocons," *antiwar.com*, June 13, 2003; Bill King, "Neoconservatism and Trotskyism," *EnterStageRight.com*, March 22, 2004; and Joshua Muravchik, "The Neoconservative Cabal," in *The Neocon Reader*, ed. Irwin Stelzer (New York: Grove Press, 2004).

58. See Stefan Halper and Jonathan Clarke, *America Alone: The Neoconservatives and the Global Order* (Cambridge: Cambridge University Press, 2004), for one of the best discussions.

59. See, for example, Irving Kristol, *Neoconservatism: The Autobiography of an Idea* (Chicago: Ivan R. Dee, 1999), and Peter Steinfels, *The Neoconservatives: The Men Who Are Changing America's Politics* (New York: Simon & Schuster, 1979).

60. Irving Kristol, "What Is a Neoconservative?" *Newsweek*, January 19, 1976. Some may raise questions about whether the use of quotations from so long ago accurately represents the current views of the people quoted. Many of the people discussed in

this book have been politically active for a long time. Accordingly, I will be using quotations covering a wide time period. These quotations have been selected on the basis of (a) recentness, whenever possible, and (b) clear coverage of the topics being discussed. In all cases where a quotation is not of recent vintage, it has been selected either because (1) it is the most recent statement of the person's position on the topic, or (2) it is a statement that clearly reflects the continued viewpoint of the person or group being discussed, and (3) it has not been repudiated or contradicted by the person who said it. In short, every effort has been made to confirm that the quotation continues to inform the basis of big-government conservatism and faithfully represents the position of the person or group discussed.

61. Quoted in Murray Friedman, *The Neoconservative Revolution: Jewish Intellectuals and the Shaping of Public Policy* (Cambridge: Cambridge University Press, 2005), p. 134.

62. Norman Podhoretz, "Neoconservatism: A Eulogy" (American Enterprise Institute Bradley Lecture, Washington, DC, January 15, 1996).

63. Jeane Kirkpatrick interviewed by Adam Myerson in "Welfare State Conservatism," *Policy Review* 44 (Spring 1988): 2.

64. Irving Kristol, *Two Cheers for Capitalism* (New York: Basic Books, 1978), p. 119.

65. John Micklethwait and Adrian Woolridge, *The Right Nation: Conservative Power in America* (New York: Penguin Books, 2004).

66. Irving Kristol, "American Conservatism, 1945–1995," *The Public Interest* (Fall 1995): 80–91.

67. Irving Kristol, "A Conservative Welfare State," *Wall Street Journal*, June 14, 1993.

68. Ibid.

69. Ibid.

70. Gary Dorrien, *The Neoconservative Mind: Politics, Culture, and the War of Ideology* (Philadelphia: Temple University Press, 1993), p. 16.

71. Nathan Glazer, "Neoconservative from the Start," *The Public Interest* (Spring 2005): 16. Glazer was summarizing his own writings in "Reform Work—Not Welfare," *The Public Interest* (1975).

72. Irving Kristol, *Two Cheers for Capitalism* (New York: Basic Books, 1978), p. 145.

73. James Piereson, "Investing in the Right Ideas," *Wall Street Journal*, May 27, 2005.

74. Irving Kristol, "Capitalism, Socialism, and Nihilism," *The Public Interest* 31 (Spring 1973): 5–7.

75. Ludwig von Mises, *Human Action: A Treatise on Economics* (New Haven, CT: Yale University Press, 1949), p 10.

76. Irving Kristol, "Capitalism, Socialism, and Nihilism," *The Public Interest* 31 (Spring 1973): 4.

77. Michael Joyce, "The Common Man's Uncommon Intellectual," in *The Neoconservative Imagination: Essays in Honor of Irving Kristol*, ed. Christopher DeMuth and William Kristol (Washington: AEI Press, 1995).

78. Irving Kristol, *Two Cheers for Capitalism* (New York: Basic Books, 1978).

79. Quoted in David Frum, "The Libertarian Temptation," *Weekly Standard*, April 21, 1997.

80. See Dinesh D'Souza, *The Virtue of Prosperity: Finding Values in an Age of Techno-Affluence* (New York: Free Press, 2000); Irving Kristol, *Two Cheers for Capitalism* (New York: Basic Books, 1978).

81. See Daniel Bell, *The Cultural Contradictions of Capitalism* (New York, Basic Books, 1976).

82. Gertrude Himmelfarb, *The Demoralization of Society: From Victorian Virtues to Modern Values* (New York: Alfred Knopf, 1995), p. 36.

83. See Joseph Schumpeter, *History of Economic Analysis. Capitalism, Socialism and Democracy* (New York: Harper and Brothers, 1950), p. 84.

84. David Bosworth, "The Spirit of Capitalism, 2000," *The Public Interest* (Winter 2000): 3–28.

85. Irving Kristol, "Capitalism, Socialism, and Nihilism," *The Public Interest* 31 (Spring 1973): 4, 6–7.

86. See, for example, Irving Kristol, "Pornography, Obscenity, and the Case for Censorship," *New York Times Magazine*, March 28, 1971.

87. Quoted in Doug Bandow, "Can Unbridled Capitalism Be Tamed," *Wall Street Journal*, March 26, 1997.

88. Daniel Mahoney, "Can Compassionate Conservatism Govern," *The Public Interest* 142 (Winter 2001): 124.

89. Irving Kristol, "Is the Welfare State Obsolete?" *Harpers*, June 1963.

90. Irving Kristol is quoted as saying: "There are in Washington today people who are married with children and religiously observant. Do they have faith? Who knows? They just believe that it is good to go to church or synagogue. Whether you believe or not is not the issue—that's between you and God—whether you are a member of a community that holds certain truths sacred, that is the issue.' Neoconservatives are 'pro-religion even though they themselves may not be believers.'" Ron Bailey, "The Voice of Neoconservatism," *Reason*, October 17, 2001.

91. Irving Kristol, "The Neoconservative Persuasion," *Weekly Standard*, August 11, 2003. The two groups also share a strongly pro-Israel stance on foreign policy.

92. See Ron Bailey, "Origin of the Specious: Why Do Neoconservatives Doubt Darwin?" *Reason* (July 1997): 22–28. This position is interesting for neoconservatives to take because they are not believers in creationism themselves, but they are concerned that Darwinism will undermine the religious foundations of moral values. Bailey quotes Kristol as saying, "If there is one indisputable fact about the human condition it is that no community can survive if it is persuaded—or even if it suspects—that its members are leading meaningless lives in a meaningless universe."

93. Norman Podhoretz, "The Christian Right and Its Demonizers," *National Review*, April 3, 2000.

94. Irving Kristol, "Christmas, Christians, and Jews," *National Review*, December 30, 1988.

95. Murray Friedman, *The Neoconservative Revolution: Jewish Intellectuals and the Shaping of Public Policy* (Cambridge: Cambridge University Press, 2005), p. 183.

96. Gary Dorrien, *The Neoconservative Mind: Politics, Culture, and the War of Ideology* (Philadelphia: Temple University Press, 1993), p. 102.

97. Irving Kristol, "A Conservative Welfare State," *Wall Street Journal*, June 14, 1993.

98. Irving Kristol, "American Conservatism, 1945–1995," *The Public Interest* (Fall 1995): 80–91.

99. Quoted in Sam Tanenhaus, "When Left Turns Right, It Leaves the Middle Muddled," *New York Times*, September 19, 2000.

100. David Brooks, "How to Reinvent the GOP," *New York Times Magazine*, August 29, 2004.

101. Quoted in Karl Zinsmeister, "Respect the Limits That Made the USA," *American Enterprise*, January/February 2006.

102. William Kristol and Robert Kagan, "Toward a Neo-Reaganite Foreign Policy," *Foreign Affairs* 75 (July/August 1996): 31.

103. Ibid.

104. David Brooks, "How to Reinvent the GOP," *New York Times Magazine*, August 29, 2004.

105. Ibid.

106. David Brooks, "A Vision Bruised and Dented," *New York Times*, March 23, 2006.

107. William Kristol, "On the Future of Conservatism," *Commentary*, February 1997.

108. David Brooks, "Older & Wiser? A Weekly Standard 10th Anniversary Symposium," *Weekly Standard*, September 19, 2005.

109. David Brooks, "Up from Libertarianism," *Weekly Standard*, August 19, 1996; David Frum, "The Libertarian Temptation," *Weekly Standard*, April 21, 1997.

110. David Brooks, "How to Reinvent the GOP," *New York Times Magazine*, August 29, 2004.

111. Ibid.

112. Bill Kristol and David Brooks, "What Ails Conservatism," *Wall Street Journal*, September 15, 1997.

113. David Brooks, "One Nation Conservatism," *Weekly Standard*, September 13, 1999.

114. Ibid.

115. Ibid.

116. Cited in Fareed Zakaria, "Whimper on the Right," *The New Yorker*, June 5, 2000.

117. "Michael J. Petrilli vs. Neal McCluskey on National Standards," *edspresso.com*, April 28, 2006, http://www.edspresso.com/2006/04/day_3_michael_j_petrilli_vs_ne_1.htm.

118. David Brooks, "Love the Service around Here," *New York Times*, November 11, 2001.

119. Ibid.

120. Quoted in Edward Epstein, "New Push for National Service: Sept. 11 Revives Interest in Citizenship Duty for Youth," *San Francisco Chronicle*, September 11, 2002.

121. Quoted in Jonah Goldberg, "The Meaning of McCain," *National Review*, February 3, 2000.

122. John McCain (address to Annual City Year Convention, Phoenix, AZ, June 15, 2001).

123. John McCain and Evan Bayh, "A New Call to Service," *New York Times*, November 6, 2001.

124. *Roe v. Wade*, 410 US 113 (1973).

125. William Martin, *With God on Our Side: The Rise of the Religious Right in America* (New York: Broadway Books, 1996), p. 192.

126. See Steve Bruce, *The Rise and Fall of the New Christian Right* (Oxford: Clarendon Press, 1988).

127. Jn. 15:19

128. Cited in Erin O'Donnell, "Twigs Bent Left or Right," *Harvard Magazine*, January–February 2006.

129. Pew Research Center, *Religion and Public Life: A Faith-Based Divide* (Washington: The Pew Forum on Religion & Public Life, 2005).

130. Quoted in Michael Cromartie, "Religious Conservatives in American Politics, 1980–2000: An Assessment" (Family Research Council, Witherspoon Lecture, Washington, DC, April 12, 2001).

131. Nathan Glazer, "Toward a New Concordat," *The World* (Summer 1982): 113.

132. David Wilhelm, "Presidential Politics and Mainline Protestants," *The Common Good* 2, no. 21 (October 14, 2003).

133. Pew Research Center, *Religion and Public Life: A Faith-Based Divide* (Washington: The Pew Forum on Religion & Public Life, 2005).

134. Ibid.

135. Ibid., p. 2.

136. John Petrocik, "Reformulating the Party Coalitions: The 'Christian Democratic' Republicans" (address to the American Political Science Association Annual Meeting, Boston, MA, August 1998).

137. Peter Berger, "Democracy and the Religious Right," *Commentary*, January 1997, pp. 53–56.

138. Thomas Frank, *What's the Matter with Kansas? How Conservatives Won the Heart of America* (New York: Henry Holt & Co., 2004).

139. Walter Shapiro, "Presidential Election May Have Hinged on One Issue: Issue 1," *USA Today*, November 4, 2004.

140. Quoted in Walter Shapiro, ibid.

141. Pew Research Center, *Religion and Public Life: A Faith-Based Divide* (Washington: The Pew Forum on Religion & Public Life, 2005).

142. William Bole, "Communitarian Lite: American Catholics & Their Politics," *Commonweal*, September 13, 2002.

143. Pew Research Center, *Religion and Public Life: A Faith-Based Divide* (Washington: The Pew Forum on Religion & Public Life, 2005).

144. Stephen Hart, *What Does the Lord Require? How American Christians Think about Economic Justice* (New Brunswick, NJ: Rutgers University Press, 1992), p. xiv.

145. Adam Wolfson, "Not Your Father's Republican Party," Claremont Institute, November 14, 2005, http://www.claremont.org/writings/051031wolfson.html.

146. Quoted by Adam Wolfson in remarks to the 13th International Annual Meeting in Political Studies, Estoril, Portugal, June 29, 2005, http://www.claremont.org/writings/051031wolfson.html.

147. Ross Douthat, "Theocon Moment," *Wall Street Journal*, April 6, 2006.

148. *New York Times*, August 17, 1999, cited on http://www.ontheissues.org/Celeb/Gary_Bauer_Principles_+_Values.htm.

149. "Dobson Defends Senator Santorum against Gay Activists," Focus on the Family, April 24, 2003, http://www.family.org/welcome/press/a0025665.cfm.

150. Letter from Louis Sheldon to Arthur Schlesinger, October 27, 2004, posted at http://www.traditionalvalues.org/modules.php?sid=1982.

151. Ryan Sager, *The Elephant in the Room: Evangelicals, Libertarians and the Battle to Control the Republican Party* (Hoboken, NJ: John Wiley & Sons, 2006), pp. 142–43.

152. See, for example, Gerald Twomey, "The Preferential Option for the Poor," in *Catholic Social Thought from John XXIII to John Paul II* (Ceredigion: The Edwin Mellen Press, 2004), http://amywelborn.typepad.com/openbook/2005/06/preferential_op.html.

153. United States Conference of Catholic Bishops, *Moral Principles and Policy Priorities for Welfare Reform* (Washington, DC: United States Conference of Catholic Bishops, 1995.

154. Quoted in E. J. Dionne, "The Great Republican Rebranding," *Washington Post*, May 6, 2006.

155. Quoted in Naomi Schaefer Riley, "Mr. Compassionate Conservative," *Wall Street Journal*, October 21, 2006.

156. "The Prolife Movement and the New Right," *Conservative Digest*, December 1992.

157. Gary Bauer, fundraising letter, Campaign for Working Families, February 18, 2004.

158. Ibid.

159. Frank Bruni, "Gary Bauer, No. 4 in Iowa Poll, Casts Himself as Heir to Reagan," *New York Times*, September 24, 1999.

160. Gary Bauer, "Save Social Security, Save Our Families," *New York Times*, January 23, 1997.

161. See, for example, Amy Fagan, "Conservative Groups Warn GOP," *Washington Times*, March 27, 2006.

162. Jude Wanniski, "Sketching the Laffer Curve," *Yorktown Patriot*, June 14, 2005.

163. Arthur Laffer, "The Laffer Curve: Past, Present, and Future," Heritage Foundation Backgrounder no. 1765, June 1, 2004.

164. Ibid.

165. Bruce Bartlett, "Supply-Side Economics: 'Voodoo Economics' or Lasting Contribution?" *Laffer Associates Supply-Side Investment Research*, November 11, 2003.

166. Jude Wanniski, "Taxes and a Two-Santa Theory," *National Observer*, March 6, 1976. Emphasis in original.

167. Ed Crane, "The GOP: Slouching toward Irrelevance," *Cato Institute Policy Report* 20, no. 3 (May/June 1999).

168. *The Economic Recovery Tax Act of 1981*, Public Law 97-34, *U.S. Statutes at Large* 95 (1981): 172.

169. William A. Niskanen and Stephen Moore, "Supply Side Tax Cuts and the Truth about the Reagan Economic Record," Cato Institute Policy Analysis no. 261, October 22, 1996.

170. Alvin Toffler, *The Third Wave* (New York: Bantam Books, 1980).

171. Newt Gingrich, "Foreword," in Alvin and Heidi Toffler, *Creating a New Civilization: The Politics of the Third Wave* (Atlanta: Turner Publishing, 1994), p. 8.

172. Alvin Toffler, *The Third Wave* (New York: Bantam Books, 1980), p. 417.

173. Ibid.

174. Newt Gingrich et al., *Contract with America* (New York: Times Books, 1994).

175. Quoted in Jerry Taylor, "GOP Has a New Newt," *Cleveland Plain Dealer*, May 24, 1994.

176. Remarks by Newt Gingrich, *Fox News Sunday*, April 16, 2006.

177. Newt Gingrich, "The Conservative Movement at the Crossroads," April 18, 2004, http://www.newt.org/backpage.asp?art=1703.

178. Newt Gingrich, "The Republican Imperative to Govern," *Wall Street Journal*, January 2, 2001.

179. Newt Gingrich, "A New Approach to Cutting Government," *Wall Street Journal*, February 27, 2001.

180. Newt Gingrich (speech to American Association for the Advancement of Science, Washington, DC, April 13, 2000).

181. Quoted in "Newt's Turn to Ride the Highway," *Washington Technology*, January 15, 1995.

182. Quoted in Scott Schoenberg, "The New Newt," *Atlanta Business to Business*, May 2000.

183. Gingrich (speech to American Association for the Advancement of Science, April 13, 2000).

184. Newt Gingrich, "The Age of Transitions," http://www.newamerican leadership.com.

185. Nicholas Mokhoff, "Gingrich's Rx for U.S. Competitiveness: 'Real Change,'" *Embedded.com*, January 16, 2006, http://www.embedded.com/showArticle.jhtml? articleID=177100506.

186. Annette Meeks, "Keep Winning the War of Ideas," *Minneapolis Star Tribune*, October 31, 2005.

187. Todd Lindberg, "Gingrich Lost and Found," *Policy Review* 94 (April–May 1999): 10.

188. Quoted in Jerry Taylor, "GOP Has a New Newt," *Cleveland Plain Dealer*, May 24, 1994.

189. Newt Gingrich, "The Conservative Movement at the Crossroads," April 21, 2005, http://www.newt.org/backpage.asp?art=1703.

190. Ibid.

191. From an interview in Todd Datz, "Old Pol, New Gig," *CSO Magazine*, April 2001.

192. Quoted in Kara Swisher, "Gingrich Wants the Government to Act More Like Tech Firms," *Wall Street Journal*, July 19, 2000.

193. Newt Gingrich (remarks to the American Enterprise Institute, Washington, DC, February 28, 2005).

194. Newt.org, "Winning in a Global Economy."

195. Quoted in Annette Meeks, "Keep Winning the War of Ideas," *Minneapolis Star Tribune*, October 31, 2005.

196. www.newt.org.

197. Andrea Stone, "Former Foes Clinton, Gingrich Band Up on Health Care Plan," *USA Today*, May 11, 2005.

198. Debra Rosenberg, "A New Contract?" *Newsweek OnLine*, July 5, 2006, http://www.msnbc.msn.com/id/13718956/site/newsweek/.

Chapter 3

1. Major Garrett, *The Enduring Revolution: How the Contract with America Continues to Shape the Nation* (New York: Crown Forum, 2005), p. 26.

2. Dan Balz, "Democrats Take House," *Washington Post*, November 7, 2006; Kristin Jensen and William Roberts, "Democrats Clinch Full Control of U.S. Congress with Senate Win," Bloomberg, November 9, 2006.

3. Ed Gillespie and Bob Schellhas, eds., *Contract with America: The Bold Plan by Rep. Newt Gingrich, Rep. Dick Armey, and the House Republicans to Change the Nation* (New York: Basic Books, 1994), p. 22.

4. John Samples, "Same as the Old Boss? Congressional Reforms under the Republicans," in Chris Edwards and John Samples, *The Republican Revolution 10 Years Later: Smaller Government or Business as Usual* (Washington: Cato Institute, 2005), p. 27.

5. The Contract with America called for votes on the following items: (1) the Fiscal Responsibility Act: a balanced budget/tax limitation amendment and a legislative line-item veto; (2) the Taking Back Our Streets Act: an anti-crime package including stronger truth in sentencing, "good faith" exclusionary rule exemptions, effective death penalty provisions, and cuts in social spending from the summer's "crime" bill to fund prisons; (3) the Personal Responsibility Act: welfare reform, including provisions to prohibit welfare for minor mothers and denying increased AFDC for

additional children while on welfare, cuts in spending for welfare programs, and a tough two-years-and-out provision with work requirements; (4) the Family Reinforcement Act: child support enforcement, tax incentives for adoption, strengthening rights of parents in their children's education, stronger child pornography laws, and an elderly dependent care tax credit; (5) the American Dream Restoration Act: a $500 per child tax credit, repeal of the marriage tax penalty, and creation of American Dream Savings Accounts; (6) the National Security Restoration Act: prohibiting the placement of U.S. troops under U.N. command and increasing defense spending; (7) the Senior Citizens Fairness Act: raising the Social Security earnings limit, repealing the 1993 tax hikes on Social Security benefits, and providing tax incentives for private long-term care insurance; (8) the Job Creation and Wage Enhancement Act: a variety of tax cuts, including a reduction in the capital gains tax, rollback of some business regulations, and unfunded mandate reform; (9) the Common Sense Legal Reform Act: civil justice reform, including "loser pays" laws, limits on punitive damages, and reform of product liability laws; and (10) the Citizen Legislature Act: establishing congressional term limits. The only item not to pass the House was term limits (see Chapter 11). However, many of these items failed to pass the Senate.

6. Fred Barnes, "The Governing Party," *Weekly Standard*, December 1, 2003.

7. Ariel Cohen and William L. T. Schirano, "The Real Culprit behind Price Gouging: OPEC," Heritage Foundation WebMemo no. 102, May 31, 2006, http://www.heritage.org/Research/EnergyandEnvironment/wm1102.cfm.

8. See, for example, HR 4043, sponsored by Rep. Darell Issa (R-CA) and HR 5058, sponsored by Rep. Tom Tancredo (R-CO).

9. Jerry Taylor and Peter Van Doren, "Strategic Petroleum Reserve Inflating Oil Prices," *Environment News*, January 1, 2005.

10. Carl Hulse and David Kirkpatrick, "Sharp Reaction to GOP Plan on Gas Rebate," *New York Times*, May 1, 2006.

11. Fred Barnes, "A Big Government Conservatism," *Wall Street Journal*, August 15, 2003. Emphasis added.

12. David Brooks, "The Promised Land," *New York Times*, November 29, 2003.

13. Quoted in Michael Dorning, "One for the Gipper," *Chicago Tribune*, October 26, 2005.

14. Peter Sepp, "Congressional Perks: How the Trappings of Office Trap Taxpayers," National Taxpayers Union Foundation Policy Paper no. 131, November 1, 2000.

15. Quoted in Jonathan Rausch, "Is There an Excuse for George Nethercutt?" *Reason*, August 12, 2000. Nethercutt had made term limits one of the centerpieces in his successful 1994 campaign to unseat then Democratic House Speaker Tom Foley. For years he featured his term limit pledge on his official website. But when the time came for him to leave Congress in 2000, he abandoned the pledge. He is now serving his seventh term.

16. Nicholas Confessore, "Welcome to the Machine," *Washington Monthly*, July/August 2003.

17. Elizabeth Drew, "Selling Washington," *New York Review of Books*, June 23, 2005.

18. David Maraniss and Michael Weisskopf, *Tell Newt to Shut Up* (New York: Touchstone, 1996), p. 117.

19. Quoted in Peter Perl, "Absolute Truth," *Washington Post Magazine*, May 13, 2001.

20. Nicholas Confessore, "Welcome to the Machine," *Washington Monthly*, July/August 2003.

21. Elizabeth Drew, "Selling Washington," *New York Review of Books*, June 23, 2005.

22. Jim Drinkard and Andrea Stone, "Abramoff Pleads Guilty to More Charges," *USA Today*, January 5, 2006.

23. R. Jeffrey Smith, "DeLay Indicted in Texas Finance Probe," *Washington Post*, September 29, 2005.

24. Susan Schmidt and James Grimaldi, "Abramoff Pleads Guilty to 3 Counts," *Washington Post*, January 4, 2006.

25. Ibid.

26. "Ohio Rep. Ney Pleads Guilty to False Statements," Associated Press, September 14, 2006.

27. R. Jeffrey Smith and Susan Schmidt, "Bush Official Arrested in Corruption Probe," *Washington Post*, September 20, 2005.

28. Randy "Duke" Cunningham, a seven-term Republican representative for California's 50th district in Orange County, pleaded guilty in November of 2005 to accepting $2.4 million in bribes in exchange for helping a defense contractor. He received a sentence of eight years and four months in prison and an order to pay $1.8 million in restitution. William Jefferson, an eight-term Democratic member of Congress from Louisiana, is accused of accepting $100,000 in exchange for assisting a company in getting a Nigerian telecommunications contract. Although videotaped accepting the money, he has not, as of this writing, been indicted.

29. For example, not long after Republicans took control of Congress in 1994, Norquist helped his old friend Jack Abramoff get a lobbying job with the law firm of Preston Gates Ellis. Susan Schmidt and James Grimaldi, "The Fast Rise and Steep Fall of Jack Abramoff," *Washington Post*, December 29, 2005.

30. A report by the Senate Finance Committee concluded that these groups "appear to have perpetrated a fraud" by laundering money for Abramoff. James Grimaldi and Susan Schmidt, "Report Says Nonprofits Sold Clout to Abramoff," *Washington Post*, October 13, 2006. Abramoff even referred to Americans for Tax Reform as a "hard-won asset" of his lobbying operation. Ibid.

31. In the interest of full disclosure, one of those who admitted accepting payments from Abramoff was Doug Bandow, who at the time was a senior fellow at the Cato Institute. As soon as the allegation came to light, Bandow was asked to resign from Cato. He is no longer associated with the institute. The other columnist was Peter Ferrara. Ferrara has written for many think tanks in the past, including the Cato Institute, but is currently a fellow with the Institute for Policy Innovations in Texas. Eamon Javers, "Op-Eds for Sale," *Business Week*, December 16, 2005.

32. Andrea Stone and William Welch, "GOP Comes Around to a Majority View," *USA Today*, June 17, 2004.

33. John Samples, "Same as the Old Boss? Congressional Reforms under the Republicans," in Chris Edwards and John Samples, *The Republican Revolution 10 Years Later: Smaller Government or Business as Usual* (Washington: Cato Institute, 2005), p. 29.

34. "Hastert Is Longest-Serving GOP Speaker," Associated Press, June 21, 2006.

35. Bruce Bartlett, *Imposter: How George W. Bush Bankrupted America and Betrayed the Reagan Legacy* (New York: Doubleday, 2006), p. 17.

36. Gingrich admitted doing this during an interview on *Fox News Special Report*, April 18, 2006.

37. Linda Killian, *The Freshmen: What Happened to the Republican Revolution* (Boulder, CO: Westview Press, 1998).

38. Quoted in Stephen Slivinski, *Buck Wild: How Republicans Broke the Bank and Became the Party of Big Government* (Nashville: Nelson Currant, 2006), p. 111.

39. Quoted in Nicole Rae, *Conservative Reformers: The Republican Freshmen and the Lessons of the 104th Congress* (Armonk, NY: M.E. Sharpe, 1998), p. 184.

40. Robin Toner, "Changing Prospects for Medicare Drug Benefits," *New York Times*, June 15, 2002; "Bush Eager for Congress to Send Him Medicare Bill," Associated Press, June 29, 2003; Robert Novak, "Signing Any Health Bill," *Washington Post*, June 7, 2003.

41. Newt Gingrich, "Conservatives Should Vote 'Yes' on Medicare," *Wall Street Journal*, November 20, 2003.

42. 527 committees, named for a section of the income tax code, are tax-exempt organizations that use voter mobilization and issue-based ads to influence federal elections. Thomas Edsall, "Campaign Finance Measure Approved," *Washington Post*, April 6, 2006.

43. Jeffrey Birnbaum and Jonathan Weisman, "GOP Seeks Curbs on 527 Groups," *Washington Post*, March 16, 2006.

44. Quoted in Robert Bluey, "Hypocritical Republicans Attack 527s," *Human Events*, April 3, 2006.

45. See, for example, Donald Deere, Kevin M. Murphy, and Finis Welch, "Sense and Nonsense on the Minimum Wage," *Regulation* 18, no. 1 (1995).

46. Jonathan Weisman, "Minimum Wage Hike Passed By House," *Washington Post*, July 29, 2006.

47. In the end, the bill passed the House and failed in the Senate. Democrats almost unanimously opposed the bill. Republicans were left in the bizarre position of supporting a minimum-wage hike in the face of Democratic opposition.

48. Jonathan Weisman, "Minimum Wage Hike Passed By House," *Washington Post*, July 29, 2006.

49. Stephen Moore and Stephen Slivinski, "A GOP Surrender on Social Security," *National Review Online*, September 18, 2002.

50. Mike Allen, "Hastert Doubtful on Social Security Bill," *Washington Post*, April 1, 2005.

51. "Poll: About Half Think Hastert Should Resign," *www.cnn.com*, October 9, 2006.

52. Bruce Reed, "Bush's War against Wonks," *Washington Monthly*, March 2005.

53. Quoted in E. J. Dionne, "Base Assumptions," *Washington Post*, June 6, 2006.

54. Brian De Bose and Stephen Dinan, "Martinez Says His Staffer Produced Schiavo Memo," *Washington Times*, April 6, 2005.

55. Quoted in Joe Klein, "The Perils of the Permanent Campaign," *Time*, October 30, 2005.

56. John Harris, "Clintonesque Balancing of Issues, Polls," *Washington Post*, June 21, 2001.

57. Quoted in Ron Suskind, "Why Are These Men Laughing," *Esquire*, January 2003.

58. Bob Dole, *One Soldier's Story: A Memoir* (New York: Harper Collins, 2005), p. 265.

59. Timothy Carney, "Specter for Hire," *Human Events*, April 26, 2004, citing Specter's memoir, *A Passion for Truth*.

60. For example, Pete Roskam, running for the open seat vacated by Rep. Henry Hyde (R-IL), said that he supports budget earmarks "to make sure projects like fixing the dangerous railroad crossing at Irving Park and Wood Dale roads continue to get funded." Eric Krol, "Roskam Defends Federal Pork Support," *Daily Herald*, August 22, 2006.

61. Aaron Steelman, "Term Limits and the Republican Congress: The Case Strengthens," Cato Institute Briefing Paper no. 41, October 28, 1998; Stephen Moore

and Aaron Steelman, "Antidote to Federal Red Ink: Term Limits," Cato Institute Briefing Paper no. 21, November 3, 1994; James Payne, *The Culture of Spending: Why Congress Lives beyond Our Means* (San Francisco: ICS, 1991).

62. "The First 18 Months of the 108th Congress: Ghosts of the Revolution," National Taxpayers Union Foundation Policy Paper no. 184, October 7, 2004, http://www.ntu.org/pdf/pp_ntuf_154.pdf.

63. Tucker Carlson, "The Decline and Fall of the GOP," *Cato's Letter*, Spring 2006.

64. Timothy Carney, "Santorum Beats Conservatives," *National Review Online*, April 28, 2004.

65. Brian Naylor, "GOP Faces Dilemma on Sen. Chafee," National Public Radio, September 11, 2006.

66. Michelle Smith, "R.I. Senator May Leave Republican Party," Associated Press, November 10, 2006.

67. Amy Ridenour, "The Story of the Three Hour Roll Call," National Center for Public Policy Research Blog, December 5, 2003, http://www.nationalcenter.org/2003/12/story-of-three-hour-roll-call.html. Feeney, a principled conservative, refused to budge.

68. David Keane, "GOP Leaders Are Naked," *The Hill*, September 29, 2005.

69. Bruce Bartlett, *Imposter: How George W. Bush Bankrupted America and Betrayed the Reagan Legacy* (New York: Doubleday, 2006), pp. 29–31.

70. Rep. Mark Foley was forced to resign his congressional seat after the discovery that he had sent lascivious and inappropriate e-mails and text messages to congressional pages. Subsequent news reports revealed that several members of the Republican leadership were at least vaguely aware of Foley's conduct but failed to take any action against him. Charles Babington and Jonathan Weisman, "Rep. Foley Quits in Page Scandal," *Washington Post*, September 30, 2006.

71. Robert Novak, "Rejected Speaker Goes Missing in Campaigns," *Houston Chronicle*, October 12, 2006.

72. John O'Sullivan, "O'Sullivan's First Law," *National Review*, October 27, 1989.

73. Dick Polman, "Republicans Have Deserted Their Core Principles, Critics Say," Knight Ridder, March 23, 2005.

74. Dick Armey, "Where We Went Wrong," *Washington Post*, October 29, 2006.

Chapter 4

1. Testimony of Robert Rector, Senior Research Fellow, The Heritage Foundation, "The Size and Scope of Means-Tested Welfare Spending," before the Committee on the Budget, U.S. House of Representatives, August 1, 2001; Testimony of Robert Rector, Senior Research Fellow, Domestic Policy Studies, The Heritage Foundation, before the Subcommittee on Human Resources of the House Committee on Ways and Means, February 10, 2005; U.S. Census Bureau, "Income Stable, Poverty Rate Increases, Percentage of Americans without Health Insurance Unchanged," *Census Bureau News*, August 30, 2005, http://www.census.gov/Press-Release/www/releases/archives/income_wealth/005647.html.

2. "Income Stable, Poverty Rate Increases, Percentage of Americans without Health Insurance Unchanged," *Census Bureau News*, August 30, 2005.

3. "Poverty Rate at 12.7 Percent, 4th Straight Rise," Associated Press, August 30, 2005.

4. For a complete discussion of welfare and its failures, see Michael Tanner, *The Poverty of Welfare: Helping Others in the Civil Society* (Washington: Cato Institute, 2003).

5. See Robert Moffitt, "The Effect of Welfare on Marriage and Fertility: What Do We Know and What Do We Need to Know?" University of Wisconsin–Madison, Institute for Research on Poverty, Discussion Paper no. 1153-97, December 1997; Jeff Groger and Stephen Bronars, "The Effect of Welfare Payments on Marriage and Fertility Behavior of Unwed Mothers: Results from a Twins Experiment," National Bureau of Economic Research Working Paper no. 6047, Cambridge, MA, May 1997; Marianne Bitler et al., "The Impact of Welfare Reform on Marriage and Divorce," Federal Reserve Bank of Atlanta Discussion Paper no. 2002-9, May 2002; Francine Blau, Lawrence Kahn, and Jane Waldfogel, "The Impact of Welfare Benefits on Single Motherhood and Headship of Young Women: Evidence from the Census," National Bureau of Economic Research Working Paper no. 9338, Cambridge, MA, November 2002; Hilary Williamson Hoynes, "Does Welfare Play Any Role in Female Headship Decisions?" *Journal of Public Economics* 26, no. 3 (1991): 545–61; Ron Haskins, "Does Welfare Encourage Illegitimacy? The Case Just Closed. The Answer Is Yes," *American Enterprise* 7 (July/August, 1996): 48-49; Charles Murray, "Does Welfare Bring More Babies?" *Public Interest* 115 (Spring 1994): 17–30.

6. Richard Vedder, Lowell Gallaway, and Robert Lawson, "Why People Work: An Examination of Interstate Variation in Labor Force Participation," *Journal of Labor Research* 12, no. 1 (Winter 1991): 47–59. See also, Ken Auletta, *The Underclass* (New York: Random House, 1982).

7. Public Law 104-193, *U.S. Statutes at Large* 110 (1996): 2105.

8. Section 401(B) states, "No Individual Entitlement—This part shall not be interpreted to entitle any individual or family to assistance under any State program funded under this part." However, Kent Weaver of the Brookings Institution suggests that in some states an individual entitlement may still exist under state law. R. Kent Weaver, *Ending Welfare as We Know It* (Washington: Brookings Institution, 2000), p 328.

9. States may not use TANF funds to substitute for current state spending on teen pregnancy prevention efforts. TANF dollars may be used only to deliver special services over and above the programs generally available to other state residents without cost and regardless of income.

10. Later legislation restored food stamp eligibility for most immigrants.

11. Michael Tanner, "Welfare Reform: Less than Meets the Eye," Cato Institute Policy Analysis no. 473, April 1, 2003; Jenifer Zeigler, "Implementing Welfare Reform: A State Report Card," Cato Institute Policy Analysis no. 529, October 19, 2004.

12. Congress did finally reauthorize welfare reform in 2006 after nearly five years of deadlock. The reauthorization legislation contained some good elements, such as strengthened work requirements, but also wasteful new spending (a massive increase in child-care spending, for example), and new programs such as the Healthy Marriage Initiative (see below).

13. Dennis Cauchon, "Federal Aid Programs Expand at Record Rate," *USA Today*, March 13, 2006.

14. George W. Bush, *A Charge to Keep* (New York: William Morrow, 1999), p. 235.

15. Daniel Mahoney, "Can Compassionate Conservatism Govern?" *Public Interest* (Winter 2001): 126–27.

16. See, for example, Richard Neuhaus and Peter Berger, *To Empower People: The Role of Mediating Structures in Public Policy* (Washington: American Enterprise Institute, 1976).

17. Richard Neuhaus, "The Public Square," *First Things* 112 (April 2001): 63–80, http://www.firstthings.com/ftissues/ft0104/public.html#while.

18. Charles Murray, *What It Means to Be a Libertarian: A Personal Interpretation* (New York: Broadway Books, 1996), p. 59.

19. Sen. Rick Santorum (remarks to the First International Conference on Social Justice, Washington, DC, September 27, 2005), http://www.townhall.com/columnists/RickSantorum/2005/11/17/the_conservative_future_compassion.

20. Nedra Pickler, "More Gov't Funds Go to Faith-Based Charities," Associated Press, March 9, 2006.

21. Robert Rector, "Understanding Poverty and Economic Inequality in the United States," Heritage Foundation Backgrounder no. 1796, September 15, 2004.

22. Robert Rector, "A Comprehensive Urban Policy: How to Fix Welfare and Revitalize America's Inner Cities," Heritage Foundation Memo to President-Elect Clinton no. 12, January 18, 1993.

23. James Q. Wilson, *On Character: Essays by James Q. Wilson* (Washington: AEI Press, 1991), p. 22.

24. Quoted in Fred Barnes, *Rebel in Chief: Inside the Bold and Controversial Presidency of George W. Bush* (New York: Crown Forum, 2006), p. 128.

25. Quoted in "Politics and Policymakers," *Philanthropy Magazine*, January 1, 2006.

26. David Seifman and Frankie Edozien, "Newt Hails Mayor's Poverty Plan," *New York Post*, September 20, 2006. Not surprisingly, the evidence from a similar program in Chicago is that such payments do little to actually change behavior. Individuals who take care of themselves do not need a financial incentive to do so. Those who are incapable of making doctor appointments or sending their children to school do not change their habits based on a $50 check. Jonathan Eig, "Poverty Program Gives Points to Do the Right Thing," *Wall Street Journal*, July 7, 2006.

27. Lawrence Mead, *The New Paternalism: Supervisory Approaches to Poverty* (Washington: Brookings Institution Press, 1997).

28. Significant portions of this section are drawn from Michael Tanner, "Corrupting Charity: Why Government Should Not Fund Faith-Based Charities," Cato Institute Briefing Paper no. 62, March 22, 2001.

29. For an excellent discussion of the history of faith-based charity activity in the United States and its success, see Marvin Olasky, *The Tragedy of American Compassion* (Washington: Regnery, 1992).

30. Some of the efforts of government to distance itself from involvement with religion were almost comic in their extremism. In one perhaps apocryphal story, reported by columnist George Will, an official with the Department of Housing and Urban Development wrote to the bishop in charge of the St. Vincent de Paul Housing Center in San Francisco asking him to rename the building the *Mister* Vincent de Paul Center. George F. Will, "Keeping Faith behind Initiatives" *Washington Post*, January 28, 2001. In another case, a city agency notified the local branch of the Salvation Army that it would be awarded a contract to help the homeless, but only on the condition that the organization remove the word "salvation" from its name. Could the organization, perhaps, be known as some other kind of army, a government official wondered. Stanley Carlson-Thies, "Faith-Based Institutions Cooperating with Public Welfare: The Promise of the Charitable Choice Provision," in *Welfare Reform and Faith-Based Organizations*, ed. D. Davis and B. Hankins (Waco, TX: J. M. Dawson Institute of Church-State Studies, Baylor University, 1999), p. 38. As late as 1986, HUD proposed a total ban on grants to churches and other religious organizations.

Department of Housing and Urban Development, "Emergency Shelter Grants Program," *Federal Register* 51 (1986): 45277.

31. Public Law 104-193, § 104a(1)(a).

32. Specifically, states could involve faith-based organizations in providing subsidized jobs, on-the-job-training, job search, job-readiness assistance, community service positions, vocational educational training, job skills training, and GED programs. Faith-based organizations could provide meals and run food pantries. In addition, states could place unmarried minor mothers and expectant mothers who could not remain with their parents in maternity homes, adult-supervised residential care, second-chance homes, or other facilities operated by faith-based organizations. And last, faith-based groups could provide abstinence education, provide drug counseling and treatment, and operate health clinics.

33. "Agency Responsibilities with Respect to Faith-Based and Community Initiatives," White House News Release, January 29, 2001, http://www.whitehouse.gov/news/releases/2001/01/20010129-3.html.

34. Spencer Hsu, "Bush Orders DHS to Create Center for Faith-Based Aid," *Washington Post*, March 8, 2006.

35. "HHS Awards $49 Million from Compassion Capital Fund," U.S. Department of Health and Human Services, Press Release, September 29, 2005, http://www.hhs.gov/news/press/2005pres/20050929.html.

36. Much of the discussion in this chapter concerns faith-based or religious charities, because they are the focus of the Bush administration and a relatively new innovation in government policy. But many of the same arguments would apply to secular charities as well. In short, government funding of *any* private charitable program is not a good idea.

37. The general legal rule is known as the "*Lemon* test," after the 1971 Supreme Court decision in *Lemon v. Kurtzman*. Under the *Lemon* test, government may provide aid to a religious organization, provided it meets three criteria: (1) the government program must have a secular purpose; (2) it must not have a primary effect of either advancing or inhibiting religion; and (3) it must not foster "excessive entanglement" between church and state. 403 U.S. 602 (1971), as cited in William Van Alstyne, *First Amendment Cases and Materials* (Westbury, NY: Foundation Press, 1995), pp. 909–15. Most jurisprudence surrounding government funding of religious activities has centered on aid to religious schools. However, the courts have occasionally addressed government funding of charitable activities. The Supreme Court first ruled on the issue in 1899, in the case of *Bradfield v. Roberts*, holding that the District of Columbia could use public funds to subsidize the construction of a hospital that was owned by the Catholic Church, because, despite the religious affiliation of the ownership and corporate board, no direct connection between the hospital and the church was to exist. "The property and its business were to be managed in its own way, subject to no visitations, supervision or control by any ecclesiastical authority whatever." 175 U.S. 291 (1899), as cited in Melissa Rogers, "The Wrong Way to Do It Right: Charitable Choice and Churches," in *Welfare Reform and Faith-Based Organizations*, ed. Derek Davis and Barry Hankins (Waco, TX: J. M. Dawson Institute of Church-State Studies, Baylor University, 1999), pp. 61–88. In *Raemer v. Board of Public Works* (1976), the court ruled that no federal funds could go to an institution that was so "pervasively sectarian" that religious activities cannot be separated from secular ones. 426 U.S. 736 (1976), as cited in Jim Castelli and John Mcarthy, "Religion-Sponsored Social Services: The Not-So-Independent Sector," Aspen Institute Nonprofit Sector Research

Fund, March 1998, p. 29. However, the court said that if secular activities can be separated out, they may be funded. This holding was reaffirmed in the 1988 case of *Bowen v. Kendrick*, the Supreme Court ruling that government may fund social service agencies with religious ties, again provided that those agencies are not "pervasively sectarian." 487 U.S. 589 (1988), as cited in Carl Esbeck, *The Regulation of Religious Organizations as Recipients of Governmental Assistance* (Washington: Center for Public Justice, 1996). The court failed to define "pervasively sectarian," but a clue may be found in the earlier case of *Hunt v. McNair*, when the court concluded that "Aid may normally be thought to have a primary effect of advancing religion when it flows to an institution in which religion is so pervasive that a substantial portion of its functions are subsumed in the religious mission or when it funds a specifically religious activity in an otherwise substantially secular setting." 413 U.S. 734 (1973), as cited in ibid. This finding has been generally taken to mean that such activities as prayer, bible study, and proselytizing may not be conducted with government funds, but the provision of social services—food, clothing, shelter, education, counseling—may be. In the end, the arguments over funding of faith-based charities boil down to two issues. While critics of Charitable Choice point to the Establishment Clause of the First Amendment, supporters cite the Free Exercise Clause, arguing that government should not discriminate against faith-based organizations in giving out government grants and contracts. John DeIulio, the first director of the president's Office of Faith-Based Initiatives, called it "leveling the playing field." John DeIulio, "Know Us by Our Works," *Wall Street Journal*, February 14, 2001. This latter position is not without merit, but it does not change any of the policy arguments against government-funded charity discussed in this chapter.

38. Diana Etendi, "Charitable Choice and Its Implications for Faith-Based Organizations," *Welfare Reformer* 1 (1999): 6–11.

39. Alan Cooperman, "Losing Faith in the President," *Washington Post*, October 17, 2006.

40. *U.S. Code* 42 (Supp. 1998), § 609a(j).

41. Statement of President George W. Bush, January 29, 2001, http://www.whitehouse.gov/news/releases/2001/01/.

42. Stephen Burger, "New Hope for Gospel Missions: The Devil's in the Details," *USA Today*, September 3, 1996.

43. *U.S. Code* 42 (Supp. 1998), § 609a(h).

44. Melissa Rogers, "The Wrong Way to Do It Right: Charitable Choice and Churches," in *Welfare Reform and Faith-Based Organizations*, ed. D. Davis and B. Hankins (Waco, TX: J. M. Dawson Institute of Church-State Studies, Baylor University, 1999), pp. 61–88.

45. The Civil Rights Restoration Act does specify that the anti-discrimination laws will apply only to "the geographically separate plant or facility which receives the federal funds," but the legislative history makes clear that a geographically separate facility refers to "facilities located in different localities and regions," not facilities that are part of a complex or proximate to each other in the same city. Melissa Rogers, "The Wrong Way to Do It Right: Charitable Choice and Churches," in *Welfare Reform and Faith-Based Organizations*, ed. Derek Davis and Barry Hankins (Waco, TX: J. M. Dawson Institute of Church-State Studies, Baylor University, 1999). Therefore, depending on how the courts or government agencies interpret the laws, the regulations could go well beyond the program receiving government funds and subject the entire church or organization to government oversight. Richard Hammar, author

of *Pastor, Church & Law,* for one, suggests: "In most cases, church programs and activities are conducted in the church facility itself, not in a geographically separate facility. In such cases, [government regulation] will apply to the entire church and all of its programs and activities." Richard Hammar, *Pastor, Church & Law,* 5th ed. (Matthews, NC: Christian Ministry Resources, 1991), p. 592.

46. For example, under federal anti-discrimination statutes, organizations must: (a) "Keep such records and submit to the responsible Department official . . . timely, complete, and accurate compliance reports at such times, and in such form, and containing such information as the responsible Department official may determine to be necessary to enable him to ascertain whether the recipient has complied or is complying with [the regulation]." Recipients are specifically required to maintain "racial and ethnic data, showing the extent to which members of minority groups are beneficiaries of and participants in federally-assisted programs." *Code of Federal Regulations,* title 45, sec. 80.6(b) (1997). (b) "Make available to participants, beneficiaries, and other interested persons, such information regarding the provisions of [federal regulations] and its applicability to the program for which the recipient receives federal financial assistance." *Code of Federal Regulations,* title 45, sec. 80.6(b) (1997). (c) "Make available to participants, beneficiaries, and other interested persons, such information regarding the provisions of [federal regulations] and its applicability to the program for which the recipient receives federal financial assistance." *Code of Federal Regulations,* title 45, sec.45. 80.7(a) (1997). (d) Permit access by federal government officials to its "books, records, accounts, and other sources of information and its facilities as may be pertinent to ascertain compliance." *Code of Federal Regulations,* title 45, sec.45. 80.6(c) (1997). Civil rights issues may be further extended because the courts have held that accepting government money can transform an organization from a private association to a "state actor," bringing the Fourteenth Amendment into play and imposing equal protection and due process obligations that can frequently conflict with church doctrines. Carl Esbeck, *The Regulation of Religious Organizations as Recipients of Governmental Assistance* (Washington: Center for Public Justice, 1996), pp. 45–47. For example, the courts have held that a religious foster home that received substantial state funding may not prohibit foster children under its control from having access to contraceptives. *Arneth v. Gross,* 699 F. Supp. 450 (S.D. N.Y. 1988), as cited in ibid. And although Charitable Choice legislation contains language exempting faith-based organizations from civil rights prohibitions against discrimination on the basis of religion, the courts have said that accepting state funds can subject a church's hiring practices to scrutiny. In one case, the Salvation Army was prohibited from discharging an employee who was a Wiccan because the employee's position was largely paid for by public funds. *Dodge v. Salvation Army,* U.S. Dist. Lexis 4797 (S.D. Miss. 1989), as cited in Melissa Rogers, "The Wrong Way to Do It Right: Charitable Choice and Churches," in *Welfare Reform and Faith-Based Organizations,* ed. Derek Davis and Barry Hankins (Waco, TX: J. M. Dawson Institute of Church-State Studies, Baylor University, 1999).

47. Mark Chaves, "Religious Congregations and Welfare Reform," *Social Science and Modern Society* 38 (January–February 2001): 22.

48. Jim Castelli and John McCarthy, "Religion-Sponsored Social Services: The Not-So-Independent Sector," Aspen Institute Nonprofit Sector Research Fund, p. 4, http://www.nonprofitresearch.org/usr_doc/25356.pdf.

49. *U.S. Code* 40 (Supp. 1994), §§ 276(a)–276(a)-5.

50. Joe Loconte, *Seducing the Samaritan: How Government Contracts Are Reshaping Social Services* (Boston: Pioneer Institute for Public Policy Research, 1997), appendix B.

51. Stephen Monsma, *When Sacred and Secular Mix: Religious Non-Profit Organizations and Public Money* (Lanham, MD: Rowman & Littlefield, 1997).

52. Cited in Joe Loconte, *Seducing the Samaritan: How Government Contracts Are Reshaping Social Services* (Boston: Pioneer Institute for Public Policy Research, 1997), p. 41.

53. Robert Sirico, "Charities on the Dole," *Wall Street Journal*, March 31, 1995.

54. Stanley Carlson-Thies, "Faith-Based Institutions Cooperating with Public Welfare: The Promise of the Charitable Choice Provision," in *Welfare Reform and Faith-Based Organizations*, ed. D. Davis and B. Hankins (Houston: Baylor University, 1999), p. 36.

55. Quoted in Joe Loconte, *Seducing the Samaritan: How Government Contracts Are Reshaping Social Services* (Boston: Pioneer Institute for Public Policy Research, 1997), p. 41.

56. David Kelley, *A Life of One's Own: Individual Rights and the Welfare State* (Washington: Cato Institute, 1998), p. 118.

57. Tibor Machan, *Generosity: Virtue in Civil Society* (Washington: Cato Institute, 1998), p. 70.

58. Arthur Brooks, "Public Subsidies and Charitable Giving: Crowding Out, Crowding In or Both?" *Journal of Policy Analysis and Management* 19, no. 3 (2000): 451–64.

59. Christopher Horne, David Van Slyke, and Janet Johnson, "Attitudes for Public Funding for Faith-Based Organizations and the Potential Impact on Private Giving" (paper presented to a conference on The Role of Faith-Based Organizations in the Social Welfare System, Washington, DC, March 7–8, 2003).

60. Lisa Montiel, *The Use of Public Funds for Delivery of Faith-Based Human Services* (Albany, NY: The Roundtable on Religion and Social Welfare Policy, 2004), table 2, p. 10.

61. Patrick Fagan, Robert Patterson, and Robert Rector, "Marriage and Welfare Reform: The Overwhelming Evidence That Marriage Education Works," Heritage Foundation Backgrounder no. 1606, October 25, 2002.

62. Cheryl Wetzstein, "Marriage Advocates Eye Federal Funding," *Washington Times*, August 26, 2006.

63. Robert Rector, "Using Welfare Reform to Strengthen Marriage," *American Experiment Quarterly* 4 (2001): 64.

64. Theola Labbe, "Federal Program Would Give D.C. Couples Impetus to Marry," *Washington Post*, July 31, 2005.

65. See, for example, William Julius Wilson, *When Work Disappears: The World of the Urban Poor* (New York: Alfred Knopf Press, 1996); William Julius Wilson and Kathleen Neckerman, "Poverty and Family Structure: The Widening Gap between Evidence and Public Policy Issues," in *The Truly Disadvantaged: The Inner City, The Underclass, and Public Policy*, ed. William Julius Wilson (Chicago: University of Chicago Press, 1987); Kathryn Edin, "Few Good Men: Why Poor Mothers Don't Marry or Remarry," *American Prospect*, June 2, 2000.

66. Sara McLanahan et al., *The Fragile Families and Child Well-Being National Baseline Report* (Princeton, NJ: Princeton University, 2001); Irwin Garfinkle et al., *Fathers under Fire: The Revolution in Child-Support Payments* (New York: Russell Sage Foundation, 1998).

67. Sara McLanahan et al., *The Fragile Families and Child Well-Being National Baseline Report* (Princeton, NJ: Princeton University, 2001); Irwin Garfinkle et al., *Fathers under Fire: The Revolution in Child-Support Payments* (New York: Russell Sage Foundation, 1998).

68. Marc Mauer and Tracy Huling, *Young Black Americans and the Criminal Justice System: Five Years Later* (Washington: The Sentencing Project, 1995).

69. Cynthia Miller and Virginia Knox, *The Challenge of Helping Low-Income Fathers Support Their Children: Final Lessons from Parents Fair Share* (New York: Manpower Demonstration Research Project, 2001).

70. Theodora Ooms, "Marriage and Government: Strange Bedfellows," Center for Law and Social Policy, Policy Brief no. 1, August 2002, p. 3.

71. Sara McLanahan, Irwin Garfinkle, and Ronald Mincy, "Fragile Families, Welfare Reform, and Marriage," Brookings Institution, Welfare Reform and Beyond, Briefing Paper no. 10, November 2001.

72. Robert Lerman, "Marriage as a Protective Force against Economic Hardship" (paper presented at the 23rd Annual Research Conference of the Association for Public Policy and Management, Washington DC, November 1, 2001).

73. Theodora Ooms, "Marriage and Government: Strange Bedfellows," Center for Law and Social Policy, Policy Brief no. 1, August 2002, p. 3.

74. See, for example, Mary Jo Bane, "Household Composition and Poverty," in *Fighting Poverty: What Works and What Doesn't*, ed. Sheldon Danziger and Daniel Weinberg (Cambridge, MA: Harvard University Press, 1986).

75. Theodora Ooms, "Marriage and Government: Strange Bedfellows," Center for Law and Social Policy, Policy Brief no. 1, August 2002.

76. V. Joseph Hotz et al., *The Costs and Consequences of Teenage Childbearing for Mothers* (Chicago: University of Chicago Press, 1995).

77. Neil Gilbert, "The Unfinished Business of Welfare Reform," *Society* 24, no. 3 (March–April 1987): 511.

78. Suzanne Bianchi, "Children of Poverty: Why Are They Poor?" in J. Chafel, *Child Poverty and Public Policy* (Washington: The Urban Institute, 1993), table 4.2, p. 100.

79. Ibid.

80. Isabel Sawhill, "Welfare Reform and the Marriage Movement," Welfare Reform and Beyond Brief no. 8, Brookings Institution, Washington, DC, October 2001.

81. Ibid., p. 4.

82. U.S. Census Bureau, *Fertility of American Women: June 2004*, Current Population Report P20-555, Washington, DC, December 2005.

83. Debra Kalmuss, "Subsequent Childbearing among Teenage Mothers: The Determinants of a Closely-Spaced Second Birth," *Family Planning Perspectives* 26, no. 4 (July 1994): 149–53.

84. Steven McLaughlin et al., "The Effects of Sequencing of Marriage and First Birth at Adolescence," *Family Planning Perspectives* 18, no. 1 (Jan.–Feb. 1986): 12–18.

85. Naomi Seiler, *Is Teen Marriage a Solution?* (Washington: Center for Law and Social Policy, 2002).

86. Isabel Sawhill, "Welfare Reform and the Marriage Movement," Welfare Reform and Beyond Brief no. 8, Brookings Institution, Washington, DC, October 2001, p. 7.

87. Daniel Lichter, Deborah Roemke Graefe, and J. Brian Brown, "Is Marriage a Panacea? Union Formation among Economically-Disadvantaged Unwed Mothers," *Social Problems* 50, no. 1 (2003).

88. I am setting aside the entire question of whether marriage is desirable in and of itself. However, evidence certainly exists that both the Left and Right have allowed their views toward marriage, the roles of women in society, and the propriety of sex outside of marriage to color their views on the economic effect of marriage and the desirability of the federal government's promotion of it.

89. See Patrick Fagan, Robert Patterson, and Robert Rector, "Marriage and Welfare Reform: The Overwhelming Evidence That Marriage Education Works," Heritage Foundation Backgrounder no. 1606, October 25, 2002, for a detailed list of the literature on various marriage initiatives.

90. Significant portions of this section are drawn from Jagadeesh Gokhale and Michael Tanner, "KidSave: Real Problem, Wrong Solution," Cato Institute Policy Analysis no. 562, January 24, 2006.

91. *America Saving for Personal Investment, Retirement, and Education Act of 2005* or *ASPIRE Act of 2005*, S 868, 209th Cong., 1st sess., http://thomas.loc.gov/cgi-bin/bdquery/z?d109:s.00868. It was read twice by the Senate on April 21, 2005. See Rick Santorum, "Kids Accounts: To Nurture Investors," *The Hill*, July 25, 2005.

92. Russ Wiles, "New Programs Launch Savings Plans for Kids," *Arizona Republic*, October 1, 2006.

93. David Brooks, "Mr. President, Let's Share the Wealth," *New York Times*, February 8, 2005.

94. David John, "Congress Should Revive KidSave as an Innovative Step toward Retirement Security," Heritage Foundation Executive Memorandum no. 899, September 17, 2003; Norman Ornstein, "Good (and Not Good) Reasons to Overhaul Social Security," *Roll Call*, February 2, 2005.

95. Michael Sherraden, *Assets and the Poor: A New American Welfare Policy* (Armonk, NY: M.E. Sharpe, 1991).

96. Marvin Oliver and Thomas Shapiro, *Black Wealth/White Wealth* (New York: Rutledge, 1996), p. 2.

97. Robert Havemann and Barbara Wolfe, "Who Are the Asset Poor? Levels, Trends, and Composition, 1983–1998" (paper presented to the Symposium on Asset Building: Research and Policy, Washington University in St. Louis, Center for Social Development, St. Louis, MO, 2000).

98. Ibid.

99. Dalton Conley, *Being Black, Living in the Red: Race, Wealth and Social Policy in America* (Berkeley: University of California Press, 1999).

100. According to population projections of the Social Security Administration, 4.05 million children were born in 2006. That number times $2,000 per newborn child yields $8 billion in the annual cost of the KidSave program (leaving out administrative costs for the sake of simplicity).

101. The cost would be proportionately smaller or larger depending on the size of the initial deposit for each newborn child. Present values are calculated at a discount rate of 3 percent, reflecting the government's opportunity cost of funds for long-term borrowing. (Note: a risk-adjusted discount rate is used.) Proponents of KidSave-type proposals may argue that the investments would earn returns at market rates—more than 5 percent per year. That would incorrectly suggest that a higher discount rate should be used to reduce the present value of the program's cost. The correct discount rate should reflect the government's long-term opportunity cost of funds.

102. Jami Curley and Michael Sherraden, "The History and Status of Children's Allowances: Policy Background for Children's Savings Accounts," Policy Report, Center for Social Development, Washington University, St. Louis, MO, 1998.

103. This is the cost, in present-value terms, of providing a seed account of $2,000 for every child age 18 and younger alive today and every newborn child (at birth) in the future.

104. Jami Curley and Michael Sherraden, "The History and Status of Children's Allowances: Policy Background for Children's Savings Accounts," Policy Report, Center for Social Development, Washington University, St. Louis, MO, 1998.

105. Letter from Congressional Budget Office to Rep. Jerry Weller, July 7, 2005, http://www.cbo.gov/ftpdoc.cfm?index=6523&type=1.

106. Ibid. This sum represents the net present value of the borrowing cost of a $2,000 loan repaid interest free after 30–34 years.

107. Any future fiscal adjustment to resolve the existing imbalances in entitlements must involve a sizable reduction in federal payment commitments on account of entitlements. To the extent we are unable or unwilling to reduce those commitments, national saving needs to be increased to improve the economy's productive capacity to pay for projected retirement and health care costs. KidSave accounts are certainly motivated by the need to increase saving. The key question, therefore, is whether establishing such accounts would help do so. Unfortunately, mandating saving on behalf of children by imposing higher taxes on adults is unlikely to work. Why? For the same reason that imposing higher taxes for financing entitlement commitments will not successfully finance those outstanding commitments. Specifically, higher taxes would cause negative incentive effects on labor supply, capital accumulation, productivity, and output. For those reasons, KidSave accounts might achieve exactly the opposite of what's required. Jagadeesh Gokhale and Michael Tanner, "KidSave: Real Problem, Wrong Solution," Cato Institute Policy Analysis no. 562, January 24, 2006.

108. For a detailed discussion of the administrative structure options for KidSave accounts, see Fred Goldberg and Jodi Berk Cohen, "The Universal Piggy Bank: Designing and Implementing a System of Savings Accounts for Children," Center for Social Development, Washington University in St. Louis, MO, September 2000.

109. In the case of home purchases, however, whether a subsequent home sale would trigger a reversion of the released home equity into KidSave accounts remains unclear. If not, this loophole could be exploited for premature consumption of assets accumulated in KidSave accounts. But requiring such reversions would also entail greater complexity in the tax code. There are additional complications as well: For example, what would be the tax treatment of interest earned on KidSave accounts? Would it be tax free? If so, parents may exploit those accounts to hold their own savings in KidSave accounts and earn returns tax free. However, making interest earnings on KidSave accounts taxable to the parents (as is done in the United Kingdom, for example) would eliminate the benefits of child credits in the federal income tax and increase the complexity of the tax code.

110. KidSave accounts would allow tax-free accumulations of assets until the money is withdrawn (for retirement or earlier for emergency spending needs). To the extent parents were heretofore unable to access tax-free investment vehicles to save for their children's future needs, such accounts would provide it. Access to a tax-subsidized account would enable the parents not only to save more for their children, but also to consume more themselves by reducing their own saving on behalf of their children. Offsetting this increase in consumption would be a reduction in the consumption of those who would bear higher tax burdens but don't have children eligible to receive KidSave accounts. Such individuals generally tend to

be older, high-saving, and wealthy individuals—whose consumption is unlikely to decline by much because of the higher taxes they would pay to finance KidSave accounts. Quite possibly, therefore, total national consumption would increase from introducing KidSave accounts and national saving would *decline*—ultimately causing lower investment, productivity, and output for future generations. The possibility cannot be ruled out that KidSave accounts would cause an outcome precisely the opposite of what is intended.

111. Empirical evidence that parents' consumption would increase following the introduction of KidSave accounts, although indirect, is quite strong. Studies have shown that "effective" transfers of resources from younger to older generations have, over time, increased the consumption of older generations—as would be expected in theory. The transfer itself is the result of the political process whereby older generations have voted for redistributing resources from younger and future generations toward themselves. Such transfers have occurred in two ways: directly, by providing older generations more by way of entitlement benefits than their past payroll tax contributions, and indirectly, through the forced annuitization of benefits that, by insuring retirees against outliving their resources, enables them to consume at a faster rate and reduces involuntary bequests. The studies also confirm that retirees have not undone their forced annuitization of resources through Social Security and Medicare by increasing their purchases of life insurance. See, for example, Alan Auerbach, Jagadeesh Gokhale, Lawrence Kotlikoff, et al., "The Annuitization of Americans' Resources: A Cohort Analysis," in *Essays in Saving, Bequests, Altruism, and Life-Cycle Planning*, ed. Lawrence Kotlikoff (Cambridge, MA: MIT Press, 2001), and Jagadeesh Gokhale, Lawrence Kotlikoff, and J. Sabelhaus, "Understanding the Postwar Decline in U.S. Saving: A Cohort Analysis," in *Brooking Papers on Economic Activity 1996:1, Macroeconomics*, ed. William C. Brainard and George L. Perry (Washington: Brookings Institution Press, 1996), pp. 315–407. The transfer in the reverse direction (that is, from older to younger generations) appears unlikely to be similarly effective because older generations would retain control over the transferred resources directly (as account guardians and managers) or indirectly (through the political process), thereby dictating the future tax burdens to be imposed on children when they become adults.

112. The child tax credit was increased from $500 to $1,000 per child in the Economic Growth and Tax Relief Reconciliation Act of 2001, but the increase is scheduled to expire at the end of tax year 2010.

113. The labor-market effect would be different for those with and without children. The latter would face higher taxes but would not receive any benefit from KidSave accounts. By implication, households facing higher taxes but receiving no benefits from KidSave accounts would reduce their labor-force participation and after-tax earnings in response to higher taxes. Recent literature on how higher taxes affect labor supply points to sizable (uncompensated) elasticities—as high as 0.5. See Alan Krueger and Bruce Meyer, "Labor Supply Effects of Social Insurance" (Working Paper No. 9014, National Bureau of Economic Research, Cambridge, MA, June 2002).

114. See, for example, http://registeredrep.com/mag/finance_college_smarts/index.html; http://www.discovercolleges.com/college_tips/financial_aid_overview.cfm.

115. Several effective private efforts to increase savings exist among the poor. For example, several nonprofit organizations are contributing funds to a program known as SEED (Savings for Education, Entrepreneurship, and Downpayment), a partnership

of the Aspen Institute Initiative for Financial Security, the Center for Social Development of Washington University, CFED, the New America Foundation, and the University of Kansas School of Social Welfare. This program provides an initial deposit and then matches family contributions for four years—up to $1,200. So far, several hundred children in several dozen communities are participating. Among those funding the initiative are the Charles and Helen Schwab Foundation, Citigroup Foundation, the Ford Foundation, MetLife Foundation, and the Richard and Rhoda Goldman Fund. In another example, the St. Louis–based Jim Casey Youth Opportunities Initiative offers "opportunity passports" to teenagers leaving foster care. The program, currently operating in 12 communities around the country, provides $1,000 in matching funds for money these young people save for college, an apartment security deposit, or a car. Amy Goldstein, "Initiatives to Promote Savings from Childhood Catching On," *Washington Post*, August 20, 2005.

Chapter 5

1. "Nobel Prize in Physiology or Medicine Winners 2006–1901," The Nobel Prize Internet Archive, http://almaz.com/nobel/medicine/medicine.html.

2. Pharmaceutical Manufacturers Association, "Facts about the U.S. Pharmaceutical Industry," 2002.

3. *Economic Report of the President* (Washington: Government Printing Office, 2004), p. 192.

4. Gerard Anderson et al., "It's the Prices Stupid: Why the United States Is So Different from Other Countries," *Health Affairs* 22, no. 3 (May/June 2003): 99.

5. Miranda Mugford, "A Comparison of Reported Differences in Definitions of Vital Events and Statistics," *World Health Statistics Quarterly* 36 (1983), cited in Nicholas Eberstadt, *The Tyrany of Numbers: Measurements & Misrule* (Washington: American Enterprise Institute press, 1995), p. 50.

6. Take prostate cancer, for example. Even though American men are more likely to be diagnosed with prostate cancer than their counterparts in other countries, Americans are less likely to die from the disease. Fewer than one of five American men with prostate cancer will die from it, but 57 percent of British men and nearly half of French and German men will. Even in Canada, a quarter of men diagnosed with prostate cancer die from the disease. Similar results can be found for other forms of cancer. For instance, just 30 percent of U.S. citizens diagnosed with colon cancer die from it, compared with fully 74 percent in Britain, 62 percent in New Zealand, 58 percent in France, 57 percent in Germany, 53 percent in Australia, and 36 percent in Canada. Similarly, less than 25 percent of U.S. women die from breast cancer, but 46 percent of British women, 35 percent of French women, 31 percent of German women, 28 percent of Canadian women, 28 percent of Australian women, and 46 percent of women from New Zealand die from it. The same type of results can be seen for diseases ranging from heart disease to AIDS. Gerard Anderson, Varduhi Petrosyan, and Peter Hussey, *Multinational Comparisons of Health Systems Data, 2002* (New York: The Commonwealth Fund, 2002), pp. 55–62; Gerard Anderson and Peter Hussey, *Multinational Comparisons of Health Data Systems Data, 2000* (New York: The Commonwealth Fund, 2000), pp. 17–18; Gerard Anderson and Bianca Frogner, *Multinational Comparisons of Health Data Systems Data, 2005* (New York: The Commonwealth Fund, 2006).

7. Carmen DeNavas-Walt, Bernadette Proctor, and Cheryl Hill Lee, "Income, Poverty, and Health Insurance Coverage in the United States, 2004," U.S. Census Bureau, August 2005, http://www.census.gov/prod/2005pubs/p60-229.pdf.

8. Dick Armey, "Just Gotta Learn from the Wrong Things You've Done," *Cato Journal* 22, no. 1 (2002): 7.

9. "National Health Expenditures," Centers for Medicare and Medicaid Services, 2005, www.cms.hhs.gov/statistics/nhe/.

10. "National Health Expenditures," Centers for Medicare and Medicaid Services, 2005, www.cms.hhs.gov/statistics/nhe/.

11. Cited in Ronald Bailey, "Is *Brave New World* Inevitable?" *Reason*, April 24, 2002.

12. See Michael Tanner, "Individual Mandates for Health Insurance: Slippery Slope to National Health Care," Cato Institute Policy Analysis no. 565, April 5, 2006.

13. Robert Hartman and Paul van de Water, "The Budgetary Treatment of an Individual Mandate to Buy Health Insurance," Congressional Budget Office Memorandum, August 1994.

14. Scott Helman, "Mass Bill Requires Health Insurance," *Boston Globe*, April 4, 2006. For a detailed critique of the Massachusetts plan, see Michael Tanner, "No Miracle in Massachusetts: Why Governor Romney's Health Care Reform Won't Work," Cato Institute Briefing Paper no. 97, June 6, 2006.

15. Scott Helman, "Mass Bill Requires Health Insurance," *Boston Globe*, April 4, 2006.

16. Heidi Przybyla, "Romney Targets Democrats' Turf on Health and Education for 2008," Bloomberg News, March 30, 2006, bloomberg.com.

17. The Heritage Foundation first spelled out the details of its proposal in 1994. Stuart Butler, "The Heritage Foundation Proposal" (presentation to Heritage Foundation conference, "Is Tax Reform the Key to Health Care Reform," Heritage Lectures no. 298, October 23, 1990). However, it has reaffirmed its support for an individual mandate as recently as 2003. Stuart Butler, "Laying the Groundwork for Universal Health Care Coverage," Testimony before the Special Committee on Aging, U.S. Senate, 108th Congress, 1st sess., March 10, 2003, http://aging.senate.gov/public/_files/hr95sb.pdf. The Heritage Foundation hosted a forum for Governor Romney in 2006 during which it implied support. This support should not be surprising. The Heritage Foundation is generally acknowledged to have been involved in drafting Governor Romney's proposal, and Ed Haislmaier, a Heritage Foundation research fellow, wrote in favor of Romney's plan for NationalReviewOnline. Edmund Haislmaier, "Mitt's Fit," *NationalReviewOnline*, January 27, 2006.

18. Bill Frist, "Transforming Health Care: A Patient-Centered, Consumer-Driven and Provider-Friendly Vision" (address to National Press Club, Washington, DC, July 12, 2004).

19. Katie Merx, "Health Cost Savings Backed: Gingrich Calls for National Reform," *Detroit Free Press*, April 2, 2006.

20. Ross Douthat and Reihan Salam, "The Party of Sam's Club," *Weekly Standard* 11, no. 9, November 14, 2005, http://www.weeklystandard.com/Content/Public/Articles/000/000/006/312korit.asp.

21. Far too many conservatives appear to have bought into the idea of universal coverage as the primary focus of health care policy. A better approach would be to shift the health care debate away from its single-minded focus on expanding coverage to the bigger question of how to reduce costs and improve quality.

22. For example, 1 million Britons are waiting for admission to National Health Service hospitals at any given time, and shortages force the National Health Service to cancel as many as 100,000 operations each year. Roughly 90,000 New Zealanders are facing similar waits. In Sweden, the wait for heart surgery can be as long as 25 weeks, while the average wait for hip replacement surgery is more than a year. And in Canada, more than 800,000 patients are currently on waiting lists for medical procedures. See Michael Cannon and Michael Tanner, *Healthy Competition: What's Holding Back Health Care and How to Free It* (Washington: Cato Institute: 2005), pp. 36–37.

23. See, for example, Helen Levy and David Meltzer, "What Do We Really Know about Whether Health Insurance Affects Health?" in *Health Policy and the Uninsured*, ed. Catherine McLaughlin (Washington: Urban Institute, 2004), pp. 179–204.

24. Jack Hadley and John Holahan, *The Cost of Care for the Uninsured: What Do We Spend, Who Pays, and What Would Full Coverage Add to Medical Spending?* Kaiser Commission on Medicaid and the Uninsured, Issue Update, Washington, DC, May 10, 2004.

25. Rob Stewart and Jeffrey Rhoades, "The Long-Term Uninsured," Research Note, U.S. Census Bureau, http://aspe.hhs.gov/health/long-term-uninsured04/report.pdf.

26. This argument is true only if cross subsidies occur in existing pools. If everyone's rates are actuarially fair, then young people's explicit or implicit premiums do not result in lower or higher premiums for anyone else. These two views of health insurance—*ex ante* versus no *ex ante* redistribution—are actually the basis for much analysis and policy prescription in health care.

27. Greg Scandlen, "The Pitfalls of Mandating Health Insurance," *Council for Affordable Health Insurance's Issues & Answers*, no. 135 (April 2006).

28. Greg Kelly, "Can Government Force People to Buy Insurance?" *Council for Affordable Health Insurance's Issues & Answers*, no. 123 (March 2004), citing data from the Insurance Research Council, http://www.cahi.org/cahi_contents/resources/pdf/n123GovernmentMandate.pdf.

29. Stephanie Jones, "Uninsured Drivers Travel under the Radar," *Insurance Journal*, August 18, 2003. In fact, in some areas of Los Angeles, the uninsured rate reaches an astounding 75 percent!

30. Greg Kelly, "Can Government Force People to Buy Insurance?" *Council for Affordable Health Insurance's Issues & Answers*, no. 123 (March 2004).

31. Ibid.

32. 32 "Hawaii: Health Insurance Coverage of the Total Population, States (2003–2004), U.S. (2004)," Kaiser statehealthfacts.org, Urban Institute and Kaiser Commission on Medicaid and the Uninsured estimates based on the Census Bureau's March 2004 and 2005 Current Population Survey (CPS: Annual Social and Economic Supplements).

33. Heather Kent, "BC Doctor Seeks Class-Action Suit over Payment for Uninsured Patients," *Canadian Medical Association Journal* 163, no. 9: 1184.

34. Peter Orszag and Matthew Hall, "Nonfilers and Filers with Modest Tax Liabilities," *Tax Notes*, Tax Policy Center, Urban Institute and Brookings Institution, August 4, 2003, http://www.urban.org/UploadedPDF/1000548_TaxFacts_080403.pdf.

35. Nina Olsen, *National Taxpayer Advocate 2003 Annual Report to Congress*, Taxpayer Advocate Service, Internal Revenue Service, December 31, 2003, http://www.irs.gov/pub/irs-utl/nta_2003_annual_update_mcw_1-15-042.pdf.

36. Michael Calabrese and Laurie Rubiner, "Universal Coverage, Universal Responsibility: A Roadmap to Make Coverage Affordable for All Americans," New America Foundation Universal Health Insurance Program Working Paper no. 1, January 2004, p. 4, http://www.newamerica.net/Download_Docs/pdfs/Pub_File_1443_1.pdf.

37. David R. Guarino, "Six House Reps Fail to File Income Tax Returns," *Boston Herald*, March 10, 2005.

38. Lyle Nelson, *How Many People Lack Health Insurance and for How Long?* Congressional Budget Office, May 12, 2003, http://www.policyalmanac.org/health/archive/health_insurance.shtml.

39. C. Eugene Steuerle, "Implementing Employer and Individual Mandates," *Health Affairs* (Spring II, 1994): 54.

40. Ibid.: 62.

41. *The Uninsured: A Primer, Key Facts about Americans without Health Insurance*, Kaiser Commission on Medicaid and the Uninsured, Washington, DC, December 2003, http://www.kff.org/uninsured/7451.cfm.

42. Michael Calabrese and Laurie Rubiner, "Universal Coverage, Universal Responsibility: A Roadmap to Make Coverage Affordable for All Americans," New America Foundation Universal Health Insurance Program Working Paper no. 1, January 2004, p. 5.

43. Julie Appleby, "Average Family Health Policy Nears $11,000," *USA Today*, September 14, 2005. Of course for most people, much or all of this cost is hidden, paid by their employer. But people who do not receive employer-paid health insurance—the subjects of an individual mandate—would have to bear the cost themselves.

44. For example, the average cost of a Health Savings Account–qualified family policy is roughly $7,900. "Employer Health Benefits 2005 Annual Survey," Kaiser Family Foundation, p. 97, http://kff.org/insurance/7315/upload/7315.pdf.

45. Kenneth Thorpe, "An Analysis of the Costs and Coverage Associated with Blue Shield of California's Universal Health Insurance Plan for All Americans," Emory University, June 11, 2003.

46. Scott Helman and Liz Kowalczyk, "Joy, Worries on Health Care," *Boston Globe*, April 13, 2006.

47. Massachusetts also expects to receive approximately $610 million annually in federal funds under a Medicaid waiver.

48. "Health Care Access and Affordability Conference Committee Report," April 3, 2006, http://www.mass.gov/legis/summary.pdf. Even these estimates may be based on unrealistic assumptions. For example, medical inflation in Massachusetts has been running between 10 and 14 percent annually. The bill's projected costs are based on a medical inflation rate of 10 percent. Higher inflation would drive subsidy costs to more than $800 million per year. Lawmakers also assumed that use of "the state's 'free care pool,'" a pot of money used to pay hospitals for treating uninsured residents, will drop dramatically as more uninsured residents buy insurance. The savings would go toward subsidies to help low-income uninsured residents buy health plans. But if, for reasons discussed above, the mandate fails to significantly reduce the number of uninsured, the savings will be less than projected. Scott Helman and Liz Kowalczyk, "Joy, Worries on Health Care," *Boston Globe*, April 13, 2006.

49. Victoria Colliver, "High Cost for Health Insurance/Massachusetts Plan Would Run Billions More in California," *San Francisco Chronicle*, April 27, 2006.

50. Michael Cannon, "Medicaid's Unseen Costs," Cato Institute Policy Analysis no. 548, August 18, 2005.

51. Massachusetts has some 40 mandated benefits, including treatment for alcoholism, blood lead poisoning, bone marrow transplants, breast reconstruction, cervical cancer/human papillomavirus screening, clinical trials, contraceptives, diabetic supplies, emergency services, hair prostheses, home health care, in vitro fertilization, mammograms, mastectomy, maternity care and maternity stays, mental health generally (in addition there is a requirement for mental health parity), newborn hearing screening, off-label drug use, phenylketonuria/formula, prostate screening, rehabilitation services, and well-child care. Services for the following providers must also be covered: chiropractors, dentists, nurse anesthetists, nurse midwives, optometrists, podiatrists, professional counselors, psychiatric nurses, psychologists, social workers, and speech or hearing therapists. Insurance policies must provide coverage to adopted children, handicapped dependents, and newborns. Victoria Craig Bunce, J. P. Wieske, and Vlasta Prikazky, "Health Insurance Mandates in the States, 2006," Council for Affordable Health Insurance, March 2006, http://www.aba.com/NR/rdonlyres/7DEC4FCA-57A0-4CC5-834A-22C9AB859D37/43015/CAHIStateMandates32006.pdf.

52. Michael Calabrese and Laurie Rubiner, "Universal Coverage, Universal Responsibility: A Roadmap to Make Coverage Affordable for All Americans," New America Foundation Universal Health Insurance Program Working Paper no. 1, January 2004.

53. "Blue Shield Offers Healthcare Plan for Universal Coverage with Universal Responsibility," Blue Shield Association of California, press release, December 3, 2002. See also, Kenneth Thorpe, "An Analysis of the Costs and Coverage Associated with Blue Shield of California's Universal Health Insurance Plan for All Americans," Blue Shield Association of California, June 11, 2003.

54. Stuart Butler, "The Heritage Foundation Proposal" (presentation to Heritage Foundation conference, "Is Tax Reform the Key to Health Care Reform," Heritage Lectures no. 298, October 23, 1990), p. 18. Although 16 years old, this formulation remains the clearest presentation of the Heritage Foundation's position, which has not changed.

55. Victoria Craig Bunce, J. P. Wieske, and Vlasta Prikazky, "Health Insurance Mandates in the States, 2006," Council for Affordable Health Insurance, March 2006, http://www.cahi.org/cahi_contents/resources/pdf/MandatePubDec2004.pdf.

56. Ibid.

57. *Prioritization of Health Services: A Report to the Governor and Legislature*, Oregon Health Services Commission, 1991.

58. *Evaluation of the Oregon Medicaid Proposal*, United States Office of Technology Assessment (1992), quoted in Jonathan Oberlander, Theodore Marmor and Lawrence Jacobs, "Rationing Medical Care: Rhetoric and Reality in the Oregon Health Plan," *Canadian Medical Association Journal* 164, no. 11 (2001): 1586.

59. Scott Helman, "Lobbyists Took in $7.5 Million on Health Bill," *Boston Globe*, April 5, 2006.

60. To see this process in action, one only has to look at the details of the comprehensive proposals containing individual mandates. For example, many supporters of an individual mandate also would require insurers to accept all comers without any waiting period for preexisting conditions. They embrace community rating (a prohibition on charging different premiums based on factors such as age, sex, occupation, or health status) and would prohibit any risk rating of premiums. In addition, we

have already seen that enormous special-interest pressure will exist to add benefits to the mandated package. As more benefits are added, the cost of the mandate would increase. That will place legislators in a very difficult position. If they increase subsidies to keep pace with the rising cost of the mandate, the cost of the program will explode. If they hold subsidies steady, the increased cost will be borne by consumers, who would have no choice but to continue purchasing the ever more expensive insurance. Because the consumers would have little or no leverage over insurers (they can no longer refuse to buy their products), they can eventually be expected to turn to the only entity that can hold down their costs—the government. Attempts to scale back benefits would certainly meet political opposition from powerful constituencies complaining about "cuts." The only other alternative would be for the government to intervene directly by capping premiums. Insurers unable to charge more for an increasingly expensive product can be expected to trim costs by cutting back on their reimbursement rates to hospitals and physicians. The result will ultimately be rationing, the lack of available health care goods and services.

61. See Alain Enthoven, "The History and Principles of Managed Competition," *Health Affairs* 12 supplement 1 (1993): 24–48.

62. Richard Epstein, "Unmanageable Care," *Reason*, May 1993.

63. Chapter 58 of the Acts of 2006, section 101. The law defines the connector as "a body politic and corporate and a public instrumentality." It is designed to operate independent of any other government agency and has a corporate charter, but its board consists of the Massachusetts secretary of administration and finance, the state Medicaid director, the state commissioner of insurance, the executive director of the group insurance commission, three members appointed by the governor, and three members appointed by the attorney general. As an entity it falls somewhere between a government agency and a private corporation. One useful analogy would be the Federal Reserve Board.

64. Robert Moffit and Nina Owcharenko, "Understanding Key Parts of the Massachusetts Health Plan," *Human Events Online*, April 21, 2006, http://www.humanevents.com/article.php?id = 14200.

65. Chapter 58 of the Acts of 2006, sections 101 and 76.

66. See Tom Miller, "Nickles-Stearns Is Not the Market Choice for Health Care Reform," Cato Institute Policy Analysis no. 210, June 13, 1994.

67. Edmund Haislmaier, "The Significance of Massachusetts Health Reform," Heritage Foundation WebMemo no. 1035, April 11, 2006, http://www.heritage.org/Research/HealthCare/wm1035.cfm.

68. See, for example, Robert Moffit, "Promoting Choice and Controlling Cost: What Congress Can Learn—Again—from Its Own Health Insurance Program," Heritage Foundation WebMemo no. 146, September 20, 2002, http://www.heritage.org/Research/HealthCare/wm146.cfm.

69. U.S. General Accounting Office, *Federal Employees' Health Plans: Premium Growth and OPM's Role in Negotiating Benefits*, Report to the Subcommittee on International Security, Proliferation, and Federal Services, Committee on Governmental Affairs, U.S. Senate, GAO-03-236, December 2002.

70. Conover estimates the total cost of regulation at $339.2 billion but suggests that the regulations provide benefits equal to $170.1 billion, leaving a net cost of $169.1 billion. Christopher Conover, "Health Care Regulation: A $169 Billion Hidden Tax," Cato Institute Policy Analysis no. 527, October 4, 2004.

71. Jennifer Anne Perez, "Association Health Plans: A Godsend, or a Recipe for Disaster?" *Entrepreneur Extra*, February 20, 2003.

72. *Health Care Choice Act of 2005*, HR 2355, 109th Cong., 1st sess., May 12, 2005, http://thomas.loc.gov/cgi-bin/bdquery/z?d109:h2355.

73. See, for example, Al Dobson, "A Comparative Study of Patient Severity, Quality of Care, and Community Impact at MedCath Heart Hospitals," The Lewin Group, February 2004, http://www.medcath.com/corp/content/Lewin-executive-summary-5-13-03.pdf.

74. General Accounting Office, "Specialty Hospitals: Information on National Market Share, Physician Ownership, and Patients Served," letter to Reps. Bill Thomas and Jerry Kleczka, April 18, 2003. Copy in author's files.

75. Newt Gingrich, "A Health Threat We're Not Treating," *Washington Post*, November 12, 2005.

76. "Medicare Drug Act Imposes Moratorium on Physician-Owned Specialty Hospitals," *BNA's Health Care Fraud Report*, February 4, 2004.

77. Federal Trade Commission and Department of Justice, *Improving Health Care: A Dose of Competition* (Washington: FTC, July 23, 2004), Executive Summary, p. 20, note 22.

78. Newt Gingrich, *Winning the Future: A 21st Century Contract with America* (New York: Regnery, 2005), p. 117.

79. Kate Schuler, "White House Looks to Price Transparency to Lower National Health Care Costs," *CQ Today*, March 13, 2006.

80. Gardiner Harris, "U.S. Rules Morning After Pill Can't Be Sold over the Counter," *New York Times*, May 7, 2004.

81. Christine Hall, "Pro-Life Groups Petition FDA to Revoke RU 486 Approval," CNS News Service, August 21, 2002.

82. Julia Duin, "Teen Dead after Abortion Pill," *Washington Times*, September 22, 2003. Approximately seven deaths have been linked to RU-486 through mid-2006, though in some cases the cause of death is disputed. "Deaths after RU-486," *New York Times*, April 10, 2006. However, experts who track outcomes associated with RU-486 continue to maintain that the drug is safe for use. Michael Greene, "Fatal Infections Associated with Mifepristone-Induced Abortion," *New England Journal of Medicine* 353, no. 22 (2005): 2317–18.

83. S 581, "RU-486 Suspension and Review Act of 2003," 108th Cong., 1st sess., November 21, 2003, http://thomas.loc.gov/cgi-bin/bdquery/z?d108:SN01930:. A House version of the bill has 80 cosponsors. HR 3453, 108th Cong., 1st sess., November 6, 2004, November 14, 2004, http://thomas.loc.gov/cgi-bin/bdquery/z?d108:h3453.

84. Gardiner Harris, "2 Republicans in Senate Vow to Block F.D.A. Pick," *New York Times*, September 15, 2006.

85. Gardiner Harris, "FDA Dismisses Medical Benefit from Marijuana," *New York Times*, April 21, 2006.

86. "Frist Calls for Two Year Moratorium on Direct-to-Consumer Drug Advertising for New Drugs" (press release, July 1, 2005, http://frist.senate.gov/index.cfm?FuseAction = PressReleases.Detail&PressRelease_id = 1988&Month = 7&Year = 2005).

87. Reimportation is technically permitted from 25 named countries by the manufacturer, wholesalers, or licensed pharmacists, but only after the secretary of health and human services has certified that certain safety and cost-saving requirements have been met. Under the Bush administration, Health and Human Services has refused to issue such certification, effectively blocking commercial reimportation.

Individuals are prohibited from reimporting drugs under any circumstances, but the FDA has not attempted to enforce this provision against people who bring in small amounts of a drug (less than a 90-day supply) for personal use.

88. For a discussion of how reimportation could be done properly, see Roger Pilon, "Drug Reimportation: The Free Market Solution," Cato Institute Policy Analysis no. 521, August 4, 2004.

89. Sen. John Kyl, "Pharmaceutical Price Controls Abroad: An Unfair Trade Policy," Republican Policy Committee, November 6, 2003.

90. Milton Friedman, "Milton Friedman and the Reimportation Debate," Tech Central Station, February 2, 2004; Richard Epstein, "A Perversion of Free Trade," Tech Central Station, July 24, 2003, http://www.tcsdaily.com/article.aspx?id=020204D.

91. Quoted in Jim Abrams, "Import Drug Bill Clears House," Associated Press, July 25, 2003.

92. Nina Owcharenko, "Time to Stop Drug Reimportation," Heritage Foundation Commentary, August 25, 2004. Emphasis added.

93. Robert Goldberg, "Drug Reimportation Makes No Sense," *Chicago Tribune*, August 23, 2002.

94. "Former House Speaker Newt Gingrich Calls for Increased Investment in Health Care Information Technology," *California Healthline*, May 10, 2005.

95. Andrea Stone, "Former Foes Clinton, Gingrich Band Up on Health Care Plan," *USA Today*, May 11, 2005.

96. Bill Crounse, "Electronic Medical Records: The Right Medicine for an Ailing Healthcare System," Microsoft News for Healthcare Providers, November 22, 2005, http://www.microsoft.com/industry/healthcare/providers/businessvalue/housecalls/emr.mspx.

97. Andrea Stone, "Former Foes Clinton, Gingrich Band Up on Health Care Plan," *USA Today*, May 11, 2005.

98. "Widespread Adoption of Health Information Technology Could Save $162 Billion a Year, Says Rand Study, but the Federal Government Needs Help," *Health Affairs*, September 14, 2005.

99. Bernie Monegain, "Datamonitor: Physicians to Drive Healthcare IT Spending Growth," *Health Care IT News*, February 2, 2006.

100. "How Much Is Really Being Spent on IT?" The Health Care Blog, February 7, 2004, http://www.thehealthcareblog.com/the_health_care_blog/2004/06/technology_how_.html.

101. Neil Versel, "Tech Spending Grows Fastest in Health Care," *Modern Physician*, November 19, 2003.

102. Bill Crounse, "Electronic Medical Records: The Right Medicine for an Ailing Healthcare System," Microsoft News for Healthcare Providers, November 22, 2005.

103. http://www.teladoc.com/home.php; http://www.pinnaclecare.com.

104. "What All Americans Should Consider Regarding H.R. 2234," *Health Freedom Watch*, May 2005.

105. Amy Goldstein, "Medical Privacy Changes Proposed," *Washington Post*, March 22, 2002.

106. Charlotte Twight, "Prying Eyes: The End of Medical Privacy," *FoxNewsOnline*, January 22, 2003.

Chapter 6

1. In the context of government spending, "entitlements" are those programs that do not require an annual appropriation by Congress. Funding levels are automatically

set by the number of eligible recipients or other formulas and are not subject to congressional discretion. Each person eligible for benefits by law receives them unless Congress changes the eligibility criteria. The three largest entitlement programs are Social Security, Medicare, and Medicaid. But many other programs, including veterans' benefits and even agricultural subsidies, are also entitlements.

2. Brian Reidl, "The President's Budget: Strong on Short-Term Spending, but Long-Term Challenges Remain," Heritage Foundation Web Memo no. 990, February 6, 2006, http://www.heritage.org/Research/Budget/wm990.cfm.

3. *Budget of the United States, Fiscal Year 2007* (Washington: Executive Office of the President, Office of Management and Budget, 2006), p. 18.

4. Ibid.

5. Congressional Budget Office, *The Long-Term Budget Outlook*, December 2003.

6. Ibid.

7. Brian M. Riedl, "Entitlement-Driven Long-Term Budget Substantially Worse Than Previously Projected," Heritage Foundation Backgrounder no. 1897, November 30, 2005.

8. Medicaid is not strictly speaking a program for the elderly. It is a means-tested program for low-income individuals. However, more than a quarter of Medicaid spending is attributable to the elderly, primarily for long-term care. Kaiser Commission on Medicaid and the Uninsured, "Medicaid Program at a Glance," January 2005, http://www.kff.org/medicaid/upload/The-Medicaid-Program-at-a-Glance-Fact-Sheet.pdf.

9. Congressional Budget Office, *A 125-Year Picture of the Federal Government's Share of the Economy, 1950 to 2075*, Long-Range Fiscal Policy Brief No. 1 (June 14, 2002; revised July 3, 2002).

10. Social Security Administration, *2006 Annual Report of the Board of Trustees of the Federal Old-Age and Survivors Insurance and Disability Insurance Trust Funds* (Washington: Government Printing Office, 2006).

11. This figure is in present-value terms over an infinite horizon. That is, $85 trillion would have to be saved today, earning 2.9 percent interest, to pay all the promised future benefits. Social Security Administration, *2006 Annual Report of the Board of Trustees of the Federal Old-Age and Survivors Insurance and Federal Disabilities Insurance Trust Fund* (Washington: Government Printing Office, 2006); U.S. Department of Health and Human Services, Centers for Medicare & Medicaid Services, *2006 Annual Report of the Board of Trustees of the Federal Hospital Insurance and Federal Supplemental Medical Insurance Trust Funds Fund* (Washington: Government Printing Office, 2006). This amount is in addition to the "official" national debt of $8.4 trillion. Given that the total U.S. GDP in 2005 was only $11.75 trillion, the magnitude of the problem is easy to see. "Rank Order: GDP (Purchasing Power Parity)," in *World Factbook* (Washington: Central Intelligence Agency, 2006).

12. Brian M. Riedl, "Entitlement-Driven Long-Term Budget Substantially Worse Than Previously Projected," Heritage Foundation Backgrounder no. 1897, November 30, 2005.

13. "Preface," in *21st Century Challenges: Reexamining the Base of the Federal Government*, GAO-05-325SP (Washington: Government Accountability Office: 2005).

14. Congressional Budget Office, *The Long-Term Budget Outlook*, December 2005.

15. Bruce Bartlett, *Imposter: How George W. Bush Bankrupted America and Betrayed the Reagan Legacy* (New York: Doubleday, 2006), p. 157.

16. Alan Greenspan (remarks to the Federal Reserve Bank of Philadelphia, December 2, 2005).

17. Bipartisan Commission on Entitlement and Tax Reform, *Final Report to the President* (Washington: Government Printing Office/Diane Pub Co., 1995), p. 8.

18. National Bipartisan Commission on the Future of Medicare, "Building a Better Medicare for Today and Tomorrow", March 16, 1999, http://medicare.commission.gov/medicare/index.html.

19. U.S. Department of Health and Human Services, Centers for Medicare & Medicaid Services, *2005 Annual Report of the Board of Trustees of the Federal Hospital Insurance and Federal Supplementary Medical Insurance Trust Funds* (Washington: Government Printing Office, 2005), p. 107.

20. David Walker, "Budget Process: Long-Term Focus Is Critical," statement before the House Committee on Rules, Subcommittee on Legislative and Budget Process, 108th Cong., 2nd sess., March 23, 2004, GAO-04-585T.

21. Joseph Antos and Jagadeesh Gokhale, "Medicare Prescription Drugs: Medical Necessity Meets Fiscal Insanity," Cato Institute Briefing Paper no. 91, February 9, 2005.

22. Irving Kristol, "Is the Welfare State Obsolete," *Harper's*, June 1963.

23. Irving Kristol, "A Conservative Welfare State," *Wall Street Journal*, June 14, 1993.

24. Heidi Przybyla, "Evangelicals Cool to Bush's Focus on Social Security Accounts," Bloomberg, April 19, 2005.

25. John Mueller, *Winners and Losers from Privatizing Social Security* (Washington: National Committee to Preserve Social Security and Medicare, 1999). A summary is available at http://www.eppc.org/publications/pubID.2369/pub_detail.asp.

26. John Mueller, "Taxes, Social Security & the Politics of Reform," *Weekly Standard*, November 29, 2004.

27. David Kirkpatrick and Sheryl Stolberg, "Backers of Gay Marriage Ban Use Social Security as Cudgel," *New York Times*, January 25, 2005. Among those signing the letter were Gary Bauer, James Dobson, Jerry Falwell, Tony Perkins, Richard Viguerie, and Paul Weyrich.

28. Richard Brookhiser, "Call Me Pete. (Pierre S. Du Pont IV)," *National Review*, December 31, 1987.

29. Ramesh Ponnuru, "Ponzi's Revenge—Social Security," *National Review*, February 24, 1997.

30. Newt Gingrich, "Promoting Active, Healthy Aging," *Newt.org*.

31. Dan Goodgame, "Reining in the Rich," *Time*, December 19, 1994.

32. Newt Gingrich, testimony before the House Committee on Ways and Means, Hearing on the Use of an Expert Panel to Design Long-Range Social Security Reform, 105th Cong., 2nd sess., April 1, 1998, http://waysandmeans.house.gov/legacy/fullcomm/105cong/4-1-98/4-1ging.htm.

33. Newt Gingrich, "Promoting Active, Healthy Aging," *Newt.org*.

34. Social Security Administration, *2003 Annual Report of the Board of Trustees of the Federal Hospital Insurance and Federal Supplemental Medical Insurance Trust Funds Fund* (Washington: Government Printing Office, 2003).

35. Ibid.

36. U.S. Department of Health and Human Services, Centers for Medicare & Medicaid Services, *2006 Annual Report of the Board of Trustees of the Federal Hospital Insurance and Federal Supplemental Medical Insurance Trust Funds Fund* (Washington: Government Printing Office, 2006).

37. Douglas Holtz-Eakin, "The Medicare Challenge: It's Not Just about Prescription Drugs," statement before the Senate Special Committee on Aging, 108th Cong., 1st sess., March 20, 2003, http://frwebgate.access.gpo.gov/cgi-bin/getdoc.cgi? dbname = 108_senate_hearings&docid = f:87355.pdf.

38. We set aside for the moment the question of deteriorating quality in the Medicare system. However, the system remains troubled in many ways beyond cost. See Sue Blevins, *Medicare's Midlife Crisis* (Washington: Cato Institute, 2001).

39. Jagadeesh Gokhale, testimony before the Committee on Homeland Security and Government Affairs, Subcommittee on Federal Financial Management, Government Information, and International Security, 107th Cong., 1st sess., September 22, 2005, http://www.gao.gov/new.items/d01713t.pdf.

40. Bruce Bartlett, *Impostor: How George W. Bush Bankrupted America and Betrayed the Reagan Legacy* (New York: Doubleday, 2006), p. 64.

41. See William J. Scanlon, "Cost Sharing Policies Problematic for Beneficiaries and Program," testimony before the Subcommittee on Health, House Committee on Ways and Means, 107th Cong., 1st sess., May 9, 2001, http://www.gao.gov/new.items/d01713t.pdf.

42. Dan Crippen, Director, Congressional Budget Office, statement before the Senate Finance Committee, 107th Cong., 1st sess., March 22, 2001, http://www.senate.gov/~finance/72755.pdf.

43. "Bad Medicare Math," *Wall Street Journal*, March 17, 2004.

44. Amy Goldstein, "Foster: White House Had Role in Withholding Medicare Data," *Washington Post*, March 19, 2004.

45. Majority Leader Tom DeLay (R-TX) was later "admonished" by the House Ethics Committee for offering retiring Rep. Nick Smith (R-MI) financial support and endorsements for his son, who Smith hoped would succeed him in Congress. Charles Babington, "Ethics Panel Rebukes Delay," *Washington Post*, October 1, 2004. Smith courageously resisted and voted no. His son was defeated in the party primary.

46. Norman Ornstein, " . . . And mischief," *Washington Post*, November 26, 2003.

47. Medicare Part A, the Hospital Insurance program, pays for inpatient hospital, skilled nursing facility, and hospice care. Accounting for 45 percent of spending in 2005, Part A is funded by a dedicated tax of 2.9 percent of wages paid by employers and employees. Medicare Part B, Supplementary Medical Insurance, pays for physician, outpatient, and preventive services. Part B is funded by general revenues and beneficiary premiums. Medicare Part C refers to private Medicare Advantage Plans, such as HMOs, which provide benefits through contracts with private insurance companies, and accounted for 15 percent of benefit spending in 2005.

48. The Henry J. Kaiser Family Foundation, *Fact Sheet: The Medicare Prescription Drug Benefit*, September 2005, http://www.kff.org/medicare/upload/7044-04.pdf; Jim Mays and Monica Brenner et al., *Estimates of Medicare Beneficiaries Out-of-Pocket Spending; Modeling Impact of MMA* (Washington: The Henry J. Kaiser Family Foundation), 2004, p. 5.

49. Sheryl Stolberg and Milt Freudenheim, "AARP Support for Medicare Bill Came as Group Grew 'Younger,'" *New York Times*, November 26, 2003.

50. *Medicare-Guaranteed Prescription Drug Act of 2006*, S 2342, 109th Cong., 2nd sess., March 1, 2006, http://thomas.loc.gov/cgi-bin/bdquery/z?d109:s.02342.

51. The Congressional Budget Office estimates that as many as one-fourth of the participants in the new entitlement would have had private drug coverage anyway.

A Detailed Description of CBO's Cost Estimate for the Medicare Prescription Drug Benefit (Washington: Congressional Budget Office, 2004).

52. Theo Francis, "Retiree Costs Get Recalculated," *Wall Street Journal*, March 2, 2004.

53. Ibid.

54. Tracy Correa, "Companies Back Off on Health Care," *Fresno Bee*, October 28, 2005.

55. Congressional Budget Office, *A Detailed Description of CBO's Cost Estimate for the Medicare Prescription Drug Benefit* (Washington: CBO, 2004).

56. Cost estimate by Michael Cannon, Cato Institute, based on Congressional Budget Office figures. Michael Cannon, "Eight Reasons to Delay the Imprudent Drug Program," *The Hill*, November 9, 2005.

57. See http://newmeds.phrma.org/.

58. Alex Berenson, "Cancer Drugs Offer Hope, but at Huge Expense," *New York Times*, July 12, 2005.

59. Quoted in ibid.

60. See Christopher Lee, "Problems Cited in Medicare Prescription Drug Sign-Up," *Washington Post*, November 16, 2005; Robert Pear, "Confusion Is Rife about Drug Plan as Sign Up Nears," *New York Times*, November 13, 2005. However, polls indicate that most seniors who have enrolled in the program say they had no trouble using—or signing up for—the prescription drug benefit. Bill Brubaker, "Survey Refutes Criticism of Medicare Drug Plan," *Washington Post*, March 13, 2006.

61. Amy Goldstein and Shailagh Murray, "New Medicare Drug Plan Is Called a Success," *Washington Post*, May 17, 2006.

62. Ibid.

63. Robert Pear, "Bipartisan Senate Group Seeks to Lift Late Fees on Medicare Drug Plan," *New York Times*, May 17, 2006.

64. Ibid.

65. The Department of Health and Human Services has issued rules requiring insurers to grandfather plan participants until the next open-enrollment period when formularies are changed. However, changes from brand name to generic drugs are not covered under this rule. Robert Pear, "Medicare Rule Guarantees Continuity of Drugs," *New York Times*, April 27, 2006.

66. Jeffrey Birnbaum and Claudia Deane, "Most Seniors Enrolled Say Drug Benefit Saves Money," *Washington Post*, April 12, 2006.

67. Richard Wolf, "1 in 5 Pay More in Medicare Rx Plan," *USA Today*, April 27, 2006.

68. Kate Schuler, "Critics Renew Call for Delay or Repeal of Medicare Drug Benefit," *Congressional Quarterly*, October 8, 2005.

69. Peter Baker and Mike Allen, "President Vows to Veto Any Changes to Medicare," *Washington Post*, February 12, 2005.

70. Quoted in Major Garrett, *The Enduring Revolution: How the Contract with America Continues to Shape the Nation* (New York: Crown Forum, 2005), p. 270.

71. Social Security Administration, *2006 Annual Report of the Board of Trustees of the Federal Old-Age and Survivors Insurance and Disability Insurance Trust Funds* (Washington: Government Printing Office, 2006).

72. Social Security Administration, *2006 Annual Report of the Board of Trustees of the Federal Old-Age and Survivors Insurance and Disability Insurance Trust Funds* (Washington: Government Printing Office, 2006).

73. *Budget of the United States Government, Fiscal Year 2000: Analytical Perspectives* (Washington: Executive Office of the President, Office of Management and Budget, 1999), p. 337. Emphasis added.

74. Social Security Administration, *2006 Annual Report of the Board of Trustees of the Federal Old-Age and Survivors Insurance and Disability Insurance Trust Funds* (Washington: Government Printing Office, 2006).

75. *Flemming v. Nestor*, 363 U.S. 603 (1960). For a fuller discussion of this issue, see Charles Rounds, "Property Rights: The Hidden Issue of Social Security Reform," Cato Institute Social Security Paper no. 19, April 19, 2003.

76. See Michael Tanner, "Disparate Impact: Social Security and African-Americans," Cato Institute Briefing Paper no. 61, February 5, 2001.

77. William Jefferson Clinton (speech to the Great Social Security Debate, Albuquerque, NM, July 27, 1998, http://www.ssa.gov/history/clntstmts.html#forum72798).

78. Quoted in Jim VandeHei and Mike Allen, "In GOP, Resistance on Social Security," *Washington Post*, January 11, 2005.

79. *Fox News Sunday*, May 1, 2005. This pronouncement was just one among many.

80. Cited in Caroline Baum, "Bush Elicits Third-Rail Sparks from Left, Right," Bloomberg, May 4, 2005.

81. Quoted in Jim VandeHei and Peter Baker, "Bush Struggles to Regain His Pre-Hurricane Swagger," *Washington Post*, September 24, 2005.

82. Quoted in Jim VandeHei and Mike Allen, "In GOP, Resistance on Social Security," *Washington Post*, January 11, 2005.

83. Quoted in ibid.

84. George W. Bush (remarks to the press aboard Air Force One, April 8, 2005), http://www.whitehouse.gov/news/releases/2005/04/20050408.html.

85. Mike Allen, "Hastert Doubtful on Social Security Bill," *Washington Post*, April 1, 2005.

86. David Espo, "Parties Hope to Win on Social Security," Associated Press, February 21, 2005.

87. Jonathan Weisman, "Social Security Legislation Could Be Shelved," *Washington Post*, September 16, 2005.

88. *Social Security Personal Savings Guarantee and Prosperity Act of 2004*, HR 4851, 108th Cong., 2nd sess., http://thomas.loc.gov/cgi-bin/bdquery/D?d108:69:./temp/~bdafBE. This legislation would still have been *far* superior to the current system. Many of the bill's supporters were traditional small-government conservatives who believed that (a) benefit changes were politically impossible, (b) the higher rate of return from private investment would render benefit reductions unnecessary, or (c) both. Although I disagree with this approach, I do not doubt the sincerity of the bill's sponsors or their commitment to reform. What is unfortunate is the intemperate language used by some of the bill's nonlegislative supporters.

89. Memorandum from Stephen C. Goss to Representative Paul Ryan, "Estimated Financial Effects of the 'Social Security Personal Savings and Prosperity Act of 2004,'" July 19, 2004, http://www.ssa.gov/OACT/solvency/PRyan_20040719.html.

90. Peter Ferrara, "Charge of the Light Brigade," *Washington Times*, January 10, 2005.

91. Peter Ferrara, "Personal Accounts Preferred," *Washington Times*, May 27, 2005.

92. For a detailed critique of the administration's approach, see Ed Crane, "Memo to Karl Rove," *Wall Street Journal*, April 18, 2005.

93. Susan Page, "Conflict Will Define Bush's Role in History," *USA Today*, March 13, 2006. Even President Bush admits that he is "spending my political capital on Iraq." Presidential press conference, March 21, 2006.

94. This failure is a particular shame because Social Security reform was once a bipartisan issue. Democrats like Sens. John Breaux (LA), Bob Kerrey (NE), and Daniel Patrick Moynihan (NY) were outspoken in warning about the program's looming insolvency and calling for innovative approaches to fixing it. The Democratic Leadership Council and its think-tank arm, the Progressive Policy Institute, explored ideas including personal accounts. Representatives like Charlie Stenholm (D-TX) reached across the aisle in search of compromise. Even President Clinton led a national debate to "Save Social Security First."

95. Former representative Charlie Stenholm, among others, tells the author that the administration failed to take even the bare minimum steps necessary to build support among moderate Democrats.

96. S 1302 and HR 3304 (known as GROW for Growing Real Ownership for Workers), 109th Cong., 1st sess., http://thomas.loc.gov/cgi-bin/bdquery/z?d109:h.r.03304. See Michael Tanner, "The Personal Lockbox: A First Step on the Road to Social Security Reform," Cato Institute Social Security Paper no. 36, September 13, 2006.

97. As Federal Reserve Chairman Alan Greenspan has suggested, "If those funds had been removed from the unified budget and 'locked up' . . . a reasonable hypothesis is that Congress would, in fact, have responded by taking actions to pare the deficit." Alan Greenspan, testimony before the Senate Special Committee on Aging, 109th Cong., 1st sess., March 15, 2005, http://www.federalreserve.gov/BoardDocs/Testimony/2005/20050315/default.htm. Indeed, the overwhelming body of recent research suggests not only that Congress increases its spending to offset every dollar of trust fund accumulations, but also that the availability of Social Security surpluses actually encourages Congress to increase its non–Social Security spending even beyond the size of the surplus. That is, studies indicate that for every dollar of Social Security surplus, Congress increases non–Social Security spending by $1.50–$2.00. Sita Nataraj and John Shoven, "Has the Unified Budget Destroyed the Federal Government Trust Funds?" (paper presented at a conference sponsored by the Office of Policy, Social Security Administration, and Michigan Retirement Research Consortium, Washington, DC, August 12–13, 2004); Kent Smetters, "Is the Social Security Trust Fund a Store of Value," *American Economic Review* 94, no. 2 (May 2004): 176–81. As Cato Senior Fellow Jagadeesh Gokhale notes, "Social Security's current institutional setup promotes *negative* savings." Jagadeesh Gokhale, "Social Security Status Quo versus Reform: What's the Tradeoff?" Cato Institute Social Security Paper no. 35, July 12, 2005, p. 4 (emphasis in original).

98. Amy Fagan, "Social Security Reform Rejected," *Washington Times*, March 20, 2006.

99. Patrick Wetherille and Chris Schrimpf, "Senators Turn Their Backs on Seniors," *Human Events*, March 17, 2006.

100. Social Security Administration, *2006 Annual Report of the Board of Trustees of the Federal Old-Age and Survivors Insurance and Federal Disabilities Insurance Trust Fund* (Washington: Government Printing Office, 2006). The total unfunded obligations of the system over an infinite horizon actually increased by nearly $2 trillion, but much of that change was from a recalculation of future bond rates (which also changed the discount rate in making present-value calculations). The $550 billion represents the portion of increased liabilities due to inaction.

101. For a detailed discussion of the program, its problems, and proposals for reforming it, see Michael Cannon, "Medicaid's Unseen Costs," Cato Institute Policy Analysis no. 548, August 18, 2005.

102. Donald Marron, acting director, Congressional Budget Office, "Medicaid Spending Growth and Options for Controlling Costs," testimony before the Senate Special Committee on Aging, 109th Cong., 2nd sess., July 13, 2006, http://www.cbo.gov/ftpdocs/73xx/doc7387/07-13-Medicaid.pdf.

103. Ibid.

104. *The Fiscal Survey of the States: December 2004* (Washington: National Governors Association and National Association of State Budget Officers, 2004), http://www.nasbo.org/Publications/fiscalsurvey/fsfall2004.pdf.

105. *2003 State Expenditure Report* (Washington: National Association of State Budget Officers, 2004).

106. Net Reported Medicaid and SCHIP Expenditures, http://www.cms.hhs.gov/MedicaidBudgetExpendSystem/Downloads/2004to1997.pdf.

107. "Federal Medicaid Commission Named; Former Tennessee Governor to Lead Panel," *Medical News Today*, July 12, 2005.

108. "Gingrich Recommends Reforms to Address Disparities in Medicaid," *Medical News Today*, April 5, 2005.

109. This analysis holds true even though many Medicaid recipients are not actually poor, at least not in the way the term is commonly thought of. In 2003, for example, 36 million Americans were living in poverty, but 52 million were on Medicaid. This disparity stems in part from the State Children's Health Insurance Program which extends eligibility for children well up the income ladder. In addition, a substantial portion of Medicaid recipients are actually the elderly, who rely on the program to pay for long-term care or nursing-home stays. In fact, although a majority of Medicaid *recipients* are low-income workers or children, nearly 70 percent of Medicaid *spending* goes for the elderly and disabled. Many of these recipients have assets or income that they have sheltered through their families.

110. See, for example, Aaron Yelowitz, "Evaluating the Effects of Medicaid on Welfare and Work: Evidence from the Past Decade," Employment Policies Institute, December 2000.

111. Richard Wolf, "Deficit-Reduction Package Squeaks through in House," *USA Today*, February 1, 2006.

112. See http://www.house.gov/pence/rsc/doc/RSC_2007_BUDGET.pdf.

Chapter 7

1. *Historical Tables, Budget of the United States, Fiscal Year 2007* (Washington: Executive Office of the President, Office of Management and Budget, 2006), Table 1.1: Summary of Receipts, Outlays, and Surpluses or Deficits, 1789–2011.

2. Stephen Slivinski, "Grand Old Spending Party: How Republicans Became Big Spenders," Cato Institute Policy Analysis no 543, May 3, 2005, using *Historical Tables, Budget of the United States FY2005* and *Budget of the United States, FY2006*.

3. *Historical Tables, Budget of the United States, Fiscal Year 2007* (Washington: Executive Office of the President, Office of Management and Budget, 2006), Table 1.1: Summary of Receipts, Outlays, and Surpluses or Deficits, 1789–2011.

4. The very first budget put forward by the new House majority abolished more than 200 programs and three cabinet agencies, the Departments of Commerce, Education, and Energy. See "Is This for Real?" *Wall Street Journal*, June 15, 1995.

5. Sheryl Stolberg and David Kirkpatrick, "GOP Rebellion Threatens to Derail Efforts to Adopt Budget," *New York Times*, March 15, 2005.

6. Janet Hook, "President Putting 'Big' Back in Government," *Los Angeles Times*, February 8, 2005.

7. *Historical Tables, Budget of the United States, Fiscal Year 2006* (Washington: Executive Office of the President, Office of Management and Budget, 2005).

8. Rich Lowry, "Say It Ain't So: How the GOP Majority Lost Its Way," *NationalReviewOnline*, January 30, 2006, citing comments by former House majority leader Dick Armey, http://article.nationalreview.com/?q = NjM4OTUwMzI1OTBkZjk3ZjIwZT ZiNWIwZGNjOTA1OGY.

9. The only other real budgetary confrontation between Clinton and the Republicans came in 1997, when Republicans tried to attach a partisan census provision to a disaster-relief bill. Clinton, accusing them of playing politics with aid to flood victims, again forced an ignominious retreat. Tod Lindberg, "Gingrich Lost and Found," *Policy Review* 94 (April–May 1999): 8–23.

10. Clinton vetoed a total of 19 spending bills, some for policy or other reasons to be sure, but many for excess spending. Bruce Bartlett, *Impostor: How George W. Bush Bankrupted America and Betrayed the Reagan Legacy* (New York: Doubleday, 2006), p. 127.

11. *Historical Tables, Budget of the United States, Fiscal Year 2007* (Washington: Executive Office of the President, Office of Management and Budget, 2006), Table 1.1: Summary of Receipts, Outlays, and Surpluses or Deficits, 1789–2011.

12. William Niskanen, "A Case for Divided Government," *Cato Policy Report* 25, no. 2 (March/April 2003).

13. Rich Lowry, "Say It Ain't So: How the GOP Majority Lost Its Way," *National ReviewOnLine*, January 30, 2006, http://article.nationalreview.com/?q = NjM4O TUwMzI1OTBkZjk3ZjIwZTZiNWIwZGNjOTA1OGY.

14. Quoted in Richard Wolf, "Fastest Rise in Federal Spending since FDR," *USA Today*, April 3, 2006.

15. Quoted in Ramesh Ponnuru, "Swallowed by Leviathan: Conservatism versus an Oxymoron: Big-Government Conservatism," *National Review*, September 29, 2003.

16. Stephen Slivinski, *Buck Wild: How Republicans Broke the Bank and Became the Party of Big Government* (Nashville: Nelson Current, 2006).

17. *Historical Tables, Budget of the United States, Fiscal Year 2007* (Washington: Executive Office of the President, Office of Management and Budget, 2006), Table 1.1: Summary of Receipts, Outlays, and Surpluses or Deficits, 1789–2011.

18. *Budget of the United States, Fiscal Year 2006* (Washington: Executive Office of the President, Office of Management and Budget, 2005), Table 1.2—Summary of Receipts, Outlays, and Surpluses or Deficits(–) as Percentages of GDP: 1930–2010, http://www.gpoaccess.gov/usbudget/fy06/sheets/hist01z2.xls. See also, Brian Faler, "Republican Voters Dismayed by Biggest Spending Rise since 1990," Bloomberg, September 15, 2006.

19. Richard Wolf, "Fastest Rise in Federal Spending since FDR," *USA Today*, April 3, 2006.

20. Calculations by Stephen Slivinski based on Congressional Budget Office data. Stephen Slivinski, "Grand Old Spending Party: How Republicans Became Big Spenders," Cato Institute Policy Analysis no. 543, May 3, 2005.

21. Stephen Moore, "The Federal Budget 10 Years Later: The Triumph of Big Government," in *The Republican Revolution 10 Years Later: Smaller Government or Business as Usual*, ed. Chris Edwards and John Samples (Washington: Cato Institute, 2005), p. 65.

22. "McCain Criticizes Pork in Defense Bill," *New York Daily News*, February 27, 2006.

23. Winslow T. Wheeler, "Defense Pork: Putting Lipstick on a Pig," *Mother Jones*, March 21, 2006.

24. "McCain Criticizes Pork in Defense Bill," *New York Daily News*, February 27, 2006.

25. Charles Pena, "$400 Billion Defense Budget Unnecessary to Fight War on Terrorism," Cato Institute Policy Analysis no. 539, May 28, 2005.

26. *Historical Tables, Budget of the United States, Fiscal Year 2007* (Washington: Executive Office of the President, Office of Management and Budget, 2006), Table 1.1: Summary of Receipts, Outlays, and Surpluses or Deficits, 1789–2011.

27. Quoted in Gail Russell Chadock, "Bush's $5 Trillion Problem: Rising Deficit Troubles GOP," *Christian Science Monitor*, January 23, 2004.

28. These calculations exclude spending for defense, homeland security, and entitlements. Stephen Slivinski, *Buck Wild: How Republicans Broke the Bank and Became the Party of Big Government* (Nashville: Nelson Current, 2006).

29. Veronique de Rugy, "The Republican Spending Explosion," Cato Institute Briefing Paper no. 87, March 3, 2004.

30. "Bogus Budgeting," *Washington Post*, February 3, 2004.

31. Amy Goldstein, "Foster: White House Had Role in Withholding Medicare Data," *Washington Post*, March 19, 2004.

32. National Taxpayers Union, NTUF Releases Bill Tally for the 109th Congress, 1st Seven Months: House Members Sorted by Spending Totals and Senators Sorted by Spending Totals, March 9, 2006. The six senators who sponsored net reductions in spending were: Tom Coburn (R-OK), Saxby Chambliss (R-GA), Larry Craig (R-ID), Richard Shelby (R-AL), Craig Thomas (R-WY), and surprisingly Arlen Specter (R-PA).

33. Bruce Bartlett, *Imposter: How George W. Bush Bankrupted America and Betrayed the Reagan Legacy* (New York: Doubleday, 2006), pp. 131–32.

34. Chris Edwards, "Pork: A Microcosm of the Overspending Problem," *Cato Institute Tax and Budget Bulletin* 24 (August 2005).

35. Chris Edwards, "Nearly 14,000 Pork Projects in Federal Budget This Year," *Budget & Tax News*, October 1, 2005.

36. "Highway Bill Has Record Number of Lawmaker-Requested Projects," *CNN.com*, August 2, 2005.

37. Jeffrey Birnbaum, "House Votes to Disclose Earmarks," *Washington Post*, September 15, 2006. One of those appropriators, Rep. James Walsh (R-NY), pointed with pride to pet projects for his district that he managed to slip into spending legislation without debate. One of his campaign leaflets refered to Walsh as "The $125 Billion Man," the amount his House Appropriations subcommittee controls each year. Jonathan D. Salant, "Walsh, Congress's '$125 Billion Man,' Boasts of Pet Projects," Bloomberg, September 27, 2006.

38. "At Congress 'Favor Factory' Revolving Door Keeps Spinning," *USA Today*, September 18, 2006.

39. Elana Schor, "Loopholes in Earmark Reform Bills," May 11, 2006; William Roberts and Charles R. Babcock, "Congress's Failure to Curb Pet Projects Good News for Lobbyist," Bloomberg, September 19, 2006.

40. Chris Edwards, "Pork: A Microcosm of the Overspending Problem," *Cato Institute Tax and Budget Bulletin* 24 (August 2005).

41. Stephen Slivinski, "Grand Old Spending Party: How Republicans Became Big Spenders," Cato Institute Policy Analysis no. 543, May 3, 2005; Stephen Moore and Steve Slivinski, "The Return of the Living Dead: Federal Programs That Survived the Republican Revolution," Cato Institute Policy Analysis no. 375, July 24, 2000.

42. Amy Fagan and Stephen Dinan, "DeLay Declares 'Victory' in War on Budget Fat," *Washington Times*, September 14, 2005.

43. David Holman, "The Jeffersonian," *American Spectator*, July 18, 2006.

44. George Melloan, "Washington's Spending Spree and the Dangers It Poses," *Wall Street Journal*, July 12, 2005.

45. Jonathan Weisman, "In Congress, the GOP Embraces Its Spending Side," *Washington Post*, August 4, 2005.

46. Alan Reynolds, "Kerry's Social Security Plan," *Washington Times*, October 2, 2004.

47. Federation of Tax Administrators, "State Individual Income Taxes (Tax rates for tax year 2006—as of January 1, 2006)," http://www.taxadmin.org/FTA/rate/ind_inc.html.

48. Effectively, the worker would pay the full 12.4 percent Social Security and 2.9 percent Medicare taxes, because most economists believe that the employer's share of those taxes is ultimately passed on to the worker through lower compensation.

49. Marilyn Geewax, "Federal Budget Deficit Declines," *Atlanta Journal-Constitution*, October 12, 2006.

50. *Historical Tables, Budget of the United States, Fiscal Year 2007* (Washington: Executive Office of the President, Office of Management and Budget, 2006), Table 1.1: Summary of Receipts, Outlays, and Surpluses or Deficits, 1789–2011.

51. Ibid. Some conservatives have suggested that cutting taxes is a form of "starving the beast." That is, by depriving the government of revenue, we can force it to cut back on spending. So far, at least, no evidence indicates this tactic has been successful. William Niskanen, "Comment," in *American Economic Policy in the 1990s*, ed. Jeffrey Frankel and Peter Orszag (Cambridge, MA: MIT Press, 2002); William Niskanen, "'Starve the Beast' Does Not Work," *Cato Policy Report* 26, no. 2 (March/April 2004).

52. Marilyn Geewax, "Federal Budget Deficit Declines," *Atlanta Journal-Constitution*, October 12, 2006.

53. Ron Suskind, *The Price of Loyalty: George W Bush, the White House, and the Education of Paul O'Neill* (New York: Simon & Schuster Paperbacks, 2004), p. 291.

54. "However the government gets the money it spends, the goods and services that it buys, or that are bought by the people to whom it transfers money, are thereby not available for other use. Those goods and services—not the pieces of paper that pay for them—are the real cost of government to the taxpayers." Milton Friedman and Rose Friedman, *Tyranny of the Status Quo* (New York: Harcourt, 1984), p. 8.

55. Douglas Holtz-Eakin, testimony before the House Committee on the Budget, 109th Cong., 2nd sess., February 15, 2006, http://www.house.gov/budget/hearings/holtzeakinstmnt021506.pdf.

56. Public Law 109-59.

57. In the early years of the Republic, federal road building was rare, and many—including Presidents Jefferson, Madison, Monroe, Jackson, Tyler, Polk, Pierce, and Buchanan—expressed doubts as to whether the federal government could actually build roads as opposed to merely designating post roads. Although considerable

debate took place about whether Congress actually had constitutional authority, the question appears to have been settled when the Supreme Court ruled in the case of *Searight v. Stokes* that being "charged . . . with the transportation of the mails," Congress could enter into a compact with the state of Pennsylvania regarding the use and upkeep of the Cumberland Road. *Searight v. Stokes*, 44 U.S. (3 How.) 151, 166 (1845).

58. Interestingly, the program was intended to be limited and temporary, scheduled to expire in 1972.

59. George H. W. Bush (address on signing the Intermodal Surface Transportation Efficiency Act of 1991, Ft. Worth, TX, December 18, 1991, http://www.fhwa.dot.gov/byday/fhbd1218.htm).

60. The Mass Transit Account receives a portion of the motor fuel taxes, usually 2.86 cents per gallon, as does the Leaking Underground Storage Tank Trust Fund, usually 0.1 cent per gallon. The General Fund receives 2.5 cents per gallon of the tax on gasohol and some other alcohol fuels plus an additional 0.6 cent per gallon for fuels that are at least 10 percent ethanol. The Highway Account receives the remaining portion of the fuel tax proceeds.

61. Joe Grata, "Wage Ruling May Raise Road Costs," *Pittsburgh Post-Gazette*, April 8, 2006.

62. Gabriel Roth, "Liberating the Roads: Reforming U.S. Highway Policy," Cato Institute Policy Analysis no. 538, March 17, 2005.

63. Ibid.

64. Nick Jans, "Alaska Thanks You," *USA Today*, May 17, 2005.

65. Gabriel Roth, "Liberating the Roads: Reforming U.S. Highway Policy," Cato Institute Policy Analysis no. 538, March 17, 2005.

66. *Transportation Empowerment Act*, S 2861 and HR 3113, 108th Cong., 2nd sess., September 1, 2002, http://thomas.loc.gov/cgi-bin/bdquery/D?d107:14:./temp/~bd16Sj.

67. The "no" votes were cast by Sens. John Cornyn (R-TX), Judd Greg (R-NH), John Kyl (R-AZ), and John McCain (R-AZ).

68. Shailagh Murray, "Some in GOP Regretting Pork-Stuffed Highway Bill," *Washington Post*, November 5, 2005.

69. Ronald Reagan (Statement on Returning without Approval the Surface Transportation and Uniform Relocation Assistance Act of 1987, March 27, 1987), http://www.reagan.utexas.edu/archives/speeches/1987/032787c.htm.

70. *RSC Budget Options: Summary and Explanation of Offsets*, Republican Study Committee, September 21, 2005.

71. Ronald Utt, "The Bridge to Nowhere; A National Embarrassment," Heritage Foundation WebMemo no. 889, October 20, 2005, http://www.heritage.org/Research/Budget/wm889.cfm. As the "bridge to nowhere" became a national embarrassment, Congress attempted to defuse the issue with a budgetary subterfuge. The specific earmark for the bridge was eliminated, but the money to build it was still approved, supposedly leaving the eventual decision on what to do with the money to Alaska authorities. They still plan to build the bridge. Shailagh Murray, "Funding for Alaskan Bridges Eliminated," *Washington Post*, November 17, 2005.

72. Nick Jans, "Alaska Thanks You," *USA Today*, May 17, 2005.

73. "Highway Bill Criticized for Special Projects," Associated Press, August 2, 2005.

74. Jeff Jacoby, "The Republican Pork Barrel," *Boston Globe*, August 4, 2005.

75. Bill Nichols, "$268 Billion Highway Bill Signed amid Criticism," *USA Today*, September 10, 2005.

76. Jeff Jacoby, "The Republican Pork Barrel," *Boston Globe*, August 4, 2005.

77. Bill Nichols, "$268 Billion Highway Bill Signed amid Criticism," *USA Today*, September 10, 2005.

78. Ibid.

79. Ibid.

80. "Highway Bill Criticized for Special Projects," Associated Press, August 2, 2005.

81. "CCAGW Slams Highway Bill," press release, Council for Citizens against Government Waste, July 27, 2005, http://councilfor.cagw.org/site/News2?page=NewsArticle&id=9162&news_iv_ctrl=0&abbr=CCAGW_&JServSessionIdr007=nnfyolmgi5.app20a.

82. "Highway Bill Loaded with Pork," *CNN.com*, April 7, 2004.

83. "Group Says Big Profitable Operations Collect Most Farm Subsidies," Associated Press, November 30, 2004, citing figures from the Environmental Working Group. See also, General Accounting Office, *Farm Programs: Information on Recipients of Federal Payments*, GAO-01-606 (Washington: GAO, 2001), p. 22.

84. Brian Riedl and John Frydenlund, "At the Federal Trough: Farm Subsidies for the Rich and Famous," Heritage Foundation, November 26, 2001. Among others receiving federal farm subsidies are Charles Schwab; Scottie Pippen; David Rockefeller; Sam Donaldson; Sen. Blanche Lincoln; Reps. Doug Ose (R-CA), Tom Latham (R-IA), and Marion Berry (D-AR); and Chevron, DuPont Chemical, Caterpillar, Westvaco Corporation, Cargill, and Hancock Mutual Life Insurance.

85. David Aftandilian, "Farm Bill 2002: Corporate Welfare or Farmer's Friend," *Chicago Conscious Choice*, July 2002.

86. Gilbert Gaul, Dan Morgan, and Sarah Cohen, "Farm Program Pays $1.3 Billion to People Who Don't Farm," *Washington Post*, July 2, 2006.

87. John Boehner and Cal Dooley, "This Terrible Farm Bill," *Washington Post*, May 2, 2002.

88. U.S. Department of Agriculture, *Food and Agriculture Policy: Taking Stock for the New Century*, September 2001, p. 47, http://www.usda.gov/news/pubs/farmpolicy01/fullreport.pdf.

89. Dan Griswold, Stephen Slivinski, and Chris Preble, "Six Reasons to Kill Farm Subsidies and Trade Barriers," *Reason*, February 2006.

90. Two classic examples of how U.S. agricultural policy impoverishes other countries are cotton and sugar. A 2002 study found that although subsidies will protect cotton growers in America from falling world prices, they will further depress prices by encouraging continued production, and thus cripple growers in Third World countries with no subsidies. U.S. farmers harvested a record crop of 9.74 billion pounds of cotton in 2001, aggravating a U.S. glut and pushing prices far below the breakeven price of most growers around the world. These depressed prices cost African countries $250 million each year, according to a World Bank study published last February. The report estimates that the removal of U.S. subsidies would produce a drop in U.S. production that would lead to a short-term rise in the world price of cotton and in turn would increase revenue to west and central African countries by about $250 million. Roger Thurow and Scott Kilman, "U.S. Subsidies Create Cotton Glut That Hurts Foreign Cotton Farms," *Wall Street Journal*, June 26, 2002. Former World Bank president James Wolfensohn warns that "these subsidies are crippling Africa's chance to export its way out of poverty." Quoted in Nicholas Kristof, "Farm Subsidies That Kill," *New York Times*, July 5, 2002. Similarly, the U.S. Department of Agriculture not only provides direct subsidies to sugar producers but also imposes

a 16 percent tariff on sugar imports. As a result, although no growth occurred in demand for sugar between 1981 and 1991, U.S. sugar cane production surged by approximately 26 percent. This production led to a nearly 10-fold increase in the land devoted to sugar cane and sugar beet production. "Farm Subsidies: A Harvest of Environmental Sorrows," National Center for Policy Analysis, 2002. U.S. sugar policies keep developing countries in the Caribbean out of U.S. markets, leading to increased poverty and crime in those countries, and indirectly to increased illegal immigration to the United States. Tom Carter, "U.S Farm Policy Sows Ire in Africa," *Washington Times*, July 2, 2003.

91. Daniel Griswold, Stephen Slivinski, and Christopher Preble, "Ripe for Reform: Six Good Reasons to Reduce U.S. Farm Subsidies and Trade Barriers," Cato Institute Trade Policy Analysis no. 30, September 14, 2005, citing Organization for Economic Cooperation and Development figures.

92. Unfortunately, Congress's courage in taking on the farm lobby did not last long. Every year since 1998, Congress ignored agreed-upon subsidy limits and passed huge supplemental spending bills containing increased farm subsidies. As a result, total farm subsidies have soared to more than $20 billion per year, up from an average of $9 billion per year in the early 1990s. Chris Edwards and Tad DeHaven, "Farm Bill Reversal," Cato Institute Tax and Budget Bulletin no. 2, March 2002.

93. John Boehner and Cal Dooley, "This Terrible Farm Bill," *Washington Times*, May 2, 2002.

94. Stephen Moore, "The Federal Budget 10 Years Later: The Triumph of Big Government," in *The Republican Revolution 10 Years Later: Smaller Government or Business as Usual*, ed. Chris Edwards and John Samples (Washington: Cato Institute, 2005), p. 66. These estimates assume price increases among certain commodities— assessments with which few independent agricultural economists agree. If these estimates are wrong, the bill could end up costing taxpayers $10 billion to $20 billion more than projected. John Boehner and Cal Dooley, "This Terrible Farm Bill," *Washington Times*, May 2, 2002.

95. Quoted in Mike Allen, "Bush Signs Bill Providing Big Farm Subsidy Increases," *Washington Post*, May 14, 2002.

96. Quoted in Caroline Baum, "Monstrous Farm Bill Turns Freedom to Farm into Freedom to Fleece Taxpayers," Bloomberg, June 12, 2002.

97. Gilbert Gaul, Dan Morgan, and Sarah Cohen, "No Drought Required for Federal Drought Aid," *Washington Post*, July 18, 2006.

98. Ibid.

99. Chris Edwards and Tad DeHaven, "Corporate Welfare Update," Cato Institute Tax and Budget Bulletin no. 7, May 2002. Some analysts suggest a broader definition of corporate welfare that includes targeted corporate tax loopholes. But allowing corporations to keep more of their own earnings is not a form of welfare. It is their money, after all. To label such loopholes as corporate welfare essentially suggests that all money belongs to the government, and thus any portion that government allows you to keep is a form of welfare. Furthermore, simply closing tax loopholes would just put more money into the hands of the federal government while doing nothing to reduce the size of government. That should not be taken as a blanket defense of special-interest tax breaks. As a matter of public policy they are usually a bad idea. Because they provide special treatment for politically powerful industries, such tax breaks run counter to the notion that all taxpayers should be treated the same. Furthermore, special-interest tax breaks distort the economy by creating an

uneven playing field for particular industries. As a result, our economic resources do not go toward their most efficient use, costing workers, business, and consumers in the long run.

100. Quoted in Richard Wolf, "Bush Set for Battle over Spending and Tax Cuts," *Financial Times*, March 1, 2001.

101. Chris Edwards and Tad DeHaven, "Corporate Welfare Update," Cato Institute Tax and Budget Bulletin no. 7, May 2002.

102. Jeffrey Birnbaum, "Boeing Has a Powerful Ally with Hastert," *Washington Post*, July 18, 2004.

103. Quoted in Carl Pope and Paul Rauber, "Bright Light Must Shine on Energy Policy," *Los Angeles Times*, December 21, 2003.

104. Jerry Taylor and Peter Van Doren, "Mighty Porking Power Rangers: Scanning the Energy Bill," *NationalReviewOnline*, November 19, 2003.

105. Moreover, ethanol is three times more expensive to produce than gasoline (which is why it has to be mandated upon an unwilling fuels industry), and it cannot be shipped in pipelines used for standard gasoline. This factor makes ethanol even more expensive and renders the nation more vulnerable to occasional regional supply shocks.

106. Cited by Rep. Ed Royce (R-CA), *Congressional Record* 147, no. 96 (July 11, 2001): H 3916.

107. "Welfare Kings," *Forbes*, June 15, 2005.

108. James K. Jackson, *Export-Import Bank: Background and Legislative Issues*, Congressional Research Service Report for Congress 98-568E, January 19, 2001, p. 5.

109. Bernie Sanders, "The Export-Import Bank: Corporate Welfare at Its Worst," CommonDreams.org, May 15, 2002.

110. Ian Vasquez and John Welborn, "Reauthorize or Retire the Overseas Private Investment Corporation," Cato Institute Foreign Policy Briefing Paper no. 78, September 15, 2003.

111. *Emergency Supplemental Appropriations Act to Meet Immediate Needs Arising from the Consequences of Hurricane Katrina, 2005*, HR 3645, 109th Cong., 1st sess., September 2, 2005, http://thomas.loc.gov/cgi-bin/bdquery/z?d109:h.r.03645:; *Second Emergency Supplemental Appropriations Act to Meet Immediate Needs Arising from the Consequences of Hurricane Katrina, 2005*, HR 3673, 109th Cong., 1st sess., September 7, 2005, http://thomas.loc.gov/cgi-bin/bdquery/z?d109:h.r.03673:.

112. Jackie Calmes, "Much of Katrina Aid Remains Unspent," *Wall Street Journal*, October 25, 2005.

113. Stephen Moore, "Welcome to the GOP's New New Deal," *Wall Street Journal*, September 19, 2005.

114. Reps. Mike Pence and Jeb Hensarling, "RSC Budget Options 2005," September 22, 2005, http://johnshadegg.house.gov/rsc/RSC_Budget_Options_2005.doc.

115. Robert Novak, "GOP in Turmoil," *Washington Post*, September 22, 2005.

116. Quoted in Shailagh Murray, "For a Senate Foe of Pork Barrel Spending, Two Bridges Too Far," *Washington Post*, October 21, 2005.

117. Ibid.

118. Eric Lipton, "Breathtaking Waste and Fraud in Hurricane Aid," *New York Times*, June 27, 2006.

119. President Bush (address, September 15, 2005); for transcript see *PBS Online News Hour: A NewsHour with Jim Lehrer Transcript*, http://www.pbs.org/newshour/bb/weather/july-dec05/bush_9-15.html.

120. Scott Stearns, "Bush Calls for Massive Katrina Spending," *voanews.com*, September 22, 2005.

121. William Niskanen, "The End of Small Government," *American Spectator*, September 20, 2005.

122. Michael Tackett, "Bush Speech Was Part Franklin Roosevelt, Part Lyndon Johnson," *Chicago Tribune*, September 16, 2005.

123. "The GOP's New New Deal," *Wall Street Journal*, September 19, 2005.

124. Michael Tanner and Michael Cannon, "Katrina's Medicaid Boondoggle," *Washington Times*, October 21, 2005.

125. Karl Zinsmeister, "Respect the Limits That Made the USA," *American Enterprise*, January/February 2006.

126. Ibid.

127. Gingrich admitted doing this during an interview on *Fox News Special Report*, April 18, 2006.

128. James Pinkerton, "The Bush Budget, All Bulked Up," *Washington Post*, February 8, 2004.

129. "You've Got to Stand for Something," by Aaron Tippin.

130. A program's benefits often go to a narrow few individuals who benefit substantially, while the costs are spread over a wide population, meaning each individual's contribution will be relatively small. Thus the program's recipients will put much more effort into securing the program than the financers will put into opposing it. For example, assume a proposal to give the city of Cincinnati $10 million for a new bridge; $10 million is a lot of money to Cincinnati. The city will testify before Congress, hire lobbyists, produce reports showing the need for the project, and generally do whatever is necessary to obtain the money. In contrast, the additional taxes needed to pay for the project will cost each taxpayer only a few pennies. Few taxpayers will go to the expense or effort of opposing the project. That is why nearly all witnesses at congressional hearings testify in *favor* of additional spending. The problem, from the taxpayer's point of view, is that eventually all those few pennies add up to a very real tax burden.

131. Jacob Weisberg, "Interest Group Conservatism," *Slate*, May 4, 2005.

Chapter 8

1. Ronald Reagan (State of the Union address, Washington, DC, January 26, 1982, http://www.presidency.ucsb.edu/ws/index.php?pid=42687).

2. The 1996 Republican Platform, adopted August 12, 1996, http://www.du.edu/orgs/ducr/rplat.htm.

3. "2004 Republican Party Platform: A Safer World and a More Hopeful America," reported by full committee August 26, 2004, http://www.gop.com/media/2004platform.pdf.

4. Quoted in Fred Barnes, *Rebel in Chief: Inside the Bold and Controversial Presidency of George W. Bush* (New York: Crown Forum, 2006), p. 165.

5. Annie E. Casey Foundation, *Children at Risk: State Trends 1990–2000* (Baltimore: Annie E. Casey Foundation, 2001), citing Census Bureau data.

6. Lawrence Mishel, Jared Bernstein, and John Schmitt, *The State of Working America, 2000–2001* (Ithaca, NY: Cornell University Press, 2001), p. 153.

7. Phillip Kaufman, Martha Naomi Alt, and Christopher Chapman, *National Dropout Rates in the United States: 2000* (Washington: National Center for Education Statistics, 2001), p. viii.

8. Uri Bronfenbrenner et al., *The State of Americans* (New York: Free Press, 1996), pp. 176–77.

9. Phillip Kaufman, Martha Naomi Alt, and Christopher Chapman, *National Dropout Rates in the United States: 2000* (Washington: National Center for Education Statistics, 2001).

10. Phillip Kaufman, Martha Naomi Alt, and Christopher D. Chapman, *Dropout Rates in the United States: 2001* (Washington: National Center for Education Statistics, 2004), Table A: "Student Dropout Rates by Race/Ethnicity, October 2001."

11. *Rising above the Gathering Storm: Energizing and Employing America for a Brighter Economic Future*, Committee on Prospering in the Global Economy of the 21st Century (Washington: National Academies Press, 2006).

12. Patrick Rooney, William Hussar, Michael Planty, et al., *The Condition of Education 2006* (Washington: National Center for Education Statistics, 2006).

13. "Tests Expose Flawed Diplomas," *USA Today*, July 25, 2006.

14. Milton Friedman, "Public Schools: Make Them Private," Cato Institute Briefing Paper no. 23, July 23, 1995.

15. 418 U.S. 717, 741–42 (1974).

16. Newt Gingrich (remarks to the American Enterprise Institute, February 28, 2005, http://www.aei.org/events/filter.all,eventID.1016/transcript.asp).

17. Mitt Romney, "Reforming Education," *Washington Times*, April 10, 2006.

18. *Historical Tables, Budget of the United States Government, Fiscal Year 2006* (Washington, Executive Office of the President, Office of Management and Budget, 2005), Table 8.7—Outlays for Discretionary Programs: 1962–2006, http://www.gpoaccess.gov/usbudget/fy06/sheets/hist08z7.xls.

19. Ibid.

20. John Boehner, "House Republicans Vote to Provide Third Major Increase in Education Funding since No Child Left Behind, Linked to Reform" (press release, December 8, 2003, http://matheson.house.gov/ed_workforce/press/press108/12dec/omnibus120803.htm).

21. Diane Long, "Frist Defends No Child Left Behind," *The Tennessean*, September 20, 2003.

22. Eric Hanushek, "The Economics of Schooling: Production and Efficiency in Public Schools," *Journal of Economic Literature* 24 (September 1986): 1161–62.

23. John E. Chubb and Terry M. Moe, *Politics, Markets, and America's Schools* (Washington: Brookings Institution, 1990), p. 193.

24. Bruce Bartlett, *Imposter: How George W. Bush Bankrupted America and Betrayed the Reagan Legacy* (New York: Doubleday, 2006), p. 131.

25. "No Child Left Behind—Strengthening America's Education System," White House News, http://www.whitehouse.gov/infocus/education/.

26. George W. Bush (remarks to J.E. B. Stuart High School in Falls Church, VA, January 12, 2005, http://www.whitehouse.gov/news/releases/2005/01/20050112-5.html).

27. Public Law 107-110, *U.S. Statutes at Large* 115 (2002): 1425.

28. George W. Bush (speech to the 2004 Republican National Convention, New York, NY, September 2, 2004, http://www.whitehouse.gov/news/releases/2004/09/20040902-2.html).

29. *RickSantorum.com*, http://www.ricksantorum.com/Record/Read.aspx?ID=4&TypeID=7.

30. George W. Bush, "A Culture of Achievement" (speech delivered to the Manhattan Institute, New York, NY, October 5, 1999, http://www.manhattan-institute.org/html/bush_speech.htm).

31. Andrew Rudalevige, "The Politics of No Child Left Behind," *Education Next* no. 4 (2003), Hoover Institution.

32. As the President's undersecretary of education Eugene Hickock put it, the president would not "sacrifice accountability on the altar of choice." Quoted in Andrew Rudalvige, "The Politics of No Child Left Behind," ibid.

33. *No Child Left Behind Act*, Public Law 107-110, *U.S. Statutes at Large* 115 (2002): 1425, http://www.ed.gov/policy/elsec/leg/esea02/107-110.pdf.

34. The Department of Education has estimated that approximately 1,700 public schools either currently fit this category or shortly will. Press release, "Secretary Spellings Delivers Remarks on School Choice," U.S. Department of Education, April 5, 2006, http://www.ed.gov/news/pressreleases/2006/04/04052006.html.

35. Stephen Arons, quoted in Lawrence Uzzell, "No Child Left Behind: The Dangers of Centralized Education Policy," Cato Institute Policy Analysis no. 544, May 31, 2005.

36. Rick Santorum, *It Takes a Family: Conservatism and the Common Good* (Wilmington: ISI Books, 2005), pp. 351–59.

37. American Institute of Physics, *FYI: Bulletin of Science Policy News*, June 28, 2001, http://aip.org/fyi/2001/081.html.

38. David Salisbury, "Bush Confusing 'Freedom' with 'Service,'" *FoxNews.com*, June 27, 2002.

39. See, for example, Sandra Cimbricz, "State Mandated Testing and Teachers' Beliefs and Practices," *Educational Policy Analysis Archives* 10, no. 2 (January 9, 2002); Linda McNeil and Angela Valenzuela, "The Harmful Impact of the TAAS System of Testing in Texas: Beneath the Accountability Rhetoric," Rice University, 2000; Linda McNeil, *The Contradictions of School Reform: Educational Costs of Standardized Testing* (New York: Routledge, 2000); Mary Smith and Claire Rottenberg, "Unintended Consequences of External Testing in Elementary Schools," *Educational Measurement: Issues & Practices* 10, no. 4 (1991): 7–11; Stuart Yeh, "Limiting the Consequences of High-Stakes Testing," *Educational Policy Analysis Archives* 14, no. 43 (October 28, 2005); Audrey Noble and Mary Smith, *Old and New Beliefs about Measurement Driven Reform: "The More Things Change, the More They Stay the Same"* (Los Angeles: National Center for Research on Evaluation, Standards, and Student Testing, University of California, Los Angeles, 1994).

40. See, for example, "National Assessment Education Progress: Precursor to a National Test," *National Center for Home Education Current Issue Analysis*, April 1, 2002, http://www.hslda.org/docs/GetDoc.asp?DocID=215&FormatTypeID=PDF.

41. Chester E. Finn Jr. and Frederick M. Hess, "On Leaving No Child Behind," *The Public Interest* (Fall 2004): 35–56.

42. Diane Ravitch, "Every State Left Behind," *New York Times*, November 7, 2005.

43. Kirk Johnson, "A National Test Would Lift All Boats," *The World & I*, November 2001.

44. William Bennett and Ronald Paige, "Why We Need a National School Test," *Washington Post*, September 21, 2006.

45. See, for example, R. J. Dietel, J. A. Knuth, and J. L. Herman, *What Does Research Say about Assessment?* (Oak Brook, IL: North Central Regional Educational Laboratory, 1991); Charles Rooney and Robert Schaeffer, *Test Scores Do Not Equal Merit: Enhancing Equity and Excellence in College admissions by De-emphasizing SAT and ACT Results*

(Cambridge, MA: FairTest, 1998); Noe Medina and Monty Neill, *Fallout from the Testing Explosion: How 100 Million Standardized Exams Undermine Equity and Excellence in America's Public Schools* (Cambridge, MA: FairTest, 1990); R. G. Lomax et al., "The Impact of Mandated Standardized Testing on Minority Students," *Journal of Negro Education* 64, no. 2 (1992): 171–85.

46. Monty Neill, "Let Students Graduate," *USA Today*, July 25, 2006.

47. See, for example, Lawrence Lashway, "Holding Schools Accountable for Achievement," *Education Resources Information Center Digest* 130 (1999); Helen Ladd, *Holding Schools Accountable* (Washington: Brookings Institution Press, 1999).

48. Gail Sunderman and Jimmy Kim, *Expansion of Federal Power in American Education: Federal-State Relationships under the No Child Left Behind Act, Year One* (Cambridge, MA: The Civil Rights Project at Harvard University, 2004).

49. William Sanders and June Rivers, "Cumulative and Residual Effects of Teachers on Future Student Academic Achievement," Research Progress Report, University of Tennessee Value-Added Research and Assessment Center, Knoxville, November 1996.

50. "Demanding vs. Doing," *New York Times*, July 26, 2006.

51. Sam Dillon, "Most States Fail Demands Set Out in Education Law," *New York Times*, July 25, 2006.

52. Christina Gheen, "State Legislatures Attack Constitutionality of Bush Education Plan," *The Jurist*, February 23, 2005.

53. Pam Solo, "NCLB Left Behind: Understanding the Growing Grassroots Rebellion against a Controversial Law," Civil Society Institute, August 2005, http://www.nclbgrassroots.org/landscape.php#.

54. *School District of the City of Pontiac et al. v. Margaret Spellings* (U.S. Dist. Ct., E.D. Mich., 2005). On March 22, 2006, the plaintiffs filed their opening brief with the U.S. Court of Appeals for the Sixth Circuit, asking that the decision of District Court Judge Friedman dismissing the complaint be reversed. Little action has occurred since then.

55. Erin Cassan, "States Cry Foul over Bush Education Policy," *New Standard*, April 22, 2005. Connecticut also points out that students in that state have been tested in grades 4, 6, 8, and 10 for two decades, with positive results. Connecticut students consistently rank near the top of the nation in academic performance. The state argues that NCLB's requirement for additional tests in grades 3, 5, and 7 is arbitrary and unnecessary.

56. Opinion and Order Granting Defendant's Motion to Dismiss, http://www.nea.org/lawsuit/images/nclbdismiss.pdf.

57. Michelle R. Davis, "Bush Proposes Steps to Boost Math and Science Teaching," *Education Week*, February 1, 2006.

58. Sam Dillon, "College Aid Plan Widens U.S. Role in High Schools," *New York Times*, January 22, 2006.

59. Karen Arenson, "Panel Explores Standard Tests for Colleges," *New York Times*, February 6, 2006.

60. Ibid.

61. Newt Gingrich (remarks to the American Enterprise Institute, Washington, DC, February 28, 2005, http://www.aei.org/events/filter.all,eventID.1016/transcript.asp).

62. Newt Gingrich, *Winning the Future: A 21st Century Contract with America* (New York: Regnery, 2005), p. 100.

63. Ibid., p. 95.

64. Ibid.

65. Timothy Starks, "Congress Weighs Anti-U.S. Biases at Key Colleges Columbia, NYU Cited in Testimony," *New York Sun*, June 20, 2003.

66. Ironically—and sadly—although Clinton appropriated and took credit for the 100,000 new teachers proposal, it was actually first suggested by a Republican, Rep. Bill Paxon (NY). David Winston, "The GOP's Two Brands," *Policy Review* 99 (February–March 2000).

67. Michelle R. Davis, "Bush Proposes Steps to Boost Math and Science Teaching," *Education Week*, February 1, 2006.

68. An important debate remains among school-choice advocates about whether vouchers or tax credits represent the best approach. Some suggest that tax credits are more effective at putting into place the freedoms and incentives necessary to the effective operation of the market, offer greater resistance to new regulation, decrease the risk of fraud and corruption, and avoid problems that might arise from state funding of religious schools. In particular, they point out that voucher programs are almost always accompanied by a myriad of new federal and state regulations, often effectively bringing private schools that accept voucher students under the regulatory eye of state authorities. Others worry that tax credits do not provide a steady and predictable funding source. Tax credits against income taxes are little use in states without a state income tax and may be worth relatively little to low-income parents with little income or tax liability. Critics of tax credits also point out that they represent another form of social engineering through the tax code. Taxes should be a neutral system for generating government revenue not an instrument used to achieve social policy aims. For more on this debate, see Andrew Coulson, "Toward Market Education: Are Vouchers or Tax Credits the Better Path," Cato Institute Policy Analysis no. 392, February 22, 2001; Joseph Bast, "Tax Credits versus Vouchers: Time to Decide," *The Heartlander*, March 1, 2002; and John Goodman and Matt Moore, "School Choice vs. School Choice," National Center for Policy Analysis Policy Backgrounder no. 155, February 1, 2005.

69. U.S. Department of Education, "Choices for Parents: America's Opportunity Scholarships for Kids," February 2006, http://www.ed.gov/nclb/choice/schools/choice-parents.pdf; Dan Lips, "America's Opportunity Scholarships for Kids: School Choice for Students in Underperforming Public Schools," Heritage Foundation Backgrounder no. 1939, May 30, 2006.

70. Lois Romano, "GOP Unveils Voucher Plan," *Washington Post*, July 19, 2006.

71. Andrew Coulson, "Why Federal School Vouchers Are a Bad Idea," Cato Institute Daily Commentary, April 8, 2006, http://www.cato.org/pub_display.php?pub_id=6342.

72. Major Garrett, *The Enduring Revolution: How the Contract with America Continues to Shape the Nation* (New York: Crown Forum, 2005), p. 238.

Chapter 9

1. *New State Ice Co. v. Liebmann*, 285 U.S. 262 (1932), Brandeis dissenting, at 311.

2. "Federalist no. 45," in *The Federalist*, ed. Clinton Rossiter (New York: Signet Classics, 2003), p. 238.

3. "Federalist no. 51," in *The Federalist*, ed. Clinton Rossiter (New York: Signet Classics, 2003), p 294.

4. Thomas Jefferson, "First Inaugural Address" (Washington, DC, March 4, 1801, http://www.bartleby.com/124/pres16.html).

5. See Roger Pilon, "Congress, the Courts, and the Constitution," in *Cato Handbook for Congress: 105th Congress*, ed. Ed Crane and David Boaz (Washington: Cato Institute, 1997), pp. 26–27. In general Congress has based its authority to enact legislation that goes beyond its enumerated powers and intervenes in areas traditionally left to the states on the General Welfare and Commerce Clauses of the Constitution. In reality, however, both of those clauses were intended as restraints on federal power, not authorizations for it. The General Welfare Clause was meant to serve as a brake on the power of Congress in the exercising of its enumerated powers. That is, the exercise of an enumerated power had to be for the *general* welfare rather than the welfare of particular factions or regions. The Commerce Clause was to ensure the free flow of commerce among the states. It was primarily a means for Congress to prevent states from erecting trade barriers with other states.

6. Richard Nathan, Thomas Gais, and James Fossett, "Bush Federalism, Is There One, What Is It, and How Does It Differ?" (presentation to the Annual Research Conference of the Association for Public Policy Analysis and Management, Washington, DC, November 7, 2003).

7. Barry Goldwater, *Conscience of a Conservative* (Shepherdsville, KY: Victor Publishing, 1960), p. 24.

8. Executive Order no. 12612, *Federal Register* 52 (October 26, 1987): 41685, http://www.blm.gov/nhp/news/regulatory/EOs/eo_12612.html.

9. Jim Abrams, "Bush, Hill Allies Seen Eroding States' Rights," *Washington Times*, January 4, 2004.

10. At least this is the theory. In practice, politics often undermine redistribution goals. Because almost every member of Congress fights for his or her state's portion of funds, Congress ends up distributing money as widely as possible to buy support for a program. The result is that more-populous states (with larger congressional delegations) or states with legislators sitting on key committees often receive funds at the expense of poorer states.

11. Chris Edwards, "Federal Aid to the States Ripe for Cuts," Cato Institute Tax and Budget Bulletin no. 20, May 2004.

12. George W. Bush (remarks at the National Governors' Association Meeting, February 26, 2001, http://www.whitehouse.gov/news/releases/2001/02/20010226-8.html).

13. Richard Nathan, Thomas Gais, and James Fossett, "Bush Federalism, Is There One, What Is It, and How Does It Differ?" (presentation to the Annual Research Conference of the Association for Public Policy Analysis and Management, Washington, DC, November 7, 2003).

14. Jim VandeHei, "Blueprint Calls for Bigger, More Powerful Government," *Washington Post*, February 9, 2005.

15. *Special Report with Brit Hume*, Fox News Network, March 18, 2005.

16. David Brooks, "One Nation Conservatism," *Weekly Standard*, September 13, 1999.

17. 125 S. Ct. 2195 (2005).

18. 125 S. Ct. 94 (2006).

19. Quoted in David Savage, "Roberts Questions Lawyers on Oregon's Assisted-Suicide Law," *Los Angeles Times*, October 4, 2005.

20. See *Raich v. Ashcroft*, Amicus Curiae Brief in Support of the Respondents from the State of Alabama, Louisiana, and Mississippi, citing *Alden v. Maine*, 527 U.S. 706, 748 (1999).

21. Ibid.

22. *Raich v. Ashcroft*, 125 S. Ct. 2195 (2005), Thomas dissenting.

23. *United States v. Lopez*, 115 S. Ct. 1624 (1995).

24. Only in Massachusetts have the courts ruled that gays must be allowed to marry. The New Jersey Supreme Court has ruled that gay couples are entitled to an arrangement giving all the rights of married couples but left it up to the legislature whether that arrangement should be marriage or some form of civil union. Connecticut and Vermont have legalized civil unions through the legislative process.

25. The amendment reads: "Marriage in the United States shall consist only of the union of a man and a woman. Neither this Constitution or [sic] the constitution of any State, nor state or federal law, shall be construed to require that marital status or the legal incidents thereof be conferred upon unmarried couples or groups."

26. See Alan Cooperman, "Little Consensus on Marriage Amendment: Even Authors Disagree on the Meaning of Its Text," *Washington Post*, February 14, 2004.

27. Dale Carpenter, "The Federal Marriage Amendment: Unnecessary, Anti-federalist, and Anti-democratic," Cato Institute White Paper, September 23, 2004.

28. "Federalist no. 47," in *The Federalist*, ed. Clinton Rossiter (New York: Signet Classics, 2003), p. 298.

29. *Youngstown Sheet & Tube Company vs. Sawyer*, 343 U.S. 579, 587 (1952), cited in Gene Healy and Timothy Lynch, *Power Surge: The Constitutional Record of George W. Bush* (Washington: Cato Institute, 2006), p. 7.

30. James Risen and Eric Lichtblau, "Bush Lets US Spy on Callers without Courts," *New York Times*, December 16, 2005.

31. Christopher Kelly, "Faithfully Executing and Taking Care: The Unitary Executive and Presidential Signing Statements" (paper presented at the American Political Science Association, Boston, MA, August 29, 2002).

32. Ibid.

33. Neil Kinkopf, "Signing Statements and the President's Authority to Refuse to Enforce the Law," American Constitution Society for Law and Policy, June 15, 2006.

34. Bob Egelko, "Executive Authority: How Bush Redefines the Intent of the Law. Instead of Vetoing Bills, He Officially Disregards Portions with Which He Doesn't Agree," *San Francisco Chronicle*, May 7, 2006.

35. Christopher Kelly, "Faithfully Executing and Taking Care: The Unitary Executive and Presidential Signing Statements" (paper presented at the American Political Science Association, Boston, MA, August 29, 2002).

36. Bob Egelko, "Executive Authority: How Bush Redefines the Intent of the Law. Instead of Vetoing Bills, he Officially Disregards Portions with Which He Doesn't Agree," *San Francisco Chronicle*, May 7, 2006.

37. Christopher Kelly, "Faithfully Executing and Taking Care: The Unitary Executive and Presidential Signing Statements" (paper presented at the American Political Science Association, Boston, MA, August 29, 2002).

38. Neil Kinkopf, "Signing Statements and the President's Authority to Refuse to Enforce the Law," American Constitution Society for Law and Policy, June 15, 2006.

39. Jennifer Van Bergen, "The Unitary Executive: Is the Doctrine behind the Bush Presidency Consistent with a Democratic State?" *FindLaw*, January 9, 2006, http://writ.news.findlaw.com/commentary/20060109_bergen.html.

40. Christopher Yoo, Steven Calabresi, and Anthony Colangelo, "The Unitary Executive in the Modern Era: 1945–2004," *Iowa Law Review* 90, no. 2 (2005): 601.

41. Neal Devins, "Defending Congress' Interests in the Courts: How Lawmakers and the President Bargain over Department of Justice Representation," *Presidential Studies Quarterly* 32, no. 1 (March 2002): 158.

42. Michael Stokes Paulsen, "The Most Dangerous Branch: The Executive Power to Say What the Law Is," *Georgetown Law Review* 83 (December 1994): 322.

43. Christopher Yoo, Steven Calabresi, and Anthony Colangelo, "The Unitary Executive in the Modern Era: 1945–2004," *Iowa Law Review* 90, no. 2 (2005): 601.

44. George W. Bush, "Statement on Signing the Department of Defense, Emergency Supplemental Appropriations to Address Hurricanes in the Gulf of Mexico, and Pandemic Influenza Act," *Weekly Compilation of Presidential Documents* (December 12, 2005). This statement is clearly consistent with the Bush administration's long-held belief that "Any effort by the Congress to regulate the interrogation of battlefield combatants would violate the Constitution's sole vesting of the Commander in Chief authority in the President. . . . Congress can no more interfere with the President's conduct of the interrogation of enemy combatants than it can dictate strategic or tactical decisions on the battlefield." U.S. Department of Justice, "Memorandum for Alberto R. Gonzales, Counsel to the President, Re: Standards of Conduct under 18 USC Secs. 2340-2340A," August 1, 2002, p. 39.

45. Christopher Kelly, "A Comparative Look at the Constitutional Signing Statement: The Case of Bush and Clinton" (paper presented at the Annual Meeting of the Midwest Political Science Association, Chicago, IL, April 3, 2003).

46. Ibid.

47. George W. Bush, "Statement on Signing the Medicare Prescription Drug, Improvement, and Modernization Act," *Weekly Compilation of Presidential Documents* (December 8, 2003), p. 1774.

48. Charlie Savage, "Bush Challenges Hundreds of Laws," *Boston Globe*, April 30, 2006.

49. U.S. Constitution, art. 1, sec. 7.

50. *Clinton v. New York*, 524 U.S. 417 (1998).

51. American Bar Association Task Force on Presidential Signing Statements and the Separation of Powers Doctrine, *Report* (presented to the ABA House of Delegates at the 2006 Annual Meeting in Honolulu, Hawaii, August 7, 2006), p. 27, http://www.abanet.org/op/signingstatements/aba_final_signing_statements_recommendation-report_7-24-06.pdf.

52. Ibid.

53. James Bennet, "True to Form, Clinton Shifts Energies Back to U.S. Focus," *New York Times,* July 5, 1998.

54. U.S. Constitution, art. 1, sec. 9: "The Privilege of the Writ of *Habeas Corpus* shall not be suspended, unless when in Cases of Rebellion or Invasion the public Safety may require it."

55. *Hamdi v. Rumsfeld,* 542 U.S. 507 (2004).

56. "Two Groups Sue over NSA Wiretap Program," CNN, January 17, 2006.

57. *Hamdan v. Rumsfeld,* 126 S. Ct. 2749 (2006)

58. Thomas E. Mann and Norman J. Ornstein, *The Broken Branch: How Congress Is Failing America and How to Get It Back on Track* (New York: Oxford University Press, 2006), p. 376.

59. Ibid.

60. "Federalist no. 62," in *The Federalist*, ed. Clinton Rossiter (New York: Signet Classics, 2003), p. 81.

61. David Schoenbroad and Jerry Taylor, "The Delegation of Legislative Powers," in *Cato Institute Handbook for Congress, 108th Congress* (Washington: Cato Institute, 2002), p. 155.

62. Jacob Weisberg, "Leaner, Cleaner, Liberals," *The New Republic,* April 1, 1996.

63. Gene Healy and Timothy Lynch, *Power Surge: The Constitutional Record of George W. Bush* (Washington: Cato Institute, 2006), p. 3.

64. Quoted in Charlie Savage, "Bush Challenges Hundreds of Laws," *Boston Globe,* April 30, 2006.

65. David Brooks, "One Nation Conservatism," *Weekly Standard,* September 13, 1999.

66. "Federalist no. 48," in *The Federalist*, ed. Clinton Rossiter (New York: Signet Classics, 2003), p. 308.

Chapter 10

1. "Federalist no. 17," in *The Federalist*, ed. Clinton Rossiter (New York: Signet Classics, 2003), p. 115.

2. Quoted in David Nielsen, "Congress, Baseball Rumble over Steroids," Scripps Howard News Service, March 18, 2005.

3. Remarks made at hearing by the Senate Committee on Commerce, Science, and Transportation on "Steroid Use in Professional and Amateur Sports," 108th Cong., 2nd sess., March 10, 2004.

4. "Tom Davis, Grandstander," *NationalReviewOnline,* March 14, 2005, http://www.nationalreview.com/editorial/editors200503140922.asp.

5. "New Specter Rears Head in Owens Case, but Senator Backs Off," Associated Press, November 29, 2005.

6. "House Subcommittee to Tackle BCS," Associated Press, December 3, 2005.

7. Frank Ahrens, "Congress Agrees to Raise Broadcast-Indecency Fines," *Washington Post,* May 20, 2006.

8. Todd Shields, "Activists Dominate Content Complaints," *MediaWeek,* December 6, 2004.

9. Frank Ahrens, "Senator Bids to Extend Indecency Rules to Cable," *Washington Post,* March 2, 2005.

10. Brooks Boliek, "Sensenbrenner to Cable Execs: Indecency Is Criminal Act," *Hollywood Reporter,* April 5, 2005.

11. Barton Gellman, "Recruits Sought for Porn Squad," *Washington Post,* September 20, 2005.

12. Brooks Barnes, "For Nielsen, Fixing Old Ratings System Causes New Static," *Wall Street Journal,* September 16, 2004.

13. Shailagh Murray and James Grimaldi, "House Passes Bill to Restrict Internet Poker," *Washington Post,* July 12, 2006.

14. Ibid.

15. Nancy Zuckerboard, "Frist Targets Internet Gambling," *Washington Post,* September 13, 2006.

16. A legal disagreement has been ongoing about whether Internet gambling is illegal under the Wire Act of 1961. Both the Clinton and Bush Justice Departments have taken the position that the Wire Act applies to all forms of Internet gambling,

and therefore it is illegal under existing law. However, the Fifth Circuit Court of Appeals, in the case of *Thompson v. MasterCard International et al.* (2003), held that the Wire Act prohibits only sports betting, meaning that casino games such as poker and blackjack are legal.

17. George W. Bush (address to the Front Porch Alliance, Indianapolis, IN, July 22, 1999). Available at http://www.cpjustice.org/stories/storyreader$383.

18. "The State Is Looking After You," *The Economist*, April 6, 2006.

19. David Brooks, "From Freedom to Authority," *New York Times*, May 14, 2006.

20. Newt Gingrich, with Dana Pavey and Anne Woodbury, *Saving Lives, Saving Money: Transforming Health and HealthCare* (Washington: Gingrich Communications, 2003), p. 94.

21. Ceci Connolly, "More U.S. Teens Delay Having Sex, Study Finds," *Washington Post*, December 11, 2004.

22. Les Christi, "Crime Rate Drops Again," *CNN.com*, October 17, 2005.

23. Susan Whitney, "Commitment: Divorce Rate in the U.S. Is Declining," *Deseret News*, March 7, 2005.

24. Jay Greene and Marcus Winters, "Public School Graduation Rates in the United States," Manhattan Institute for Policy Research Civic Report no. 31, November 2002.

25. Lawrence Finer and Stanley Henshaw, "Estimates of US Abortion Incidence, 2001–2003," Guttmacher Institute, August 3, 2006, http://www.guttmacher.org/pubs/2006/08/03/ab_incidence.pdf.

26. "The State Is Looking After You," *The Economist*, April 6, 2006.

27. Daniel Akst, "Long Live the Nanny State," *New York Times*, July 23, 2006.

28. Paternalists generally argue that people often do not act rationally and thus markets do not maximize public welfare. Government must intervene, therefore, to correct for individual myopia. In reality, however, studies suggest that government actors appear to be no more rational than economic actors. Indeed, the government may actually be more likely to err because it is susceptible to several forms of manipulation and lacks strong corrective mechanisms. Edward Glaeser, "Paternalism and Psychology," *Regulation* 29, no. 2 (Summer 2006): 32–38.

29. Charles Murray, *What It Means to Be a Libertarian* (New York: Broadway Press, 1997).

30. Sarah Schweitzer, "Card Says President Sees America as a Child Needing a Parent," *Boston Globe*, September 2, 2004.

31. For a history of the Schiavo case, see http://news.findlaw.com/legalnews/lit/schiavo.

32. Charles Babbington, "Viewing Videotape, Frist Disputes Fla. Doctors' Diagnosis of Schiavo," *Washington Post*, March 19, 2005.

33. Jon Thogmartin, "Report of Autopsy for Theresa Schiavo, Case #5050439," Pasco & Pinellas Counties Medical Examiner's Office, June 13, 2005. http://www.abstractappeal.com/schiavo/autopsyreport.pdf.

34. *An Act for the Relief of the Parents of Theresa Marie Schiavo*, Public Law 109-3, March 21, 2005.

35. Congress also attempted to subpoena Terri Schiavo to testify at a congressional hearing, http://abstractappeal.com/schiavo/HouseSubpoenas.pdf. Because taking any action that prevents a congressional witness from testifying is illegal, the effect of the subpoena, if enforced, would have been to prevent removal of the feeding tube. Apparently Congress eventually recognized the absurdity of the idea, and no attempt was made to enforce the subpoena.

36. "No Bill of Attainder or ex post facto Law will be passed." U.S. Constitution, art. 1, sec. 9.

37. "Federalist no. 44," in *The Federalist*, ed. Clinton Rossiter (New York: Signet Classics, 2003), p. 279.

38. *United States v. Brown*, 381 U.S. 437, 440 (1965).

39. "Some Conservatives Bothered by Intervention of Bush, Congress in Terri Schiavo Case," *ABC News*, March 23, 2005.

40. Erwin Chemerinsky, "Ignoring the Constitution for Political Gain," *Duke University News & Communications*, March 22, 2005, http://dukenews.duke.edu/2005/03/schiavo.html.

41. Charles Fried, "Federalism Has a Right to Life, Too," *New York Times*, March 23, 2005.

42. Quoted in Dick Polman, "Republicans Have Deserted Their Core Principles, Critics Say," Knight Ridder, March 23, 2005.

Chapter 11

1. George Will (address to the Cato Institute's 2006 Friedman Prize Awards Dinner, Chicago, IL, May 18, 2006).

2. Scott Hodge, Scott Moody, and Wendy Warscholik, "The Rising Cost of Complying with the Federal Income Tax," Tax Foundation Special Report no. 138, December 2005, http://www.taxfoundation.org/publications/show/1281.html.

3. Joint Economic Committee, *Taxes and Long-Term Economic Growth*, February 1997.

4. Congressional Budget Office, "2001 Budget Options Report," 2001.

5. Richard Vedder, "Why Government Job Training Fails," *Investor Business Daily*, January 10, 1996.

6. Jagadeesh Gokhale and Kent Smetters, "Measuring Social Security's Financial Outlook within an Aging Society," *Daedalus* (Winter 2006): 91–106.

7. Ronald Reagan, "Farewell Address to the Nation" (Washington, DC, January 11, 1989, http://www.reaganlibrary.com/reagan/speeches/farewell.asp).

8. The quote is widely attributed to Goldwater (http://en.wikiquote.org/wiki/Barry_Goldwater), but it may be apocryphal. Other sources attribute it to Davy Crockett.

9. These powers are set out in article 1, section 8: (1) To lay and collect Taxes, Duties, Imposts and Excises, to pay the Debts and provide for the common Defence and general Welfare of the United States; but all Duties, Imposts and Excises shall be uniform throughout the United States; (2) To borrow Money on the credit of the United States; (3) To regulate Commerce with foreign Nations, and among the several States, and with the Indian Tribes; (4) To establish an uniform Rule of Naturalization, and uniform Laws on the subject of Bankruptcies throughout the United States; (5) To coin Money, regulate the Value thereof, and of foreign Coin, and fix the Standard of Weights and Measures; (6) To provide for the Punishment of counterfeiting the Securities and current Coin of the United States; (7) To establish Post Offices and Post Roads; (8) To promote the Progress of Science and useful Arts, by securing for limited Times to Authors and Inventors the exclusive Right to their respective Writings and Discoveries; (9) To constitute Tribunals inferior to the supreme Court; (10) To define and punish Piracies and Felonies committed on the high Seas, and Offences against the Law of Nations; (11) To declare War, grant Letters of Marque and Reprisal, and make Rules concerning Captures on Land and Water; (12) To raise and support

Armies, but no Appropriation of Money to that Use shall be for a longer Term than two Years; (13) To provide and maintain a Navy; (14) To make Rules for the Government and Regulation of the land and naval Forces; (15) To provide for calling forth the Militia to execute the Laws of the Union, suppress Insurrections and repel Invasions; (16) To provide for organizing, arming, and disciplining the Militia, and for governing such Part of them as may be employed in the Service of the United States, reserving to the States respectively, the Appointment of the Officers, and the Authority of training the Militia according to the discipline prescribed by Congress; (17) To exercise exclusive Legislation in all Cases whatsoever, over such District (not exceeding ten Miles square) as may, by Cession of particular States, and the Acceptance of Congress, become the Seat of the Government of the United States, and to exercise like Authority over all Places purchased by the Consent of the Legislature of the State in which the Same shall be, for the Erection of Forts, Magazines, Arsenals, dock-Yards, and other needful Buildings; And (18) To make all Laws which shall be necessary and proper for carrying into Execution the foregoing Powers, and all other Powers vested by this Constitution in the Government of the United States, or in any Department or Officer thereof.

10. U.S. Constitution, amend. 10.

11. Thomas Jefferson, "First Inaugural Address" (Washington, DC, March 4, 1801). Available at http://usinfo.state.gov/usa/infousa/facts/democrac/11.htm.

12. Barry Goldwater, *Conscience of a Conservative* (Shepherdsville, KY: Victor Publishing, 1960), p. 7.

13. Ibid., p. 8.

14. Fred Barnes, *Rebel in Chief: Inside the Bold and Controversial Presidency of George W. Bush* (New York: Crown Forum, 2006), pp. 175–76.

15. In particular, Bartlett favors a value added tax.

16. Michael Shear and Tim Craig, "Allen Blasts Webb Novels for Sex Scenes," *Washington Post*, October 28, 2006.

17. Fred Barnes, *Rebel in Chief: Inside the Bold and Controversial Presidency of George W. Bush* (New York: Crown Forum, 2006), p. 176.

18. Stephen Slivinski, *Buck Wild: How Republicans Broke the Bank and Became the Party of Big Government* (Nashville: Nelson Currant, 2006).

19. Linda Killian, *The Freshmen: What Happened to the Republican Revolution* (Boulder, CO: Westview Press, 1998), pp. 407–13, 441–43.

20. Dick Armey, "Where We Went Wrong," *Washington Post*, October 29, 2006.

21. Dan Casse, "What Is a Bush Republican?" *Commentary*, April 10, 2006.

22. David Brooks, "From Freedom to Authority," *New York Times*, May 14, 2006.

23. Karlyn Bowman, "Attitudes toward the Federal Government," American Enterprise Institute Studies in Public Opinion, August 6, 2003, http://www.aei.org/publications/pubID.18988/pub_detail.asp.

24. Rasmussen Reports, February 16, 2004.

25. Darren Carlson, "Big Government, Big Threat?" Gallup News Service, December 28, 2004.

26. "Poll: Majority Believes Government Doing Too Much," *CNN.com*, October 27, 2006.

27. Ibid.

28. http://www.smallgovernmentact.org.

29. E. J. Dionne, "Lessons for Liberals in California," *Washington Post*, June 9, 2006.

30. David Boaz, "Libertarian Orphans," *Wall Street Journal*, January 31, 2006.

31. Scott Keeter and Gregory Smith, "In Search of Ideologues in America: It's Harder than You Think," Pew Research Center, April 11, 2006, http://pewresearch.org/obdeck/?ObDeckID = 17.

32. Dick Armey, "Where We Went Wrong," *Washington Post*, October 29, 2006.

33. Scott Keeter and Gregory Smith, "In Search of Ideologues in America: It's Harder Than You Think," Pew Research Center, April 11, 2006, http://pewresearch.org/obdeck/?ObDeckID = 17.

34. Even if these libertarian-leaning voters do not actually vote Democratic, evidence indicates that they may be sufficiently disillusioned to just stay home. In his excellent book, *The Elephant in the Room*, Ryan Sager points out that the desertion of libertarian conservatives poses a serious threat to Republicans, particularly in western states such as Arizona, Colorado, Idaho, Montana, Nevada, New Mexico, Utah, Wyoming, and Alaska. He also suggests that Republican losses in California, Oregon, and Washington are partially caused by the alienation of libertarian-leaning voters. Ryan Sager, *The Elephant in the Room: Evangelicals, Libertarians, and the Battle to Control the Republican Party* (Hoboken, NJ: John Wiley & Sons, 2006).

35. Richard Weaver, *Ideas Have Consequences* (Chicago: University of Chicago Press, 1948).

36. George Will (address to the Cato Institute's 2006 Friedman Prize Awards Dinner, Chicago, IL, May 18, 2006).

37. William Clinton, "State of the Union Address" (Washington, DC, January 23, 1996, http://www.gpoaccess.gov/sou/index.html).

38. Martin Luther King, "Beyond Vietnam: A Time to Break Silence" (speech to a meeting of Clergy and Laity Concerned at Riverside Church in New York City, April 4, 1967). Available at http://www.informationclearinghouse.info/article2564.htm.

39. Barry Goldwater, *Conscience of a Conservative* (Shepherdsville, KY: Victor Publishing, 1960), p. 23.

40. *Transportation Equity Act,* HR 3, 109th Cong., 1st sess., February 9, 2005, http://thomas.loc.gov/cgi-bin/bdquery/z?d109:h.r.00003:.

41. Chris Edwards, *Downsizing the Federal Government* (Washington: Cato Institute, 2006).

42. For a discussion of these state spending restrictions, see Michael New, "Proposition 13 and State Budget Limitations: Past Successes and Future Options," Cato Institute Briefing Paper no. 83, June 19, 2003.

43. See Chris Edwards, "Capping Federal Spending," Cato Institute Tax & Budget Bulletin no. 32, March 2006.

44. Donald B. Marron, "Medicaid Spending Growth and Options for Controlling Costs," testimony before the Senate Special Committee on Aging, 109th Cong., 2nd sess., July 13, 2006, http://www.cbo.gov/ftpdocs/73xx/doc7387/07-13-Medicaid.pdf.

45. Michael Cannon, "Medicaid's Unseen Costs," Cato Institute Policy Analysis no. 548, August 18, 2005.

46. See, for example, Aaron Yelowitz, "Evaluating the Effects of Medicaid on Welfare and Work: Evidence from the Past Decade," Employment Policies Institute, December 2000.

47. Michael Cannon of the Cato Institute has laid out an excellent proposal for how this can be done. See "Medicaid's Unseen Costs," Cato Institute Policy Analysis no. 548, August 18, 2005.

48. See Shaila Dewan, "In Mississippi, Soaring Costs Force Deep Medicaid Cuts," *New York Times*, July 2, 2005; Tim Hoover, "System Will Be Restructured: Medicaid Panelists Start Task," *Kansas City Star*, June 29, 2005; Anita Wadhwani, "Bresden's 2003 Revisions to TennCare Now Block Him," *Tennessean*, July 6, 2005.

49. U.S. Department of Health and Human Services, Centers for Medicare and Medicaid Services, *2006 Annual Report of the Board of Trustees of the Federal Hospital Insurance and Federal Supplemental Medical Insurance Trust Funds Fund* (Washington: Government Printing Office, 2006).

50. Jagadeesh Gokhale, testimony to the Committee on Homeland Security and Government Affairs, Subcommittee on Federal Financial Management, Government Information, and International Security, 109th Cong., 1st sess., September 22, 2005, http://hsgac.senate.gov/_files/092205Gokhale.pdf.

51. National Bipartisan Commission on the Future of Medicare, "Building a Better Medicare for Today and Tomorrow," March 16, 1999, http://medicare.commission.gov/medicare/index.html.

52. See Martin Feldstein, "Prefunding Medicare," NBER Working Paper no. 6917, National Bureau of Economic Research, Cambridge, MA, January 1999.

53. Social Security Administration, *2006 Annual Report of the Board of Trustees of the Federal Old-Age and Survivors Insurance and Disability Insurance Trust Funds* (Washington: Government Printing Office, 2006).

54. The Cato Institute has recommended that workers be allowed to invest their half of the payroll tax (6.2 percent of taxable wages). See Michael Tanner, "The 6.2% Solution: A Plan for Reforming Social Security," Cato Institute Social Security Paper no. 32, February 17, 2004.

55. As part of this process, Congress should resist the temptation to guarantee workers the currently promised level of Social Security benefits. In practice, lowering those expectations will mean shifting government-provided benefits toward a sustainable level. One method of doing so is to change the benefit formula from wage indexing to price indexing, either in full or in part.

56. William Niskanen, "Comment," in *American Economic Policy in the 1990s*, ed. Jeffrey Frankel and Peter Orszag (Cambridge, MA: MIT Press, 2002); William Niskanen, "Starve the Beast Does Not Work," *Cato Institute Policy Report* 26, no. 2 (March/April 2004).

57. William Gale and Brennan Kelly, "The No New Taxes Pledge," *Tax Notes*, July 12, 2004. Although these statistics may be somewhat distorted because Democrats, who did not sign the pledge, frequently voted against these and other spending bills for purely partisan reasons or because they actually sought *more* spending than was contained in the bills, they nonetheless show that many of the most fervent anti-tax Republicans were, in fact, big spenders.

58. Stephen Erickson, "The Entrenching of Incumbency: Reelection in the US House of Representatives, 1790–1994," *Cato Journal* 14, no. 3 (Winter 1995): 397–420.

59. See Jonathan Ferry, "Coming to Terms with Term Limits: A Summary of State Term Limit Laws," U.S. Term Limits Foundation, Term Limits Outlook series 3, no. 4, December 1994. Term limits for Congress were also passed by the Utah state legislature.

60. *U.S. Term Limits, Inc., et al. v. Thornton et al.*, 514 U.S. 779 (1995).

61. See, for instance, John G. Kester, "State Term-Limits Laws and the Constitution," in *The Law and Politics of Term Limits*, ed. Edward H. Crane and Roger Pilon (Washington: Cato Institute, 1994), pp. 109–24; Ronald Rotunda, "A Commentary

on the Constitutionality of Term Limits," in *The Law and Politics of Term Limits*, pp. 141–55; and John Armor, *Why Term Limits? Because They Have It Coming* (Ottawa, IL: Jameson Books, 1994), pp. 120–26.

62. Quoted in Doug Bandow, "Real Term Limits Now More Than Ever," Cato Institute Policy Analysis no. 221, March 28, 1995.

63. Kenneth J. Cooper, "House Rejects Measures to Require Term Limits," *Washington Post*, March 30, 1995.

64. Albert Eisele, "Term Limits RIP," *The Hill*, March 9, 2005.

65. Ibid.

66. James Payne, *The Culture of Spending: Why Congress Lives beyond Our Means* (San Francisco: ICS, 1991), p. 71.

67. See, for example, Aaron Steelman, "Term Limits and the Republican Congress: The Case Strengthens," Cato Institute Briefing Paper no. 41, October 28, 1998; Stephen Moore and Aaron Steelman, "Antidote to Federal Red Ink: Term Limits," Cato Institute Briefing Paper no. 21, November 3, 1994.

68. Quoted in "Classic Quotes from Citizen Legislators," *No Uncertain Terms* 8, no. 1 (January 2000), http://www.ustl.org/Press/No_Uncertain_Terms/2000/0001nut.html.

69. Ibid.

70. Andrew Busch, "After Compassionate Conservatism," *Wall Street Journal*, August 1, 2006.

Chapter 12

1. Cait Murphy, "Why the Republicans Need to Lose," *CNNMoney.com*, October 25, 2006, http://money.cnn.com/2006/10/23/news/economy/pluggedin_murphy_election.fortune/index.htm?cnn=yes.

2. Ibid.

3. Bruce Bartlett, *Impostor: How George W. Bush Bankrupted America and Betrayed the Reagan Legacy* (New York: Doubleday, 2006), p. 209.

4. Cait Murphy, "Why the Republicans Need to Lose," CNNMoney.com, October 25, 2006, http://money.cnn.com/2006/10/23/news/economy/pluggedin_murphy_election.fortune/index.htm?cnn=yes.

5. Robert Higgs, *Crisis and Leviathan: Critical Episodes in the Growth of American Government* (New York: Oxford University Press, 1989)

6. Andrew Busch, "After Compassionate Conservatism," *Wall Street Journal*, August 1, 2006.

7. Stephen Slivinski, "Fiscal Policy Report Card on America's Governors: 2006," Cato Institute Policy Analysis no. 581, October 24, 2006.

8. Scott Allen, "Romney Details Repair Plan for Tunnel Ceiling," *Boston Globe*, July 18, 2006.

9. Eric Pfeiffer, "Gingrich on Conservatives' Radar," *Washington Times*, July 31, 2006.

10. http://www.ntu.org/downloads/BT109-1_Senate.pdf; http://www.ntu.org/downloads/BT108-2_Senate.pdf; http://www.ntu.org/downloads/BT107-2_Senate.pdf.

11. *Imus in the Morning*, May 28, 2006

12. Stephen Slivinski, "Fiscal Policy Report Card on America's Governors: 2006," Cato Institute Policy Analysis no. 581, October 24, 2006.

13. http://www.ntu.org/downloads/BT109-1_Alpha.pdf.

14. http://www.ntu.org/downloads/BT109-1_Alpha.pdf.

15. http://www.ntu.org/misc_items/rating/VS_2005.pdf.

16. Shalia Dewan and Anne Kornblut, "In Key House Races, Democrats Run to the Right," *New York Times*, October 30, 2006.

17. Joe Conason, "Spinning Election Day in Advance," *New York Observer*, November 2, 2006.

18. Quoted in Peter Baker, "The GOP Leans on a Proven Strategy," *Washington Post*, October 25, 2006.

19. Tom Hamburger and Peter Wallsten, "Conservative Leaders Plan a Comeback," *Los Angeles Times*, November 9, 2006.

20. Quoted in David Kirkpatrick, "Republican Woes Lead to Feuding by Conservatives," *New York Times*, October 20, 2006.

21. David Brooks, "The Middle Muscles In," *New York Times*, November 9, 2006.

22. Jim VandeHei and Peter Baker, "Bush, GOP Congress Losing Core Supporters," *Washington Post*, May 11, 2006.

23. Susanna Schrobsdorff, "It's the War, Stupid—And the Youth Vote, And Angry Indies, And . . . ," Newsweek Online, November 9, 2006.

24. Poll conducted by the Club For Growth, November 7, 2006, http://www.clubforgrowth.org/2006/11/new_poll_people_want_limited_g.php.

25. Dick Armey, "Where We Went Wrong," *Washington Post*, October 29, 2006.

26. Ibid.

27. Thomas Jefferson, Letter to E. Carrington, May 27, 1788, http://odur.let.rug.nl/~usa/P/tj3/writings/brf/jefl52.htm.

28. Ronald Reagan, "A Time for Choosing" (address to the nation, NBC, October 27, 1964).

Index

(G. W.) Bush's executive signing statements and, 191–92
(G. W.) Bush's expansion of entitlements with, 3
Congressional Republicans on opposition to, 72
drug costs for seniors under, 129
enrollment statistics, 128
Gingrich on, 57
Medicare funding and, 124
national-greatness conservatives on, 40
passage of, 124–25
politicization of policy process and, 68
projected costs for, 121–22, 125–26, 127–28
reelection pressures on, 67
small government and repeal of, 220–21
prescription drug reimportation, 115
privacy, national health-information system and, 116–17
private charitable giving, government welfare and, 15, 88–89
privatization, of government services under Reagan, 23
progressive conservatives, 7–8
Progressive Era, expansion of federal power and, 182
progressivism, Americans' attitudes toward government and, 19–20
Protestant evangelicals. *See* evangelical Protestants
Public Interest, The, 26
public opinion polls, 10, 70, 213–15
public schools. *See also* education programs
failures of, 166

radio, Congressional legislation regarding, 198–99
Rahall, Nick J. II, 154
Raich v. Ashcroft, 185–86
Rand, Ayn, 21
Rangel, Charles, 232
Rasmussen, Scott, 213
rationalism, Strauss on, 29
Rauch, Jonathan, 15
Ravitch, Diane, 173
Ready-to-Learn Television, 170
Reagan, Nancy, 32
Reagan, Ronald

conservative philosophy of governing, 4, 7, 13, 199, 205
on constitutional government, 209
defense spending by, 143
on Department of Education, 165
domestic discretionary spending under, 145
earmarks in highway bill vetoed by, 153
election of 1994 and, 61–62
executive signing statements and, 190
federal control of education and, 179
federal spending under, 141
on federalism, 183–84
Goldwater's defeat and, 23, 215–16, 229
on limited government and personal freedom, 209
nature of conservatism and, 24
neoconservatives and, 31
on separation of powers, 181
small-government conservatism and, 212, 230
"Reagan Democrat" voters, 31
Reagan's Victory: The Presidential election of 1980 and the Rise of the Right (Busch), 226
Real ID, 187
Rebel in Chief (Barnes), 11
Rector, Robert, 12, 81, 82
Rehabilitation Act, 85
Rehnquist, William, 187
Reidl, Brian, 159
religion. *See also* faith-based charities
neoconservatives on support for institutions of, 38
Strauss on United States and, 28–29
Supreme Court and Religious Right on, 44
Religious Right.
big-government conservatism and, 8–9, 43–50
on economic issues, 49–50
election of 2006 and, 233
federal involvement in education and, 172
on government, 46–47
indecency legislation and, 198–99
on Medicare and Social Security, 122, 123
neoconservatives on, 38–39
political agenda of, 48–49
on RU-486, 114

About the Author

As director of Cato's health and welfare studies, Michael Tanner heads research on new market-based approaches to health, welfare, and Social Security. Under Tanner's direction, Cato launched the Project on Social Security Choice, which is widely considered the leading impetus for transforming the soon-to-be-bankrupt system into a private savings program. *Time* magazine calls Tanner "one of the architects of the private accounts movement," and the *Congressional Quarterly* named him one of the nation's five most influential experts on Social Security. In addition to his work on Social Security, Tanner oversees Cato's research on new market-based approaches to health care reform and social welfare programs. He is the author or coauthor of several books, including *Healthy Competition: What's Holding Back Health Care and How to Free It*, *A New Deal for Social Security*, and *The Poverty of Welfare: Helping Others in Civil Society*. A prolific writer and frequent guest lecturer, Tanner appears regularly on network and cable news programs. His writings have appeared in nearly every major American newspaper, including the *New York Times*, *Washington Post*, *Los Angeles Times*, *Wall Street Journal*, and *USA Today*. He currently lives with his wife, Ellen Maidman-Tanner, in Takoma Park, Maryland.

Cato Institute

Founded in 1977, the Cato Institute is a public policy research foundation dedicated to broadening the parameters of policy debate to allow consideration of more options that are consistent with the traditional American principles of limited government, individual liberty, and peace. To that end, the Institute strives to achieve greater involvement of the intelligent, concerned lay public in questions of policy and the proper role of government.

The Institute is named for *Cato's Letters,* libertarian pamphlets that were widely read in the American Colonies in the early 18th century and played a major role in laying the philosophical foundation for the American Revolution.

Despite the achievement of the nation's Founders, today virtually no aspect of life is free from government encroachment. A pervasive intolerance for individual rights is shown by government's arbitrary intrusions into private economic transactions and its disregard for civil liberties.

To counter that trend, the Cato Institute undertakes an extensive publications program that addresses the complete spectrum of policy issues. Books, monographs, and shorter studies are commissioned to examine the federal budget, Social Security, regulation, military spending, international trade, and myriad other issues. Major policy conferences are held throughout the year, from which papers are published thrice yearly in the *Cato Journal.* The Institute also publishes the quarterly magazine *Regulation.*

In order to maintain its independence, the Cato Institute accepts no government funding. Contributions are received from foundations, corporations, and individuals, and other revenue is generated from the sale of publications. The Institute is a nonprofit, tax-exempt, educational foundation under Section 501(c)3 of the Internal Revenue Code.

CATO INSTITUTE
1000 Massachusetts Ave., N.W.
Washington, D.C. 20001
www.cato.org